Seventh Edition

Teaching and Learning Elementary Social Studies

Arthur K. Ellis

Seattle Pacific University

Allyn and Bacon

Boston ▪ London ▪ Toronto ▪ Sydney ▪ Tokyo ▪ Singapore

Series Editor: *Traci Mueller*
Vice President, Editor in Chief, Education: *Paul A. Smith*
Editorial Assistant: *Bridget Keane*
Marketing Manager: *Brad Parkins*
Editorial-Production Administrator: *Annette Joseph*
Editorial-Production Coordinator: *Holly Crawford*
Editorial-Production Service: *Lynda Griffiths, TKM Productions*
Text Designer: *Denise Hoffman, Glenview Studios*
Composition Buyer: *Linda Cox*
Electronic Composition and Art: *Omegatype Typography, Inc.*
Manufacturing Buyer: *Suzanne Lareau*
Cover Administrator: *Linda Knowles*

Between the time Website information is gathered and then published, it is not unusual for some
sites to have closed. Also, the transcription of URLs can result in unintended typographical errors.
The publisher would appreciate notification where these occur so that they may be corrected in
subsequent editions. Thank you.

Library of Congress Cataloging-in-Publication Data

Ellis, Arthur K.
  Teaching and learning elementary social studies / Arthur K. Ellis.—7th ed.
    p. cm.
  Includes bibliographical references (p.) and index.
  ISBN 0-205-33752-X
  1. Social sciences—Study and teaching (Elementary)

LB1584 .E39 2002
372.83'044—dc21

                                                                    2001022746

Printed in the United States of America

10 9 8 7 6 5 4   RRD-VA   06 05 04

Photo Credits: Brian Smith: pp. 5, 16, 227; Will Faller: pp. 10, 67, 79, 100, 120, 127, 134, 147, 181, 246,
265; Gary Shelly: pp. 44, 186, 195, 200, 217, 224; Library of Congress: pp. 47, 324; Lyrl Ahearn: pp. 58,
68, 70, 74; Will Hart: pp. 66, 97, 129; © Jay Gardner, Courtesy of Perseus Basic Books: p. 76; Stephen
Marks: p. 202 *(top)*; Jim Pickerell: pp. 318, 358, 359; North Wind Picture Archives: p. 354.

Other Credits: Quote on p. 208: From *The Family Guide to Children's Television* by Evelyn Kaye,
Text copyright © 1974 by Action for Children's Television, Inc. Used by permission of Pantheon
Books, a division of Random House, Inc. Cartoon on p. 336: Arthur Poinier, Courtesy of *The Detroit
News*. Figure 16.1 on p. 352: From *Leading the Cooperative School* by D. W. Johnson and R. T.
Johnson, 1989, Edina, MN: Interaction Book Company. Reprinted by permission.

Contents

Chapter 3

The Knowledge Base for Elementary Social Studies   28

Chapter 4

Theory: Developmental and Psychological Dimensions   55

Chapter 7

Teaching and Learning Strategies   **124**

Chapter 8

Assessing Student Progress   **158**

Chapter 9

Inquiry and Discovery: Children as Researchers   177

Chapter 14

Social Studies and Literacy   313

Preface

Children need models rather than critics.
—Joseph Joubert

Welcome to the seventh edition of *Teaching and Learning Elementary Social Studies*. The field changes, sometimes rapidly, as new ideas emerge. It is always a wonderful challenge to remain current while deciding which new ideas are worth incorporating and which old ideas are worth saving. Whatever the issue, the innovation, or the insight, three areas of concern predominate for the teacher of elementary social studies: the nature of childhood, the nature of teaching, and the nature of learning.

What is the nature of childhood? The Japanese proverb says, "It is like the springtime to be a child"—such wisdom in such simple words. Spring is a short season; it lasts only for a while and then it is gone. Wise teachers know this, and they act accordingly. They celebrate childhood—they share in its joys as well as in its more difficult moments. They know that children are playful by nature. Plato made note of this centuries ago, when he wrote that play is the work of childhood. Jean Piaget observed that organization and adaptation are two of childhood's primary tasks. This means that children's play is meaningful in that they are trying their best to figure out how things work. The poet William Wordsworth wrote of childhood:

> *There was a time when meadow, grove and stream,*
> *The earth and every common sight,*
> > *To me did seem*
> > *Appareled in celestial light,*
> *The glory and the freshness of a dream.*

What is the nature of teaching? Good teachers understand dreams. They know something about wonder. They realize that life's little moments are truly "appareled in celestial light." This is why their classrooms are places of trust, respect, happiness, caring, and loving discipline. Teaching has been called a science. It is true that certain principles of effective teaching have been derived through research, and we will explore them. In this book, however, we will also think of teaching as an art form. Good teachers are artists who understand and use principles derived from research, but ultimately they teach because they love teaching, they love children, and they themselves have an unquenchable thirst for learning. The word *passion* comes to mind. In an attempt to merge passion with excellence, we will explore the foundations of the social studies; that is, the knowledge base of content, method, and organization. This takes us to key concepts and skills in history, geography, and citizenship; and into the realms of planning, assessment, and teaching strategies. Through it all, more than anything, I want you to remember why you entered this calling in the first place. You and I both know you decided to become a teacher because you care about children and want the best for them.

What is the nature of learning? How do children learn best? What knowledge is worth learning? What is developmentally appropriate practice? What do we mean by multiple intelligences? Learning styles? Inquiry and discovery? Project learning? Cooperative learning? Integrated studies? We will explore these matters together along with ideas such as active learning, reflective thinking, motivation, interest, concept acquisition, and metacognition. What do we know from brain research about learning? What should teachers know about social growth and development? About concrete and abstract learning? What basic skills are needed to enable children to learn on their own? We will investigate the role of the social sciences in social studies, the role of content standards and performance standards, and the role of assessment techniques designed to help us document what we know. And not least of all, how can learning social studies make students and teachers better citizens in a democratic society?

Finally, this book is organized around three simple principles:

1. Good teaching is a *means* to a *goal* called learning. Never lose sight of the goal.
2. Active learning accompanied by reflective thinking represents the best social studies environment you can create.
3. Meaningful learning is at once social, moral, and academic. You must not separate the seamless cloak of learning.

Social studies is the most integrative, connected subject in the curriculum. Its focus is on people and their activities. Thus, the same challenges that have confronted human beings throughout history come to life in the classroom. Those challenges are self-realization, the dreams of the individual; citizenship, the role of the contributing person in the lives of others; and scholarship, the knowledgeable person who loves to learn.

Among the changes I've made in this new edition are strategies for building a good foundation for social studies learning; attention to new developments in learning theory from work in cognitive psychology and brain function; the addition of many new lesson plans and examples; developing insights to citizenship and character education; strengthened materials on the social sciences and on emerging standards; new ideas on reflective thinking, metacognition, and constructivism; and careful attention to the integration of assessment with teaching and learning. Always the approach is to amplify theory with numerous examples of practice.

I assume full responsibility for the contents of this book, especially any unintended shortcomings. As to the book's strengths, I owe much to good friends and colleagues who have contributed a great deal to my own teaching and learning over the years. I acknowledge with gratitude the many contributions children have made to this book in the form of maps, drawings, activities, essays, and artwork. I also wish to thank such people as John Cogan, JoAnne Buggey, David and Roger Johnson, Patricia Hammill, N. J. Petersen, Gary Shelly, Richard Scheuerman, and Jim LeGette for their contributions, which came in many forms. Traci Mueller, my editor at Allyn and Bacon, has proven to be very supportive and patient along the way. Thanks, finally, to my family for all they do.

> *Listen and learn, and in the end you will be wise.*
> —The Book of Proverbs, Chapter 19

Ideas, Definitions, and Trends

Where do we begin in the wonderful world of social studies? Let's try some word association. Write down several impressions that come quickly to mind when you think of the term *social studies*. Are your impressions positive, negative, or neutral? When you are teaching social studies to children, it is useful to think of the experience from their perspective. What impressions would you hope for them to have? No doubt you want them to have positive impressions.

This chapter will get you started in the right direction. We will address a number of ideas, search for meaning, and examine important trends—specifically, the following:

- The meaning of social studies
- A rationale for social studies
- Curriculum patterns
- Classroom environments
- Higher-order thinking
- Provisions for learner differences
- The role of the teacher

Or set upon a golden bough to sing ... Of what is past,
or passing, or to come.

—William Butler Yeats, *Sailing to Byzantium*

Take a moment to consider two characters portrayed in children's fiction: Alice, in *Alice's Adventures in Wonderland,* and Dorothy, in *The Wonderful Wizard of Oz.* Each of them was trying to find her way: Alice, out of Wonderland, and Dorothy, to the Emerald City. Each met a rather bizarre set of folks along the way. Each of them finally accomplished her objective. Poor Alice kept asking highly unreliable characters for directions, while Dorothy had only to follow the Yellow Brick Road. Their experiences were different, to be sure. Alice was in a state of

1

perpetual uncertainty, and Dorothy knew all along exactly what needed to be done. We could safely say that Alice had a maze, while Dorothy had a map. The philosopher Alexander Pope once observed that learning should be a map rather than a maze. A well-taught social studies curriculum is just that—a map that helps make sense of the human experience.

Social studies is the study of human beings. Specifically, social studies focuses on human activities in the past, present, and emerging future. It is the study of other people, places, and events across time and space. And, at the same time, it is direct life experience in what it means to be a citizen, a participant, and a self-realized individual. In other words, you don't just *learn* social studies as a school subject; you *take part* in it. In that sense, social studies demands of teachers and students a deeper level of knowledge. It demands knowledge lived, not just information studied. The skills and ideas learned in social studies should be put to direct and practical use in the form of classroom and school governance, of realizing one's unique potential, of growing awareness of others and concern for their welfare, and for free and full participation in the group. Abraham Lincoln's well-chosen phrase, "of the people, by the people, and for the people," goes to the very heart of an uplifting social studies experience. My task in this book is to facilitate your journey, not to give you easy answers, but to challenge you and your students to rise to the occasion of making social studies eminently rewarding, enjoyable, and worthwhile.

"Butterfly and Flower" by 6-year-old child

Although the term *social studies* was coined in the second decade of the twentieth century, it was not until 1993 that a final version or official definition was ratified by the National Council for the Social Studies (NCSS). Of course, there was no hurry; but, on the other hand, it's nice to know what this area of the curriculum is officially all about. Just imagine: You may have gone through some of your school years studying an area of the school curriculum that had not been officially defined. Horrors! So, at long last, here it is:

> *Social studies* is the integrated study of the social sciences and humanities to promote civic competence. Within the school program, social studies provides coordinated, systematic study drawing upon such disciplines as anthropology, archaeology, economics, geography, history, law, philosophy, political science, psychology, religion, and sociology, as well as appropriate content from the humanities, mathematics, and natural sciences. The primary purpose of social studies is to help young people develop the ability to make informed and reasoned decisions for the public good as citizens of a culturally diverse, democratic society in an interdependent world.

There are elements of this definition that are particularly appealing. Notice the commitment to integrated studies. This makes good sense when the subject matter is people. Notice also the emphasis on civic duty, the public good, and the individual as decision maker, as well as the attention paid to democracy, cultural diversity, and interdependence. In my opinion, this is good and noble rhetoric. Any teacher who takes these ideas seriously will no doubt do worthwhile things with children. My only reservation with this definition, although perhaps it's implied, is the lack of a statement about the personal fulfillment of the individual. I firmly believe that social studies can do much to help a child along the road to self-realization, through the soaring vision found in biographies, the arts, and music; through the great mysteries unlocked for a child who discovers the world of maps, stories, and histories; and, most of all, in the wonderful realm of group activities, projects, and shared experience.

Nevertheless, the official definition of social studies represents a useful point of departure, a place from which to begin the journey. After all, it wouldn't be social studies in a democracy if we all agreed on every aspect of this wonderful area of the curriculum. Take a few moments to study Figure 1.1. This gives you an overview of an exemplary social studies program. We will spend the course of this book attempting to bring the ideas in Figure 1.1 to life.

A Rationale

From time to time, someone will question the validity of social studies as an elementary school subject. Some critics would prefer to see social studies replaced with history, geography, and perhaps civics as separate subjects. At another extreme are those who feel that social studies ought to be combined with science and taught as environmental studies.

The first group argues that social studies is a watered-down form of several subjects brought together under the umbrella of "people-related" topics and that history and geography, in particular, suffer as a result. These critics point to the widespread

FIGURE 1.1

An exemplary social studies program should involve social studies teachers and curriculum that engage students according to the following criteria:

The Teacher
- demonstrates both scholarship and expertise in the curriculum
- participates in all aspects of the development of the curriculum, including setting goals and objectives, implementation, evaluation, and revision
- uses sound instructional theory and practice

The Curriculum
- is guided by thoughtfully selected as well as clearly stated and defined goals and objectives
- is based on sound scholarship from the content areas relative to the social studies
- sets high expectations for students and uses a variety of systematic and valid measures to assess student performance
- relates appropriately to the age, maturity, interests, and needs of the students for whom it is designed
- incorporates effective instructional strategies and techniques that engage students directly and actively in the learning process both in and out of the classroom
- provides valid evidence that the outcome of the program is consistent with the stated goals and objectives
- is consistent with the 10 thematic strands identified by NCSS Curriculum Standards for Social Studies (see Figure 3.3 on page 34)

The Students
- critically examine significant content, issues, and events from a variety of perspectives
- participate actively in their school community and world
- engage in focused systematic observations and comprehensive decisions
- understand democratic principles and participate in the democratic process

Source: Based on criteria outlined by the National Council for the Social Studies Curriculum Awards, available at http://www.ncss.org/awards/curriculum.html.

historical and geographic illiteracy among today's students. The second group complains that it is unrealistic to expect elementary teachers (especially at primary levels) to have to prepare lessons in both social studies and science when there is so much reading, language, spelling, math, and so forth that must be covered. If social studies and science were combined, they argue, the teacher would have more time in the day and would probably do a better job of teaching the combined subject.

Both of these criticisms of social studies are reasonable, and they ought to be considered fairly. I agree with futurist Alvin Toffler's point that *every* subject in the school curriculum ought to be continually reexamined and not taken for granted. It is, therefore, healthy to question the appropriateness of social studies, or any other subject.

Some elementary school teachers teach social studies each day with great earnestness; and some teachers, feeling considerable pressure to produce results in other areas, say they work social studies in when and where they can. So it goes.

*The goals of social studies encompass
a wide range of knowledge, skills,
and values.*

Of course, social studies has been around as a school subject for some time (since about 1918), so it does have the force of tradition behind it. Therefore, the search for a rationale may lead teachers initially to say: Why wouldn't we have social studies? We've always had it! After all, social studies is largely an adapted, interdisciplinary form of two subjects, history and geography, that have been considered important for centuries.

Our search for a rationale begins with the premise that a number of unique characteristics of social studies must be identified—things that only social studies can do for young learners. The reasons are listed here, not necessarily in order of their importance.

1. *Social studies provides a forum for children to learn about and practice democracy.* From ancient Athens, to the English Magna Carta, to the councils of the Iroquois nation, to the Constitution of the United States, to Martin Luther King Jr.'s "I Have a Dream" speech, the idea of participatory government and freedom for the individual represents one of humankind's noblest achievements. Surprisingly few people in the world today have the opportunity to live in democratic societies. This precious heritage of Americans is, as Thomas Jefferson said, "renewed with each succeeding generation." The rights and responsibilities of adults living in a democratic society include freedom of speech, worship, assembly, the press, and so on. You have the privilege—and mandate—to set those rights and responsibilities in motion through stories, activities, discussions, and projects with the children you teach.

2. *Social studies is designed to help children explain their world.* Jean Piaget wrote that the two most important tasks of childhood are organization and adaptation. By *organization*, he basically meant the ability to understand and classify things with respect to how they work. For example, a child's initial insights to

the U.S. economic system or to the location of continents on the world map represent examples of organization. *Adaptation* refers to the process of accommodating oneself to one's environment. A child who enters school has already adapted considerably to the environment through speech, dress, rules at home, and so forth, but school is designed to expand such adaptation greatly through formal learning processes. These processes are intellectual, social, emotional, and physical. A good social studies program provides insights to one's history, culture, and landscape—in short, to the world and how it works. Jerome Bruner wrote that most of what happens appears as chaos to children because they don't understand how things work. An effective teacher replaces chaos with understanding. Figure 1.2 illustrates an attempt by a child to explain her world through systematic observation and recording.

3. *Social studies can help children along the road to positive self-development.* People who reflect on their school days often speak about teachers who really affected their lives. One teacher characteristic inevitably comes to the fore in such conversations—something like: "He [She] showed a personal interest in me." The research literature in effective teaching frequently uses the term *pervasive caring* as an important characteristic of good teachers. Thus, both anecdote and research bear testimony to the teacher who cares. Because social studies is the area of the curriculum dedicated to the study of human beings, it lends itself quite naturally to the care and nurturing of the individual child. After all, you would not want to be accused of spending time teaching children about community helpers, economic systems, other cultures, and so on without first tending to the needs of the children in your own classroom. Unless the lives of the children you come in contact with daily are touched by you in a positive way, they will be hard pressed to learn anything meaningful about the lives of others.

4. *Social studies should help children acquire a foundational understanding of history, geography, biography, and the social sciences.* It is difficult to say exactly how much knowledge of history or of the other disciplines children ought to acquire in their elementary school years. The sources of children's knowledge are sev-

---

FIGURE 1.2

A Child's Drawing of Herself Preparing to Make a Sketch of the School She Attends. Perspective Taking Is Fundamental to Map Making.

eral, and school alone will not account for their knowledge of the world. Indeed, teachers carry far too heavy a burden when they assume responsibility for *all* learning that children achieve. The best access to knowledge is found in listening and speaking, reading and writing, and observing and recording. You will need to give serious consideration to how you will build the knowledge base most effectively. But clearly, you are the one who is responsible for teaching children the basics of history, geography, and citizenship.

5. *Social studies ought to promote in children a genuine sense of the social fabric.* Children come to school from increasingly smaller families. The one-parent, one-child family is not uncommon. Opportunities for give-and-take within the family structure are lessened not only because there are fewer family members but also because people within a family spend less time interacting with each other in task-related activities (chores, etc.) than they used to. But the social needs and potential of human beings remain constant. The question is: What will you do to promote a sense of others in your classroom? From the day they enter school, children need to be supported and guided in their attempts to cooperate, share, and contribute. A sense of others includes respect for and tolerance of the child at the adjoining desk, an openness to alternative points of view, a willingness to take part in group efforts, and an expanding view of the community as something the child is not merely a part of, but as something he or she can make better through participation in it. Cooperative learning ideas introduced over the past few decades offer virtually unlimited possibilities for you to develop the social fabric with your social studies program as its centerpiece.

The Social Studies Curriculum

Let's come back to the idea of social studies as the study of human beings. First, social studies is the only curriculum subject with people as its subject matter. People are often considered in language arts and science, but in social studies, people remain the constant focus. Social studies deals directly with the basic needs of human beings: food, clothing, shelter, belonging, security, and dreams. Everyone, everywhere, throughout history has had these needs, but it takes a good teacher to help students understand and recognize these needs in themselves and in others.

Social studies, like other subjects of the elementary school curriculum, is designed to be taught in increments, or in a developmental sequence. This means that instruction proceeds from the simple to the complex, from the familiar to the remote, from the known to the unknown. Thus, kindergarten and first-grade students spend much social studies time studying self-awareness and families because these two topics have a sense of relevance and immediacy to young children. In time, the horizons widen to neighborhoods, communities, cities, regions, the nation, and the western and eastern hemispheres. Such a progression from self to the world in the study of people is known as the *widening horizons* or *expanding environments* curriculum (see Figure 1.3).

Integrated with the idea of widening horizons is a second thought. Called the *spiral* curriculum, it is designed to enhance such key factors as reinforcement of knowledge and ideas, concept and skill development, and transfer of learning. Thus, even though self-awareness and family studies are found in the early primary years, they are not abandoned as topics of later study. They are too important to

FIGURE 1.3

The Widening Horizons or Expanding Environments Curriculum

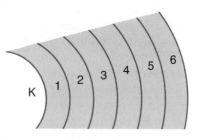

Key:

K – Self and Others   4 – Regions
1 – Families   5 – United States and Canada
2 – Communities   6 – World
3 – Cities

set aside. Instead, the spiral curriculum calls for introducing concepts and skills at simple levels, to be pursued at deeper levels of sophistication each time they are revisited. Therefore, sixth-graders ought to be capable of conducting relatively sophisticated neighborhood studies if the concept of a neighborhood has been sequentially reinforced in a variety of settings over the years.

The other facet of the spiral curriculum that needs to be developed is the early introduction of topics that experts once thought were beyond young children. Through television, young children are aware of elections, space travel, unemployment, and global conflicts. It would be folly to ignore these national and global events; they can, at the very least, be treated impressionistically.

Thus, the spiral and the widening horizons curricula work in concert. Let's take a look at each idea in greater detail.

The Widening Horizons Curriculum

The widening horizons philosophy states that the study of human beings should begin with examples from the local environment. Thus, first-graders might find themselves learning about the family and the neighborhood. Certainly these are two aspects of humanity that are within the realm of the daily experience of young learners. Each day they interact with family members. They walk or ride through neighborhoods on the way to school, and they play there during their free time. Thus, when thoughts about families and neighborhoods are presented in the classroom, students can relate them to their own life experiences. After a study of the family and the neighborhood, students expand their horizons to the community, the city, the state, the region, the United States, and finally the wider world. Each new area of study is an outgrowth of those that preceded it. In moving from the close and familiar examples of people to those further away and more remote in terms of experience, students are following what seems to be a logical progression. Notice the relationship between the specific curriculum topics illustrated in Figure 1.4 and the widening horizons graphic shown in Figure 1.3.

FIGURE 1.4   *Outline of Social Studies Content*

Kindergarten

Tools for learning about the
    world: maps, photos, globe
The *individual* and others
Living in a family
Going to school
Changes in seasons, animals,
    people
Need for food, clothing, shelter
Need for rules
Different places to live

Grade 1

Tools for learning about the
    world: maps and photos
The individual and the *family*
Needs of families:
    Food
    Clothes
    Shelter
Families in neighborhoods
Living in the United States

Grade 2

Tools for learning about the
    world: map, photos, graphs
Setting for *communities:* the
    earth, North America, the
    United States
Large and small communities
    made up of neighborhoods
Community services
Different kinds of work in
    communities
Rules in communities
Communities long ago in our
    country
Celebrating holidays in
    communities

Grade 3

Tools for learning about the
    world: maps, photos, graphs,
    time lines, diagrams, tables
How to study a particular
    community
Representative communities in
    the United States:
    Cities, towns, and suburbs
    Farms and ranches
    Fishing communities
Need for rules
Communication

Grade 4

Tools for learning about the
    world: maps, photos, time lines,
    diagrams, tables
Forest *regions* in Washington
    state, Hawaii, Puerto Rico,
    Russia, Amazon Basins
Desert regions in southwestern
    United States, Africa, Arabian
    Peninsula
Plains regions in central and
    coastal United States, China,
    Kenya, Australia
Mountain regions in Colorado,
    West Virginia, Switzerland
Interdependence of regions
Materials for learning about
    one's own state

Grade 5

Tools for learning about the
    world: maps, graphs, photos,
    time lines, diagrams, tables
Ways of learning about the past
Chronological history of the
    United States
An overview of the geography of
    the United States
Geography of:
    New England states
    Middle Atlantic states
    Southeast states
    South Central states
    North Central states
    Mountain West states
    Pacific states
History and geography of
    Canada and Latin America

Grade 6

Tools for learning about the
    world: maps, photos, graphs,
    time lines, diagrams, tables
Beginnings of Western
    Civilization:
    Mesopotamia and Ancient
        Egypt
    Ancient Greece
    Ancient Rome and the
        Roman Empire
Geography and history of:
    Western Europe
    Eastern Europe and Russia
    Middle East and North
        Africa
    Africa south of the Sahara
    South Asia, East Asia, and
        Australia

Source: Adapted from *The World and Its People* (Glenview, IL: Silver Burdett).

Even though it remains essentially intact as the dominant curricular pattern for
elementary social studies, the widening horizons approach has its detractors. In a
simpler era, when travel and television were less influential for some and nonexis-
tent for others, perhaps it was reasonable to expect children to learn more gradually about worldwide events. But much has changed since the widening horizons

curriculum was proposed half a century ago. Further, not one shred of empirical evidence has ever been produced to substantiate its structure. Obviously, it is difficult for very young children to understand events that occur in remote corners of the globe or that occurred centuries ago. But we know that they are indeed interested in other peoples and other times, and that there is much they can understand through stories, film, and play. The other side of this issue is that older children ought to study families and neighborhoods. Those are not exclusively topics for primary school children to study. If they were, sociologists, geographers, and historians wouldn't study them.

The Spiral Curriculum

Perhaps the most intriguing new curricular approach to social studies is the spiral curriculum. The basic idea of the spiral curriculum is that within each discipline of the social sciences there exists a basic structure, composed of concepts and processes, that can be adapted for use in the teaching of elementary social studies. Proponents of this point of view suggest that the social sciences contain the fundamental ideas (concepts) and procedures (processes) a learner needs to become an independent problem solver.

The presentation of ideas from social science to young learners can be accomplished in a number of ways, including 50-minute lectures each day, but why would any teacher want to do that? The key to the spiral curriculum is to identify and teach real social science concepts in a developmentally appropriate way. Thus, children are recognized and respected as *young* learners who need active experience in order to build up their schema, or knowledge base, yet meaningful content is not sacrificed. Therefore, you can expect that I will keep reminding you of terms such as *experience*, *activities*, and *inquiry*. The concepts you will teach remain essentially the same from kindergarten to sixth grade. That is how the spiral works. Teachers and students keep revisiting the same important ideas at increasingly sophisticated levels over time. This makes it easier for a school faculty to work to-

A Japanese proverb says: "It is like the springtime to be a child."

gether to articulate the curriculum. Of course, the content is different each year, but the ideas or concepts are the same. Chapter 3 is important in this regard because it introduces and explains these key concepts.

Here is a brief example of how the spiral curriculum works (see Figure 1.5). Perhaps you wish to teach children the historical concept of the *oral tradition*, which is the handing down of life activities and patterns through the spoken word (stories, reminiscences, and so on). It is an important source of knowledge of the past, especially knowledge of everyday life patterns. A primary teacher might introduce the concept by asking children if they know stories about their parents' or grandparents' childhoods. The teacher then shares a family story or two that was told (and perhaps retold) to him or her, working a little geography into the story, showing where incidents took place (perhaps in another state). Later that day, as the children prepare to go home, the teacher hands out a letter for parents, which asks them to share a story from their childhood with their child. When the children return to school, the teacher asks them to discuss and draw pictures about something from their parents' childhood stories. The teacher takes time to explain the idea of traditions, relating this experience to larger, shared traditions such as

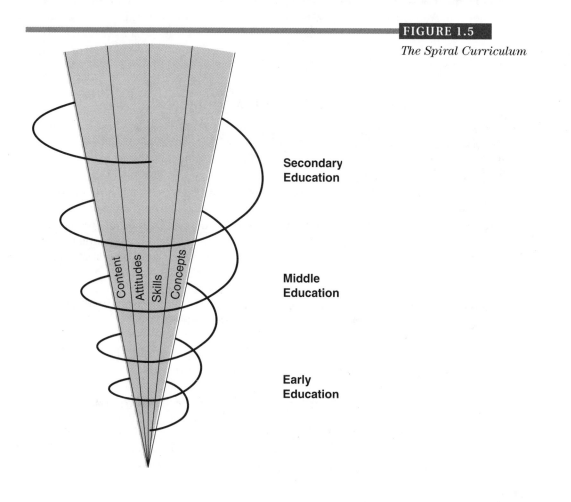

FIGURE 1.5

The Spiral Curriculum

Secondary
Education

Middle
Education

Early
Education

Content Attitudes Skills Concepts

Thanksgiving, as well as stories about famous people from history. After the stories are collected and illustrated, the class prepares to compile them into a history book. The teacher introduces the rich oral traditions of certain Native American tribes and other groups that depended more on the spoken than the written word.

Now all of this is rather simple and introductory, which is exactly the right idea. This teacher has done a good job of setting the stage for the concept of oral tradition to emerge. As students progress through the year and through the grades beyond, the concept is revisited time and again in different contexts. It is compared and contrasted with the written tradition and other ways of preserving the past. Students become historians who investigate and re-create the past through stories handed down. They write plays, put on pageants, listen to storytellers and guest speakers, read the work of other historians, and build the concept deeper and deeper. Philosopher Jean Jacques Rousseau wrote more than two centuries ago, "Teachers, teach less, and teach it well." This is the essence of the spiral approach to the curriculum: to identify a few key concepts and to teach them well with depth.

Classroom Environments

For effective social studies learning to take place, the environment must be conducive to free and open inquiry. The chemistry or mix of basic ingredients is something that will be examined later, but for now, here is a brief look at several aspects of a supportive social studies learning environment: a constructivist environment for learning, higher-level thinking, and provisions for differences in learners.

A Constructivist Environment for Learning

Most teachers would agree that students should become increasingly self-sufficient and less dependent on direct supervision as they progress through the grades. Curiously, however, it is not uncommon to find that precisely the opposite occurs. A certain type of teacher—the teacher whose presence dominates the classroom, who passes judgment on every pupil response, who always decides who will or will not be called on, who asks questions that have "right" and "wrong" answers, and who reduces the students' concept of learning to paper and pencil, read and recite, listen and give back—causes students to become directly dependent on him or her and not on their own latent powers. Eventually, students construct their own knowledge.

Teachers must make a conscious attempt to help students become confident in their own abilities by assuming less directive postures and by seeing themselves in the role of facilitators of learning and not dispensers of information. A teacher must be open to the students' views even when those views fail to coincide with the teacher's own. A teacher must ensure that students acquire the skills necessary to survive and prosper as inquirers (see Figure 1.6). The following goals are directed toward the concept of increased learner independence:

- To recognize that human beings actively construct knowledge and that they should not be viewed merely as passive receivers
- To teach a research methodology that enables children to look for information to answer questions they have raised, and to use the conceptual framework developed in the course (e.g., to apply the concept of system to new areas)

FIGURE 1.6 *The California Framework for History and the Social Sciences:*
A Graphic Illustration of the Goal Structure of the Social Studies

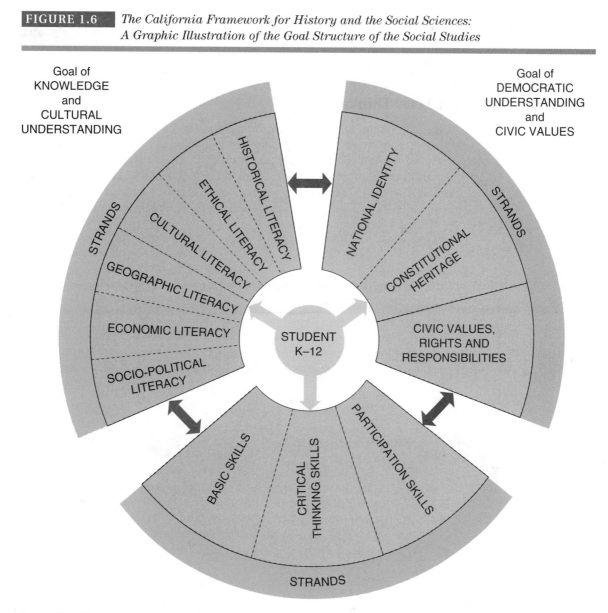

Source: The History–Social Science Framework for California Public Schools (Sacramento: California State Department of Education).

- To help youngsters develop the ability to use firsthand sources—both the materials provided and the materials they gather in their communities—as evidence from which to develop hypotheses and draw conclusions
- To conduct classroom discussions in which youngsters learn to listen to others as well as to express their own views
- To legitimize the search—that is, to give sanction and support to open-ended discussions where definitive answers to many questions are *not* found

- To encourage children to reflect on their own experiences
- To create a new role for the teacher, in which he or she becomes a resource rather than an answer giver
- To utilize people in the community as resources

Higher-Level Thinking

To ensure the intellectual growth and development of learners, the classroom teacher must challenge students to move beyond lower-level mental exercises, such as the memorization of specific facts, to higher-level thought processes, such as explanation, evaluation, and hypothetical thought. It is particularly crucial to ask questions and assign tasks involving students in exploring relationships among social phenomena. Take a moment to explore the intellectual hierarchy developed in the following questions and tasks.

At the memory level, a teacher might ask students to name the capital of California. Although it could be useful to know that bit of information (most likely in order to pass a test), it would be a greater test of students' intellectual prowess to ask them to explain why Sacramento was chosen as the capital of California and to determine the criteria that have been used to choose capitals of different states. Or a teacher might ask students to evaluate the choice of Sacramento as a state capital in light of today's needs. In a hypothetical mode, students might be given the task of establishing criteria and selecting a site for the capital of California based on present and future considerations. Throughout such a series of exercises, a

*"Still Life with Flowers and Vase" by
7-year-old child*

teacher might have as a primary objective getting students to see that a capital location is or ought to be related to the several functions a seat of government needs to perform, and that a capital is more than a name to be memorized.

Differences among Learners

Every teaching situation involving two or more students contains a number of learner differences; these may be intellectual, experiential, social, emotional, preferential, or developmental. To provide for these differences while presenting a cohesive program is one of the great challenges of teaching social studies—or any other subject, for that matter. Even if a teacher had diagnostic instruments available for determining which particular learning situation would suit which particular student(s) at which particular time, there would be no way to guarantee delivery of the many possible alternatives. The more reasonable course of action, given present possibilities, is to become acquainted with each student as a person with unique *as in any subject* needs, interests, and learning styles rather than as a potential reservoir of information, and to provide for a variety of different learning styles.

For example, for a primary class studying the Japanese family, typical alternative activities might include viewing a film on family life in Japan, inviting a Japanese person to visit the classroom, preparing and eating food similar to that eaten by people in Japan, role-playing various roles in the Japanese family, putting together a photomural of life in Japan from magazine pictures, listening to the teacher read about various tasks performed in a Japanese household, writing letters to children in a Japanese school, and making charts on differences and similarities between our lives and those of the Japanese. Although this type of planning certainly does not provide for every type of individual difference, it does provide the variety necessary to ensure that a number of basic skills are developed while different interests are taken into account.

A Good Social Studies Teacher

As a school subject in the context of the school day, social studies is one of perhaps 5 to 10 subjects you teach. It therefore must compete for your energy and time on your schedule with reading, mathematics, science, and language. You are, of course, expected to teach all these subjects well.

Following are 12 jobs of the social studies teacher. They span the range of expectations held for you as measures of competence. How competent are you? Your skills as a social studies teacher can hardly be viewed apart from your competencies as a teacher, in general. But social studies is fundamental as a school subject because of its commitment to the fulfilled person, the informed citizen, and the contributing individual. To the extent that these ideals become reality for your students, they will improve their performance throughout the entire curriculum. Check yourself against these 12 jobs as you reflect on your role as a teacher of elementary social studies. Each job is explained in greater detail in various portions of this book.

1. *Use a variety of teaching strategies.* Variety accomplishes at least two things. First, it makes learning more enjoyable because it resists the boredom of a set, highly predictable routine. Second, it increases your chances of reaching the wide

range of learning styles found in every classroom. Think for a moment of the possibilities: small-group discussion, whole-class discussion, committee work, drama, construction, drawing, films, speakers, silent reading, problem solving, and so on.

2. *Build bridges to other subjects.* Social studies is inherently interdisciplinary. It is possible to make logical and useful connections between social studies and almost any other subject. Cultural areas such as art and music, skill areas such as reading and math, and inquiry areas such as science are all natural subjects for integration with social studies. When you build these bridges, you achieve a natural reinforcement of subject matter, learning seems more real, and you present students with many opportunities to experience learning transfer.

3. *Teach to the real world.* Applications ought to be built into every lesson. The best applications tie school learning into the real world. The subject matter of social studies is people, so you should be able to apply ideas about individuals and groups of any size to the real world of your students.

4. *Emphasize hands-on experiences.* Most children of elementary age are in stages of intuitive and concrete learning. Such direct, active experiences as making things, investigating, and play can form the basis for learning more remote and abstract ideas.

5. *Keep the focus on people.* Human beings are the subject matter of social studies. Sometimes those people live far away or existed long ago. Do not forget that you have a group of human beings in your classroom. Provide time for sharing, for

A good teacher cares deeply about children's freedom, interests, belongingness, and dreams.

cooperating, for expressing feelings, and for caring about each other. Research shows a steady decline in students' concepts of themselves as learners as they progress through the school years. Resolve to turn that around.

6. *Gather materials.* It's true that a good social studies teacher is a scrounge. You need to be on the alert for copies of used *National Geographic*, old maps, books, pictures, construction materials, games, and any other materials you can beg, borrow, or purchase reasonably. When your friends know it is for a worthy cause, they may be able to help.

7. *Encourage reflective thinking.* The value of experience increases to the extent that children reflect on it. They need to talk about, plan, assess, and thoughtfully consider the conceptual, moral, and social aspects of the time you and they spend together learning. Are the children learning ideas? Are the experiences purposeful and socially redeeming? Are lives being improved?

8. *Teach values.* Integrity, trust, cooperation, respect, and dignity can be modeled, talked about, and expected in your classroom. Do not shy away from these basic values. Instead, take every opportunity to explore them with your students.

9. *Give students freedom.* It is a curious fact that freedom is encouraged and expected in our Western societies, but we give little of it to the students in our schools. Where will they learn to use freedom in a responsible way? Give your students a certain amount of free time, perhaps on one day a week, just to see what they will do with it. If you have developed a rich environment and modeled learning well, they will use it productively.

10. *Create a sense of place.* If your students must spend six hours a day in your room, make it a challenging, attractive place to be. Do not overlook the value of displays, bulletin boards, interest centers, game tables, reading corners, and privacy areas. It does not take much to make a place magic for a young child.

11. *Promote success.* Many of your children will have an almost desperate need to experience success. Some will view themselves as largely unsuccessful. For a few children, you may need to scale down the amount and difficulty of the work. For others, you may have to intensify the complexity of the work. All people need to experience success or they tend to give up, become apathetic, and cease to learn.

12. *Reward excellence.* If you seriously consider these jobs, you will have some amazing outcomes in social studies. Do not let the fine work of your students go unnoticed. Inform them of their progress. Let parents know how well their children are doing. Display your students' work in the hallway or media center. Promote a sense of public recognition and appreciation for excellence.

Summary

Social studies is the study of human beings. The purpose of social studies in the elementary school curriculum is to introduce children to the world of people. Your task as a teacher of social studies is to make this world come alive. You need to share with children the excitement and creativity that are generated by inquiry, projects, cooperative efforts, integration of the arts, and other imaginative strategies. It isn't easy. It takes much thought and energy to move away from a worksheet-centered, read-around-the-room, emotionless approach to this subject.

The challenge of this first chapter has been to open up to you the world of possibilities inherent in the social studies curriculum. Think of yourself as an explorer on the edge of a great adventure as you approach this complex, intriguing subject. As you catch a glimpse of the vision of what social studies can become in the hands of a caring teacher, you are on the threshold of limitless possibilities.

ACTIVITIES

1. Talk to elementary school children about what they are doing in social studies. Try to piece together the scope and sequence of the social studies curriculum from their perspective.
2. Compare an elementary social studies textbook with a recent copyright to one at the same level that was published several years ago. Make your own inferences about the changes that have taken place in social studies curricula.
3. Interview an elementary school teacher who has taught for a number of years. Ask about changes that have occurred in social studies.
4. Review several new social studies programs. Analyze the contents to see which one best suits your perspective. If you are currently teaching, see what it would take to get that program for your classroom.
5. Try to imagine a classroom where social studies was being taught really well. What would it be like? How would you describe the teacher's behavior? In what kinds of activities and experiences would the students be involved?

SUGGESTED READINGS

Brandt, R., ed. (2000). *Education in a New Era: ASCD Yearbook 2000.* Alexandria, VA: Association for Supervision and Curriculum Development.

Gavin, C., et al. (1999). "Essential Questions for Elementary Social Studies: Curricular Reform for Social Action." *Social Studies and the Young Learner, 11* (Jan./Feb.): 12–15.

National Council for the Social Studies. Visit NCSS on the World Wide Web at *www.socialstudies.org.*

National Task Force for Social Studies Standards. (1994). *Expectations of Excellence: Curriculum Standards for Social Studies.* Washington, DC: National Council for the Social Studies.

Social Education. Official journal of the National Council for the Social Studies.

Social Studies and the Young Learner. Published by the National Council for the Social Studies. This journal is devoted to theory and practice of elementary social studies.

Building the Foundation for Social Studies

In this chapter, we will spend time establishing the foundation for meaningful social studies teaching and learning. I will keep this chapter brief, but I will also ask you to return to it from time to time as a means of reflecting on your own growth and development as a teacher. If we are successful, this chapter will become your compass, your map, your guide, and your lodestar to purposeful thought and action. Specifically, the chapter addresses the following points:

- Research-based findings teachers ought to know about
- Children's natural tendencies as learners
- Characteristics of higher-achieving students
- Encouraging thoughtfulness
- Keys to creativity

A rising tide lifts all boats.
—John F. Kennedy

Sometimes the question arises: Does educational research reveal anything that classroom teachers really need to know?" It is a fair question. It ought to be asked. The answer is *yes, we do.* Here, we will concentrate on seven principles that are supported in one way or another by thoughtful research. I am convinced that if you take these findings seriously and act on them routinely, yours will be a greatly enhanced social studies experience. All your students, not just a select few, will be the real winners.

Research Findings That Will Enhance the Social Studies Experience
- *Higher-order thinking.* Challenge your students to think, to question ideas, to put ideas to use, and to search for meaning. In a practical sense, this means moving beyond "what" and "how" to "why." Your questions should include "What do you think?" "Why do you think so?" You will have to model this behavior. It is also important to give your students time to think, to read, to work together, and to solve complex problems.

■ *The doctrine of interest.* This very old idea states that children should study those things that interest them most. It is easily misunderstood. People's interests arise when they find something compelling, fascinating, and worth wondering about. Childhood is on your side in this regard because children are quickly drawn to imaginative stories, projects, ideas, and activities. The question to ask yourself is: How do I make learning come alive? Three ways to create interest include (1) showing a personal interest in each child, (2) being genuinely enthusiastic about the material you teach, and (3) providing choices for students within the framework of the curriculum.

■ *Active learning.* Everything we know from child development tells us that elementary-age children need to learn through the five senses. They need to explore, create, build, talk, act, sing, dance, pretend, draw, paint, play, and perform. This does not mean there is no time for other forms, such as reading and listening to teacher talk, but the emphasis should be on activity. Freedom of movement is closely related to freedom to learn. Children need to be *doing* things, especially in cooperation with one another.

■ *Project learning.* Projects create complex syntax. They defeat the simple syntax of students sitting in rows doing seatwork. Projects call for collaboration, planning, building, and real assessment. People are basically project animals. We think and act in terms of projects quite naturally. Projects bring meaning to learning. It is certainly good as well as necessary to read about the Renaissance, but a project of a Renaissance Fair brings the Renaissance to life because knowledge is put to use.

■ *Parent involvement.* Achievement will increase, discipline problems will decrease, and classroom life will become more productive when you actively involve parents in their children's learning. Parents need to participate in certain homework assignments, they need to feel welcome in your room, and they can be a tremendous resource if you will invite them on board. I have heard pessimistic people say that parents don't care anymore. You and I are optimists. We know better.

■ *Collaborative learning.* It is a documented fact that students do not get to talk enough during the school day. They are too often denied the opportunity to share their ideas, to test them with others, and to work as part of a team. A classroom must be a place of social activity. It must be a friendly, supportive place where children want to go. Life is about working, playing, and getting along with others. The best classrooms, like the best of life, are always based on team building, sharing, and caring.

■ *Reflective practice.* It is tempting to try to cover too many things. The problem with doing so is that nothing takes hold at deeper levels. Children and teachers need time to search for meaning, to share thoughts and feelings, and to plan and assess together. Reflective practice will take you and your students to the truth of situations. Your classroom will be a more honest, open, and supportive place. Reflection takes time and patience. Don't get caught up in the coverage mentality.

These seven principles of teaching and learning are foundational elements of a meaningful social studies curriculum. Certainly, there is more to teaching social studies than this, but if you leave these ideas behind or neglect them, your efforts will be considerably diminished. As you plan, as you practice, and as you assess, ask yourself: Am I doing what I can to ensure that these elements of teaching and learning are built into the routine of classroom life?

John Dewey wrote a book called *The School and Society* more than 100 years ago. Much of what he noted has been validated over time, but curiously, many of his better ideas continue to elude our grasp at the level of school practice. I wish to spend a little time illuminating some of his thoughts as guides to productive teaching and learning in social studies. His ideas are quite powerful, but like most truly powerful ideas, they are also rather simple. They serve as reminders to us—reminders of certain foundational elements needed to support the growth and development of young learners. Dewey referred to these natural tendencies of children as "instincts" because his own observation and reflection led him to conclude that they tend not only to be universal but qualities that we do not have to teach because they are already there. I like to think of them as gifts of childhood. These tendencies are gifts to us as teachers. We only need to act on them. Sadly, some teachers see these tendencies not as opportunities but as problems to be overcome. Keep these four tendencies in mind for every lesson you teach:

1. *Conversation.* Surprise, children like to talk. They want to talk. They spend much of their early childhood asking questions, chattering, and developing the art of conversation. When they come to school, they find themselves in group settings that unfortunately are not always supportive of this tendency. In my own teaching at the college level, I often find myself reflecting on the difference between my classroom when I am lecturing and students are supposedly listening and my classroom when I involve my students in an activity of some kind. Everything changes. Time passes more quickly. People are sharing their thoughts. Problems are being solved. Language develops. Of course, there is a time to talk and a time to listen. Balance is the key, but the evidence shows that students are not given enough time to talk to one another during the school day.

2. *Construction.* Yes, I'm saying your room ought to become a construction zone. Kids need to build things, to take things apart, to work as little artists, architects,

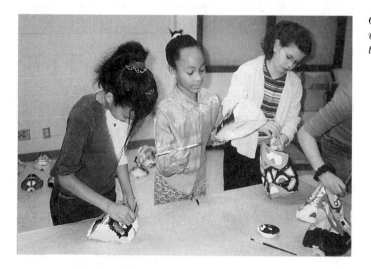

Children are naturally curious. They want to learn. Our task is to nurture the possibilities.

engineers, builders, and designers. They learn this way. You need manipulatives, equipment, and interest centers in your classroom. The construction needs to be related to topics of study, and social studies offers virtually unlimited opportunities in this regard. Maps, models, puppet theatres, dioramas, and villages are waiting to be built. This is constructivism in its most literal sense. Children are natural constructivists. Take advantage of the opportunity.

3. *Inquiry.* Curiosity, discovery, and good old poking around all come rather naturally to children. Your job and mine is to use this instinct to good advantage. This means involving students in problem-solving activities, in asking good questions, in seeking answers to questions posed, and in finding out on their own as opposed to being told. Much of what people learn comes from being told, reading, and so on, but this type of learning takes on deeper meaning when it relates to our one's own inquiry. The knowledge is useful. Knowledge discovered is always more powerful because it is knowledge owned by the inquirer. Self-confidence deepens when we learn to depend on ourselves.

4. *Artistic expression.* Every child is an artist—so is every adult, for that matter—but we sometimes seem to forget that. Our artistic interests take different forms, but we all have an ability to express ourselves creatively. In social studies, artistic expression takes on such forms as drawing, painting, sculpting, making models, writing play scripts, producing plays, role-playing, keeping a journal, writing stories, writing and playing music, sewing, cooking, recreating historical characters, making videos, building villages, creating time lines, and so on.

These four tendencies, viewed as solutions to making social studies come alive, handed to us by children as gifts, need-to become imbedded in practice. Conversation, construction, inquiry, and artistry ought to be the essence of the day-to-day routine in your classroom. You and your students should come to expect this as a matter of course. Classrooms where these things happen regularly are places of active learning, places of freedom of movement and expression, and places where opportunity prevails over restraint.

Characteristics of Higher-Achieving Students

Every student can be a higher achiever in the sense that every individual can always do better. From the struggling child who can barely read to the child who regularly achieves the highest grades, the challenge is one of self-improvement. But what is different about highly successful students? Can we identify the salient characteristics of those children who do well in school and in life in general? And can the classroom teacher who knows about those characteristics foster them in all students? It is a bit of a challenge, but good teaching, though never easy, brings its own rewards. Researcher Howard Johnston has investigated the patterns or characteristics of higher achievers and has identified eight such characteristics. You can take full advantage of these findings through social studies experiences and throughout the entire curriculum for that matter. The point is that some children already exhibit the attributes. But for the good teacher, this is not enough. We want to extend the opportunities to all our students. As you read through the list, challenge yourself to think of ways in which you could ensure that all your students and their parents become aware of these characteristics.

▪ Hold more conversations with adults. You can give assignments that require children to interview other teachers, their parents, and people in the neighborhood. These are modest ideas, but they represent a beginning.

▪ Develop skills and interests outside of school (hobbies, drama, sports, music, etc.). Anything you can do to encourage your students to take up hobbies, to become involved in school music programs, or to join after-school clubs will pay great dividends. Some teachers go so far as to start after-school extracurricular groups, such as drama clubs, chess clubs, and the like.

▪ Have more consistent life patterns. Letters home to parents urging them to provide definite times and places to do homework, place restrictions on the amount of television time, and encourage family activities related to social studies and other curricular areas will give you a place to start the process.

▪ Spend time planning for the future. Students need to think, draw, write, and talk about their futures. They need to talk with responsible adults and older students about how to go about planning for life beyond the present moment.

▪ Are involved in academically challenging activities. You need to set whole-class challenges as well as challenges for each individual student. Contracts, work plans, and goal setting represent concrete means of doing this.

▪ Have purpose within their families (chores, responsibilities, etc.). Again, there is nothing like a letter home to parents encouraging them to find tasks, chores, and meaningful responsibilities that enable your students to feel as though they are contributing to family life.

▪ Spend more time in supervised settings (home, church, clubs, sports, etc.). Children need models of positive adult leadership. This is crucial to their development as fully functioning individuals and as citizens of the community.

▪ Spend more time reading. Set the tone. Talk to your students about the many books you read. Talk about going to the library and looking for good material learning. Require each of your students to read at least 30 books per year.

Keep in mind the quote from the beginning of this chapter: "A rising tide lifts all boats." We want all your students to succeed. Now that you have had a chance to read through the list, you need to ask yourself whether you can play a significant role in encouraging the traits of high achievers in *all* your students. Notice that money, expenses, and so on, are not issues here. What does come through is a sense of a more ordered, consistent, supervised, and adult-connected childhood. Nurturing is the key. Children need love, structure, and patience. In a perfect world, all the kids you teach would already exhibit these characteristics, and your job would be far easier than in fact it is. But short of that, you can begin by informing the parents of your own students. They need your help. Good information in invaluable. You might be surprised how many parents are perfectly willing to try to improve their child's opportunities to become a better student and a better person.

Encouraging Thoughtfulness

As you walk down the halls of a school and look into the classrooms, you get different feeling about each one. Why is it that some are inviting and others are not? Why is it that some are places of thoughtfulness, reflection, and coherence and others simply are not? And why is it that you find yourself thinking that you'd like to be a student in this classroom, but you're not so sure about that one? Onosko and Newmann (1994), two eminent researchers, have identified certain attributes of classrooms where thoughtfulness prevails. The work in this area by Berliner and Biddle (1997) is also very useful to teachers who wish to make their classrooms places of reflection and deeper thought. Here are a few ideas around which you can build a foundation of thoughtfulness for social studies.

■ *Treat students' ideas and contributions with respect.* It is a fragile thing to be a student. Students respond to encouragement, to civil behavior, and to kindness. They tend to pass it along to others. You need to make it clear through your behavior that you welcome ideas from your students. You want them to feel that they can contribute. More than this, you want them to feel that their contributions are genuinely *needed* in order to make this a better place. It takes a gifted teacher to create such an atmosphere.

■ <u>*Encourage students to justify their contributions*</u>. Just as you want your students to feel free to contribute their ideas, so too will you want them to think through what they are doing and to learn to make a case for their efforts. They need this. Think of it as high expectations, of asking each student to do his or her best work. When students are required to analyze and assess their own ideas, they become more reflective in their own practice. Administrators, parents, and the general public expect this of you as a teacher, and you should expect it of your students.

■ *Maintain sustained involvement with a smaller number of topics.* A criticism of teaching in U.S. schools is that we tend to try to "cover" too many topics, resulting in superficial treatment of subject matter. The saying "Less is more" is certainly true. Depth of coverage is the key. One teacher spent a great deal of time with her class studying the Hopi Nation. The class built a model village. They made kuchina dolls. They assumed Hopi names during the study. They made food from Hopi recipes. They wrote letters to the Hopi Nation, asking for information. They did a great deal of reading. Another teacher, thinking this was too much attention to one group, had his students "cover" all the Native American nations of North America. Think about it.

■ *Plan challenging activites.* Psychologist Lev Vygotsky described the Zone of Proximal Development as the space between which a child can learn on his or her own and in which a child can learn with guidance. This is the realm of challenge for a learner. The challenge for the teacher is to figure out what experiences students need to truly challenge their intellectual and social skills. In this sense, a good teacher is like a good coach, observing, diagnosing, and advising. A perfect example of this happens when a teacher says to a student, "You know, there's a book I've been thinking about that I'd love to have you read." Such a comment, given lovingly and sincerely, has all the qualities of personalizing, of interest, and of desire to help a young person grow.

■ *Exhibit coherence, continuity, and a progression of ideas in your lessons.* *Coherence* means that things stick together, they make sense, they are thought out. You'll find that your teaching achieves greater coherence if you involve the students in planning. *Continuity* means that one day flows naturally from the day before and so on. It implies a plan from beginning to end, with flexibility along the way. You begin to achieve continuity when you are willing to slow down the process and ask your students to reflect on meaning, purpose, and interest. We talk about a *progression of ideas* in the sense of a spiral; that is, we have a few powerful ideas and we keep returning to them with new examples that allow children to probe them in greater depth over time.

Thoughtfulness begins with you. As you model this behavior, your students will begin to get the idea. Talk about the books you are reading. Talk about the things you are learning. Convey to your class a sense of excitement about your own journeys of discovery. Take time to reflect with individuals and with the class as a whole. Take time to find out how students feel, what they think, and what they are interested in. And above all, don't fall victim to the coverage mentality. Take the advice of the great philosopher Alfred North Whitehead, who said simply, "Don't try to teach too much."

Keys to Creativity

In this book and from other sources, you will learn about constructivism, multiple intelligences, learning styles, thinking styles, individual differences, and other characteristics of learners that speak to their uniqueness. I wish to close this foundational chapter by addressing the issue of creativity—a topic dear to the heart of social studies. It has been observed that creative people have an ability to make the familiar strange and the strange familiar. What does this mean to you? What does this have to do with teaching and learning social studies? I won't tell you because I think your own sense of creativity will enable you to answer the question. For now, let's explore some fundamentals to making your classroom a place where creativity is encouraged and found.

■ *Give children freedom and space.* A school and the classrooms within a school should be places of opportunity over restraint, places of freedom over coercion. In recent times, we have seen a shift in the business world from top-down authoritarian management to relaxed, playful atmospheres in which people are encouraged think for themselves, show initiative, and take chances with ideas. This is a remarkable change, and believe me, businesses would not do this if they weren't getting good results.

■ *Encourage projects.* Please forgive me if I begin to sound like a broken record to you at some point because my feelings are so strong on this matter. Projects help us apply knowledge; they get us beyond learning information for information's sake. Projects are something we *do*. They involve construction, building, performing, and, above all, teamwork. A class play or pageant; a display of maps, drawings, and models; a neighborhood cleanup campaign; the "adoption" of a nearby retirement home—all are examples of ways to involve students in something bigger than any individual can do alone. Philosopher Jurgen Habermas has raised the question, "What happens when interest in performance is not accompanied by corresponding participation?" The answer is disaster. Projects are about participation.

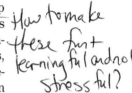
How to make these fun + learning ful and not stress ful?

■ *Encourage good literature.* Active learning does not mean that we do not read and write. Biographies, histories, novels, and poetry are essential to the growth and development of learners. Children watch too much television and they do not read enough. As I mentioned earlier, there is no reason to think in terms of anything less than each of your students reading one book a week (at least 30 per year) as a goal, regardless of their age. Beyond reading, students should write every day. We get good at what we practice, especially with expert help. Two of the best ways for people to expand their horizons are friendship and books. Working and playing together, reading good literature, and writing about your ideas represent fast tracks to improved achievement and social/moral growth.

■ *Encourage the arts and music.* Don't even think about putting together a social studies unit devoid of drawing, sketching, mapping, designing, painting, sculpting, drama, and singing. These are not frills. They are essentials. Your students need to listen to good music and study good artwork. They need to draw every day, because learning to draw is the best way of learning to see and create. The arts can bring a social studies program to life, whether at the level of appreciating good work done by experts or at the level of childhood performance.

Social studies is the study of human beings. Human beings are natural creators. It's what we do. It is difficult even to imagine the potential creativity lying dormant in a typical class of 25 to 30 students. Your task is to unleash it, to nourish it, to encourage risk taking, and to help each child find his or her unique gifts. As you support your students in their creative efforts, you will find your own creativity coming to the surface. It will manifest itself undeniably in the variety of lessons you teach and in the freedom you give yourself and your students to explore, to dream, and to discover the pleasures of learning together.

Summary

My purpose in this chapter has been to introduce the underlying foundational aspects of teaching and learning social studies. Much of the rest of this book is devoted to coverage of these same basic themes in greater depth. Thus, the book itself is based on the idea of the spiral curriculum. Using the spiral, we will limit ourselves to a few powerful ideas that we will study over and over. You don't want too many themes, too many ideas. When that happens, you are left with a laundry list. Your own teaching should be limited to a small number of truly important ideas, skills, and values that you and your students return to over and again. Instead of going down the tempting road of broad and superficial coverage, we will continue to pursue these themes with expanded analysis; with numerous examples of activities, lessons, and units; and with strategies for planning, teaching, learning, and assessment.

ACTIVITIES

1. Engage a fellow educator in a reflective discussion on the nature of childhood learning. What are the priorities?
2. I made the statement that drawing, mapping, drama, painting, singing, and so on, are not frills in a good social studies program. To what extent do you agree?
3. Who should plan the social studies curriculum? Should students be involved in planning, and if so, to what extent?

4. Some people will say that if you give children freedom to engage each other in conversation and to move about the room, then management problems will inevitably result. Do you agree?

SUGGESTED READINGS

Beane, J. (1997). *Curriculum Integration: Designing the Core of Democratic Education.* New York: Teachers College Press.

Berliner, D., and Biddle, B. (1997). *The Manufactured Crisis.* White Plains, NY: Longman.

Dewey, J. (1899). *The School and Society.* Boston: Houghton Mifflin.

Ellis, A. (2001). *Research in Educational Innovations* (3rd ed.). Larchmont, NY: Eye on Education.

Johnston, J. H. (1995). "Climate: Building a Culture of Achievement." *Schools in the Middle* (Nov./Dec.): 10–15.

Onosko, J., and Newmann, F. (1994). "Creating More Thoughtful Learning Environments," In J. Mangieri and C. Block, eds., *Creating Powerful Thinking in Teachers and Students.* Fort Worth, TX: Harcourt Brace.

3

The Knowledge Base for Elementary Social Studies

The content, concepts, and methods of elementary social studies are derived primarily from history, geography, and the social sciences. Social studies is both integrative and broad in scope by its very nature. After all, when the subject matter is human beings and their interaction with environments, then we have a wide ranging course of study. This is both a strength and a weakness of this area of the curriculum. It is a strength because human behavior takes so many forms over time and place that we are never at a loss for interesting material. The weakness may be that there is so much to learn that it seems at times overwhelming. Children are all too easily overwhelmed by names, dates, facts, and so on. The secret is to bring meaning to knowledge. Good teachers have always known that. This chapter focuses on the following related topics:

- Thoughts on the nature of knowledge
- A review of the National Council for the Social Studies standards
- Remarks about what elementary students should know
- A brief description of the structure of history, geography, and the social sciences

> *Knowledge is of two kinds. We know a subject ourselves, or we know where we can find information upon it.*
> —Samuel Johnson

You can see from the 1775 Samuel Johnson quote (by the way, he wrote the first dictionary of the English language) that there is an age-old perception of the differences people have in mind when they speak about knowledge. In a nutshell, the argument is over whether knowledge is strictly content, strictly process, or, as Dr. Johnson suggests, both. A recurring issue in teaching and learning social studies is that of what and how much children should know about history, geography, and the social sciences. It is easy to find critical commentaries regarding how little today's students know, especially compared to students of generations past. Similarly, it is not particularly difficult to find commentaries arguing that the amount of content knowledge someone has is insignificant. This argument holds that the important thing is that people have process skills that enable them to locate and use knowledge when needed. Each of these arguments contains a certain measure of truth and a good dose of exaggeration.

Actually, the content versus process debate will probably never be completely solved, simply because it hinges so much on opinion and philosophy of teaching and learning. Let me illustrate the point by asking you to examine Figures 3.1 and 3.2. They present the basic argument from the progressive (process orientation) and essentialist (basic skills and knowledge) points of view, respectively. Take a moment to consider each and whether you favor one perspective more than the other or whether perhaps you see certain advantages in each.

The Nature of Knowledge

Who was the first president of the United States? Who is the woman whose profile has recently appeared on a U.S. coin? How many time zones does the United States have? Which state is bordered by more states than any other? What were the principal causes of the Civil War? Perhaps you think I'm trying to draw you into a game of Trivial Pursuit. No, on the contrary, I'm merely bringing up an issue that has become one of paramount debate in recent years—that of what and how much children ought to know as a result of their experiences with elementary social studies.

FIGURE 3.1

Basic Assumptions of Progressive Education

- Learning how to learn is at the heart of the matter. Students need to learn how to deal with unknown outcomes and challenges. In this sense, knowledge is seen as dynamic and ever changing rather than as static.

- Subject matter does not represent an end in itself; rather, it provides the raw material for learning and is relevant when it can be put to use. Textbooks, lectures, and formal examinations are considered artificial; true learning takes place when real problems of living are engaged and subject matter is used as a tool or instrument for learning.

- Experience is the key to productive learning. Learning should be active, exploratory, and socially engaged. A school should be a miniature democracy, a community, where citizenship is learned through experience.

- Learner interest is significant. Human beings learn best when they have the opportunity to study those things that interest them most.

- Project learning is productive because of its practical, problem-solving, creative, social, and open-ended attributes.

- Real-world connections provide a sense of relevance and enable students to feel that they are taking part in public life.

- Reflective thinking should accompany active learning in order to provide a sense of purpose, balance, and assessment.

- The process of education should take precedence over the product. Learning represents continuous growth and is a complex enterprise.

FIGURE 3.2

*Basic
Assumptions
of Essentialist
Education*

- We have lost sight of the true purpose of education, which is intellectual and academic, not social and emotional.

- Education should be rigorous and demanding. The teacher's role is that of scholar who challenges students to higher levels of academic achievement.

- Academically talented students should especially be challenged because they represent the nation's future talent pool in a meritocratic society.

- The core disciplines, such as history and geography, should represent the essence of the curriculum. Activities in peer relations, life adjustment, and so on should be downplayed.

- Standards are necessary, as are standardized tests of achievement. Standards help teachers and students focus on essential knowledge and skills.

- Educational fads—such as learning styles, self-esteem curricula, and so on—are distractions from the real issue, which is to provide each student with the basic skills and knowledge necessary to achieve in life.

- Traditional forms—including textbooks, examinations, grades, graded schools, standards for promotion, and the like—are of proven worth and should be maintained.

At the heart of this matter is the process/product controversy, the essence of which is whether greater emphasis should be placed on *how* to learn or *what* to learn. Everyone agrees that both are important, but the argument is focused more on where the appropriate balance lies than on anything else.

What do you think about this? Perhaps your opinion is influenced by your own experience with social studies during your school years. Maybe you were the type of person who enjoyed learning the names of rivers and mountains, about the way people made a living in distant lands, or about life in ancient times. Maybe you weren't. Take a moment to write briefly your own recollections of social studies, especially how you felt about it:

_____

_____

_____

_____

Whether your memories were positive, negative, or mixed is no doubt influenced by (1) your attitude toward the subject matter itself, (2) the kinds of experiences you had in learning the subject matter, and (3) who taught you. In most cases, the subject matter itself is the least important of the three considerations. One person may remember studying Latin America and how boring it was. Another person may remember studying Latin America and how much fun it was when the class got to fix a Latin American meal and how kind and enthusiastic the teacher was about things. Elements such as these tend to interact and influence how a person feels, not just about social studies but about school learning in general.

Each of us has a certain amount of portable knowledge of history, geography, and the like. This knowledge belongs to us, and we carry it around with us inside our heads. It is committed to memory. Of course, memory fits into two categories:

long term and short term. Some things we seem to remember all our lives, and other things, well, we just hope we can remember them for the big test! But whatever we know, we had to *acquire* the knowledge, because we weren't simply born with it.

There are three ways that people know what they know. The first way, and the most common, is *knowledge received*. People receive knowledge from many sources: lecture, explanation, story, sermon, song, textbook, film, and so on. The point is that the knowledge first belongs to someone else, and it is then transmitted to another through some medium. This is essentially a passive view of knowledge acquisition. That, however, can be misleading because the level of a person's motivation will determine his or her level of involvement. Perhaps you can recall being told a story when you were a child and your own imagination was participating actively along with the storyteller. Knowledge received implies that experts are at the source and novices who need to know something are on the receiving end. The expert may be a lecturer, the author of a textbook, a gifted storyteller, or whatever, but the point is that the relationship between an expert and the learner is unequal. Another point worth considering about knowledge received is that it is secondhand knowledge. The learner generally trusts the accuracy of the authority because the learner is dependent on the expert source of information.

Most of your knowledge and mine is knowledge received. We didn't create it, and we probably had no way to verify it; rather, we tend to trust its accuracy. For example, you may know some things about life in ancient Greece or colonial America. It is likely that you received that knowledge from some source or perhaps a number of sources. It is important for a teacher to convey to students that no text on any subject is entirely accurate. There is no such thing as complete accuracy; only degrees of accuracy are found.

A second way people know what they know is *knowledge discovered*. This means of knowing is quite different from knowledge received. The implication of knowledge discovered is that some thing, event, circumstance, or whatever exists that you do not know about; however, by applying yourself, you can find out. In a nutshell, the difference between these first two forms is as simple as the difference between being told by someone else and finding out for yourself. In essence, this changes the learning equation fundamentally. The center of gravity shifts to the learner. The teacher, or other expert source, becomes a facilitator. This puts the teacher in an extremely important role because he or she must arrange the environment for learning in such a way as to be challenging, motivating, and filled with possibilities. Discovery learning assumes that students will investigate, experiment, use trial and error, and reach conclusions for themselves. Thus, in their quest for knowledge, students become historians, geographers, and so on. The teacher who involves students in knowledge discovered must create a rich environment, know when to ask questions, know when to lend support and cues, and, most difficult of all, know when not to intervene. All this raises teaching to a higher art form.

The third way people know what they know is *knowledge constructed*. Here, there is no assumption of the prior existence of certain knowledge; that is, being told or even finding out will not work at this level. At a simple level, imagine an empty lot with little on it. You decide to build a house there. You change things as a result of your effort. Now knowledge of a house in that part of town is common—others know about it, too. Knowledge constructed implies the building of new structures, the writing of new stories or accounts, the reassembling of existing knowledge into new forms, and so on. Creativity and originality are keys to knowledge constructed, although the creativity may exist within an already developed pattern. Projects, plays, building, and drawings are examples of knowledge constructed.

Knowledge of this third kind also exists as a social construction. Children working together will talk about what they are doing. They will make decisions, have agreements and disagreements, organize themselves, socialize, reflect, and find themselves linked to something greater than that which exists when people work alone. Thus, a far more subtle kind of knowledge emerges. It is a knowledge of friendship, collaboration, and teamwork. This kind of knowledge must be experienced in order for it to be real. To deny this kind of knowledge to children in the name of teaching social studies would be ironic, to say the very least.

Russian psychologist Lev Vygotsky noted the importance of language and thought as dependent on each other for their development. When children work together on a project, a mural, a play, or a construction activity, they will have the opportunity to express their ideas and feelings during the process. They are engaged in constructing knowledge as they talk and listen to each other. The importance of this can hardly be underestimated. When people express themselves verbally in connection with their involvement in an activity, they have the possibility to reach higher levels of consciousness about what they are doing. They can reflect, decide, evaluate, and employ a range of metacognitive strategies that are not available to the person working alone.

In summary, it is fair to say that all three ways of knowing are strategic and complementary. People simply cannot discover or create everything they need to know, so received knowledge plays a vital role in human development. On the other hand, knowledge received must be balanced with knowledge discovered and constructed. The wise teacher understands the relationship among all three and uses all three. When President Thomas Jefferson sent Lewis and Clark on their three-year expedition to the West of North America, he chose them because they were well read and had received knowledge from multiple sources over the years. He also chose them because he knew they were discoverers, and, indeed, they discovered many plants, animals, rivers, mountain passes, and so on along the way. But Jefferson also knew these expedition leaders would construct new knowledge of the West as a result of their experiences. Their maps, charts, and descriptions created new knowledge of a landscape known well perhaps to certain Native Americans, but hardly at all to European Americans. Today, their journal accounts are considered to be one of the great epic stories of the nineteenth century. A gifted teacher is aware that the well-known journeys of discovery found in text and film are qualitatively no different from the journeys of discovery that his or her students are involved in as they learn about their world and construct both personal and collective meanings of it.

The National Council for the Social Studies Standards as a Guide to the Knowledge Base

The past decade has seen the development of national standards in all the major areas of school curriculum. The standards for social studies were completed under the aegis of the National Council for the Social Studies (NCSS) in 1994. The standards serve as a general framework for the knowledge and experiential basis of social studies. The purpose of the standards is not, as some have feared, to create a national curriculum. Rather, the intent is to establish a sense of direction and a goal structure. The NCSS notes that the standards should

1. Serve as a framework for K–12 social studies program design through the use of 10 thematic strands.
2. Serve as a guide for curriculum decisions by providing performance expectations regarding knowledge, processes, and attitudes essential for all students.
3. Provide examples of classroom practice to guide teachers in designing instruction to help students meet performance expectations.

Let's take a look at each of the three intended outcomes, beginning with the 10 thematic strands (listed in Figure 3.3). The strands represent broad categories of teaching and learning and are meant to provide only the most general sense of coverage. However, they convey the essence of the spiral curriculum concept of visiting and revisiting a few key ideas from kindergarten through twelfth grade.

The 10 key strands from the NCSS standards represent powerful ideas about human behavior. As you examine them carefully, you will see that they are concept statements from history, geography, and the social sciences. They are a logical place for you to begin thinking about the spiral curriculum and its potential to build a schema for young learners. These ideas need to be emphasized and reemphasized each year at increasing levels of sophistication. The standards are, in fact, the cornerstone of the social studies goal structure. As you plan lessons, units, and experiences, you should seriously consider them. I would go so far as to say that every social studies experience should relate to one or more of the strands. The point that must be underscored, however, is that the ideas need to be taught and learned in developmentally appropriate ways.

The thematic strands also serve as a guide for curriculum decision making. At one level, decisions about what textbooks to adopt, which materials to use, and so on should focus on the knowledge, processes, and attitudes exemplified in the 10 concept statements. The hope is that commercial textbook companies and experimental projects alike will take the standards into account so that a measure of commonality will emerge. This is not to say that every program should look alike, especially in a day of site-based decision making. Rather, the point is that educators can begin to address the fundamental questions of (1) What knowledge of history, geography, and social science should children possess? (2) What skills of critical thinking and problem solving should children attain? and (3) What values of citizenship and self-fulfillment are basic to positive growth and development for children in a democratic society?

The third use of the strands is that they can serve as a guide to classroom practice. As you design lessons and units, you will want to take into account the performance expectations implied in the strands. In order to give you a clearer idea of this, Figures 3.4 and 3.5 illustrate, at primary and intermediate levels, *performance expectations* (i.e., what should students know and be able to do as a result) and *classroom examples* showing how teachers can bring the NCSS standards to life.

FIGURE 3.3

I. Culture

Human beings create, learn, and adapt culture. Human cultures are dynamic systems of beliefs, values, and traditions that exhibit both commonalities and differences. Understanding culture helps us understand ourselves and others.

II. Time, Continuity, and Change

Human beings seek to understand their historic roots and to locate themselves in time. Such understanding involves knowing what things were like in the past and how things change and develop—allowing us to develop historic perspective and answer important questions about our current condition.

III. People, Places, and Environment

Technological advancements have insured that students are aware of the world beyond their personal locations. As students study content related to this theme, they create their spatial views and geographic perspectives of the world; social, cultural, economic, and civic demands mean that students will need such knowledge, skills, and understandings to make informed and critical decisions about the relationship between human beings and their environment.

IV. Individual Development and Identity

Personal identity is shaped by one's culture, by groups and by institutional influences. Examination of various forms of human behavior enhances understanding of the relationships between social norms and emerging personal identities, the social processes which influence identity formation, and the ethical principles underlying individual action.

V. Individuals, Groups, and Institutions

Institutions exert enormous influence over us. Institutions are organizational embodiments to further the core social values of those who comprise them. It is important for students to know how institutions are formed, what controls and influences them, how they control and influence individuals and culture, and how institutions can be maintained or changed.

VI. Power, Authority, and Governance

Understanding of the historic development of structures of power, authority, and governance and their evolving functions in contemporary society is essential for the emergence of civic competence.

VII. Production, Distribution, and Consumption

Decisions about exchange, trade, and economic policy and well-being are global in scope and the role of government in policy making varies over time and from place to place. The systematic study of an interdependent world economy and the role of technology in economic decision making is essential.

VIII. Science, Technology, and Society

Technology is as old as the first crude tool invented by prehistoric humans, and modern life as we know it would be impossible without technology and the science which supports it. Todays technology forms the basis for some of our most difficult social choices.

IX. Global Connections

The realities of global interdependence require understanding of the increasingly important and diverse global connections among world societies before there can be analysis leading to the development of possible solutions to persisting and emerging global issues.

X. Civic Ideals and Practices

All people have a stake in examining civic ideals and practices across time, in diverse societies, as well as in determining how to close the gap between present practices and the ideals upon which our democratic republic is based. An understanding of civic ideals and practices of citizenship is critical to full participation in society.

Source: Expectations of Excellence: Curriculum Standards for Social Studies, Bulletin 89, Fall 1994, Washington, DC: NCSS.

FIGURE 3.4

Social studies programs should include experiences that provide for the study of *how people organize for the production, distribution, and consumption of goods and services,* so that the learner can:

Performance Expectations
a. give examples that show how scarcity and choice govern our economic decisions;
b. distinguish between needs and wants;
c. identify examples of private and public goods and services;
d. give examples of the various institutions that make up economic systems such as families, workers, banks, labor unions, government agencies, small businesses, and large corporations;
e. describe how we depend upon workers with specialized jobs and the ways in which they contribute to the production and exchange of goods and services;
f. describe the influence of incentives, values, traditions, and habits on economic decisions;
g. explain and demonstrate the role of money in everyday life;
h. describe the relationship of price to supply and demand;
i. use economic concepts such as supply, demand, and price to help explain events in the community and nation;
j. apply knowledge of economic concepts in developing a response to a current local economic issue, such as how to reduce the flow of trash into a rapidly filling landfill.

Focus on the Classroom: Standards into Practice

Performance Expectations: e, i
At the beginning of a unit on economic specialization in production, Mark Moran's early primary class is divided into two teams of cookie makers. Both teams make gingerbread cookies. One team works as an assembly line, each person having a special job—rolling out the dough, cutting the basic shape, making the almond mouth, locating raisin buttons, etc. The second team works as individuals, each person creating his or her own gingerbread cookies. Both teams have the same supplies to work with.

After they have finished baking their cookies, the students examine the cookies and identify the advantages and disadvantages of each method of producing cookies. Ideas that emerge relate to division of labor, pride, creativity, independence, specialization, and quality control.

Students subsequently prepare summaries in writing about how they produced their cookies. Moran evaluates the quality of the student writing by determining how accurate the students are in detailing the production process and the extent to which evidence of key concepts is present.

In the weeks that follow this lesson, students examine other situations involving assembly line production, including a field trip to a local plant where pickup trucks are assembled.

Source: Adapted from *Expectations of Excellence: Curriculum Standards for Social Studies* (p. 65), Bulletin 89, Fall 1994, Washington, DC: NCSS. © National Council for the Social Studies. Reprinted by permission.

FIGURE 3.5

Culture: Middle Grades

Social studies programs should include experiences that provide for the study of *culture and cultural diversity,* so that the learner can:

Performance Expectations

a. compare similarities and differences in the ways groups, societies, and cultures meet human needs and concerns;

b. explain how information and experiences may be interpreted by people from diverse cultural perspectives and frames of reference;

c. explain and give examples of how language, literature, the arts, architecture, other artifacts, traditions, beliefs, values, and behaviors contribute to the development and transmission of culture;

d. explain why individuals and groups respond differently to their physical and social environments and/or changes to them on the basis of shared assumptions, values, and beliefs;

e. articulate the implications of cultural diversity, as well as cohesion, within and across groups.

Focus on the Classroom: Standards into Practice

Performance Expectations: a, c, d, e

The fifth grade students in Rose Sudmeier's class are sharing the stories behind their names in small groups. In constructing a "native culture" in their classroom, they have studied the place/environment, including descriptions, vocabulary development, visual presentations, and survival in the environment. This process led to a look at the people living in that place. They are now talking about naming traditions in general and how they came to be named.

The class researches the tools, food, and other survival necessities that would be needed in their place. They then begin to discuss what the people might do at night when it was dark or during the day when work was done and how traditions, such as the naming tradition, might be passed on. At this point, Sudmeier brings in her colleague, Dave Trowbridge, and his geography class from the high school, which has been studying traditions, storytelling, art, and music of the Northwest Coastal Indian tribes.

The high school students visit the fifth grade class on two different days, showing the elementary students how to do basic dance steps and how to make dancing masks. They also tell them stories of various legends and play musical tapes. The fifth graders continue their study for another three days on their own. The high school students plan a return visit for the end of the week, when they also invite the fifth graders to be their guests in a potlatch. At the potlatch, the high schoolers entertain the fifth graders with stories and then have them join them in dances and use the masks they had shown them how to make. In keeping with the potlatch tradition, the guests receive small gifts from the high school students at the end.

As an evaluation tool, Sudmeier has the children keep journals in which they write about their culture, traditions they started, poetry they wrote about their environment, and reflections on their participation in the various activities. She looks for the journals to be thoughtfully written, expressing positive views, accurate in the information presented, creative, and reflective.

Source: Adapted from *Expectations of Excellence: Curriculum Standards for Social Studies* (p. 79), Bulletin 89, Fall 1994, Washington, DC: NCSS. © National Council for the Social Studies. Reprinted by permission.

The years that mark the bridge between the closing of the twentieth century and the opening of the twenty-first century have been a time of great contention over the knowledge base that children ought to possess, not just in social studies but in all content areas. Part of the problem is the sheer explosion of the base itself; today there is more to know than ever before. Another aspect of the problem is the fundamental transformation in the ways in which knowledge is stored, received, and made available. This is particularly an issue with regard to the advent of video, computer technologies, and electronic databases. The book, which has been the staple of knowledge stored, is challenged by the new technologies, and no one knows for sure what it all means. One thing is certain, however: We are witnessing a return of graphic and pictorial forms (which were dominant in centuries past) to a world of education that has been dominated by print.

Who has the better sense of the events surrounding the American Revolution: the child who has read the book *Johnny Tremain* or the child who has seen the film? Who knows more about city government: the child who has read the text or the child who has played the simulation *Sim City*? Who knows more about the U.S. space program: the child who has read several books on its history or the child who uses the Internet and World Wide Web to access the daily activities of NASA? I don't think these are trivial questions. Of course, the easy answer is that teachers want children to access knowledge through multiple sources and experiences.

Setting aside for now *how* someone gains knowledge of history, geography, government, and so forth, let's return to the question of what a child completing elementary school ought to know. A number of prominent educators have addressed this question, most notably philosopher Mortimer Adler in his book *The Paideia Proposal* (Macmillan, 1982), and professor of English E. D. Hirsch Jr. in his book *Cultural Literacy* (Houghton Mifflin, 1987). I recommend that you examine both books; and because Hirsch went a step further with his *Core Knowledge Series*, books that define a knowledge base for elementary children in all disciplines, you might want to look more deeply into his work. *The Core Knowledge Series: Grades 1–6* (Delta, 1991–1995) develops content material for the social studies under the headings of Geography, World Civilization, and American Civilization. Other sources exist, certainly, but for the serious seeker of a knowledge base in elementary social studies, Hirsch's materials are probably the best place to start. In fact, it would be beneficial to you to compare Hirsch's *Core Knowledge Series* with the contents of textbooks available from such publishers as Allyn and Bacon, Macmillan, Ginn, Houghton Mifflin, Silver Burdett, Follett, and so on.

This is not the place to attempt to document everything children should know based on the social studies experience. However, I will attempt to give the flavor of such a quest—in this case, listing the historical fiction that children should have read or have had read to them about one period in American history (late colonial to Revolutionary America, 1685–1785) by the time they finish the elementary school years. The list was developed for the National Council for the Social Studies and is presented in Figure 3.6. This is not to say, however, that other books of high quality pertaining to that time period should not also be read. Part of the problem with attempting to state what should be included in a list is the predictable possibility that others might disagree. Welcome to democracy!

FIGURE 3.6

Literature Related to the Late Colonial and American Revolutionary Periods (1685–1785)	Avi	*The Fighting Ground* *Night Journeys*
	Caudill, Rebecca	*The Far-off Land*
	Clapp, Patricia	*I'm Deborah Sampson: A Soldier in the War of the Revolution* *Witches' Children: A Story of Salem*
	Collier, James Lincoln, and Collier, Christopher	*Jump Ship to Freedom* *My Brother Sam Is Dead* *War Comes to Willy Freeman*
	Forbes, Esther	*Johnny Tremain*
	Fritz, Jean	*The Cabin Faced West* *Will You Sign Here, John Hancock?*
	Gauch, Patricia	*This Time, Tempe Wick?*
	Lasky, Kathryn	*Beyond the Burning Time*
	Lawson, Robert	*Ben and Me* *Mr. Revere and I*
	Monjo, F. N.	*King George's Head Was Made of Lead*
	O'Dell, Scott	*Sarah Bishop*
	Petry, Ann	*Tituba of Salem Village*
	Rinaldi, Ann	*A Break with Charity: A Story about the Salem Witch Trials* *The Fifth March: A Story of the Boston Massacre*
	Speare, Elizabeth George	*The Sign of the Beaver* *The Witch of Blackbird Pond*

Source: Adapted from Judith Irvin, John Lunstrum, Carol Lynch-Brown, and Mary Friend Shepard, *Enhancing Social Studies through Literacy Strategies*, Bulletin 91, 1995, Washington, DC: NCSS.

Thus far, we have considered the broad guidelines of the NCSS curriculum standards as well as the knowledge base and a recommendation to research Adler's and Hirsch's viewpoints on such. The final portion of this chapter is devoted to an examination of the basic structure of history, geography, and the social science disciplines. These are the knowledge-generating scholarly disciplines from which social studies subject matter is derived.

The Social Science Disciplines

The social science disciplines of anthropology, economics, geography, history, sociology, and political science form the foundation of the elementary social studies curriculum. The social sciences are those areas of scholarly inquiry that focus in a systematic way on the study of human behavior. Social studies is that area of the elementary school curriculum that focuses on the activities of human beings.

A background in the social sciences is vital, because one task you face as a social studies teacher is to present social science to young learners in a meaningful way. Social studies is, of course, more than simplified social science. It is, above all, about the students themselves—their present needs, their possible futures, and their growing awareness of themselves and others around them. But the methods and ideas of social science can and should contribute to the intellectual and social growth of students.

Obviously, this is not the place to explore any of the social sciences in depth. Table 3.1 provides an introduction to the structure of each social science discipline. Selected sources are listed at the end of this chapter so you can pursue one or more of the disciplines in greater depth.

Anthropology

What Is Anthropology? Anthropology has been characterized as the study of culture, or the scientific study of human beings. Such a definition is obviously rather broad in scope and hardly serves to distinguish it from other social sciences. Oliver writes:

> Anthropologists occasionally cast their glance over Western Civilization, but they are mainly concerned with the history of "historyless" peoples, with the economics of communities without price-fixing market institutions, with government and politics in "stateless" societies, with social relations in places where kinship usually outweighs occupation, with the psychology of non-Westerners, with the anatomy and physiology of the whole range of mankind and its primate relatives.[1]

Thus, anthropologists incorporate elements of behavior, economics, political science, sociology, psychology, and other social sciences into their investigations. Although some anthropologists focus on Western and other technologically advanced societies—particularly on such aspects of those societies as education, vocations, religion, and families—such investigations are usually considered to be in the domain of the sociologist. The anthropologist is more commonly identified with studies of the cultural norms of so-called preliterate and emerging societies.

What Do Anthropologists Do? Anthropologists study cultures. They develop case histories of various tribal and ethnic groups, as well as descriptive accounts of the mores and patterns of different groups. Their data sources include the writings of previous investigators, plus artifacts, informants, and eye-witness accounts. Because their concern is with the concept of culture, anthropologists are generally interested in developing a total, interrelated picture of a society rather than in dealing exclusively with its economic patterns, power structure, or any other facet of that society's existence. In this respect, anthropology has been termed an *integrative science.*

Anthropologists investigate cultures using one or more of the following methods:

1. *Indirect observation.* Anthropologists pursuing indirect observation use maps, census data, the writings of previous investigators, the examination of artifacts, and interviews with informants. Indirect observation is useful for developing historical accounts of cultures and validating information obtained by other methods.

2. *Direct observation.* Anthropologists using direct observation spend time with their subjects, observing them and taking notes as they go about the business of

TABLE 3.1 A Conceptual Framework for the Social Sciences

Conceptual Schemes

Behavioral Themes: Responsibility for People and Their Environment	A: People Are the Product of Heredity and Environment	B: Human Behavior Is Shaped by the Social Environment	C: Geographic Features of the Earth Affect Human Behavior	D: Economic Behavior Depends on the Utilization of Resources	E: Political Organizations Resolve Conflict and Make Interaction among People Easier
Level Six — Through development of systems of behavior.	Physical and cultural inheritance results in variation in the people of the earth.	Social systems are affected by the values of interacting groups.	The environment is affected by the political organization of societies.	Economic systems are affected by the values of interdependent groups within societies.	Political systems depend on the interaction of groups in the societies.
Level Five — Through cultural patterns of behavior.	The interaction of physical and cultural inheritance results in people's adaptation to their environment.	People in different environments often have similar behavior patterns.	People modify their environments in order to use, increase, and conserve resources.	The patterns of buying and selling depend on the economic choices people make.	Different cultures within a society use government to meet their needs.
Level Four — Through adaptive patterns of behavior.	People inherit and learn patterns of behavior.	People learn social behavior from groups with which they interact.	People use the environment to meet their basic needs.	People interact to use resources available to them.	Peaceful interaction among people depends on social controls.
Level Three — Through adaptive patterns of the larger group.	The members of a community learn to adapt to their environment.	Community characteristics result from interactions between individuals and groups in an environment.	Communities develop different modes of adaptation to different environments.	Members of a community choose how to use resources to meet their needs.	Groups of people form governments in order to make decisions that affect all of the members of society.
Level Two — Through adaptive behavior of the basic group.	People live in a variety of environments.	Members of groups learn the social behavior of their groups.	People live in a physical environment.	People use resources to meet their needs.	Members of groups are governed by rules.
Level One — Through adaptive behavior of the individual within the group.	Individuals resemble each other.	Individuals learn from each other.	Individuals live in different environments on the earth.	Individuals, interacting to meet their needs, use resources available to them.	Individuals learn commonly accepted rules from each other.

Source: Adapted from *Living in Our World*, New York: Harcourt Brace Jovanovich.

living their lives. This method uses such tools as the camera, tape recorder, and field notebook.

3. *Participant observation.* Participant observation also depends on the investigator spending time with subjects. However, participant observers make an attempt to join their group and thereby become as inconspicuous as possible. The participant investigator often attempts to learn the language and customs of a group in order to gain some degree of acceptance. This approach was used rather effectively by an investigator who actually married the chief of a tribal group during the course of her work in Indonesia.

Selected Anthropological Concepts. Certain terms and ideas can help define the conceptual structure of anthropology.[2]

- *Acculturation.* The changes resulting when two cultures make contact with one another (e.g., the changes in European and Native American societies following the voyages of Columbus).
- *Artifacts.* Objects produced by human beings, as opposed to natural objects. Artifacts provide clues to a group's values, economic system, technological orientation, and so forth.
- *Culture.* The personality or way of life of a group of human beings; the particular set of characteristics that unify a group and make it distinguishable from other groups. The attributes of culture include language, technology, religion, food, clothing, shelter, traditions, and ideas.
- *Diffusion.* The flow of ideas, traits, and tools from one culture to another. Racial characteristics, for example, are diffused as one culture marries into and mingles with another.
- *Enculturation.* Those learning experiences a person has as a result of his or her culture. The home and school are agents of enculturation.
- *Innovation.* The introduction of new ideas, traits, and tools into a culture as a result of invention, discovery, or diffusion.
- *Personality.* Traits, behaviors, and habits a person acquires as a result of membership in and interaction with a particular culture.
- *Role.* The status of a member of a particular culture and the resulting behavior exhibited by or expected of that person in a given situation.
- *Traditions.* Customs and beliefs of a culture that are transmitted from one generation to succeeding generations.

Key Ideas about Anthropology

1. All people have universal cultural traits, such as:
   a. Language
   b. Technology
   c. Social organization
   d. Political organization
   e. Moral and legal sanctions
   f. Religion or philosophy
   g. Creative activities—art, music, dance
   h. Ways of resolving differences
   i. Methods of protection
   j. Leisure activities
   k. Methods of education or enculturation
2. All elements of culture, whether explicit or implicit, are integrated.
3. A change in one aspect of culture influences the total pattern of culture.
4. Cultural change may occur by diffusion, invention, and innovation.

Economics

What Is Economics? Economics focuses on the production and consumption of goods and services. Economists are concerned with human and material resources. Calderwood, Lawrence, and Maher write:

> Economics is concerned with all of society and with the activities of the various groups and institutions it contains—consumers, businessmen, farmers, workers, savers, investors, corporations, and federal, state, and local government. It is a social science.
>
> Economics is concerned not only with the individual parts of our economy—the consumer, the business, the union, and the market for a particular product (which we call microeconomics)—but also with the sum of these parts that together constitute the economic system of a country; that is, how the individual parts relate to form a whole. Economics is also concerned with the functioning of the economy, with how fast it is growing, and how vulnerable it is to inflation or depression (which we call macro-economics).[3]

Maher defines economics in terms of the basic economic concept of scarcity of resources and the attendant problems of their allocation.

> Ever since the spell of abundance was broken in the Garden of Eden, individuals and nations alike have confronted the fact of scarcity. It is for this reason that there are economic problems and an economic science. Scarcity means that there are not enough of the goods and services around to satisfy human wants. These goods and services are scarce because the materials from which they are made are insufficient. Thus, there is scarcity of both the resources used in production—land, machinery, equipment, and labor—and the final products into which these resources are transformed. Because of scarcity, there is a need to use to best advantage both the resources and the things produced—to economize. Economics is the science of economizing.[4]

What Do Economists Do? Economists analyze the use of various resources. Their analyses are designed to deal with the problems arising due to the scarcity of material and technical resources. Such analyses result in recommendations regarding the kinds of choices that ought to be made in order to optimize the production and consumption of goods and services. Choices must be made among alternatives, whether those choices involve buying a bracelet versus going to a movie, going to Disney World versus paneling the family room, or spending government money for foreign aid versus spending it for domestic vocational education. Economists attempt to clarify and define objectives for persons, families, and nations in order to make them better able to understand the consequences of various uses of resources. Maher provides a simple example of an economic analysis of a situation.

> The land in a pea patch together with the farmer's labor, his shovel, his hoe, and some seed are *resources*. (Sunshine and rain are resources too, but the farmer has little control over them nor does he pay to use them.) Next, the *production* process includes plowing, planting, weeding, and harvesting the peas. The *output*, of course, is the peas—if everything has gone well. But a bushel of peas is not the end of the whole activity. Rather, the satisfaction of hunger is the objective. For this satisfaction to take place, another process intervenes, namely, the process of *consumption*. When the peas are consumed, the *objective* is satisfied.[5]

The economist is faced with analytical questions regarding the allocation of resources. This abiding problem of deciding how best to use resources faces all types of economic systems: barter, capitalist, communist, socialist, and so forth. Calderwood and associates illustrate the analytical questions facing the economist.

1. How shall the economy use (allocate) its productive resources to supply the wants of its people? In commonsense terms, *what* shall be produced and *how*?
2. How fast shall the economy grow, and how shall it obtain reasonably stable growth, avoiding both depression and inflation? In other words, *how much* shall be produced in total, and how many resources shall be devoted to increasing future capacity rather than to producing goods for current consumption?
3. How shall the economy distribute money incomes, and through them the goods and services it produces, to the individual members and groups in society? For whom shall the goods be produced?[6]

Selected Economic Concepts. Here are a few selected terms and basic ideas from economics.

- *Consumer.* A person or group who uses goods and services.
- *Corporation.* A company in which people invest money and share profits and losses.
- *Demand.* The need or wish and ability to purchase goods and services.
- *Division of labor.* Assigning specific tasks to workers so each does a part of a total job.
- *Goods.* Materials produced for consumption.
- *Opportunity cost.* The trade-off that arises from choosing one good or service over other possibilities.
- *Producer.* A person who makes goods and/or services.
- *Profit.* Net income derived from the sale of goods and services.
- *Services.* Skills or abilities sold to consumers.
- *Supply.* Amount of goods and services available for consumption.

Key Ideas about Economics
1. The individual plays three roles in economic life: worker, consumer, and citizen.
2. The general social/political/economic environment affects the individual's economic opportunities and well-being.
3. An individual's economic choices and behavior may affect the system as a whole.
4. The market system is the basic institutional arrangement through which production and distribution of goods and services are determined in a free economy.

Geography

What Is Geography? Like anthropology, geography is a broad and integrative discipline. Its basic concepts are concepts of space. Greco writes that geography

is not defined by subject matter but its method or the way it looks at things. . . . Geography, as a chorological or spatial science, strives for an architecture of description in

A young geographer puts the finishing touches on her map of the school grounds.

segments of space or areas. . . . It is a synthetic areal science which utilizes the ecological aspects of all the systematic sciences—physics, biotic, or societal. . . . Explaining area differentiation is the quest of the geographer. Space, the chorology of phenomena, is his principal concern.[7]

In addition to their basic concern for describing space, geographers focus on the dynamics and interactions of variables at a particular place. Harper and Schmudde provide insight into the concept of an interconnected system.

Four variables should provide us with a basic understanding of life at any place, if we know how to relate them. They are (1) the operation of the earth environment, (2) the culture or cultures of the people living there, (3) the technological know-how possessed by the group, and (4) the ties between the people at that place and those in other areas. These are the components, or variables, with which geographers commonly work. If we are to learn to think geographically, we need to analyze each of the components and understand why they vary from place to place.[8]

Harper and Schmudde stress further the importance of recognizing the relationships among the four components cited rather than dealing with each of them in isolation. Thus, a case is made for viewing geography and geographic inquiry from a conceptual perspective—destroying the outmoded, stereotyped view of geography as a study of isolated subjects such as landforms, capital cities, and crops.

What Do Geographers Do? Geographers develop descriptions of regions or places or investigate special topics involving spatial interactions. The two major types of inquiry that geographers pursue involve regions of the world, such as the Amazon rain forest or the Pacific Northwest of the United States, and special topics, such as migration patterns or urban settlement.

Geographic methods include analyzing existing maps; developing new maps (see Figure 3.7), graphs, and charts; interpreting aerial and other photographs; using statistical techniques to analyze data; and developing descriptions of places or phenomena.

FIGURE 3.7

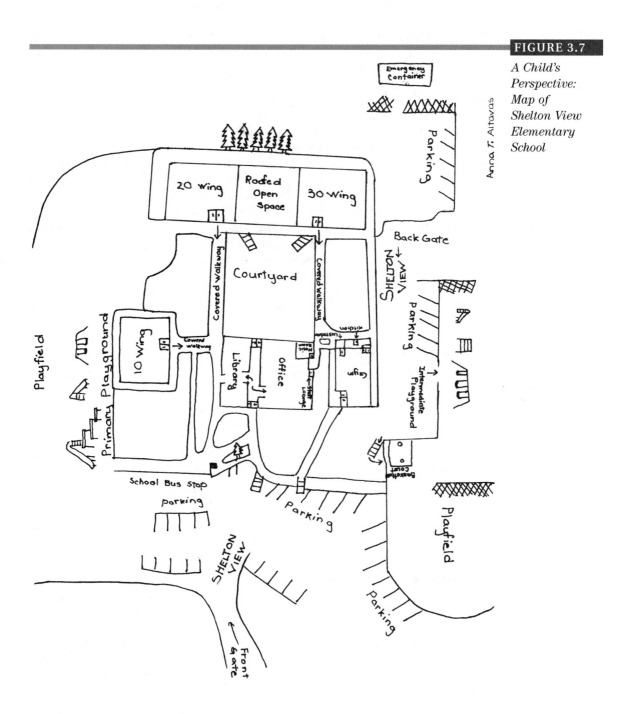

A Child's Perspective: Map of Shelton View Elementary School

Selected Geographic Concepts. These selected terms and ideas help form the conceptual structure of geography.

- *Areal association.* The relationship of phenomena on the earth's surface to one another, such as the relationship among soil, climate, and vegetation in a particular place.
- *Central place.* The focal point of a region. The central place of a region contains the specializations and services necessary to the function of that region. For example, Omaha, Nebraska, serves as a central place for the surrounding cattle country of that region.
- *Region.* An area on the earth's surface that has common properties—such as topography, climate, and soils—and that is bound together by a common focus in a particular central place. For example, the region of the Pacific Southwest has its focus in Phoenix, Arizona.
- *Situation.* The location of a place in relation to other places and the degree to which those other places are accessible. Thus, the situation of a particular place may change with the building of a railroad or with new developments in air transportation. A city such as Seattle, Washington, is in a more favorable trade situation now than it was 30 years ago. Its specific location on the earth's surface is unchanged, but the development of more efficient transportation systems makes it more accessible to Japanese as well as East Coast markets.
- *Spatial interaction.* The functional relationship between and among phenomena in a particular place. For example, textiles may be manufactured where cotton, water sources, a population of workers, and transportation networks for shipping are all available.

Key Ideas about Geography

1. Location of people and economic activities are influenced by external factors and internal value choices.
2. Environmental conditions place restrictions on cultural choices.
3. Nature and culture are interlocking components of the ecosystem.
4. Movement of cultures from subsistent economies and self-sufficient communities toward surplus-oriented, interdependent cultures means an increased technology, trade, migration, and communication network.
5. Highly specialized and specifically adapted livelihood forms have limited potential for cultural change. (Nomadic pastoralism and hunting societies are becoming extinct.)

History

What Is History? Of all the sciences that focus on human behavior, history is perhaps the broadest in scope. In fact, because its subject matter encompasses past events (and current events as they unfold and rapidly become history) in all areas of human endeavor, there is the persistent question of whether history is a science or merely a collection of stories of the past and the unfolding present. If one benchmark of a scientific endeavor is predictive capability, then history certainly does not qualify as a science to the same extent that economics or psychology does. Krug writes:

History is concerned with the totality of human experience, past and present.... It is past politics, past economics, past science, past society, past religion, past civilization— in short, past everything.... History written today records not only the story of kings, rulers, wars, and conquests, but also how men grew wheat and corn, how they sold their wares, built their homes, worshiped their gods, and how they lived and how they died. It is because of its concern with the totality of human experience that history, unlike many of the social sciences, has loosely defined boundaries.[9]

Expanding on this view, Ward notes:

History in its original meaning, everyone agrees, is inquiry.... History is inquiry into myths and folk stories that grandmothers tell. It is inquiry to find truer explanations for existing institutions and situations. It is also inquiry for the sake of inquiry, for mankind is a very interesting phenomenon. All in all, history is inquiry into the heritage and burden that society would lay on us, an inquiry that frees us to select and learn from it.[10]

An obvious point of distinction between history and the other social sciences lies in the primary focus of historical studies on the past, a concern that plays only a supportive role in the other social sciences. On the other hand, history shares with the other social sciences the function of seeking explanations of human interactions as they are exemplified by institutions and situations through processes of inquiry. Collingwood lists four characteristics of history that could well be applied to other social sciences:

1. that it is scientific, or begins by knowing something and tells what it knows.
2. that it is humanistic, or asks questions about things done by men at determinate times in the past.
3. that it is rational, or bases the answers which it gives on grounds, namely, appeal to evidence.
4. that it is self-revelatory, or exists in order to tell man what man is by telling him what man has done.[11]

Susan B. Anthony: A pioneer in the field of women's rights

What Do Historians Do? Historians pose questions about human interaction in current and past events, seek appropriate sources of data, and attempt to develop explanations and inferences to answer those questions. Krug writes that "a historian starts his inquiry basically with three questions: 'What happened? How did it happen? Why did it happen?' "[12] Such questions could, for example, serve as a guide to historical inquiry into the clashes between the executive and legislative branches of government during the Watergate inquiry.

Historians seek sources of data in a variety of places: museums, libraries, repositories, attics, archives, film depositories, and, of course, the field, where they may search for and use documents and other artifacts. Historical data consist of letters, paintings, photographs, films, charters, compacts, census tracts, financial records, household utensils, weaponry, statuaries, literature, people—there is an endless and ever growing supply of sources. Unfortunately, historians have less control over the situations they investigate than psychologists, for example. As a result, the data sources that are preserved and located often seem to be available on a random basis. Historians work with sources they can locate, which means that priceless sources of data are often irretrievably lost or destroyed.

Key Ideas about History

1. Change has been a universal characteristic of all human societies.
2. A knowledge of the past is necessary to understand present and future events.
3. No historical events have resulted from a single cause.
4. Leadership of certain individuals has had a profound influence on the course of history.
5. Interpretations of the past are constantly changing as new data and trends result in altered perspectives.

Sociology

What Is Sociology? Sociology is the study of groups and the subsequent norms of behavior that human beings exhibit as a result of their group memberships. Thus, the subject matter of sociology consists of such groups as the family, the ethnic group, the tribe or band, the society, and the nation. The subject matter of sociology also focuses on groups within larger groups—for example, suburban dwellers, business executives, migrant workers, communal groups, heads of households, or drug users.

The subject matter of sociology traditionally has been found in complex, modern, industrial societies. This distinguishes it from the subject matter of anthropology, which is often identified with preliterate cultures. Both sociology and anthropology are specialized branches of the same science, however.[13]

Sociology involves more than the mere description of groups and their resultant norms of behavior. It also involves the examination and analysis of changes that occur in group structures (e.g., changing patterns in family structures) and a study of the relationships that exist among group members and among groups.[14] Group behaviors, called *norms*, are, as Perrucci writes, clues to "the things that people invest emotional interest in—things they want, desire, consider as important, desire to become, and enjoy."[15]

The effects of groups on individual behavior—processes of socialization as exemplified by speech patterns, clothing styles, choices of food, recreation, for example—are of special interest to the sociologist. Kinch writes: "An individual is not born with a culture; he must acquire it through a process called *socialization.* In studying sociology, sociologists look at the significant points of contact between the individual and his society and the mechanisms by which he learns or acquires his culture."[16]

What Do Sociologists Do? Sociologists spend their time studying groups. They ask analytical questions about groups and group behavior that can be answered through data gathering. The sociologist gathers data through means similar to those employed by the anthropologist: direct observation, indirect observation, interviews, and examination of the writings of other social scientists. In addition, sociological research has made extensive use of the questionnaire as a data-gathering instrument. Like other social scientists, the sociologist poses researchable questions, hypothesizes, selects appropriate sources of data, gathers and processes the data, and makes inferences or statements about the data.

Selected Sociological Concepts. Here are a few selected terms and basic ideas from sociology.

- *Integrated group.* A group in which members interact and communicate with one another and in which positions of dominance and hierarchy are established—such as families, clubs, and classrooms.
- *Nonintegrated group.* A group in which members are basically interchangeable with one another and in which lines of communication and interaction are not clearly established. A group of people waiting in line for the theater or a group of people shopping in a store are examples.

An intuitive teacher knows when to lead and when to step aside.

- *Norms.* Generalizable (to most members of any given group) patterns of be-havior. Norms may be found in clothes, food, and shelter, for example.
- *Socialization.* Those things that happen to an individual as a result of his or her contacts with society and the influences that society has on the life of that individual.
- *Values.* Those beliefs that people internalize and act on as a result of their group experiences—for example, success, punctuality, generosity, and frugality.

Key Ideas about Sociology

1. Norms define the boundaries of social interaction.
2. Differentiation of social roles is based on sex, age, kinship, and occupation.
3. Complex, technological societies tend toward greater stratification.
4. Social interaction involves cooperation, conflict, assimilation, or accom-modation.
5. Each society develops institutions to aid the socialization of its members.
6. Socialization is the process by which the individual becomes a functioning member of society.
7. Human survival depends on living in groups.

Political Science

What Is Political Science? Like the other social sciences, political science has no clear-cut, one-sentence definition. However, a central focus of political science is on governing processes and the power structure found in those governing processes. As the name implies, political science involves the study of human be-havior as it relates to political systems, governments, laws, and international rela-tions. Easton writes:

> In defining political science, we are seeking concepts to describe the most obvious and encompassing properties of the phenomena we wish to describe. The idea of a *politi-cal system* proves to be an appropriate and indeed unavoidable starting point in this search. Certain kinds of activity are more prominently associated with political life than others; for example, governmental organizations, pressure groups, voting, and parties. They are, of course, part of the whole social process and, therefore, they are also rele-vant to systems other than political. Recurrent relationships among parts of the system suggest that the elements of political life have some form of determinate relationships. The task of research is to discover what they are.[17]

Thus, Easton argues that an emphasis should be placed on systems, which means essentially that the political sphere is an interrelated, dynamic set of interactions among people and the power that they exercise or that is exercised on them.

The systems approach to political science provides a rather comprehensive de-finition of the discipline; other definitions are more restrictive. Watkins writes: "The proper study of political science is not the study of the state or of any other specific institutional complex, but the investigation of all associations insofar as they can be shown to exemplify the problem of power."[18] Although such a defini-tion highlights the key political science concept of *power* and is useful in that re-gard, it fails to distinguish with any great degree of clarity between political science and other social sciences such as anthropology, sociology, and history, all of which are concerned with power. However, it does supplement Easton's definition, because power serves as the organizing concept in a dynamic political system.

What Do Political Scientists Do? Political scientists attempt to determine the existence of and analyze the relationships among the people and institutions that make up political systems. Senn offers two methods by which political scientists derive explanations for human behavior in political systems: explanations by purpose or intention and probability explanations. A statement of the basic premises of these two methods is excerpted here from Senn's book *Social Science and Its Methods.*

> *Explanation by purpose or intention.* This method explains in terms of aims, plans, goals, or intentions. Whenever human beings are studied, the social scientist must take into account the fact that they have wills and change their future.
>
> Social scientists know that whenever human behavior must be explained, either in terms of the individual or in terms of groups, the plans, intentions, and goals of individuals themselves must be taken into account. We call this explanation by purpose.
>
> Explanation by purpose is commonly used in two situations. First, a social scientist may ask a person what his purposes or intentions are or were when the purpose of the action the social scientist is attempting to explain is not clear. . . . Secondly, this kind of explanation is sought when the social scientist is ignorant of the connections between the actions of the group and the goals of the individual.
>
> *Probabilistic explanation.* Probabilistic explanations occur when a social scientist says, "If a country is attacked, it is likely that it will defend itself." . . . Probabilistic explanations use terms of probability, not certainty, and the degree to which the premises follow is sometimes called the degree of confidence, and is sometimes given as a percentage.
>
> Example: three out of four first voters select a candidate from the same party supported by their parents. . . . Therefore, we can conclude that the chances are three out of four that John (a first-time voter) will vote Democratic as his parents did.[19]

Political scientists are interested in more than the mere description of human behavior in response to political systems. Although they may attempt to develop an accurate description of human behavior—for example, voting patterns in an off-year election—such a description may serve as a prelude to the development of explanations of the purposes or intentions of voters in voting the way they did. This information could well be translated into a prediction of how voters, given certain profiles, might vote in future elections.

Selected Political Science Concepts. Here are a few selected terms and basic ideas from political science.

- *Authority.* The binding powers held by persons and/or laws over other persons. In a democracy, persons in a position of authority are either elected or appointed by elected officials and are therefore ultimately responsible to the people.
- *Government.* The officials, laws, and institutions that are responsible for maintaining social control and functions in a society.

■ *Power.* Influence held by individuals or groups over others. Persons holding power in a democratic society are bound by existing laws and the right of voters to recall such laws. Within these constraints, persons holding positions of power may determine the behavior of others. For example, Congress exercised its constitutional power in passing legislation reducing highway speed limits to 55 miles per hour and more recently raising them to 65 miles per hour. The executive branch exercises power by enforcing such a law.

■ *Political system.* The set of interactions among persons, institutions, processes, and traditions by which a society is governed, or "a set of interactions, abstracted from the totality of social behavior, through which valued things are authoritatively allocated for a society."[20]

Key Ideas about Political Science

1. The study of politics and government includes the study of the institution of government and how individuals behave as citizens.
2. Democracy is government in which the decision making is in the hands of the people, who make their demands known through voting, political parties, and pressure groups.
3. Democracy seeks to protect the rights of individuals and minority groups, although its actions are based on majority opinion.
4. Citizenship in a democracy is the exercise of duties, responsibilities, and privileges, as a reasoned and functional act of political behavior.
5. Political systems exist to make binding authoritative decisions for all citizens.

Summary

Anthropology, economics, geography, history, sociology, and political science all involve the study of human beings. Therefore, all these areas are, by definition, included in social studies. This chapter described the structure of each of these social sciences and highlighted terms and key ideas from each. The key ideas listed with each discipline in this chapter make good concept statements on which to develop lessons, activities, and even units of instruction. Go back and skim them, and you will see what I mean. Of course, when you select a key idea, you must do two things: (1) attach it to some appropriate content and (2) develop it by using an activity appropriate to certain age levels.

ACTIVITIES

1. Make a list of differences between social studies and social science. Make a list of similarities between social studies and social science. Which list is longer? Why?
2. Think about the concept of change. Identify an example of change for each of the social science disciplines.
3. Examine an elementary social studies series. Try to determine which social science disciplines are stressed at each level.

4. "Geography and history should receive far more emphasis in elementary studies than the other social sciences." Do you agree or disagree with that statement? Why or why not?

5. Use one of the key ideas listed in this chapter and develop a lesson based on it.

NOTES

1. Douglas L. Oliver, *Invitation to Anthropology* (Garden City, NY: Natural History Press, 1964), p. xii.
2. Selected social science concepts appearing throughout this chapter are adapted from *Selected Learner Outcomes for Social Studies* (St. Paul, MN: Minnesota State Department of Education, 1981, 1985).
3. J. D. Calderwood, J. D. Lawrence, and J. E. Maher, *Economics in the Curriculum* (New York: Wiley, 1970), p. 4.
4. John E. Maher, *What Is Economics?* (New York, Wiley, 1969), p. 1.
5. Ibid.
6. Calderwood et al., *Economics in the Curriculum*, p. 172.
7. Peter Greco, *Geography* (Boulder, CO: Social Science Education Consortium, 1966), p. 3.
8. R. A. Harper and T. H. Schmudde, *Between Two Worlds: A New Introduction to Geography* (Boston: Houghton Mifflin, 1973), p. 56.
9. Mark M. Krug, *History and the Social Sciences* (Waltham, MA: Blaisdell, 1967), p. 4.
10. Paul Ward, "The Awkward Social Science: History," in *Social Science in the Schools*, ed. I. Morrissett and W. Stevens (New York: Holt, Rinehart and Winston, 1971), p. 30.
11. R. G. Collingwood, in *The Idea of History*, ed. T. M. Knox (London: Oxford University Press, 1946), p. 18.
12. Krug, *History and the Social Studies*, p. 5.
13. Caroline Rose, *Sociology: The Study of Man in Society* (Columbus, OH: Merrill, 1965).
14. Ibid.
15. Robert Perrucci, *Sociology* (Boulder, CO: Social Science Education Consortium, 1966), p. 3.
16. J. W. Kinch, *Introductory Sociology: The Individual in Society* (San Rafael, CA: Individual Learning Systems, 1971), p. 3.
17. David Easton, *A Systems Approach to Political Life* (Boulder, CO: Social Science Education Consortium, 1966), p. 1.
18. Frederick Watkins, in *Political Science: A Philosophical Analysis*, ed. Vernon Van Dyke (Stanford, CA: Stanford University Press, 1960), p. 140.
19. Peter R. Senn, *Social Science and Its Methods* (Boston: Holbrook Press, 1971), pp. 145–154.
20. Easton, *A Systems Approach*, p. 5.

SUGGESTED READINGS

Atkinson, R., et al. (2000). *Hilgard's Introduction to Psychology* (13th ed.) Orlando, FL: Harcourt Brace.

Buchholz, T., and Feldstein, M. (1999). *New Ideas from Dead Economists: An Introduction to Modern Economic Thought.* New York: Penguin.

Castro, F. (1991). *A Quick Way to Learn Geography: The World.* New York: Merriam-Webster.

Ginzburg, C., et al. (1992). *Clues, Myths, and the Historical Method.* Baltimore: Johns Hopkins University Press.

Hirsch, E. (1991–1996). *The Core Knowledge Series, Grades 1–6.* New York: Delta.

Knox, P., and Marston, S. (2001). *Human Geography.* Upper Saddle River, NJ: Prentice-Hall.

National Council for the Social Studies. (1994). *Curriculum Standards for Social Studies: Expectations of Excellence.* Washington, DC: Author.

Nolan, P., and Lesch, G. (1999). *Human Societies.* New York: McGraw-Hill.

"Notable Trade Books for Young People." *Social Education.* A guide to social science and social studies-related trade books; found yearly in the May/June issue.

Park, M. (2000). *Introducing Anthropology: An Integrated Approach.* Mountain View, CA: Mayfield.

Rich, D. (1998). *Mega Skills: Building Children's Achievement for the Information Age.* Boston: Houghton Mifflin.

Theory: Developmental and Psychological Dimensions

Teachers can learn a great deal from theory and research in the areas of developmental psychology and learning theory. Learning theorists have made enormous progress, furnishing educators with new insights on how children think and learn. This chapter introduces you to the work of several theorists who have much to offer those of us who teach or will teach children. You will be exposed to the thoughts of the following writers:

- Jerome Bruner and discovery learning
- Jean Piaget and developmentally appropriate practice
- Lev Vygotsky and the zone of proximal development
- Carl Rogers and the freedom to learn
- Howard Gardner and the theory of multiple intelligence

The little world of childhood with its familiar
surroundings is a model of the greater world.

—Carl Jung

The scope and sequence of the social studies curriculum, the materials that are used, the teaching strategies that are employed—these are all crucial components of a social studies program. Once you have accounted for these factors, you are ready to go—right? Well, perhaps not quite. Let's not overlook the developmental dimension.

The finest materials, the most innovative teaching strategy, and the most interesting content become useful and meaningful only when they match the learner and that learner's ability to accommodate them. This raises the question of learning modes and readiness.

To take into account the growth and development of young learners is to recognize at the outset that not all children grow and develop at the same rate. The obvious differences in physical size ought to serve as reminders to us that differential rates of growth also occur in the social, emotional, and intellectual dimensions. Stages of development have been described at length by a number of writers. I have chosen five writers whose impact on teaching and learning social studies has been profound: Jerome Bruner, Jean Piaget, Lev Vygotsky, Carl Rogers, and Howard Gardner.

Jerome Bruner

Jerome Bruner became widely known in the field of curriculum development through his controversial elementary social studies program, *Man: A Course of Study* (MACOS). MACOS brought Bruner's fundamental ideas about children's learning to public attention, and many of those ideas were severely criticized. Despite—or perhaps because of—the controversy, no single individual has had as much influence on social studies curriculum development in recent years as has Bruner. Alone among major cognitive psychologists, Bruner moved beyond a theory of learning to a theory of instruction.

Four Key Concepts

Bruner's instructional model (see Figure 4.1) is based on four key concepts: structure, readiness, intuition, and motivation. These concepts are developed in detail in Bruner's classic book, *The Process of Education*.[1]

Structure. The concept of the structure of a discipline is not new. It is certainly as old as Aristotle, who made the case for learning significant ideas as opposed to mere facts. Bruner defines the structure of a discipline as its basic concepts and methods. The structure of anthropology, for example, is composed of its organizing concepts such as culture, beliefs, customs, and symbols, and of its methods of investigation such as direct observation and case studies.

Bruner suggests that teaching students the structure of a discipline as they study particular content leads to greater active involvement on their part as they discover basic principles for themselves. This idea, of course, is very different from the learning model that suggests that students ought to be receivers rather than developers of information. Bruner states that learning the *structure* of knowledge rather than endless sets of facts facilitates comprehension, memory, and learning transfer.

The idea of structure in learning leads naturally to the process approach, in which the process of learning (or *how* one learns) becomes as important as the content of learning (or *what* one learns). This position, misunderstood by many, has been the focus of considerable controversy. The important thing to keep in mind is that Bruner never said that content is trivial. The false dichotomy between process and content need not exist.

Readiness. Bruner states that no evidence exists to contradict the idea that any subject can be taught effectively in some intellectually honest form to any child at any stage of development. He feels that a key to readiness for learning is intellectual development, or how a child views the world. Here, he refers to the work of Piaget, stating that "what is most important for teaching basic concepts is that the

FIGURE 4.1

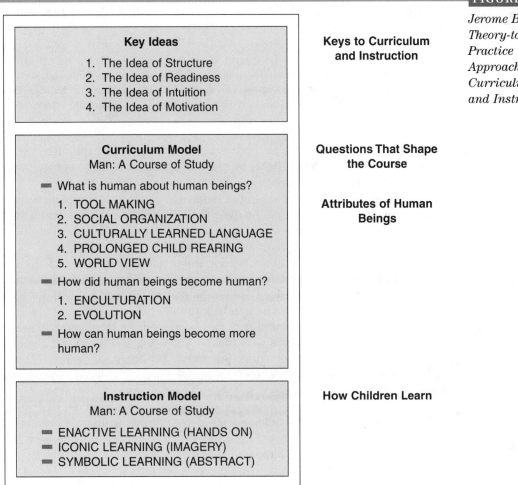

Key Ideas

1. The Idea of Structure
2. The Idea of Readiness
3. The Idea of Intuition
4. The Idea of Motivation

Keys to Curriculum and Instruction

Curriculum Model
Man: A Course of Study

■ What is human about human beings?

1. TOOL MAKING
2. SOCIAL ORGANIZATION
3. CULTURALLY LEARNED LANGUAGE
4. PROLONGED CHILD REARING
5. WORLD VIEW

■ How did human beings become human?

1. ENCULTURATION
2. EVOLUTION

■ How can human beings become more human?

Questions That Shape the Course

Attributes of Human Beings

Instruction Model
Man: A Course of Study

■ ENACTIVE LEARNING (HANDS ON)
■ ICONIC LEARNING (IMAGERY)
■ SYMBOLIC LEARNING (ABSTRACT)

How Children Learn

child be helped to pass progressively from concrete thinking to the utilization of more conceptually adequate modes of thought."[2] Thus, Bruner advocates readiness based not on waiting passively for certain stages to appear but rather on an active concept of a positively influential learning environment.

Bruner suggests that readiness depends more on an effective mix of the enactive, iconic, and symbolic learning modes (defined in a following section) than on waiting until some imagined time when children are capable of learning certain ideas. Throughout his writing is the notion that the key to readiness is a rich and meaningful learning environment coupled with an inspiring teacher who involves children in learning as a process that creates its own excitement.

Intuition. In his inclusion of intuition in his model, Bruner takes issue with the typical school pattern of formalized instruction, particularly with regard to memorizing and reproducing verbal and numerical exercises. He cautions, however, against the idea that intuition and knowledge of subject matter are diametrically opposed.

> The good intuiter may have been born with something special, but his effectiveness rests upon a solid knowledge of the subject, a familiarity that gives intuition something to work with. Certainly there are some experiments on learning that indicate the importance of a high degree of mastery of materials in order to operate effectively with them intuitively.[3]

This quotation ought to serve as a powerful argument against the often oversimplified back-to-basics theme. Higher-level thinking and knowledge of basic subject matter are partners, not opponents.

What is intuitive thinking as Bruner defines it? Perhaps it would be helpful to contrast it with analytic thinking. Analytic thinking proceeds one step at a time. It tends to be formal and therefore rather explicit. Solving a problem in a careful step-by-step approach is an example of analytic thinking.

Intuition, on the other hand, is not based on carefully designed steps. Hunches, the five senses, and unconscious maneuvers are involved in intuitive thinking. Intuition presupposes a knowledge base on the part of the learner. Without a base, the student has nothing about which to be intuitive.

Whether intuition is a natural trait can be argued. As teachers, however, we must tend toward the optimistic view that we can bring about positive changes in the way children look at their world. Bruner suggests that modeling of intuitive thinking by teachers is one way to enhance such behaviors in students. The teacher who is willing to guess, to explore, to take risks in the area of critical examination of his or her ideas by students is the type of intuitive modeler Bruner describes. In addition, he suggests that providing a wide range of investigative experiences in a free and unthreatening (in terms of right and wrong answers) atmosphere will give intuitive thinking a chance to blossom.

Bruner clearly values intuitive thinking as a learning style. He feels that it has been generally overlooked and undervalued as a legitimate tool for learning in classrooms. Real problems, particularly those with an interdisciplinary focus, seldom lend themselves to the neat, lockstep approach found in textbooks.

Jerome Bruner

Motivation. Why someone wants to learn or does not want to learn something is often difficult to figure out. Why are you reading this book? Because it was suggested or assigned to you to read? Because you really want to learn how to teach social studies and this is one tool for learning? Because you are having trouble sleeping and this, at least, is a natural aid to sleep? Other reasons? A mixture of all these reasons?

Consider for a moment the motivations of 25 children who are present in a third-grade classroom. Their motivations for being there range from a love of learning to the threat of legal sanctions. Whatever a child's initial motivation, the real question is what you can do to enhance it.

Bruner suggests that intrinsic motivation is an essential key to effective learning. John Dewey wrote about "the teachable moment," when motivation and information come together. A teacher who is curious, who values reflective thinking, and who accepts students' childlike attempts at intellectual reaching out will be a motivating presence.

Bruner clings, in antibehaviorist fashion, to the idea of intrinsic motivation—learning as its own reward. It is a refreshing thought.

Classroom Applications

Bruner presents three ways of examining one's world or of acquiring new ideas. The modes range from direct experience to abstraction. Bruner's *enactive* learning involves hands-on or direct experience. The strength of enactive learning is its sense of immediacy. Its limitation lies in failure to provide a broad basis for generalizing. The mode of learning that Bruner terms *iconic* is based on the use of visual media, such as films and pictures. In social studies, where one wishes to represent a wider world, iconic representation is particularly attractive. *Symbolic* learning is the stage at which one uses abstract symbols to represent reality. A map is an abstraction of a photograph. A passage in a textbook is a powerful way of transcending space and time with great economy. The limitations of symbolic learning for the young learner are summed up in the child's lament: "I can read what it says, but I don't know what it means." Thus, there is an increasing degree of abstraction in each of these modes. The three learning modes all have specific classroom applications. Let's examine each mode in some depth.

Enactive representation in the classroom consists of learning through sensory experiences that involve accompanying physical activity. Examples include making a pioneer encampment, playing a game that children played in colonial times, and going out into the neighborhood around the school to document evidence of pollution in the environment. Enactive representation is, however, more than mere activity. The teacher must ensure that there is something conceptual about the hands-on experience. Carving Mount Rushmore out of soap is not enactive representation unless the carver also learns about events related to the history of the Mount Rushmore project. It is important to take ample time to expand on the hands-on experience, to relate it to larger structures of learning.

The power of enactive representation is obvious—people learn by doing. Riding on a train is far different from having someone explain what it is like to ride on a train. Making a tipi and using it as a shelter in the classroom is far different from reading about tipis. But the limitations of enactive representation are obvious as well: People can't travel everywhere, and even if they could, they might miss a great deal of information. Making things in the classroom is indeed valuable, but a child can't make everything that he or she would ever need to learn about. If you recall your own social studies experiences, you know that teachers tend to err on the side of giving children far too few direct experiences. Most of social studies seems, unfortunately, to consist of reading a textbook and answering questions on worksheets.

"Place is security, space is freedom."—Yi-Fu Tuan

Iconic representation, according to Bruner, is a means of representing reality through imagery. In that sense, it is a more advanced stage of learning. An icon is a picture or image; iconic representation is concrete and not abstract. A movie is a well-known example of iconic representation. Its very concreteness leads us sometimes to say, "Oh, that wasn't how I thought of that character" or "The scenery was even more beautiful than I could have imagined." Although you would probably like to, you can't take your class to Japan to study the culture, so you show them the film (iconic representation) *A Japanese Boy: The Story of Taro.* You know that although reading about Japan is very useful, the film will do things that mere words could never do. Iconic representation furnishes our minds with mental images that become a part of our reality. In social studies, particularly, where you are trying to introduce the world of human beings to your students, iconic representation is a very powerful learning mode.

A word about learning styles is appropriate at this point. Just as the tactile learning in enactive representation is so valuable, so is the visual learning of iconic representation. By achieving a balance in the lessons you teach, you will have a much greater chance of reaching children's learning-style strengths and stretching them toward experience with alternate styles. Far too much social studies has been taught (notice I didn't say *learned*) without regard to enactive and iconic representation. To come back to the Japan example, wouldn't it be limiting for your students to learn about Japan only by studying about that country from the textbook and encyclopedias? Pictorial displays around the room, films, and other means of iconic representation will add elements of understanding that words cannot convey. And while you're at it, wouldn't preparing a Japanese meal (enactive representation) add a sparkling dimension to your study of that culture?

The most advanced learning mode in terms of abstraction is symbolic learning. *Symbolic representation* is based on the powerful tools of language and number. For example, when we write the word *whale* on the chalkboard, in one sense we have nothing more than some chalk marks on slate. But in another sense, the chalk marks direct our attention toward thoughts of great, grey, migratory marine mammals. In our mind's eye, we see these magnificent creatures spouting and diving—yet most of us have never seen a real whale. Mainly what you and I know about whales we have read about, been told about, and have seen in films and photographs.

As children develop experientially, they come to depend more and more on language as a tool for representing reality. No earthlings have ever visited another solar system, but we can imagine doing something like that. No children have ever held kindness in their hands, but they can tell you about kindness. Thus, there is a crucial interaction among experience, imagery, and language that takes place in learning. Interestingly, the sequence is not necessarily always from enactive to iconic to symbolic. If you have ever traveled to a foreign country, you may know how valuable it is to "read up" on that country prior to your visit.

Symbolic representation, through written and oral language, enables students to think abstractly beyond mere experience and pictures. In effect, it allows them to conceptualize through processes of reflective thought. Keep in mind, however, that the process is interactive and not linear. Experience, imagery, and language support each other.

Let me give you an example. I mentioned a type of shelter made by Native Americans called a tipi. Children should learn about tipis because they are an incredibly ingenious portable shelter. Most of the roving tribes of the Great Plains used them. As the tribe would follow the buffalo herds, they could actually move their villages along with them. By reading a story about the Indians of the Great Plains, the children could learn a great deal about tipis. They could make comparisons of the tipi to other portable and/or temporary structures, such as camping tents and igloos. They could also learn about the culture of nomadic Native American life on the Great Plains. These are examples of symbolic representation. Viewing a film such as *The Culture of the Plains Indians* provides the children with images. They see the Native Americans actually using their tipis, putting them up and taking them down, transporting them over distances. This is iconic representation.

A few years ago, I was teaching a course at a museum that had a hands-on Plains Indians exhibit. When I had the opportunity to help put up and take down a tipi, my knowledge of and respect for this type of architecture grew exponentially. Up to that time, what I "knew" about tipis was far more limited than I realized. This wonderful enactive experience brought to me elements of reality that I otherwise would not have known. If adults need enactive learning as part of their intellectual diet, how much more do children need such experiences to help them organize their ideas about reality?

At the elementary level in particular, there is great danger in too much emphasis on symbolic learning. Children can be marvelous little parrots if that is what we want to make of them. They can "learn" all kinds of things from their textbooks and not learn much at all, even though they give us back the facts on a test paper.

Claims of Discovery Learning

Bruner makes several significant claims on behalf of discovery learning—learning by using the senses as means of direct encounter with knowledge. He feels that as students experience success as discoverers, they will come to have a sense of efficacy about their ability to learn. This success leads to something he calls "intellectual potency." As success builds, learners are better able to organize their thought processes conceptually. They therefore become better problem solvers. You know from your own experience that this is true. If you bowl a lot, and if you get some lessons in bowling along the way, your sense of yourself as a competent bowler will improve to the point that you can laughingly remember how bad you really were the first time you went bowling. Thus, a child may not think of herself as a young geographer, but if she has practice mapping her bedroom, the playground, the way to school, and so forth, she soon will become quite good at mapping the environment.

A second claim Bruner makes about discovery learning has to do with the reward structure. He feels that discovery is itself a very rewarding process. Advocates of discovery learning have witnessed over and over the satisfaction that children evidence when they solve a problem or conduct an investigation well.

A third claim has to do with the process of discovery learning itself. Strategies for further learning on one's own emerge. These strategies are transferable to new situations beyond the classroom or the school environment. Thus, greater independence in the learning process is fostered.

The fourth claim of discovery learning has to do with memory. You have heard the Chinese proverb "I hear and I forget, I see and I understand, I do and I remember." The blend of symbolic, iconic, and enactive representation that happens in discovery learning enables learners to conceptualize what they learn, and research indicates that conceptual learning serves as a far better way to recall information than does nonconceptual or rote learning.

Learners' Minds

Bruner describes four dominant models of learners' minds that have been emphasized in recent years. These models are a useful way of thinking about balance in methods of teaching and learning social studies. Each of the models, which he calls "folk pedagogies," has quite different implications for both teacher and student role. Your task in planning, teaching, and evaluating is to consider the strategic use of each; that is, When is it appropriate to teach by telling? By showing how? By stepping back and giving children time to think for themselves? By helping children to learn to distinguish between what they know in a personal subjective sense and what they can learn from the culture? A brief description of each model follows.

1. *Children as imitative learners: the acquisition of know-how.* This model is actually the basis of apprenticeship learning. An apprentice carpenter, for example, observes and copies the methods of the master carpenter. The expert has skills that the novice needs to learn in order to succeed. Competence comes through practice. Actually, children learn much from their teachers this way. Your acts of kindness, your show of respect to all your students, your patience when someone is slow to learn—these and other modeling behaviors represent the "hidden curriculum" of this approach. We need to remember that even though we are showing children how to draw a map, for example, we are also communicating other equally important behaviors to them as well.

2. *Children as learners from didactic exposure.* This model is based on the premise that students need to receive information, facts, ideas, and rules of action in social studies. The assumption is that the teacher, text, or some other source has information that the student needs and does not know. Bruner notes that this approach is probably the most widely used teaching strategy; no doubt it is overused by many teachers. Much of what children "learn" this way they quickly forget. It is, as Bruner says, one-way teaching. Still, it is necessary because no person can discover everything he or she needs to know. Perhaps the biggest problem of this strategy is that it often is carried out in the absence of meaning for the learner.

3. *Children as thinkers.* This model views the child not merely as ignorant or in need of being told, but as a person able to reason, to exchange ideas with others, and to construct knowledge. The emphasis is on activity, collaborative learning, projects, and metacognition, or reflecting on what one is learning. Of course, this is a more active, child-centered approach than is afforded by the didactic model. Emphasis on understanding and interpretation take precedence over skilled performance or attainment of academic knowledge.

4. *Children as knowledgeable.* This model emphasizes the distinction between what children know personally and subjectively and what is known and necessary as judged by the culture. The model offers the learner the chance to test his or her ideas and beliefs against the criteria offered by scientific, literary, or other explanations of the world. To get a good idea of how this model works, ask a young child to explain to you how the seasons of the year change. He or she may have some explanation very different from that offered by a geographer. The point, however, is not that the child is wrong; rather, it is that the child can consider his or her prior understanding in the light of new evidence. It is the coming together of the child's world with that of knowledge that has stood the test of time.

In summary, Bruner notes that real schooling "is never confined to one model of the learner or one model of teaching." As a teacher, you have the responsibility to find the appropriate balance. Modern theories of teaching and learning, Bruner concludes, are "moving increasingly to the view that the child should be aware of her own thought processes." Thus, he argues for classrooms where children are active, participatory, reflective learners. There is much children do not know and much for them to learn, but it is important for us to honor them, to respect what they do know, and to involve them as they learn.

Jean Piaget

When theories of cognitive development are discussed, Jean Piaget's name is prominent. Piaget (1896–1980) was a zoologist by training. As a result of the careful note taking he did on the mental growth and development of his own children, he became interested in how children organize and adapt to their world.

Piaget's perception of human beings is that they are born as active, exploratory, and curious information processors. They have an innate need to classify, categorize, and assimilate information. According to Piaget, the two fundamental characteristics of a child's cognitive development are organization and adaptation. *Organization* is the systematizing of information into meaningful patterns or structures. A learner uses these structures or patterns that he or she has developed to organize new information and events so they do not appear random or chaotic. *Adaptation* is the process through which a person copes with the integration of new information into existing patterns and perceptions. Thus, adaptation becomes an ongoing process of assimilating and accommodating new ideas into existing ideas about the world. Adaptation, of course, is a lifelong process for all of us.

Piaget argued that a definition of intelligence can be based on the ability to organize and adapt. He viewed intelligence not as a fixed trait but rather as one's ability to organize and adapt to the environment. Piaget's concept of the learner's organization of and adaptation to the environment is a dynamic one in which continual adjustments and modifications of perceptions are required. Thus, adaptive behavior, or intelligence, results. As Seymour Papert observed, "One of the more subtle consequences of [Piaget's] discoveries is the revelation that adults fail to appreciate the extent and the nature of what children are learning, because knowledge structures we take for granted have rendered much of that learning invisible."[4] For an overview of Piaget's ideas about teaching and curriculum, see Figure 4.2.

Piaget maintained that children are not merely miniature adults. He stated that their thinking is *qualitatively* different. Children think in ways that adults can no longer remember. Piaget described states of cognitive development through which children typically progress. He emphasized that even though the stages are age related, they are not age determined. Therefore, differential rates of progress through the stages will occur.

Stages of Cognitive Development

For the person teaching social studies and other subjects to children of elementary school age, Piaget's description of developmental stages is particularly important. A knowledge of these stages is useful in determining not only the content of a program in social studies but its sequencing as well. In addition, certain teaching strategies that would be appropriate at one level may be inappropriate at another. For a description of Piaget's stages, see Table 4.1.

FIGURE 4.2

Piaget's Ideas about Teaching and Curriculum

- Teaching is the creation of environments in which students' cognitive and affective structures can emerge.
- Students grow only when they initiate their own learning experiences.
- Learning must be spontaneous and not forced and artificial.
- Verbal fluencey is not real knowledge.
- Learning is based on three types of knowledge:
    1. *Physical* (obtained from concrete experience)
    2. *Social* (obtained from interaction with others)
    3. *Logical* (obtained through reflection and abstraction)
- The teacher plays three roles:
    1. Organizer of the learning environment
    2. Assessor of students' thinking
    3. Initiator of group activities

TABLE 4.1

*Piaget's Stages
of Cognitive
Development*

Age	Stage	Typical Behaviors
Birth–2 years	Sensorimotor	Activities based on immediate experience through the senses Reflex actions Differentiating oneself from the environment Development of self-concept Trial-and-error behaviors Language to 1- or 2-word sentences
2–7 years	Intuitive or preoperational	Images stored Language development through 8- to 10-word sentences Maximum readiness to learn language; talks Spontaneous language Free association Fantasy
7–11 years	Concrete operations	Understands functional relationships Literal mindedness Does not easily change point of view in spite of new facts
12–16 years	Formal operations	Develops full formal patterns of thinking Attains logical, rational, abstract strategies Generalization Active symbolic processes

The *sensorimotor* stage covers the period from birth to 2 years old. From the initial reaching, grasping, and sucking behaviors, a child proceeds to more highly organized activities and the development of oral language. During this stage, children depend heavily on trial-and-error methods of mastering their environment.

The *preoperational* stage covers ages 2 to 7. It is usually divided into two substages: preconceptual (2 to 4 years) and intuitive (4 to 7 years). The *preconceptual* substage is characterized by dramatic growth in language development. By age 3, most children are speaking in full and often complex sentences. Experience and modeling are the keys to cognitive development at this stage. Children from ages 4 to 7 are considered by Piaget to be at an *intuitive* stage of development. Their judgments are incomplete and inconsistent. They do not think in terms of formal categories. Piaget defined intuition as something grasped by the mind immediately without the intervention of any deliberate, rational thought process. Thus, children of this age group are just beginning to bring a semblance of order to their sense of space, direction, size, number, and distance. I recall a 3-year-old who had no trouble with his idea that airplanes and the people inside them obviously became smaller as they flew higher into the sky.

The years from 7 to 11 cover the stage of *concrete operations*. Systematic, logical thought begins to supersede the impressionistic thinking of the preoperational

Piaget argued that children's thinking is qualitatively different from that of adults.

stage. Apparent discrepancies and differences no longer fool children at this stage. They are able to count, measure, weigh, calculate, and test problems. Children at this stage begin to see the world without necessarily perceiving themselves as its center. The attention span increases. Rules become more acceptable. A clear sense of time emerges. Children at this age group, however, remain unconvinced of the virtues of delayed gratification—they are essentially now centered.

The stage of *formal operations*, beginning at about age 12, is a time at which children begin to think hypothetically and abstractly. Verbal associations often take the place of direct, concrete experiences. Reasoning takes on a time dimension of past, present, and future. Ideal and abstract concepts become attractive. It should be noted, however, that a person who has entered the stage of formal operations often reverts to using earlier stage behaviors in coping and adapting to the environment. The extent to which one uses formal operations in adapting and organizing is a measure of one's success in growth and development.

Classroom Applications

In an insightful, practical book titled *Piaget for the Classroom Teacher* (Longman), Barry Wadsworth offers several suggestions to teachers who wish to implement Piagetian ideas with their students. As we examine Wadsworth's suggestions, keep in mind that Piaget was a theorist who formulated a number of useful conceptions about childhood learning, but he did not spell out specifically how a classroom should be operated. As a case in point, Piaget was apparently amused by what he called "the American question": How can we speed up this process of development?

Let's first examine the role of the teacher in a classroom where Piagetian ideas are prominent. The teacher plays three roles, each of which is crucial to the child's intellectual and social growth and development. The teacher is the *organizer of the learning environment*. The environment must be appealing, intellectually stimulating, and full of opportunities for sensory experiences. This means that there will be interesting picture displays and bulletin boards, interest centers where children can engage in hands-on activities, games, puzzles, books, easels, clay, drawing material, musical instruments, a video cassette recorder, personal computers, and so on. Of course, not all these things are required, but the point is that the physical environment must lend itself to intellectual and social stimulation. The physical environment, properly constructed, permits the promise and potential for genuine learning—but only that: the promise and potential.

The teacher's second role is that of *assessor of children's thinking*. Left alone in a stimulating environment, children will respond. But there is more to teaching and learning than eliciting responses. The teacher is there to make determinations about the progress a child is making, to mediate the child's questions, and to offer advice. The presence of a skilled, informed, interested adult is crucial. Without the adult's presence, the child is left to random experience that, although beneficial to a certain extent, is self-limiting. For example, a child who is busy playing games may never reflect on the ideas and structures of games without the teacher's help. Thus, an opportunity for new insight is lost. By interacting with the student, the teacher is able to take advantage of the child's direct experience by helping him or her search for greater meaning, thus allowing concepts to develop. The teacher's assessments and mediating questions are designed to facilitate the processes of organization and adaptation on the part of the child.

The third role of the teacher is that of *initiator of group activities*, especially play, games, and discussions. It is good to keep in mind that the classroom is a social environment and is not dedicated solely to the development of the intellect. However, social and intellectual growth are quite closely joined. The give-and-take, the shared experiences, and the opportunity to talk and listen to others who are at similar developmental levels represent the essence of true learning because they come from the child.

Teaching, then, is the creation of environments in which students' cognitive and affective structures can emerge and develop. Piaget believed that students grow only when they initiate their own learning experiences and that learning must be spontaneous and not forced and artificial. He was convinced that verbal fluency

A well-designed classroom provides many learning opportunities for children.

is not real knowledge. He felt that direct, concrete experiences are fundamental to learning and that the student's role in learning must be active, exploratory, and discovering. If you consider his ideas for a moment, you just might realize that they run counter to the classroom routines that most children experience day in and day out!

Jean Piaget

Piaget conceived of learning as being based on three types of knowledge: physical, social, and logical. Examples of *physical* learning include the following: cotton is soft, ice is cold, grain can be ground into flour, and sticks can be used to make a model house. *Social* learning, of course, can be obtained only through interaction with others. Play is especially beneficial because it affords the child opportunities to experience rules, language, norms of behavior, leadership and followership, joy, frustration, winning and losing, and so on. *Logical* knowledge develops from the experiences through the processes of reflection and abstraction. Thus, discussions about right and wrong, easy and difficult, problem solving, sharing, cooperating, insight, and so forth enable the child to look back on an experience and consider it intellectually and socially. In that sense, development ought to move from egocentric, idiosyncratic, highly personalized views toward more socially centered, publicly validated ways of thinking, feeling, and acting. Here, the role of the social environment is particularly important. The peer group provides a source of motivation and information in a linguistic form that is more appropriate to students' cognitive structures than is the teacher-to-student, workbook-centered learning that students so often encounter in elementary social studies.

Lev Vygotsky

Lev Vygotsky (1896–1934) was a Russian educator and psychologist whose ideas on teaching and learning have only recently been implemented, first in Russia and now in the Western world. Even though Vygotsky's work was carried out in the early years of the twentieth century, it has a fresh perspective that has contributed much to the constructivist movement in education. Vygotsky's theory is known as a sociohistorical approach to education, which means that he believed that human learning is too complex to reduce to simple, isolated behaviors; rather, it must be studied in the social, time-specific context in which it occurs. To reduce human learning to a set of behaviors, each of which could be studied independently, was as wrong, he thought, as to try to study water by reducing it to hydrogen and oxygen. Obviously, the result when these two elements are combined to form water is something qualitatively different from the sum of the parts. Thus, according to Vygotsky, to separate teaching and the learning in a social context is equally futile. For an overview of Vygotsky's thoughts on intellectual and social growth, see Figure 4.3.

For Vygotsky, the teaching and learning that takes place at school occurs in a primarily social setting where learners are conscious of themselves and others.

FIGURE 4.3

69

Theory

Teaching/Learning Priorities

*Vygotsky's View on
Intellectual and
Social Growth*

- ▬ Language and thought
- ▬ Social activity
- ▬ Speech and practical activity
- ▬ Use of tools
- ▬ Constructing and applying
- ▬ Modeling, tutoring, pairing/sharing
- ▬ Zone of proximal development

Human learning, especially in a school setting, is facilitated by the use of mental tools, which Vygotsky called signs. An example of such a mental tool would be a map of the playground drawn by a child. Other mental tools might include artwork, music, graphics, and the use of symbolic representation using numbers and writing—in short, anything that raises one's awareness beyond a sense of the immediate. These tools are aids to people's memories and to their abilities to communicate with others, but they are more than that. They are selective, abstracted representations. To return to the example of the playground map drawn by a child, one can readily see that the map includes only important features, not *everything* in the environment. Thus, it is both selective and abstract.

Animals can perceive, remember, express themselves, and pay attention—abilities Vygotsky called "natural mental behaviors." Human beings, however, are capable of "cultural mental behavior," behavior that transcends the immediate boundaries of time and space. Semiotics is a theory of the use of signs and symbols to represent ideas; the name Vygotsky gave to such cultural mental behaviors was *semiotic mediation*. Given this, it is not surprising that Vygotsky, in contrast to Piaget, placed great emphasis on the role of *instruction* in children's learning. This, of course, is where you come in. The teacher's role in providing instruction (either teacher directed or established by the teacher using more knowledgeable peers) is crucial. Thus, one can safely conclude that Vygotsky was more of an interventionist than was Piaget. See Figure 4.4 for practical applications of Vygotsky's ideas about teaching.

Concept Attainment

In social studies, considerable emphasis is placed on learning concepts. Typically, teachers will say that although children must learn certain facts, conceptual understanding is what is really at stake. Vygotsky had much to say about concept attainment, and his ideas have practical significance for the elementary teacher. First of all, we will examine his ideas on the four stages of concept attainment through which learners proceed. Vygotsky used very plain language in describing them. As we will see, his description of the stages proceeds from spontaneous and concrete to abstract and scientific.

FIGURE 4.4

Practical Applications of Vygotsky's Theory

- Teachers should be helpful to students but not intrusive. Let them do for themselves what they can on their own. Provide just enough guidance so that children can solve their own problems. For example, if a child is making a map showing the way to school from home, it is quite possible that he or she neglected to include a legend or key. Certain hints from the teacher could take the student to the next level.

- Your teaching should be aimed slightly ahead of the child's current level of mastery. If it is too easy or too difficult, no meaningful learning takes place. The idea is to teach within the zone of proximal development. This means that you have a good idea of the learner's strengths and weaknesses, and the only way you will have that knowledge is to spend time listening and talking with your students as individuals.

- You need to use a technique known as reciprocal teaching. This involves modeling skills—for example, showing how a map you made uses a legend, scale, and so on, and talking about it as you show your work to the students. At first, children may do a "poor" job, so you need to give them corrective feedback. This should be followed by small group "teaching" of each other by your students. (See the I Can Teach strategy in Chapter 8.)

- As you introduce concepts and skills, think in terms of simplicity at first, but try to bring your students along with you toward greater sophistication. For example, you can show examples of map legends and map scales used on professionally drawn maps.

Source: Adapted from J. Byrne, *Cognitive Development and Learning in Instructional Contexts*, 2nd ed. (Boston: Allyn and Bacon).

Vygotsky called the first stage of concept attainment *heaps*. Heaps are random categories to which the child assigns no particular hierarchy or even relationships. Thus, a very young child may know about planes, trains, and automobiles, but does not assign them to a relational category called transportation. This stage of early childhood is succeeded by a second stage, which Vygotsky called *complexes*. On the basis of the child's direct experiences, he or she begins to establish relationships among and between certain concrete categories. Now the child understands that cars, trucks, planes, and so on perform certain related functions; that is, they can carry people or things from one place to another. Vygotsky felt that concept attainment at the first two stages is not particularly stable, and such conceptual understanding as a child might have is probably not deep enough to be based on anything more than superficial similarities found among objects.

The third stage of concept attainment, which Vygotsky labeled *potential concepts*, represents a transition from a perspective of concrete, immediate, spontaneous knowledge of things and events to a more abstract, stable understanding of relationships and/or categories. The child increasingly begins to rely on symbolic representations and to begin to compare past with present events, to think about what is to come, and to

Lev Vygotsky

show an ability to reflect. It is at this stage that formal instruction (in the sense of teaching beyond direct experience) can be carried out. This stage generally lasts through early adolescence—in other words, through the remainder of the elementary school years.

Vygotsky's last stage is called *genuine concepts* or *scientific concepts*. Scientific concepts emerge on the basis of abstract, systematic knowledge. The first two stages are relatively independent of formal instruction; a child's knowledge of the world develops in the very early years in a more naturalistic, mimicking-of-others fashion. Even this, however, can be misleading if one were to conclude that no adult intervention is necessary. All educators know how important it is for adults to read to children, for example. Beyond the first two levels, potential concepts set the stage for success in attaining scientific concepts. Thus, primary-level instruction is crucial to the success of the more abstract learning that can take place if the foundation is laid carefully in the early years.

The Zone of Proximal Development

Vygotsky's best-known contribution to teaching and learning is his idea of the zone of proximal development. It is the key to clarifying the relationship between a child's developmental level and his or her instructional level. Briefly stated, the zone of proximal development is represented as "the distance between the actual developmental level as determined by independent problem solving and the level of potential development as determined through problem solving under adult guidance or in collaboration with more capable peers." In other words, what is at stake is the difference between what a child could learn on his or her own versus what a child is capable of learning when instructed by someone who knows more or who has greater skills (see Figure 4.5).

Vygotsky was concerned about the overapplication of intelligence and achievement tests to measure children's abilities. He felt that such tests yielded only a static, not a dynamic, measure of ability. For teachers, he reasoned, the question is not what a learner can do if left alone, but what he or she can do with the aid of a knowledgeable, caring teacher. Heaps and complexes, which are actually preconceptual in nature, generally develop in a bottom-up fashion as a result of concrete, day-to-day experience. But potential concepts and scientific concepts develop from the top down because they are mediated by words and other signs in the process of formal schooling. Thus, if children are to attain higher-level knowledge, there must be conscious, structured guidance.

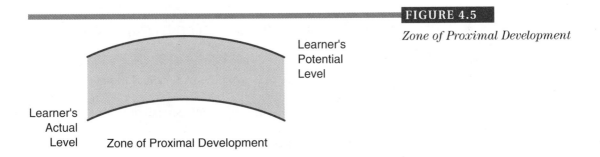

FIGURE 4.5

Zone of Proximal Development

Learner's
Potential
Level

Learner's
Actual
Level   Zone of Proximal Development

Do not assume, however, that Vygotsky concluded that adults merely have to tell children or even to show them in order for them to develop concepts. A teacher or a more advanced peer cannot do another person's thinking for him or her. Concepts emerge on the basis of experience mediated by words, sometimes in the form of key questions, prompts, additional information, and the like. In many respects, this is quite the same argument John Dewey made for reflective thinking.

Constructivist Learning

Vygotsky's ideas on childhood learning are quite compatible with constructivism, which argues that the learner is an active, meaning-making individual. In the context of the sociohistorical setting of the classroom, learning ought to be socially engaged, so that thought and expression go hand in hand. The teacher is there to facilitate the process, to ensure that learners are stretched beyond the levels they might attain if left their own. Robinson Crusoe, shipwrecked and alone on a desert island, is not the Vygotskyian model. For Vygotsky, the crucial question is environmental. A teacher who knows both subject matter and learner can create the social/intellectual atmosphere in which student learning will exceed student development. Piaget felt that language is an indicator of a child's developmental level but that it does not play a role in cognitive development. Vygotsky, on the other hand, believed that language is a tool the child uses in problem solving and planning, and that language therefore enhances cultural mental behavior.

Carl Rogers

Carl Rogers (1902–1987) firmly believed that the educational system as it exists does not meet the needs of children or of society. His view of schools was that they are essentially bureaucratic structures that cling to tradition, conservatism, and rigidity. Rogers especially took issue with the approach to education that states that educators must teach the "basics" and that students should be told what to do and how to do it. Like John Dewey before him, Rogers was a staunch advocate of democracy, and he felt that democratic thought and action should begin in the classroom. Rogers felt that the first item on the teacher's agenda ought to be the establishment of an atmosphere of trust. He saw the teacher's role as that of facilitator of learning and the student's role as an active, exploratory learner. In that sense, both Piaget and Bruner would be in complete agreement with him.

Educational Priorities

Carl Rogers's educational goals were set forth in his book *Freedom to Learn*. His goals are child centered and humanistic. Following is a list of Rogers's educational priorities:

- *A climate of trust* in the classroom in which curiosity and the natural desire to learn can be nourished and enhanced
- *A participatory mode of decision making* in all aspects of learning in which students, teachers, and administrators each have a part
- *Helping students to prize themselves*, to build their confidence and self-esteem

- *Uncovering the excitement* in intellectual and emotional discovery, which leads students to become lifelong learners
- *Developing in teachers the attitudes* that research has shown to be most effective in facilitating learning
- *Helping teachers to grow as persons,* finding rich satisfaction in their interaction with learners
- *An awareness that, for all of us, the good life is within,* not something that is dependent on outside sources[5]

Thus, Rogers sets the teaching/learning agenda quite clearly as one that aims toward personal growth, participation, the joy of learning, inner peace and tranquility, and the development of a natural desire to learn. Also, Rogers is saying that the relationship between teacher and child is at the heart of the enterprise. There must exist a condition of trust, mutual respect, and a partnership dedicated to meaningful learning. Figure 4.6 lists Rogers's educational priorities.

Classroom Applications

In *Freedom to Learn*, Rogers tells the story of a young girl who goes to school for the first time. The teacher behaves in a warm and friendly manner toward the child and introduces the girl to some of the other children. The teacher's interest in the children is genuine and obvious even to the little girl, whose fears and anxieties begin to fade. When class begins, the teacher has the children sit in a circle, and she asks each to tell about something he or she is interested in. The little girl begins to relax. The classroom is filled with interesting things: maps, books, toys, blocks, pictures, and more. Later, after the children have explored the room for a while, the teacher calls them back together. She asks the little girl if she would like to tell a story. The child tells about going shopping with her mother. The teacher prints the girl's story on the board. Rogers poses the question: "What has this small girl learned?" He answers that she has learned that:

- Her curiosity is welcomed and prized.
- The teacher is friendly and caring.
- She can learn new things, both on her own and with the teacher's help.
- There is room for spontaneity here.
- She can contribute to the group learning.

FIGURE 4.6

Rogers's Educational Priorities

- Instilling a climate of trust
- Employing a participatory mode of decision making
- Helping students to prize themselves (self-esteem)
- Uncovering the excitement in intellectual and emotional discovery
- Building lifelong learning
- Helping teachers grow as persons
- Instilling an awareness that the good life lies within us

- She is valued as a person.
- She will find a place in school for all of her many and expanding interests.
- She will develop a knowledge of resources, ways of finding out what she wants to know.
- She will read about, think about, and discuss the crucial social issues of her time.
- She will find some things very difficult to learn, requiring effort, concentration, and self-discipline.
- She finds learning very rewarding.
- She learns to attack tasks cooperatively, working with others to achieve a goal.
- She is on the way to becoming an educated person, one who is learning how to learn.[6]

By way of contrast, Rogers describes a small boy whose experience is not so happy. On his first day at school, the boy quickly learns that school means that making a mistake is very bad, that *teacher* and *disciplinarian* are synonymous terms, that most textbooks are boring, that relevant learning takes place outside of school, that original ideas have no place in school learning, that tests and grades are all-important, and that teachers are impersonal and boring.

These two contrasting views of a child's first day of school are incredibly forceful images of the potential power of a teacher, for better or for worse. Rogers's thoughts about school and about what we teachers ought to be doing in social studies are at once romantic and practical. His feelings run deep. At one point, he states, "My heart is pounding as I write this." In a section of his book subtitled "The Miracle of Childhood," Rogers describes children he has seen in a variety of situations around the world.

I see a small boy pounding nail after nail into a large wooden box until it is studded with the metal heads. I see a little girl insisting stubbornly that she will wear only the dress *she* has chosen, not the one selected by her mother. I see a child in a supermarket trying to feel every can, box, bunch of vegetables, stopped only temporarily by a mother's slap on his hands. There is a small girl trying to imitate the big words she had just heard. There is a boy turning over rocks and boards, looking for the harmless snakes he loves to collect. I see a group of children playing with clay, laughing at the forms they create. I see youngsters learning to thwart parental rules, manipulate parental behavior. I hear a small boy asking over and over, "What letter is *that*? And what letter is *that*?" I see the homeless "street children" of Brazil, unloved and unwanted, roaming the streets, stealing, struggling to survive. I see children on the beach, building sand castles, carrying buckets of water to and fro. I see children counting out pennies for a candy bar. I see and hear a small boy kicking an empty can along a city street. I hear the ever-repeated questions, "Why?" "How?" "*Why* does water run downhill?"

Carl Rogers

"*How* does the baby get inside the mother?" "*Why* is he talking so loud?" "*How* do you make it go?"

75
Theory

The activities are ceaseless, the curiosity endless. Young children are eager to find out, wanting to do, to shape, to create. They are soaking up information through eyes, ears, nose, mouth, fingers. They are moving, restless, spontaneous, determined. They are assimilating knowledge, perceiving patterns, acquiring language, improving skills.

They are learning, learning, learning—probably at a rate they will never again equal.

And then their "education" begins. Off they go to school. What will they find? The possibilities are almost endless.[7]

It is probably true that Rogers gives less in the way of a curricular prescription to the social studies teacher than do the other theorists discussed in this chapter. Certainly, he never developed a course of study for elementary levels as Jerome Bruner did. But I think he would not have done so even if he had had the time, because he would have seen it as self-defeating and even coercive in terms of his purpose, which mainly was the encouragement of learners toward self-realization. For Rogers, the key to a learning experience was that it be freely chosen; anything less than that he considered manipulative and artificial. Rogers was clearly more interested in such affective issues as self-esteem, free choice, ownership, and responsibility. More than almost any other serious thinker (A. S. Neill of Summerhill fame is an exception) on school matters, Rogers saw curriculum content as completely negotiable. In that sense, he took the doctrine of interest—a view that children ought to study whatever interests them—to extreme. I do not agree with his viewpoint that subject matter should be selected by the student exclusively. But beneath that all too easy criticism lies another issue—that is, the relationship between teacher and student. Jean Rousseau pointed out more than 200 years ago that teachers should make it their first task to know their students better. Maybe where the environment is inviting, the teacher is interesting, and relationships are caring, nurturing, and intellectually supportive, students might find great appeal in the things we think are important to study.

Howard Gardner

Howard Gardner takes issue with the conventional view of intelligence. Challenging the more narrow view of the intellect as based primarily on verbal and reasoning abilities, Gardner suggests that intelligence takes multiple forms and that each individual possesses these forms to a certain degree. What is so fundamentally appealing about Gardner's work is that it leaves in the dust the traditional notions of who is smart and who is dumb. Of course, good teachers have always known, intuitively, that every child has something special to offer and that those different gifts should be celebrated. But Gardner proposes that we teachers take a further step in which we begin to realize that the ability to relate well to others, just to take an example, is more than just a knack—it is a form of intelligence.

The Nature of Intelligence

Gardner theorizes that each form of intelligence has its unique neurological pattern as well as its own course of development. The fact that certain abilities often have not been perceived as forms of intelligence does not change their nature. Rather, the tendency to label children as unmotivated, hyperactive, or learning disabled says more about one's narrow view of what intelligence is than anything about the children. Much of one's perception of intelligence is culture bound. The U.S. culture values verbal and reasoning ability, so those forms of the intellect have been honored in the school systems. Other forms may be prized in other cultures. Certainly, Gardner's intent is not to downplay verbal or logical intelligence, which are crucial to so much of what people do. But he argues that society needs to create a much wider definition of intelligence, one that accommodates the many abilities that children and adults use in everyday life.

Howard Gardner

Think for a moment about the child who shows great ability to work with mechanical things. I recall having in class a boy named Donald who could operate a piece of equipment after watching me set it up one time, which takes a certain amount of spatial intelligence. Yet Donald, who was noticeably deficient when it came to reading and writing, had never been perceived as "intelligent" even though he was. So much of the school day favors those who are adept at reading and writing. Reading and writing are important skills, no doubt about it. But learning can be so much more. No wonder that school grades are a poor predictor of job success and success in life in general.

Perhaps one contribution that Gardner will have made with his theory of multiple intelligences is that you and I will be able to look at every child we teach and say, "My, that's an intelligent child." What a change we would begin to see in our schools and in our students! Our job is to build children up, to make them feel that they can and will learn, and that learning comes in many forms.

Types of Intelligence

Gardner offers a refreshing thought with regard to who is intelligent. Most people have grown up thinking that intelligence can be measured through the application of a test such as the Wechsler or the Stanford-Binet that yields an IQ or intelligence quotient. Gardner suggests that IQ tests actually measure only a narrow range of human ability or intelligence. As you probably know from experience, most IQ tests measure primarily verbal and problem-solving abilities. Gardner acknowledges that these are significant abilities, but he states that there is far more to human intelligence.

Gardner describes eight different "intelligences," all of which have great potential significance for the social studies curriculum (see Table 4.2). As we examine Gardner's conception, keep in mind an additional idea: These intelligences are held by all children in some measure, and they all need to be enhanced by you in the classroom. Therefore, in planning experiences for your students, you need to

TABLE 4.2 *Applications of Gardner's Multiple Intelligences*

Disposition/ Intelligence	Sensitivity to:	Inclination for:	Ability to:	Examples of Classroom Activities
Verbal-Linguistic Intelligence	The sounds, meanings, structures, and styles of language	Speaking, writing, listening, reading	Speak effectively (teacher, religious leader, politician) or write effectively (poet, journalist, novelist, copywriter, editor)	Discussions, debates, journal writing, conferences, essays, stories, poems, storytelling, listening activities, reading
Logical-Mathematical Intelligence	Patterns, numbers and numerical data, causes and effects, objective and quantitative reasoning	Finding patterns, making calculations, forming and testing hypotheses, using the scientific method, deductive and inductive reasoning	Work effectively with numbers (accountant, statistician, economist) and reason effectively (engineer, scientist, computer programmer)	Calculations, experiments, comparisons, number games, using evidence, formulation and testing hypotheses, deductive and inductive reasoning
Spatial Intelligence	Colors, shapes, visual puzzles, symmetry, lines, images	Representing ideas visually, creating mental images, noticing visual details, drawing and sketching	Create visually (artist, photographer, engineer, decorator) and visualize accurately (tour guide, scout, ranger)	Concept maps, graphs, charts, art projects, metaphorical thinking, visualization, videos, slides, visual presentations
Bodily-Kinesthetic Intelligence	Touch, movement, physical self, athleticism	Activities requiring strength, speed, flexibility, hand-eye coordination, and balance	Use the hands to fix or create (mechanic, surgeon, carpenter, sculptor, mason) and use the body expressively (dancer, athlete, actor)	Role-playing, dance, athletic activities, manipulatives, hands-on demonstrations, concept miming
Musical Intelligence	Tone, beat, tempo, melody, pitch, sound	Listening, singing, playing an instrument	Create music (songwriter, composer, musician, conductor) and analyze music (music critic)	Playing music, singing, rapping, whistling, clapping, analyzing sounds and music
Interpersonal Intelligence	Body language, moods, voice, feelings	Noticing and responding to other people's feelings and personalities	Work with people (administrators, managers, consultants, teachers) and help people identify and overcome problems (therapists, psychologists)	Community-involvement projects, discussions, cooperative learning, team games, peer tutoring, conferences, social activities, sharing
Intrapersonal Intelligence	One's own strengths, weaknesses, goals, and desires	Setting goals, assessing personal abilities and liabilities, monitoring one's own thinking	Meditate, reflect, exhibit self-discipline maintain composure, and get the most out of oneself	Student choice, journal writing self-evaluation, personal instruction, independent study discussing feelings, reflecting
Naturalist Intelligence	Natural objects, plants, animals, naturally occurring patterns, ecological issues	Identifying and classifying living things and natural objects	Analyze ecological and natural situations and data (ecologists and rangers), learn from living things (zoologist, botanist, veterinarian) and work in natural settings (hunter, scout)	Ecological field trips, environmental study, caring for plants and animals, outdoor work, pattern recognition

Source: Adapted from H. Silver, R. Strong, and M. Perini, *So Each May Learn* (Alexandria, VA: Association for Supervision and Curriculum Development, 2000).

challenge yourself to broaden those social studies experiences to include all eight intelligences, which can be summarized as follows:

1. *Linguistic intelligence,* which involves sensitivity to the meaning of words, their order and syntax, the sounds, rhythms, and inflections of language, and the uses of languages.

2. *Musical intelligence,* which consists of sensitivities to rhythm, pitch, and timbre. It also has an emotional component. Gardner relates musicians' descriptions of their abilities that emphasize an individual's natural feel for music and not the reasoning or linguistic components of musical ability.

3. *Logical-mathematical intelligence* that emerges from interaction with objects. By a sequence of stages the person is more able to perform actions on objects, understand the relations among actions, make statements about actions, and eventually see the relations among those statements.

4. *Spatial intelligence,* which is the capacity to perceive the physical world, accurately, to perform transformations and modifications on these perceptions, and to produce or recreate forms.

5. *Bodily-kinesthetic intelligence,* which involves a person's ability to use the body in highly specific and skilled ways, both for expressive (the dancer) and goal-directed (the athlete) purposes.

Personal intelligence, which takes two forms:
6. *Intrapersonal intelligence* is the ability to access one's own feelings and to label, discriminate, and symbolically represent one's range of emotions in order to understand behavior.

7. *Interpersonal intelligence* involves the ability to notice and make distinctions about others' moods, temperaments, motivations, and intentions.

8. *Naturalist intelligence* is the ability to draw on features of the natural world to solve problems (the chef, gardner, florist).

Gardner is careful to draw a distinction between an *intelligence* and a *domain.* He does this because of the confusion that seems to have arisen over the two terms to the point that many people have assumed they are the same thing. Gardner describes intelligences in terms of potential and domains in terms of activity. He writes that "an intelligence is a biological and psychological potential . . . capable of being realized to a greater or lesser extent as a consequence of the experiential cultural and motivational factors that affect a person." Thus, a person may possess a certain degree of musical intelligence with regard to his or her potential, but that potential may or may not be developed. In contrast, Gardner describes a domain as "an organized set of activities within a culture." Examples of domains include chess, physics, baseball, gardening, rap music, and so forth—in other words, culturally derived and practiced activities. He notes that any particular domain "can be realized through the use of several intelligences" and, contrariwise, any intelligence can be applied to a wide range of domains (e.g., spatial intelligence is used in navigation, billiards, sculpture, geometry, architecture, and so on).

Related to the use of the terms *intelligences* and *domains* is a third term, *field.* Gardner describes a field as "the set of individuals and institutions that judge the acceptability and creativity of products fashioned by individuals . . . within new or established domains." Within a field, then, there are critics and judges as well as institutions such as museums, institutes, universities, publishing companies, and so on that set, maintain, and adjust standards of acceptability. I was reminded of the idea of a field recently when, visiting a fair, I watched the sheep-judging exhibition in which young people who had raised sheep exhibited them to a watching gallery, but more importantly, to expert judges who made decisions about qualities that experts know to look for. You yourself are considered an expert judge in the areas of children's intellectual and social growth and development, just as a pediatrician is an expert judge of their physical well-being.

For teachers of social studies and related interdisciplinary curricula, Gardner's thoughts on problem solving and creativity are particularly insightful and practical. He cites Graham Wallas's classic conception of the four stages in the creative problem-solving process: (1) *preparation*, in which the ideas for the work are identified and considered thoughtfully; (2) *incubation*, a time of letting things sift through one's thoughts and emotions, playing with possibilities and such; (3) *illumination*, when the "lightbulb" goes on and the problem solver realizes how things come together; and (4) *verification*, in which the problem is solved, the product is constructed, the drawing executed, or whatever.

These stages tend to be generally illustrative of the behaviors of effective problem solvers. In spite of this, as many experts have noted, it is not as simple as merely teaching the stages as a rubric which can then be applied successfully to any problem. Nevertheless, you may want to consider discussing the stages with your students, posting the stages prominently in the classroom, and challenging the students to attempt to apply them to an activity such as "Draw a picture of an important event that occurred in the American Revolutionary War." Students are accustomed to drawing pictures, but they may never have associated such work with problem solving. If a child decided to portray the Battle of Lexington, he or she could, of course, merely copy from a text illustration, in which case little to no problem solving takes place. But if the child is challenged to think about what to

Collaborative learning provides opportunities for children to grow intellectually and socially.

leave in and out, whether a drawing or perhaps a diorama would be better, how concretely or abstractly to portray events, and what he or she wants the viewer to feel when observing the work, then elements of problem solving are indeed present.

Three Responsibilities of Schools

In his book *The Unschooled Mind*,[3] Gardner writes of three kinds of knowledge that teachers are responsible for teaching students. At the elementary school level, the types of knowledge take on the form of basic literacies. The elementary years are crucial because they represent the foundational elements of a child's sense of himself or herself as a scholar, as a person more or less comfortable in school environments, and as someone who possesses the knowledge and skills necessary for advanced studies at secondary and university levels. Gardner calls these three kinds of knowledge notational sophistication, concepts within the discipline, and forms of exposition and reasoning within the discipline.

Notational sophistication refers to a learner's mastery of the major written codes of the culture. There is an assumption that during the elementary school years, students will perfect their knowledge of the so-called first-order systems, including alphabet, putting letters together to read and write words and sentences, basic number facts, and the like. Having done that, students are ready to use this knowledge to comprehend more sophisticated forms of notation such as applying basic scientific concepts, solving simple equations and doing related number activities, acquiring basic computer literacy, and reading graphs, charts, and maps. In a spiral curriculum, this would imply visiting and revisiting each of these areas at increasing levels of sophistication as the elementary years progress. Thus, a young child may be taught to make and interpret picture maps that are quite literal attempts to represent a landscape, whereas a child in the intermediate grades, having learned the former, may be taught to make and interpret more abstract maps that rely on symbols, a sense of scale and distance, and selective representation of a landscape.

With respect to *concepts within a discipline*, the elementary school years set the stage for more advanced study where a set of formal ideas, concepts, methods, and examples must be mastered. Thus, children in elementary school learn about such disciplines as economics, history, and anthropology within the larger, more developmental context of social studies. Still, the elementary years are crucial because the ability to learn at sophisticated levels falls back on sound earlier learning. Young children can learn the basic idea of an economic concept such as scarcity if the examples come from their experience with the world. Historical concepts such as *chronology* are perfectly teachable if children are allowed to construct time lines, build shelters, and engage in other iconographic and enactive teaching/learning experiences. A concept such as the *anthropology of culture* begins to emerge when children compare a colonial New England family with a family living in present-day Japan. Comparisons of food, clothing, and shelter—in other words, the basics of culture—can be concretely made by children. Not surprisingly, children who participate in school and classroom government and who reflect on its meaning during the elementary school years are much better prepared experientially to study state and national government structures later on.

> *"Only if we expand and reformulate our view of what counts as human intelligence, will we be able to devise more appropriate ways of assessing it and more effective ways of educating it."*
>
> Howard Gardner

Forms of exposition and reasoning within the discipline are best approached in rudimentary fashion during the elementary grades. A child historian and a child musician are both problem solvers, but they certainly use different approaches. Young student sociologists who do a survey of play activity preferences among primary-age children will use different methods of data gathering, data analysis, and presentation of their findings than will the same students if, as geographers, they do playground observations of primary children during recess. As Gardner notes, the modeling of procedures (compared to advanced students or professionals) may be only approximate, but the idea of empirical investigation is planted. Similarly, young children can learn through experience and reflection that the artist approaches his or her tasks rather differently from the way the geographer might. By definition, the artist can take liberties with map work, introducing fantasy, exaggerating proportions, and placing beauty over accuracy, whereas the geographer's map should be accurate and factual, especially if he or she expects one to use it to find buried treasure.

In summary, Gardner's conception of knowledge forms provides a useful tool in the hands of a creative elementary teacher who realizes that he or she can teach the same curriculum that continues to exist throughout the school years, but who also realizes that it must be approached using developmentally appropriate practice. The serious elementary teacher knows as well that his or her work is truly foundational, and that children and parents alike are trusting that the foundation will be a good one.

Summary

Perhaps the most important consideration in treating the developmental dimension of learning is to relate the theory and research to the individual differences of the individual child. Individual behavioral differences are the rule rather than the exception, and not all environmental intrusions affect all children the same way. The method of presentation in the classroom and the psychology of the child always interact with respect to the mastery of intellectual material.

This is of vital importance to all teachers concerned with the child's acquisition of knowledge and with the use of inquiry in elementary social studies. The understanding of and provision for individual differences must occur for all children: those who are slow, methodical, and accurate; those who cannot tolerate ambiguity; those who seek out conflicting sources and ideas and try to resolve them; those who organize information and ideas into broad categories; those who organize information and ideas on affective, personal criteria; those who emphasize details; those who remember generalizations; those who consider a task as a whole; those who must reduce a problem to the smallest elements. These children can contribute to the elementary social studies program, especially a program emphasizing problem solving and inquiry. They can also benefit from exposure to an understanding of other cognitive styles.

Although it would be inappropriate to make sweeping conclusions about the implications of findings in the area of child development as they relate to the social studies curriculum, several tentative observations do seem in order.

1. Active or hands-on learning seems to hold a slight edge over passive learning.
2. Elementary-age students are capable of and should be given the opportunity to investigate problems that are real to them and can affect their daily lives.
3. Concrete experiences seem to be crucial to the development of abstract concepts about human beings and social systems.
4. Students should be challenged to think and act at levels that include, but also transcend, memory work. They are capable of such operations as analysis and synthesis when related tasks are presented to them in a concrete manner.
5. Elementary students are capable of carrying out data-collecting procedures depending on observation, recording, and inferencing.
6. Alternative learning styles should be recognized in students, and teachers ought not to assume one method will always be appropriate for all students.
7. Students need to feel good about themselves in order to learn effectively. This underscores the importance of the hidden curriculum in teaching.
8. Teachers need to be aware of their own behaviors in the classroom. The potential effect of modeling higher-level thinking, respect for human dignity, tolerance of ambiguity, and high standards of scholarship should not be underestimated.

ACTIVITIES

1. Discuss with a partner what you think is a key idea contributed to social studies by each of the five theoreticians listed in this chapter.
2. Examine a current primary- or intermediate-level social studies textbook and come to some conclusions about the extent to which the ideas of theoreticians have influenced its contents.
3. Of the theoretical perspectives presented in this chapter, which has the most appeal to you and which has the least? Why?
4. List at least five practical implications for your behavior as a teacher resulting from the material presented in this chapter.

NOTES

1. Jerome Bruner, *The Process of Education* (New York: Vintage Books, 1963), p. 38.
2. Ibid., p. 38.
3. Ibid., pp. 56–57.
4. Seymour Papert, *Mindstorms* (New York: Basic Books, 1984), p. 15.

5. Carl Rogers and Jerome Freiberg, *Freedom to Learn*, 3rd ed. (New York: Macmillan, 1994), p. 3.
6. Ibid., p. 341.
7. Ibid., pp. 299–300.
8. Howard Gardner, *The Unschooled Mind* (New York: Basic Books, 1991).

SUGGESTED READINGS

Bransford, J., Brown, A., and Cocking, R., eds. (2000). *How People Learn: Brain, Mind, Experience, and School.* Washington, DC: National Academy Press.

Bruner, J. (1996). *The Culture of Education.* Cambridge, MA: Harvard University Press.

Dixon-Krause, L. (1996). *Vygotsky in the Classroom.* New York: Longman.

Gardner, H. (2000). *The Disciplined Mind: Beyond Facts and Standardized Tests, the K–12 Education That Every Child Deserves.* New York: Penguin.

Rogers, C., and Freiberg, J. (1994). *Freedom to Learn* (3rd ed.). New York: Macmillan.

Sternberg, R., ed. (2000). *Handbook of Intelligence.* Cambridge: Cambridge University Press.

Wadsworth, B. (1996). *Foundations of Constructivism: Piaget's Theory of Cognitive and Affective Development.* New York: Longman.

5

Experience, Constructivism, and Reflective Thinking

Cognitive psychology in general and the constructivist movement in particular have given us major insights to how children learn and how they construct knowledge. Put simply, we know that children learn best in supportive, active, engaging environments. We also know that human beings construct knowledge both individually and socially on the basis of their experiences. And finally, we know that experience itself is not enough; human beings also need to reflect on their experiences in order to build meaningful knowledge. The topics addressed in this chapter include the following:

- How reflective thought develops
- The quest for quality in teaching and learning
- Constructivist thinking
- The coverage problem
- Thinking strategies
- Problem solving
- The social/emotional intellectual landscape

We had the experience but missed the meaning.

—T. S. Eliot

We have now examined several chapters devoted to the underlying, foundational aspects of teaching and learning social studies. We're just about to move on to such specifics as planning, teaching strategies, activities, and assessment, but before we do, I'd like to ask you to reflect on what you've learned. How will you synthesize theory and practice into your own model of teaching and learning? What steps will you take to ensure that social studies is engaging, collaborative, enjoyable, and meaningful for you and your students? To help you in your thinking, I will devote some pages to the critical issues of experience, knowledge construction by learners,

FIGURE 5.1

1. Reflective thinking takes *time.*
2. Reflective thinking requires *strategy.*
3. Reflective thinking assumes *trust.*
4. Reflective thinking requires *discipline.*
5. Reflective thinking is *social and moral.*
6. Reflective thinking assumes *experience.*

Source: Adapted from Arthur K. Ellis, *Teaching, Learning, & Assessment Together: The Reflective Classroom* (New York: Eye on Education, Inc., 2001). http://www.eyeoneducation.com.

and reflective thinking (see Figure 5.1). When you have read this chapter, you should be able to call on the theoretical and practical dimensions covered previously to help you reach some conclusions about good teaching and about children as learners. Teaching and learning are practical pursuits, but for the professional, good practice should be based on good theory.

Nurturing Experience

Teachers today have access to a variety of active teaching and learning strategies, including discovery, inquiry, cooperative learning, simulation, group investigation, and projects. These strategies have made it possible to create attractive, engaging, and potentially productive learning landscapes. Taken together and thoughtfully applied, they have the potential to remove textbooks and workbooks from their position of dominance in the social studies curriculum. These learning strategies have a common property in that they invite learners to share in active experiences, thereby creating a communal frame of reference that emanates from the investigation of an idea or problem. For children, experience is the port of entry to reflective thinking. Without experience, students are relegated to a school life of verbal knowledge, which is, as Jean Piaget noted, not *real* knowledge. Figure 5.2 is an interesting exercise that supports this point.

How Reflective Thought Develops

John Dewey addressed the crucial nature of experience in learning when he wrote that "the fundamental fallacy in methods of instruction lies in supposing that experience on the part of pupils may be assumed." Dewey went on to say that "ready-made" subject matter and delivery systems in their variety of artificial forms (textbooks, workbooks, lesson plans, etc.) are a "waste of time." That's a pretty strong statement. He stated further that experience with ideas should begin in the most concrete forms and that it should be as "unscholastic" as possible. He advised teachers who wished to involve their students in experience "to call to mind the sort of situation that presents itself outside of school."[1]

Dewey suggested that the most productive areas of endeavor in which to engage students are real problems and social issues. He said that students should begin their inquiry by poking around at a trial and error level. The important thing,

FIGURE 5.2

What Does It Mean to "Read" Something?

Take a few moments to read the following article:

England Fights Back in Tense Test

LONDON—Pace bowler Angus Fraser, not always the first choice of selectors' chairman Ray Illingworth, inspired an England fightback against West Indies in the second test at Lord's on Friday.

Fraser captured his 100th test wicket by removing Brian Lara for six and later produced a burst of two for one to cut short a recovery by Jimmy Adams (54) and captain Richie Richardson (49).

West Indies, replying to England's first innings of 283, were 209 for six at the close of a tense and absorbing second day watched by another capacity 28,000 crowd under cloudless skies.

Fraser, originally overlooked for the 1994–95 tour of Australia before being called up in an injury crisis, and left out of the team who lost the first test to West Indies by nine wickets, ended the day with three for 37 from 20 overs.

Playing on his Middlesex home ground, Fraser set the tone for a much-needed disciplined performance by England's pace bowlers on a dry pitch showing signs of disconcerting bounce.

But for four missed chances in the final session, three from Adams, England might have taken a firm grip.

After England's largely disappointing batting, the need for their bowlers to strike early was answered initially by Darren Gough and Fraser.

Gough struck with the fifth delivery off the West Indian innings, getting opener Sherwin Campbell caught behind for five by Alec Stewart with one that left the batsman a shade.

1. Did you have trouble pronouncing the words? Probably not.
2. Did you understand what you read? Probably not.
3. When I read it, I found that I could barely figure out even the simplest sense of what took place, even which side won.
4. Unless you have a background in the sport of cricket, you probably lack the schema necessary for an understanding of the story.
5. You and I need to remind ourselves that some children go down this road every day. We tend to confuse ability with prior knowledge. This is why experiential learning is so important in childhood. Words printed on a page are useful, but only if one's frame of reference can accommodate them.

he said, is the ultimate quality of a problem to be investigated because good problems "give the pupils something to do, not something to learn and the doing is of such a nature as to demand thinking, or the intentional noting of connections; learning naturally results."[2]

Dewey was convinced that much of what comprises the official learning environment is hostile to reflective thinking. He decried the "great premium put upon listening, reading, and the reproduction of what is told and read."[3] This statement is filled with irony when one considers the potential of social studies to create a sense of community. No wonder, Dewey claimed, that when children go to school, they might as well leave their minds at home, for they cannot use their minds in the abstract curriculum that prevails. Dewey's observations separate the terms *abstract* and *intellect* with surprising clarity, given the criticism of his writing as conceptually dense and often obtuse. He offers no radical argument against reading or lis-

tening as avenues to understanding; rather, his point is that these processes devoid
of an experiential backcloth leave the learner with emptiness rather than insight.

87

Experience

The Quest for Quality

John Dewey wrote much of the preceding opinions in the second decade of the
twentieth century. One might suppose that learning environments have improved
considerably over the past eight decades. In fact, they have at the level of educational theory and in the realms of research in learning and teaching and among a
relatively small but growing number of informed teachers. Reference to systematic
observation in schools, however, reveals less improvement than one might imagine. The realities of school life changed very little in the twentieth century. John
Goodlad notes that the most predictable event in secondary classrooms is the lecture, and in elementary classrooms, seat work. Both are passive, abstract pursuits
that offer little hope of intellectual or moral stimulation. Goodlad writes, "Three
categories of student activity marked by passivity—written work, listening, and
preparing for assignments—dominate in the likelihood of their occurring at any
given time at all three levels of schooling. The chances are better than 50–50 that if
you were to walk into any of the classrooms of our sample, you would see one of
these three activities under way."[4]

In a similar vein, William Glasser notes that "students in school . . . are asked
to learn well enough to remember for important tests innumerable facts that both
they and their teachers know are of no use except to pass the tests."[5] Glasser calls
this stuff "throwaway information" because it is unconnected to experience and, by
inference, to the real lives of students. Even students who receive good grades will
often remark that they do not remember much of anything about a particular subject or teacher. Glasser goes on to say that a majority of students, even good ones,
believe that much of the present academic curriculum is not worth the effort it
takes to learn it. No matter how well teachers manage them, he suggests, if students
do not find *quality* in what they are asked to do, they will not work hard enough to
learn the material.

Constructivist Thought and Social Studies

With the emergence of constructivist thought as a pervasive force in curriculum
theory, it is once again becoming easier to find teaching and learning ideas that are
based on meaningful experience and that offer the promise of quality. Figure 5.3
discusses the principles of constructivism. The basis of constructivity is that *experience precedes analysis*. The decade or more spent on such quests as time on
task, behavioral objectives, and other teacher-centered instructional protocols
proved to be a cul-de-sac along the road to inspiration in childhood learning, especially after the promise provided by the many learner-referenced social studies
curriculum projects of a generation ago.

Constructivist thought, which invests learners in a search for their own sense
of meaning based on many of the active teaching and learning strategies mentioned
earlier, meets the conditions of what could be called an experiential focus in teaching and learning. Dewey himself foreshadowed the constructivist movement when
he wrote that a person's ability to think about or apply reason to a given situation

FIGURE 5.3

Notes on Constructivism

Constructivism is a theory of knowledge with roots in philosophy, art and architecture, psychology, and cybernetics.

It asserts two main principles:

1. Knowledge is not passively received but actively built up by the cognizing subject.
2. The function of cognition is adaptive and serves the organization of the experiential world, not the discovery of ontological reality (ontological: having to do with the nature of being, existence).

The first principle represents trivial constructivism, a principle known since Socrates.

The second principle suggests that knowledge cannot and need not be "true" in the sense that it matches ontological reality. It only has to be viable in the sense that it fits within the experiential constraints that limit the cognizing organism's possibilities of acting and thinking.

The greatest impact to date has been in psychotherapy and in the empirical study of literature. In literature reading, meaning is supplied by the reader from his or her own store of experiential abstractions—thus the subjective interpretation of text.

The teacher will realize that knowledge cannot be transferred to the student by linguistic communication but that language can be used as a tool in a process of guiding a student's construction.

> What is the message for the classroom? Experiences of high quality that are at once engaging and intellectually demanding are needed. Reflective thinking, especially in regard to a search for meaning and personal, social applications are crucial.

has a constructive function. He used the term *constructive* because a person constructs an idea or plan of action "which could not be produced otherwise."[6] Social studies learning that is informal, exploratory, and interdisciplinary provides the needed conditions.

Contrasting Perspectives for Social Studies

Table 5.1 illustrates some contrasts among traditional, romantic, and emergent perspectives of social studies curricular propriety. Of course, the point is not to discard traditional and child-centered forms in favor of the emergent perspectives but rather to consider where the most appropriate balance lies.

It was noted earlier that engagement strategies are only potentially productive. Engaging students *actively* is half the battle. Active student engagement in a meaningful situation, problem, or issue makes it possible to create the conditions for reflective thinking because the students are bonded together by a common experience. The experience becomes the focal point of reflective thought. Students reconstruct, evaluate, debrief, second-guess, and otherwise mentally reorganize what they did or what they are doing. It is from that concrete, common experience that students and teachers together can build the intellectual scaffolding necessary for the creation of ideas or concepts. This is not easy to do. Goodlad said that in

TABLE 5.1

Traditional Perspective	Romantic Perspective	Emergent Perspective
Class	Individual	Flexible
Autocratic	Laissez-faire	Democratic
Subjects	Interests	Issues
Textbooks	Manipulatives	Sources
Management	Freedom	Responsibility
Skills	Discovery	Insight
Direction	Indirection	Decision making
Competitive	Individualistic	Collaborative
Tasks	Play	Growth
Reactive	Active	Initiative
Uniform	Idiosyncratic	Creative
Prescriptive	Unscripted	Emergent
Lessons	Activities	Projects
Achievement	Fulfillment	Participation
Logical	Developmental	Relational
Teaching	Exploring	Learning
Objective	Subjective	Reflective
Teacher centered	Child centered	Needs centered
Formal exams	Self-assessment	Documentation
Scheduled	Spontaneous	Contractual

Contrasting Perspectives on Educational Propriety

his seven-state study he saw virtually no evidence of teachers teaching concepts. He concluded that either they felt concepts were unimportant or that they themselves do not think conceptually. However, concept teaching through reflective thinking is, in fact, the key to the saying, "Less is more." This is because a few concepts carefully considered are worth far more as intellectual currency than the great amounts of information students are typically asked to cover. Teachers and learners must deliberately slow down, cover less, and think at length about what they are learning. Philosopher Jean Rousseau knew this, and that is why he advised teachers to teach less and teach it well. In this same spirit, Alfred North Whitehead wrote, "What you teach, teach thoroughly."[7]

Although it is imperative to include firsthand experience as an integral part of social studies learning, there should be no bias against abstract thought in constructivist classrooms. In fact, it is needed desperately. The abstract thought that one seeks, however, must be rooted in a meaningful frame of reference called experience. This was Francis Bacon's intent when he said that learning ought to be about facts—one's *own* facts and not someone else's. Bacon's Experience → Mind → Meaning model is much the same as that of Dewey.

Experience → Mind → Meaning

Constructivist learning theory states that each of us must construct our own knowledge; others cannot give it to us. The role of experience and reflection in learning has been explored at length in the annals of cognitive research. Experience and reflection are, for example, the twin pillars of significance in constructivist learning theories. But one finds similar thinking in structuralist, developmental, and information-processing literature. Robert Karplus, the director of the Science Curriculum Improvement Study (SCIS), developed a three-phase learning model consisting of preliminary exploration, invention, and discovery. Karplus notes that students need to start by exploring a concept using concrete materials. By starting an investigation in this manner, Karplus argues, a learner has a direct experience from which to begin processes of abstract thought. But to be meaningful, the learning cycle must continue beyond the direct experience.

Jerome Bruner makes a clear distinction between learning *by* experience and learning *from* experience, and the distinction lies not so much with the experience itself as with how one reflects back on the experience. Bruner notes that animals typically learn by experience. A dog that burns its paw on the stove will not repeat such a mistake. The dog is too intelligent for that. But the dog is incapable of reflecting on such ideas as heat transfer or thermodynamics as a result of its experience. So experience, valuable as it is, is not enough. A search for meaning must accompany the experience. These are the dual imperatives of constructivism. This is to say that in order for learners to think reflectively about important things, they must have direct experience. Equally important, they must also have opportunities to reconstruct their experience. The implication is that a given activity must be extended beyond the experiential phase into a time of reflection and knowledge construction.

To those who point out that there seems little new in these lines of argument, I advise a careful reading of the research-based policy guidelines that have appeared in leading educational journals and government publications over the last decade. The persuasive efforts aimed at school personnel to keep students focused on reductionist, teacher-centered, direct-instruction tasks were legion.

The Coverage Problem

Attempts to refocus social studies toward a sense of greater activity and accompanying reflective thought inevitably bring up the element of time. Ask any teacher to name sources of frustration in his or her work, and the time factor invariably appears, usually in connection with having too little of it against too much material to cover.

John Carroll suggests that time is the most problematic variable in the curriculum.[8] Most of what students are expected to learn in school settings is configured by class periods of an hour or less. This is obviously true at secondary levels where separate subjects are assigned their own time slots, but it is more true than most care to admit at elementary levels. In addition, most social studies curriculums are set on time vectors from the first day of the school year forward. Teachers feel the need to forge ahead in order to provide the coverage demanded by the textbook or the district guide. This is particularly true of basic subjects such as social studies. It is less true of so-called soft subjects such as art, physical education, and music.

Carroll implies that if educators slowed down the curriculum, most students could actually learn more. His proposition is that the curriculum favors only those who learn quickly. The problem, he believes, is that most students never have the opportunity to process or to reflect on what they are learning—in essence, what is taught never gets internalized or connected to other learning. This problem is especially vexing in social studies where so much new content involving place names, dates, and events sweeps over learners daily.

It has been noted that average and below-average learners often leave out steps when they try to solve problems. Apparently, they go too fast in their efforts to keep up, taking mental shortcuts. An example of this would be a child playing, say, checkers who rather impulsively makes what seem on the surface to him or her to be reasonable moves. Often, the moves this young checker player makes are poorly thought out and could be vastly improved by talking through a move with another person, in which case certain lapses in logic might be confronted. To those who might think that such a procedure in checkers would be unfair, it is well to keep in mind that our teaching and learning objective is not to win against an opponent but to become better at what one does.

Thinking Strategies

Robert Sternberg and others suggest that students be encouraged to think aloud with a partner in order to slow themselves down. Such a strategy allows a learner to find out how well developed his or her ideas really are.[9] Thinking aloud brings the process of coming to thought to the surface, giving learners an opportunity to compare and contrast their ideas with those of others. In other words, it provides students with the opportunity to think reflectively.

Piaget wrote about the social knowledge that develops from working and interacting with others. He was convinced that the linguistic compatibility found within the peer group enables students to teach each other quite effectively, perhaps more effectively than an adult teacher, whose language structure is quite different from that of students. Russian psychologist Lev Vygotsky wrote about the community of knowledge and insight that the members of a community must share in order for learning to come to life.[10] These insights, against the findings of educational research that show that pupils initiate talk only about seven minutes per school day, on average,[11] point to the need for major restructuring of social studies learning and teaching.

Social Studies and Problem Solving

Here is a rather simple example of how we might develop strategies for slowing down and making our thoughts more explicit in order to make them more productive. Imagine a situation of 10 apples in a sack in a ratio of 3 red apples to 2 yellow apples. How many apples would you have to take out of the sack to be certain of having a matched pair either red or yellow? This is a difficult problem for many children partly because it purposely contains some extraneous information. But is the problem inherently difficult or is it difficult because we expect students to solve it with paper and pencil after reading it from a page? Imagine two alternative methods of trying to solve the problem: (1) talking about it while drawing diagrams with a partner and (2) simply reaching into a container that held the apples, several times, and trying to construct with a partner why you got the results you did. Both of these methods take considerably more time than we generally allow for such problems, and both yield better results.

Some teachers, apparently satisfied with the results we are getting, simply do not see how we could possibly slow the curriculum down. They know they must cover a great deal of information to comply with the social studies agenda. One possible means of accommodation is for teachers to talk less. Research shows that teachers talk three times as much as their students.[12] Since students outnumber teachers by about 27 to 1, it doesn't take a mathematics genius to figure out that students are allowed very little time to practice reflective thought. A remedy for this situation, of course, is cooperative learning of some sort, where students are expected to share their thoughts and to listen to the thoughts of others. Cooperative learning not only changes the amount of student-to-student interaction so desperately needed for reflective thinking to occur but it also changes the very social fabric of classrooms. Students are given far more control over their time, and teachers are able to shift from teaching as telling to allowing learning to take place.

Of course, much of this is already known by well-informed teachers. The problem lies with their many colleagues who are less informed about how to create the proper conditions for learning. Even among those who promote active learning, however, there is a reluctance to build in the extra time needed for genuine reflection by both students and teachers. Such a need is obviously not perceived by administrators as being necessary for teachers, who have little or no time to reflect alone or with fellow teachers. Therefore, it is little wonder that teachers often neglect reflective thinking with their students.

Economist Peter Drucker[13] states in his provocative book *The New Realities* that schools will never improve until classrooms become places where people have crossed the frontier from teaching to learning. When the primary focus in a classroom is on teaching, a teacher-centered curriculum results. Teacher-centered instruction is the stuff of lesson plans, scripted activities, behavioral objectives, and predictable outcomes. When the focus in social studies is on learning, a constructivist curriculum emerges. Student-centered constructivisit learning allows students the latitude to make choices, to play to their strengths, to work at length on projects, to develop ideas, to cooperate with other students, and to reflect on the quality and meaning of their work.

Instances of crossing the frontier from teaching to learning abound, but rarely in classrooms. Rather, they are found in the real world where learners make their own connections, do their own investigations, and continuously process what they are learning. Recently, I asked a colleague for some help with a problem I was having with a computer. He patiently walked me through a series of steps that got me on the right track. I asked him how he had learned so much about computers. He replied that he had learned what he knew by hanging around, using computers, and talking to other interested people. He explained that when he was in high school, there was a computer hooked up through a terminal to a mainframe and he used to go down to the little room where it was housed, close the door, and get on line. He said he had never taken a computer class. What my friend had done unwittingly was to follow Dewey's prescription for learning: Make it experiential, make it as unscholastic as you can, and reflect on what you do with other interested people. This is how many children are learning on their own, outside of school, when they play and discuss with friends the various video games, simulations, and so on. The success of Lego blocks in actually raising children's spatial intelligence is an example.

Perhaps you could cite similar examples of real learning from your own experience. In fact, you ought to write down and share with a friend a time when you were involved in *real* learning. The point is that such examples have significance because they have the power to redirect one's sense of teaching and learning away from formal, bookish procedures to the creation of learning environments that approximate real-world learning.

The Emotional/Intellectual Landscape

One other condition essential to the establishment of classrooms where students and teachers think reflectively is that of a healthy emotional/intellectual landscape. Not long ago, I observed in a third-grade class where the teacher was doing an inquiry social studies lesson. The approach was inductive: Artifacts were available for the students to examine, the students were working in teams, and they were encouraged to make inferences from their observations and recordings. This was all to the good. Unfortunately, the atmosphere was tense and rigid. The teacher kept interrupting the students to remind them to "stay on task" even though there was no evidence of misbehavior. Additionally, it became clear that the teacher was looking for "right" answers, and the students found themselves trying to please her or second-guess her wishes. None of the spontaneity that Piaget said must be present was there. Risk taking, outlandish ideas, a sense of humor, a relaxed and friendly pace—all were lacking. In this case, what might have been a good formal curriculum was unraveled by a bad hidden curriculum. The possibility of one of those transcendent moments in teaching and learning that occur when a good experience is wedded to a good discussion was lost.

CHECK-UP

Following are a couple of simple but powerful tasks that involve writing statements of belief. First, write down several statements of belief about good teachers—in other words, some traits of good teachers. Then write down several things you believe about children.

Some Things I Believe about Good Teachers:

1. _____

2. _____

3. _____

4. _____

5. _____

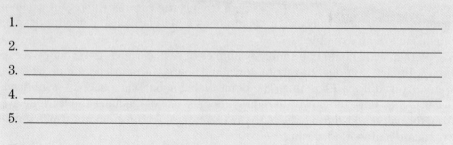

Some Things I Believe about Children:

1. _____

2. _____

3. _____

4. _____

5. _____

Take some time to share your thoughts with someone else. How are his or her statements similar to or different from yours?

Summary

The proper conditions for reflective thinking in social studies derive from a complex set of strategies developed by teachers and students. Learning by doing is simply not sufficient in itself; neither is direct experience—although both are important. You must be a guide, a fellow inquirer, an organizer of the environment, and a mediator of your students' thinking. You must establish a new set of priorities that run counter to the prevailing modes of instruction and classroom management. You must be committed to increasing the amount of student-to-student interaction, the number of decisions made by students, the amount of time given to reconstructing learning experiences, and the freedom given to your students to speak their minds and to take intellectual and emotional risks. When these conditions are met, the term *paradigm shift*—a term used so often to signal a basic transformation in what we do and what we expect to happen as a result—moves beyond the realm of cliché and into the realm of reality.

ACTIVITIES

1. Discuss with a partner how you think classrooms would have to change in order for reflective thinking to become a reality.
2. Some people might argue that children are not capable of reflective thought. Do you agree? Why or why not?
3. Many educators over the years have suggested that we teach less and teach it well. What are the implications for social studies of teaching less?
4. How can a teacher know if his or her students are thinking reflectively? What strategies are necessary to ensure that it will happen?
5. Identify at least three differences between a constructivist classroom and a traditional classroom.

NOTES

1. John Dewey, *Democracy and Education* (New York: Macmillan, 1916).
2. Ibid.
3. Ibid.
4. J. Goodlad, *A Place Called School* (New York: McGraw-Hill, 1984), p. 105.
5. W. Glasser, *The Quality School* (New York: Harper & Row, 1990), p. 7.
6. Dewey, *Democracy and Education*.
7. Alfred North Whitehead, *Aims of Education* (New York: The Free Press, 1929), p. 2.
8. J. Carroll, "A Model of School Learning," *Teachers College Record, 64* (1963): 722–733.
9. R. Sternberg, *Intelligence Applied: Understanding and Increasing Your Intellectual Skills* (San Diego: Harcourt Brace Jovanovich, 1986).
10. L. Vygotsky, *Thought and Language* (English translation by A. Kozulin.) (Cambridge, MA: MIT Press, 1986).
11. Goodlad, *A Place Called School*.
12. Ibid.
13. P. Drucker, *The New Realities* (New York: Perennial Library, 1990).

SUGGESTED READINGS

Armstrong, T. (2000). *In Their Own Way: Discovering and Encouraging Your Child's Multiple Intelligences.* New York: Tarcher/Putnam.

Crawford, D., Bodine, R., and Hoglund, R. (1993). *The School for Quality Learning.* Champaign, IL: Research Press.

Ellis, A. (2001). *Teaching, Learning, & Assessment Together: The Reflective Classroom.* Larchmont, NY: Eye on Education.

Glasser, W. (1990). *The Quality School: Managing Students without Coercion.* New York: Harper & Row.

Howard, P. (2000). *The Owner's Manual for the Brain: Everyday Applications from Mind-Brain Research.* Austin, TX: Bard Press.

Johnson, D., and Johnson, R. (1999). *Learning Together and Alone: Cooperative, Competitive, and Individualistic Learning.* Boston: Allyn and Bacon.

Matthews, D. (1999). "What We Are Learning about How Children Learn, and What This Means for Teachers." *Education Canada, 39* (Spring): 35–37.

McCombs, B., and Whisler, J. (1997). *The Learner-Centered School.* San Francisco: Jossey-Bass.

Social Studies and the Young Learner. (2000). Volume 13 (Nov./Dec.). Issue devoted to historical thinking and perspective.

Sternberg, R. (1999). *Thinking Styles.* Cambridge: Cambridge University Press.

6

Planning for Social Studies Learning

A good plan is much like a good map. It can help you get where you want to go. But a good plan is always a flexible document, open to possibilities along the way. In this chapter we will investigate a set of specific ideas designed to help you improve your planning for social studies learning. Specific points include:

- Teachers as decision makers
- Long-range goals
- Planning lessons and activities
- The events of a well-planned experience
- Sample lesson plans and activities
- How to develop a social studies unit

Mix a little foolishness with your serious plans;
it's lovely to be silly at the right moment.

—Horace (65 B.C.)

The Roman poet Horace noted that although our plans are often serious matters, it doesn't hurt to add a little humor or perhaps have a little fun along the way—wise counsel, indeed, when you remember that we're working with children. I suspect that he's also telling us that timing is everything when he uses the phrase, *the right moment*. Three centuries before Horace, the Greek philosopher Plato made it clear that the work of childhood is play. Keep it in mind. After all, you're helping to build lifelong memories and attitudes, so why not make them good ones?

A plan represents an organized way of thinking about the future. We know that one of the attributes of higher-achieving students is that they make plans for both the near and distant future. Likewise, an attribute of effective teachers is that they plan carefully and flexibly, always building in variety and choices for their students. A good plan not only guides your actions but it also allows you to reflect on what you did against some standard. A good plan exists in the future, present, and past in that it is at once a forecast, an experience, and a retrospective. A plan is speculative when it is drawn up, in motion when it is implemented, and history after it happens.

A plan for learning is therefore an enabling device that (1) helps you think about what needs to be accomplished and why, (2) guides you and your students through experiences in much the same way a map guides the traveler, and (3) provides a frame of reference for deciding to what extent the experience was meaningful. Careful planning empowers you. It makes you a true professional. Careful planning helps distinguish the teachers who do it from those who, content with mediocrity, merely make their way through textbooks with no strategic vision. That's not teaching, that's monitoring.

The Teacher as a Decision Maker

Teachers need to make several basic decisions as they plan for instruction. Those decisions relate to content, activities of the teacher, and activities of the learner.

First of all, you must make decisions about the content of your social studies program. I recommend a developmental approach to the teaching of content. This means that your instruction should proceed from what students already know toward knowledge and skills beyond their present understanding. Thus, you will want to sequence your instruction from simple to complex. Facts can lead to concepts, which, in turn, lead to generalizations. This progression happens, however, only if you are willing to make the connections. The same thing is true in the teaching of skills. Simple skills, such as measuring distances, can lead to more complex skills, such as accurately estimating distance and size.

Decision making about content also has another dimension. Suppose two fifth-grade teachers were each assigned to teach the United States as the central focus of their social studies curriculum. One teacher might give more emphasis to history; the other might choose to emphasize geography. One might spend more time on the colonial era, concentrating on the family; the other might spend more time emphasizing the settlement patterns in the New World. The point is that teachers have a

Students need time to reflect on ideas and to construct meaning.

great deal of autonomy within the prescribed curriculum, especially in social studies (as opposed to mathematics), where little agreement exists on minimal content coverage of people, places, and events.

A second instructional decision you must make is about the activities of the learners. What will your students actually do during social studies? Will they read? Orally? Silently? What will they read? Textbooks? Biographies? Resource books? Will they engage in discussion? If so, with whom? Will you lead the discussions or will students discuss ideas in small groups? Will your students be expected to listen as you lecture to them? Will they take notes? Will you have your students observe, do surveys, make maps, and draw pictures? Will they construct villages, put on plays, and tape news programs? Will they work individually? Cooperatively? Whatever your students do in social studies will be the result of decisions you have made. One thing is certain: How students spend their time will have a great effect on both their attitudes and achievements in social studies.

Your third decision is about your conduct, the activities of the teacher. As you plan for your behavior in the instructional process, keep in mind these principles of learning: motivation, retention, and transfer.

Motivation is a powerful tool in the process of learning. Consider yourself, for example. How motivated are you to be the best teacher possible? It's probably true that the level of your motivation will dictate the extent to which you succeed, assuming, of course, that you possess the basic abilities.

How well do you remember what you hear, see, and experience? The key to remembering is the learner's level of involvement in the learning process. I once worked for the National Science Foundation developing problem-solving units and training teachers to use the units in elementary classrooms. We discovered that the teachers behaved in their own classrooms essentially as we did when we taught them. If we lectured to them, they lectured to their students. If we got the teachers actively involved, they involved their students. Few of us retain all or even very much of what we learn. Our memories are less than perfect, and we may not have fully understood what we were taught in the first place. As a teacher, your responsibility is to attempt to maximize the *retention* of key ideas, skills, and values. Facts, names, dates, and places taught as items of specific knowledge are short-term memory items, at best. The keys to retention are active involvement in the learning process and emphasis on connections among ideas.

Transfer of learning simply relates to how something learned in one situation can be used in other situations. Obviously, specific facts taught without any meaningful context have little potential for transfer. Such skills as observing, recording, and communicating, however, have unlimited transfer value. Concepts also transfer well. The child who learns about supply and demand, cause and effect, roles, and interdependence has learned ideas that will apply in a variety of situations, now and in the future. You also can promote the transfer of learning by making connections between and among the subjects you teach. Challenge yourself, for example, to use ideas from mathematics in social studies. If your students are learning to make graphs in math, give them the opportunity to graph such social science data as high and low temperature readings for a week. If your students are learning to write letters in language arts, have them send real letters to cities around the country, asking for information about climate, commerce, recreation, and agriculture.

The decisions you make about content, your activities, and your students' activities will be reflected in your planning for classroom activities. Generally, when you think of planning, daily lesson plans usually come to mind. Planning is so much more than that, however. Planning encompasses long-range goals as well as short-term objectives. It is useful to think of the chunks of instruction for which you are responsible. In a global sense, you are responsible for the entire year. This is your largest chunk. Full-year planning is, by its very nature, quite general. For example, you will want to come up with four or five long-range goals for the year. Such goals might include "developing a miniature democracy in my classroom," or "imparting a knowledge of the geography of the United States," or "being committed to enhancing the self-concept of each child."

Long-range goals are not written in instructional terms, nor are they meant to be achieved quickly. The advantage to developing long-range goals is that they give you a sense of structure, a sort of intellectual scaffold from which to view learning in a meaningful, long-term perspective. You should know what your long-range goals are, and you should share them with your students. By discussing them from time to time, you and your class are able to make reflective judgments about how well you are progressing. A useful frame of reference for thinking about long-range goals for your social studies program is to consider your students' academic needs, their social development, and their personal fulfillment. By including your students in planning, you begin to get a far better sense of who they really are.

Mechanics

Every lesson plan can be analyzed from two distinct points of view: mechanics and substance. The *mechanics* are a sort of template that can be placed over any lesson. They represent the procedures one reasonably ought to follow in order to obtain measurable, effective results. Generally, these procedures are thought of as steps, although there is no need to follow them slavishly in linear fashion. The steps come principally from ideas about learning developed in psychological literature. They include ideas about the purpose of the lesson, student motivation to learn, continuity in the learning process, concept development, transfer of learning, and reflective thinking.

Let's examine the basic steps or parts of a lesson plan:

■ *Key idea.* The key idea is the social science concept or generalization you want the students to learn. It represents the single-most important thought or idea of the lesson. (See Chapter 3 for sample key ideas from each of the social sciences.) For example, a key idea from history is: *Our interpretations of the past change as new information is discovered.* The key idea is the centerpiece of the lesson. Without it, you merely have an activity. With it, you have something special: an idea about human behavior.

■ *Instructional objective.* The instructional objective is the portion of the lesson plan that establishes its intent and proposed outcome. It is the means of operationalizing the lesson's key idea. The instructional objective must be clearly stated. It should tell what the students will do (e.g., discuss, list, classify, draw) under what conditions (e.g., small group work, independent study). Students also need to know the intended purpose of the lesson. What will they know, feel, or be able to do as a result of the lesson?

■ *Set.* This stage is known variously as the *anticipatory set* or the *lesson introduction.* At this point of the lesson, you want to arouse students' attention, capture their imaginations, or indicate how today's lesson is connected to yesterday's lesson. You are putting the activity into context and making it meaningful to your students. Motivation is a crucial issue early in the lesson because at this stage, you create an appropriate mental set and an accompanying desire to learn. There are a number of ways to motivate your students. You may try to make the lesson interesting or appealing, or you may try to convince your students of the lesson's importance, or you may decide to use such extrinsic motivators as grades or special favors. In most cases, an interesting introduction designed to gain the students' attention will be sufficient.

■ *Activity.* This step represents the major teaching/learning focus of the lesson. At stake is the ratio of teacher activity to student activity: the behaviors of the teacher and students, the management of the activity and the materials, the explanations and information offered by the teacher, the tasks given to the students, and the additional help given to the students who need it. Obviously, for one adult to lead the behaviors and learning attempts of 30 children is a very complex task. Be sure that students understand specifically what they will be doing during the lesson. Clear directions are crucial to the lesson's success. Will students work together or alone? Will they make things? Do seat work? Help your students carry out the assignment. Move around the room, providing assistance as needed. Ask questions, probe, clarify, maintain order, and reassure. Of course, the nature and amount of guidance will vary with such factors as student age, ability, motivation, and the nature of the task itself.

■ *Assessment.* You have a key idea and a learning objective. Your instructional activity was designed to develop the key idea through experience. Now comes the question: What did the students learn? How will you know what they learned? What will you do to find out what your students learned? All assignments need some

Teachers who work together serve as good models of collaboration for the students they teach.

pulling together, some summarizing, or some means of looking back. In some cases, a brief discussion will be adequate. In other cases, you will need to analyze the students' work together. In another instance, you may give a quiz or test. Part of your instructional strategy should be to allow time for students to look reflectively on their work. If you don't, you may inhibit their chances of retaining key ideas and may limit the lesson's potential to achieve transfer of learning.

■ *Closure.* This is your opportunity to go over what you have accomplished. You need to spend some time reviewing what has been learned and how it is connected to what has gone before and what is yet to come. Clarify any extended expectations. There will also be times when you assign homework in connection with a lesson. When you do, be certain you are clear about what students are to do at home and what they will be expected to turn in. Remember that they are on their own, so it is not appropriate to expect them to develop new skills. They will continue or build on their classwork.

These steps give you a sense of structure or framework for lesson planning. This is not a lock-step recipe in which you must account for every point each time you work with students. The steps are based on known principles of effective learning. The sample lessons that follow illustrate the mechanics of lesson planning more concretely. Read them carefully to see how the steps are fleshed out.

Substance

The other fundamental aspect of a lesson is *substance,* or *what is learned.* A knowledge of the mechanics of lesson planning is useful because it gives you a framework within which to work. But the framework is of little value unless the substance of your lesson is worthwhile. The substance of social studies lessons is found in the four bases of content, concepts, skills, and values.

The content of a lesson involves the knowledge that you have decided is necessary for students to learn. In elementary social studies, the content of the curriculum comes primarily from the social sciences. The most dominant influences of social studies content are history and geography, but economics, government, psychology, anthropology, and sociology also contribute significantly to the content of elementary social studies. As you consider lesson content in the planning stages, you will want to ask yourself questions to clarify this area of concern. What is important about this content? In what ways is it necessary to students? What information, knowledge, and understandings should students gain from this lesson?

The content of a lesson will be adapted to the *concepts* that you want to emphasize. (The teaching of concepts is detailed in the next section.) At the planning stage, consider: What idea or ideas about human behavior are inherent in this lesson? What kinds of questions need to be raised? To what extent will the students be stimulated intellectually? Will they share their ideas? Are the ideas in this lesson transferable to other experiences?

As you plan the actual instruction for your lesson, consider what *skills* you want to reinforce or teach. A later section of this chapter gives specific recommendations addressing this concern. In planning, ask yourself questions such as: What methods and skills will the students use? Are the skills in this lesson transferable? Are students becoming increasingly independent in their problem solving?

A Sample Lesson Plan   WHAT SEASON IS IT?

Age Level. Primary

Key Idea. Each season of the year has its own unique characteristics.

Instructional Objective. Students will explore the local environments to observe, record, and gather evidence to show what season it is.

Set. Begin by showing the students a calendar (preferably one with pictures that illustrate the seasons). Ask the following questions to stimulate class discussion:

1. What is a calendar for?
2. Why do we need to keep track of time?
3. How is a calendar like a clock? How is a calendar different from a clock?
4. Calendars keep track of days, weeks, months, and years. Each year is divided into four seasons. Can anyone tell me the names of the four seasons?

Instruction. Place the names of the four seasons on the board. Ask the students to list various characteristics of the seasons (e.g., winter might be rainy or snowy). Write their responses on the board until there is a good list under each season.

Winter	*Spring*	*Fall*	*Summer*
rain	flowers	leaves	blue sky
snow	baseball	football	sunshine
skiing	green grass		vacation

"Now class, we are going to pretend that we don't know what season it is. We are going to go outside together to see if you can find evidence (define) to prove what season it is." Take the class out and see how many examples the children can find to show what season it is (e.g., leaves, weeds, kids on the playground playing football). Bring any tangible examples back to the classroom for display.

Assessment. "If someone asked us what season it is, how could we prove our answer (with evidence)?"

Closure. "The evidence we found outside shows that it is _____ (name season). When you go home today, I'd like to have you tell someone at home how you proved it was _____ (season). Also, I'd like to have you bring any new evidence that you can to prove that it is _____ ."

A Sample Lesson Plan ALEUT MAPS

Age Level. Intermediate

Key Idea. Distances can be measured in units of space or time. Each culture has invented units of space and time to keep track of those dimensions.

Instructional Objective. Students will construct and use Aleut maps to measure distances on the playground.

Set. Begin by asking students to give (or estimate) the following distances:

1. The length of a football field
2. The distance from their home to school
3. The height of the classroom door

Ask the following questions:

1. How long does it take you to get to school? Can the trip to school be measured using either distance or time?
2. How does a map help you get from one place to another?
3. How is a map like a plan? A record? A story?

Instruction. Tell the students that, in times past, when an Aleut would leave the village by kayak, he would paddle close to the shore as he voyaged from bay to bay, sometimes going great distances. Because the route was uncharted, and bays have a way of looking alike, the Aleut had to have a method of keeping track of how far away he was from his home village. So the Aleuts came up with a simple but ingenious way of doing this. They would take a stick with them, carving a notch in the stick each time they entered a new bay. So, five notches meant five bays away from home. Tell the children that they are going to make Aleut maps. Give each group of two students a stick (tongue depresser, Popsicle stick) and a pencil. Take the class out to the playground and have each pair of students make their way around the edge of the playground, making a mark for each notable tree, fence post, or whatever.

Assessment. Ask the students how such a system of keeping track of distances is similar to or different from the measures they are used to. Give each pair of students time to process this, asking them to make notes. Then, discuss insights with the class.

Closure. Assign the students a homework task of making an Aleut map that measures distances at home or in their neighborhoods.

To be complete, your planning should take into account the *values* that will be part of the lesson. Again, some suggestions for doing this are given later in this chapter. As you plan, however, ask yourself: What will the students learn about themselves? Will they be exposed to the values of others? Will they have a chance to share their values?

Obviously, not every lesson you teach will provide definitive answers to all the questions suggested here. However, every lesson ought to form a part of a total context of instructional experience designed to take all these questions into account. Regardless of whether your philosophy of lesson planning tends toward formality or informality, you need to ensure that your social studies instruction is based on a purposeful rationale rather than merely on covering topics or spending the "appropriate" amount of time with social studies (see Figure 6.1). The teaching of concepts, skills, and values is considered in greater detail in the next sections of this chapter.

Teaching Concepts

Concepts in social studies are ideas about human behavior. They transcend time and space and, in that respect, have transfer value to new situations. For example, the economic concept of *supply and demand* is a useful tool at several levels of

---

FIGURE 6.1

Keys to How to Develop a Unit

1. Choose a suitable theme—for example, "Colonial Life," "Inventions and Discoveries," "Space and Place," "A Renaissance Fair," "The Age of Exploration," "Pioneer Life and Times," "Hopi Culture," "Japanese Families," "A Better Community."
2. Spend time reading about and researching the topic. Announce the topic to the class and tell them to find out what they can in order to prepare for a planning meeting.
3. Bring the class together for a discussion of the possibilities. Involve the students in planning.
4. Collect resource materials, websites, and establish centers or focal points of learning.
5. Develop and distribute a list of differentiated activities related to the topic. The categories should include (a) academic, (b) construction, and (c) social. The expectations should be for each student to show evidence of reading, writing, drawing, building, teaching, and performance.
6. Develop strategies for involving the home. It is crucial that parents take part in some meaningful ways.
7. Meet with students to establish personal goals and responsibilities.
8. Meet with the whole class daily for times of sharing and team building.
9. Encourage freedom, responsibility, creativity, and teamwork.
10. Allow time for reflection. What are we learning?
11. Involve resource people (librarians, artists, authors, scientists, professionals, workers, parents, service groups, retired people, etc.).
12. Ensure that student work is presented, published, displayed, performed, and otherwise shared beyond the classroom.
13. Plan assessment strategies that will show evidence of academic, personal, social, and citizenship growth. Include the students in the process and expect them to assume responsibility for much of the assessment.
14. Celebrate the experience in some meaningful way—for example, a party, a performance, or a similar activity.

understanding for students attempting to learn about market systems. Concepts provide common threads of comparison and contrast that enable the student to organize data in a logical and coherent manner.

What Are Concepts?

A *concept* is an intellectual tool that provides its user with generalizable ways of dealing with reality. Anthropologists make extensive use of the concept of *culture*. Sociologists attempt to identify and describe *norms of behavior*. Concepts are ideas and not terms whose definitions are to be memorized. Therefore, they are learned only through meaningful experiences. The following is a list of social science concepts commonly taught in elementary social studies.

Rules	Problems	Probability
Change	Supply and demand	Norms
Self	Organizations	Cooperation
Adaptation	Power	Diversity
Systems	Governance	Environment
Areal association	Cause/Effect	Needs/Wants
Culture	Artifacts	Land use
Diffusion	Social interaction	Communication
Spatial interaction	Interdependence	Assimilation
Time	Community	Family
Life cycle	Seasons	Roles
Groups	Enculturation	Patterns
Tools	Technology	Markets
Resources	Conflict	Socialization
Behavior	Scarcity	Space

Concepts are best developed through experiences that are supplemented by reflective thinking. Only when people reflect on what they have done or seen do they begin to analyze and see relationships.

Developing Concepts

There are many ways to develop any given concept. However, direct experience and reflection on the experience are two proven techniques for concept building with elementary-age children. The following two examples illustrate effective ways of getting children to think conceptually. The first is a lesson in economics with primary-age children. It features the concept of *supply and demand*. As you read through the lesson, notice how the teacher creates a problem-centered experience for the students. The teacher then asks the students to think reflectively and to generalize from the specific problem of supply and demand. This is a very effective way of teaching concepts.

The second approach features the use of webbings or mind maps. In this method, the teacher and class begin their discussion with an organizing concept of theme—in this case, the concept of *culture*. Concepts have attributes or characteristics that define them. In the case of culture, some of those attributes are food, clothing, shelter, customs, work, religion, and technology. Notice the progression from the more abstract webbing that identifies a kind of rubric of culture attributes that could be applied to any study—for example, ancient Athens, a medieval village, our community, and so on—to the specific application shown in Figure 6.3, which shows the webbing applied to the Pilgrims of colonial America.

It is well to keep in mind that concepts are *ideas*. Thus, in the first example, if someone were to ask you what is the main idea of the lesson, you would reply that the main idea is the concept of *supply and demand*. In the second example, the main idea is the concept of *culture*. Teachers have been severely criticized for their failure to teach conceptually. This will not happen if you approach each experience by asking yourself: What is the main idea or concept I want the children to learn?

Teaching Supply and Demand to First-Graders

To bring this discussion of concept development into focus, let's look at an example. Suppose Ms. Jones, a first-grade teacher, wanted to develop the economic concept of *supply and demand* with her students. Since concepts are *ideas*, not isolated facts, they always transcend time and space. The concept of *supply and demand* certainly qualifies as an idea because there were supply-and-demand problems in cave days, in ancient Egypt, in the Middle Ages, in our present society, and, no doubt, in the future. Thus, we can see that supply and demand is not limited to any one place or any one time; rather, it transcends time and space.

At this point, we know that our first-grade teacher has selected a useful social science concept. But now a problem arises: Maybe the concept is too difficult for 6-year-olds to comprehend. This is where experience is crucial. Ms. Jones must develop an experience for these children that has meaning to them. She thinks about the matter and comes up with an idea to introduce the concept experientially. Let's peek in as the teacher sets up the experience.

Ms. Jones asks the students if they know what holiday (right away she has their attention) is coming up this month. Because it is mid-November, the students answer, "Thanksgiving." The teacher asks the children if they would like to make a mural depicting the first Thanksgiving held by the Native Americans and the Pilgrims. Of course they would. She reads the class the story of the first Thanksgiving and discusses the events of that time with the children. "Tomorrow," the teacher says, "we will begin our mural."

When the children arrive the next day, they are excited about the mural and want to get started. Ms. Jones shows the class two large pieces of butcher paper, each one taped up securely on either side of the room. She tells the children that the class will be divided into two groups, and that each group will make its own mural. Then she says, "Jenny, why don't you go over to the paper on this side of the room and get started?" Jenny stands up hesitantly and goes over to the piece of butcher paper. In front of her are many brushes and lots of poster paint in a rainbow of colors. Ms. Jones tells Jenny to go ahead and asks the rest of the class to come over to the other side. Thirty children crowd around the butcher paper. There is one paintbrush and one baby food jar filled with brown paint. The teacher tells the kids to go ahead and make their mural. Confusion reigns.

Finally, someone says, "This isn't fair. It won't work." Others echo those sentiments. The teacher asks the children if they have any ideas about how this situation could be improved. They suggest that half the kids go to each mural site and that the paint jars and brushes be equally distributed. The teacher agrees, and the kids make two great murals.

Later, Ms. Jones reminds the children of the problem they faced with the murals and asks if they think their solution was satisfactory. One child asks the teacher why all of this happened when things otherwise always go so smoothly. The teacher explains that it was done on purpose to help the students think about resources, human and material. The children and Ms. Jones talk about equal and unequal distribution of resources (they probably don't use the terms, at least at first). When the supply is too great for the demand (poor Jenny), and when the demand is too great for the supply (poor rest of the class), the system doesn't work very well. Can you recall the time several years ago when every child wanted a Tickle Me Elmo doll, and the supply simply wasn't great enough? Now the demand has all but disappeared and the supply is more than adequate.

important

Ms. Jones talks about water supply and the demand for water in the summer. She explains how the local grocer knows how much cold cereal to stock on the shelves. She discusses the amount of playground space and equipment available at the school and explains that that is one reason why recess occurs at different times for different classes. She solicits examples of supply and demand from the students—for example, experiences they have had with toys or playground equipment (30 kids and 3 playground balls). Last, she assigns the students the task of asking their parents if they can think of examples from life at home. The students are asked to report on these the following day.

← *real life connection*

To reconstruct this example of concept development, Ms. Jones took the students through the experience → mind → meaning continuum. An experience shared by the entire class provided a common point of reference. The teacher then helped the students to reflect on and process the experience, and developed the meaning of the concept by providing and soliciting from the children other examples of supply and demand.

The foregoing illustration raises an important point in teaching and learning social studies. Why go to all that trouble in order to introduce an economic concept to a group of 6-year-olds? Why not just read the definition from a dictionary or some other source if you really think the term is important? First of all, there was little extra work involved, assuming that the teacher was going to have the children make Thanksgiving murals anyway. What the teacher did was to capitalize on an everyday situation and teach a concept from it. Second, you can't teach concepts by reading words from the dictionary. At best, you can teach vocabulary by doing that, but the method isn't very efficient given what is known about short-term memory learning. The experience itself was the key. But the reflective thinking and mental processing of the process were also instrumental. This teacher taught the students a concept in such a way that they will probably always remember it.

The Use of Webbings

The webbing approach represents a graphic strategy for developing conceptual schemes. A *webbing*, or conceptual map, enables students to bring meaning to information at both the content and conceptual levels. Marzano and Arredondo[1] suggest that the use of webbings and other graphic approaches can lead students to generate new meaning about the material they study in several important ways:

- Webbings permit, and often encourage, nonlinear thinking.
- Webbings can be used to synthesize complex information from diverse sources efficiently, helping students to identify patterns and relationships that are otherwise difficult to apprehend.
- Webbings help the user generate information about the structure and relationships among parts that may not have been clear in the original, nongraphic information.

An example of the webbing approach may give you a clearer idea of how this process works. One of the most fundamental social science concepts is the concept of *culture*. The sociological or anthropological definition of culture is "the sum total of ways of living built up by one group of human beings and transmitted from one generation to another." But what you have just read is a definition of a term. For culture to become a concept and not just a term, you will have to develop appropriate experiences for your students.

The webbing shown in Figure 6.2 illustrates how one might begin to imagine the attributes of the concept of *culture*. If culture is about the ways of living of a group of people, then it would logically include their food, clothing, shelter, customs, and so on. The webbing in Figure 6.2 contains nine attributes of culture; certainly others could be added. But this webbing is fairly abstract because it contains no specific content about a certain group of people. In that sense, it could be used as a starting point to describe any culture.

The second webbing, shown in Figure 6.3, illustrates how one can take those attributes of the concept of *culture* and apply them to a specific culture group—in this case, the Pilgrim settlers of Plymouth Plantation in the 1620s.

FIGURE 6.2

A Webbing, or Mind Map, for the Concept of Culture

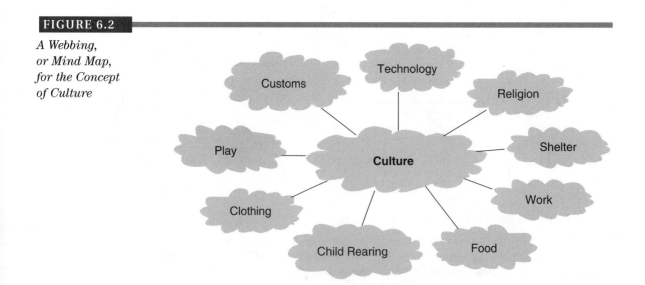

FIGURE 6.3 A Webbing, or Mind Map, for the Concept of Culture, in the Context
of the Culture of the Pilgrims

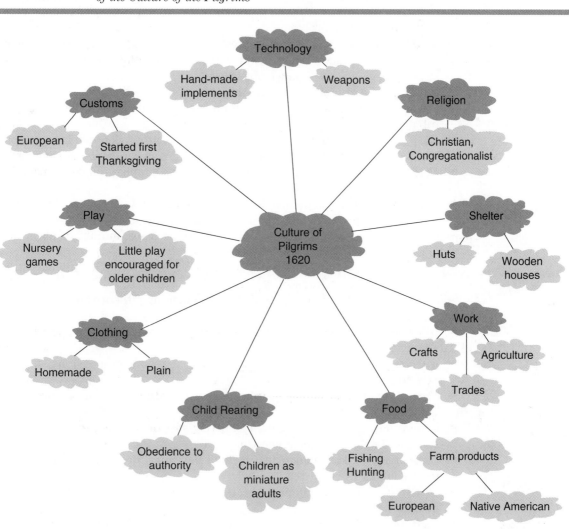

Teaching Skills

Skills are the methodological tools of social science. The ability to use them effectively sets a student free to investigate problems independently. If concepts are ideas about human behavior, then investigative skills are a primary means to the further development and expansion of those ideas. The following is a list of skills for elementary social studies:

- *Observing.* Observing phenomena, events, and interactions, both alone and with a partner; eyewitnessing; listening
- *Recording.* Recalling information or observances, photographing, mapping, drawing, illustrating, writing, tape recording, listing

need these
basic skills to
in order to
109
expand
on the
concepts

- *Describing.* Creating written, oral, photographic, and graph descriptions; identifying attributes
- *Defining.* Defining terms and procedures, developing precise meanings, communicating, stating problems
- *Measuring.* Using standard measures, developing one's own measures, counting, quantifying data, using mathematical computations, developing rating scales, using and developing map scales
- *Classifying.* Grouping, labeling, categorizing, differentiating
- *Comparing/Contrasting.* Noting differences and similarities, identifying attributes, describing
- *Data gathering.* Identifying and selecting data sources; determining appropriate methods; conducting surveys, historical studies, experiments, and interviews
- *Data processing.* Quantifying data, performing graphic analysis, mapping, making charts, writing summaries
- *Communicating.* Communicating orally and in writing, through pictures and through graphics; engaging in group activities; expressing oneself
- *Constructing.* Building models, dioramas, relief maps, murals, displays, and exhibits
- *Analyzing.* Discriminating, categorizing, finding patterns, identifying attributes, detecting structures
- *Synthesizing.* Planning, producing, documenting, theorizing, developing systems
- *Hypothesizing.* Guessing in an educated way, developing hunches, testing assumptions
- *Inferring.* Making statements from data, reaching conclusions, making decisions
- *Predicting.* Determining relationships, forecasting outcomes, correlating variables
- *Generalizing.* Conceptualizing, identifying supportive data, testing relationships, finding patterns, summarizing
- *Evaluating.* Making judgments, making decisions, determining validity, detecting errors and fallacies
- *Question posing.* Developing questions, identifying researchable problems, defining terms
- *Verifying.* Checking sources, validating ideas and sources, referring to authority

Effective teachers will plan on incorporating a variety of skills in their lessons. This variety helps keep students' interest and offers them a panoply of ways to process, interpret, apply, and share what they learn. Consider the foregoing list carefully. Every lesson you teach should incorporate one or more of these skills.

Teaching Values

The values that we teach in elementary social studies fall into three large categories, each of which is important to children's growth and development. Your task is to ensure that all three types are being learned along the way, not just in social studies, but throughout the school experience. The English philosopher John

Locke noted that teaching and learning can be approached at a simple level of just one variable, such as, the teacher who says, "I teach social studies." Or what we do can be approached from the point of view of several variables, such as the teacher who says, "I teach social studies, but I also teach children to be good citizens and to be critical thinkers." So, when we think of teaching values, skills, content, and concepts, we can see that a good teacher always thinks in terms of several variables. It is all a part of the art of good teaching.

Behavioral values are related to conduct in the classroom and at school. They are what we might consider values of good citizenship. Behavioral values include respect for others, politeness and kindness, taking turns, obeying rules, showing initiative, sharing ideas, and cooperating in group efforts, to name a few. A classroom is a crowded place, and behavioral values are at the heart of the matter of civility.

Procedural values are the values of inquiry, of scientific thinking, of critical thinking, of problem solving, of rational thought, perseverance, hard work, organization, and respect for evidence. These are the values we want children to acquire as they study, do their homework, investigate problems, and use the methods of the geographer, historian, and so on. Procedural values are obviously imbedded in the skills mentioned earlier.

Substantive values are beliefs held by individuals. These beliefs are acquired as a result of a person's experience and feelings about what is true and important. Such values range from a person's ideas of what is fun, humorous, right, and worthwhile. So, if you and I disagree over which season of the year is the best, we can say this is a difference of substantive value. Where people express religious differences, this has to do with substantive values. In a pluralistic society, we need to show tolerance and appreciation for differences.

Values are a part of every lesson and every experience at school, whether we want them to be or not. A teacher's behavior is on constant view by the students. The best way to approach values is at a level of consciousness in which you determine to teach all three types of values and to organize reflective thinking sessions in which you and your students search for meaning in the social studies experience.

How to Develop a Unit: The Design

Unit instruction is a useful approach to most teaching and learning situations, because it concentrates your efforts and those of the children in your classroom on a central theme, organizing idea, or set of concepts. The effect of such a focus is to promote systematic learning toward clearly defined objectives, thus keeping you from falling into the trap of teaching nothing more than activities, worksheets, or pages from a textbook.

What Is a Unit?

A *unit* is a sequential progression of lessons directed toward the development of a theme. Unit themes are developed through an articulation of content, concepts, skills, and values. The term *unit* implies oneness or wholeness, as opposed to fragmentation. Thus, a unit will describe its sense of coherence and oneness. In social studies, common unit titles might include "Choosing Our Leaders," "Early

Explorers," "The Pilgrims," "Learning about Latitude and Longitude," and "The Gold Rush." Of course, your textbook and district or state guides are a source of information regarding what material, and therefore what unit topics, you are to cover on your given level.

Time Allotments

How long should a unit be? How many days of instruction should be allocated to each unit? There is no predetermined amount of time that must be allocated for any given unit. You, as the instructional expert, need to make those decisions on the basis of what needs to be covered in the course of the school year.

For instance, if you have seven major topical areas in social studies to cover in one school year, and a school year is 36 weeks long, it is a matter of simply averaging about 5 weeks per unit. However, that is only an average figure, and various factors are involved. Much depends on how your units are designed—whether they are based on large themes or smaller, more focused topics. (For example, the "Transportation Revolution" could be presented independently as a week-long unit; however, it could also be taught during a broader course of study on the growth of the United States. A week-long unit on the "Puritans of Massachusetts Bay Colony" could provide a brief overview of the life of the early colonists in New England, or you might choose to broaden the scope by presenting a more comprehensive unit on the life and times in all 13 colonies. It might also become part of a Thanksgiving unit for first grade.)

Some teachers might restrict unit length. Narrowing the focus will allow more units to be covered in a single year. However, some teachers prefer to keep their unit topics more broadly focused and choose to develop and teach longer units. An example of a broader focus would be a unit titled "The Movement West" versus several smaller units titled "Life on the Prairie"; "The Trail of Tears"; "Texas, the Lone-Star State"; and "Settling the Oregon Country."

The problem with restricted topic units is that they tend to present learning in small, compartmentalized packages that do not reflect reality. The problem with too broad a topic is that it takes seemingly forever to teach—and the focus may well be lost. Developing a *balance* between the two and helping to make connections from one unit to another are among the many challenges facing the instructional expert.

How to Begin

The first step in the development of a unit is to think of it in terms of your objectives for the entire year. You will need to answer such questions as: Where does this topic logically fit in the flow of my instruction? What skills and knowledge are prerequisite to the skills and knowledge in this unit?

The second step in the development of a unit is to write the overview. A unit overview contains a rationale and a brief statement of contents. The purpose of a written rationale is to state why you are teaching a particular unit. How is the unit crucial in the process of children's learning in the social studies? This is not terribly difficult to do, because there is much agreement with the concept that children must learn to live as social beings in a civilized world; that learning about citizenship, government, history, and geography is significant to effectively function as a citizen of the world. Your statement of contents may be written in paragraph form, but more often a table-of-contents format is used. The table of contents tells what topics you intend to teach. (Many teachers map out a plan—a table of contents—for the entire year.)

Unit Objectives

Objectives for the unit should be written in clear terms; that is, each objective needs to specify exactly what is expected of the children in performance terms. Thus, while a statement such as "The children need to develop greater capabilities in the area of critical thinking" is fine as part of your rationale, it is probably better stated as a long-term goal than as a unit objective. Here are some examples of clear objectives. Note that they specify *who (the child) does what* (identifies, categorizes, etc.):

1. The child is able to identify symbols used on a map.
2. The child can verbally define, recognize, and draw a latitude and longitude line on both a globe and a map.
3. The child can locate and identify the four major directions (north, south, east, west), and develop a map key to explain directional symbols on a map.

When you develop your set of unit objectives, it is important that you consider the range of intellectual endeavor, from knowledge and comprehension through such higher-thought levels as application and analysis. Bloom's *Taxonomy of Educational Objectives* is a useful guide as you write your unit objectives. Bloom's *Taxonomy* (cognitive domain) is a hierarchical construct that is divided into six increasingly complex levels. Take a few moments to consider each level. Remember that your unit objective should reflect a representative distribution of each level.

1. *Knowledge.* The issue is recall of information. At this level, it is important that children remember what they have read, were told, or observed. This level is crucial because, if children do not possess basic skills in social studies, they are hardly in a position to eventually carry out meaningful or creative analyses of issues with a social or international scope.

2. *Comprehension.* Your objective for children at this level is to ensure that they can explain ideas. It is one thing, for example, to be able to list and identify the requirements necessary to run for president (knowledge), and quite another to be able to explain the reasoning why these requirements might be important (comprehension).

3. *Application.* Objectives developed at the application level have as their purpose something practical: actual usage. The issue at this level is whether the child can use such things as skills and concepts in new situations. For example, in spelling, one needs to know how to spell words for a spelling test (knowledge), to define words for a vocabulary test (comprehension), and to use those words appropriately in an explanation or story (application).

4. *Analysis.* Objectives written at the analysis level are designed to enable children to see relationships, make comparisons and contrasts, and look for patterns.

Analysis, as the term implies, is an attempt to break down whole entities into their component parts. For example, in a study of communities, you might want the children to identify how various communities (e.g., urban, suburban, rural) function differently to meet the needs of people living within that community, or perhaps identify how daily life might differ among communities.

5. *Synthesis*. Synthesis represents a pulling together or combining of elements. At a synthesis level, you might talk to the children about hardships of the early pioneers, and then go a step further and talk about why people might have been willing to endure such hardships (early pioneers as well as contemporary immigrants). Or, having taught the children in your classroom about freedoms in a democratic society (e.g., freedom of speech, freedom of religion), you might ask them to write a story about what might happen if one or all of those freedoms were taken away and to explain how life might be different if that were to happen.

6. *Evaluation*. Objectives for the evaluation level include those that encourage children to form their own points of view or to express their ideas on issues. For evaluation to be adequate, this level need not always take the form of the traditionally expected written test. Drawings, stories, and a class panel discussion in which the children explain and support individual opinions are examples of evaluation. At the evaluation level, divergent thinking is encouraged, and differences of opinion are to be expected.

Although you need to develop unit objectives at all six levels, you will write more objectives for knowledge and comprehension than you will for the higher categories. There are two reasons for this: Knowledge and comprehension represent the most basic skills and are therefore fundamental to the learning enterprise; additionally, the complexity of tasks at such levels as synthesis and evaluation means that those assignments will usually be of much longer duration.

It is important that you recognize the necessity of developing your unit objectives using (1) clear terms and (2) all the levels of Bloom's *Taxonomy*. These objectives will serve to guide your day-to-day instruction, and they will form the basis for your test items or other means of evaluating the child's progress. Thus, there is a natural axis that runs from planning through instruction to assessment.

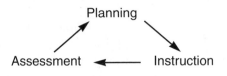

Block Plan

A block plan is a unit calendar. The scope and sequence of the unit are laid out on a grid in which each square represents one lesson. The filled-in squares show at a glance what will be taught when. Once you have chosen a unit topic that fits logically into your year's sequence of social studies instruction (whatever the level or focus—history, geography, community, or citizenship) and you have developed a set of instructional objectives to guide your teaching, you are ready to sketch your block plan for the unit.

It is quite possible that the majority of the units you develop and teach will depend heavily on textbooks and your accompanying teacher's guide both for content and direction. When this is the case, the textbook and teacher's guide will be your primary resources; however, even the teacher who takes a textbook-oriented approach to his or her units should go beyond the given, finding and developing additional source material. A textbook and teacher's guide can give basic direction, but only you, the instructional expert, can design, arrange, and implement the presentation. It is for *you* to enhance the material and develop a unit that reflects your special style and expertise as well as the needs of the children in your classroom.

As you consider the development of a unit of instruction, particularly one that goes beyond a series of textbook assignments, you will find it necessary and helpful—and challenging—to seek and collect resources that not only help strengthen your own background on the topic but also provide resource material for the children to use throughout the course of study. The following section discusses various elements involved in the development of instruction. It summarizes much of the information we just discussed and can also serve as a guide as you embark on your personal journey of instructional design.

Instructional Design and Development: Steps and Elements

After you decide on your topic, subject, or unit, then follow these steps:

1. Think of your unit in terms of a period of time you must fill from beginning to end.

2. Think of the whole as being made up of segments. Ask yourself: What do I have to cover? Make a list, then ask yourself: What do the children need to know? Make a list of that, as well.

3. Design and build a framework of ideas on how to structure—how to present—those segments. Decide exactly *what* you want to do (the approach you will use in the unit), then decide *how* you want to do it (the variety of means you will choose to utilize). *Note:* The saying "Variety is the spice of life" refers to instructional design, too!

4. Brainstorm your plan. Go through an informal planning process, moving energetically from idea, to process, to possibilities, to product. Remember: The creative process is messy! Map out ideas visually, or make lists. Dream, think, and imagine: It *will* begin to come together.

5. Organize your ideas. The unit needs to be formally organized, so from your outline of ideas or list of themes, activities, and approaches you have to decide to (a) develop your specific lesson plans; (b) prepare your lecture notes, assignments, and cooperative and individual activities; (c) develop and prepare your handouts; (d) develop and prepare assignments; and (e) don't forget—prepare your classroom to reflect the focus of study in the unit.

6. "Calendarize" your design. Organize your unit into a time frame; decide what you plan to do on a day-to-day basis (include adequate time for children to complete assignments, etc.).

Bring it to life!

7. Teach that unit! First, get the attention of your students—give them a sneak preview! Next, hit them with the hard stuff: Challenge them, raise their expectations, and explain the need to conquer certain academic material before moving on. Then, proceed through the organized design of instruction. Order and organization are not boring concepts—it's up to *you* to bring your unit to life!

Archaeology Unit: An Overview

A unit on archaeology can be an excellent opportunity to practice a variety of skills and teaching methods. It is also an ideal unit to integrate different areas of the curriculum: history, certainly, but also geography and science; language arts writing and presentation skills; artistic skills (as students "create" artifacts and record "finds" on sketch pads and graph paper); and even skills in mathematics, as children measure their dig areas or take depth measurements on site.

A unit on archaeology also lends itself (as do so many teaching units) to a wide variety of instructional strategies. For example, this unit incorporates cooperative learning, video presentations, creative group storytelling, direct instruction, and a good many hands-on activities outside of the regular classroom environment. Critical thinking and decision making are also part of the unit of study—and most of it is practiced by the children while working in their dig teams.

Exact instructions on how to teach a unit on archaeology are *not* included here; that is for you, the professional, to assemble and design. However, a good many guidelines are provided to get you started as you explore various ideas, which might spark you into adding your personal touch to the unit. I encourage you to use the suggestions offered to start your own journey toward filling in the framework. A presentation outline is provided for your reference—it will be up to you to fill in the blanks and research the content. Reading through the unit materials that follow will present some of the possibilities of what might be done with the children in your unique classroom. Figure 6.4 shows a sample webbing that you and your students might develop.

Refer to the block plan (Figure 6.5) for ideas and possible sequence, and remember that the unit can easily be adapted to the age of the children you teach. Obviously, depending on grade level, certain adjustments will have to be made in terms of content, length of time, and the explanation and execution of the actual Big Dig Event (i.e., the excavation). This particular block plan is designed for a 20-day unit, but given your particular circumstances, you may choose to use some of the ideas and teach an abbreviated unit. For example, you might arrange a simulated dig in a sandbox or in a number of sand-filled cartons in your classroom, or you might decide to teach a similar unit but with less comprehensive preparation and fewer after-dig activities.

Be creative in your use of resources; there are many possibilities for obtaining items that can be used in the dig, from your school's art department to the broken items in the storage room of a nearby art or import store. "Artifacts" can come from the most unexpected places. Also keep in mind there are vast community resources—volunteers you might ask to assist in preparing the imaginary excavation and to serve as observers at each team's dig area. Research your library and social studies publications for information on archaeological terms and for illus-

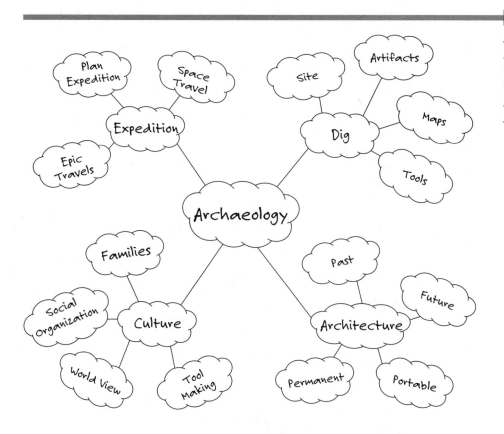

FIGURE 6.4

A Webbing Developed by Teacher and Class as Part of Planning an Archeology Unit

trations of the process of excavating. There are many resources available—you simply need to locate them.

With some effort and the application of your instructional design expertise to this model, you and your students can gain much from an archaeological experience— a motivating way to teach units in social studies.[3]

▶▶ Archaeology: Presentation Outline

Introduction. *Mysteries and Antiquities from the Past (take a good look at a garbage can . . . a what?).*

I. Historical Records
   A. What *is* history?
   B. What is history based on?
   C. Types of historical records:
      1. material remains
      2. written accounts (primary and secondary sources)

FIGURE 6.5 *Archaeology Unit: A Sample Block Plan*

Monday	Tuesday	Wednesday	Thursday	Friday
INTRODUCTION: Springboard Tell true stories of discovery Share an artifact Show opening segment "Raiders of the Lost Ark" *Start Logs*	Give a hint of upcoming BIG DIG Team Assignment Distribute presentation outline: *"HOW do archaeologists actually work?'* Reflective Thinking Log Entries	Garbage Can Analogy (classroom demonstration and home experiment) Present basic terminology Write letters to museums/ universities	VIDEO: "King Tut's Tomb" Discuss Howard Carter Talk about thrill of discovery *(use circle discussion)*	STORY IN THE ROUND: *The Mystery Dig* (must use archaeology terms learned on Wed; group activity) Introduce idea of Field Notes
GUEST SPEAKER: Archaeologist from the Children's Museum	TOPIC: Social Scientists (handout, section 2) Class discussion CREATE A POSTER (individual activity): illustrating & defining one social scientist	SNEAK PREVIEW of big Excavation Activity Talk about roles and what kinds of things they can expect to be doing CREATE DIG TEAMS Make posters	LIBRARY (cooperative and individual activity): locate and copy photos, drawings, symbols to assist students in preparing artifacts for the dig (art class tomorrow)	ART ROOM (cooperative team activity): prepare individually designed shards ('artifacts') to be used for the BIG DIG Activity *Prepare Hallway Exhibits* *(use posters made by class)*
ARMCHAIR TRAVEL: Teacher slide presentation of her travels to Greece (Mycenae, Delphi, Santorini) Share real stories about archaeologists (Handout, section III)	PREPARE DIG FOLDERS (cooperative team activity): select team name; assemble information; illustrate digging methods on graph paper	ORAL REVIEW of terms, social scientists, steps and dig methods Talk about FIELD and LAB experts *Students give briefings*	DISTRIBUTE TEAM PACKET for the BIG DIG EVENT: review all in detail; HOW will it work; time for questions, ideas, clarifications	GROUP DECISION MAKING (cooperative team meetings) *Getting Ready for the BIG DIG Event!*
THE BIG DIG EVENT (on site) Video Taping	Groups meet to PREPARE presentations Share ideas from logs	BIG DIG EXCAVATION TEAM PRESENTATIONS	DIG TEAMS CREATE CLASSROOM DISPLAYS for Parent-Friendship Night	REFLECTION: Watch Video of Dig and discuss experience

II. Social Scientists
    A. *Archaeologist*   F. Sociologist
    B. Cartographer   G. Economist
    C. Geographer   H. Psychologist
    D. Linguist   I. Historian
    E. Political scientist   J. Anthropologist
III. Some Real "Indiana Jones" Experts
    A. The Leakey family (Louis, Mary, and Richard)
    B. Heinrich Schliemann
    C. Your teacher (well, sort of . . .)
IV. Archaeology: Getting to Work
    A. The dig
    B. Plan of work: six steps, from start to finish
    C. Methodology (main ones only; there are others):
        1. trench
        2. quadrant
        3. squares
        4. numbered squares
V. Experts and Specialists Involved
    A. In the field: B. In the lab:
        1. surveyor   1. geochemist
        2. geologist   2. paleontologist
        3. photographer   3. physical anthropologist
        4. draftsperson   4. petrologist
        5. preparator   5. palynologist

➤➤ *The Dig: Your Team Packet*

When. Select a specific day; arrange it with school officials if necessary.

Where. Somewhere on the school campus; look for the marked site!

Equipment

- Your team packet (including graph paper).
- Recording material: paper, pencil, marking pen, clipboard.
- Plastic bags that zip close and a shoe box (for the finds).
- Very important: a toothbrush and a spoon. (Each member of the digging team will need both.) These will be the only pieces of digging equipment you may use. Archaeologists work slowly and carefully, not wanting to damage potential finds.

Optional Equipment. Optional, but potentially helpful in your presentation, is a Polaroid (or other type) camera to record the stages of discovery and the finished work. (An artist might choose to bring additional equipment to assist in record keeping and documentation.)

Clothing. Jeans, sweatshirt, gloves—this is going to be messy!

Basic Team Instructions. You will have some decisions to make together. By the time you locate the excavation site (as soon as possible after fourth period), you should already have decided on the method you will use first and what role each member of the team will play in the actual dig. (We have some time in class before the dig, and you can make your decisions at that time.) Begin digging immediately after you have located your site—all sites will be well marked. Have an alternative method ready should the one you select not work out. An archaeologist would be sure to dig very carefully, as there is always a chance that carelessness will destroy a priceless antiquity. You have no idea what you may find (but believe me—there is something there!), so wield that toothbrush and spoon *very* carefully!

Be sure to keep a very careful record of everything you do and everything you find. Remember, you are maintaining a complete record of your dig for next week's presentation.

Procedure. As soon as you come across the edge of something, carefully work your way around it, and it will begin to emerge. Your team may have chosen to have members take turns at various tasks, or you may have divided the work evenly so that you play the same role throughout the dig. However you chose to organize yourselves to accomplish your goal, make sure that all of the following tasks are covered:

- Some members will be engaged in the actual process of digging.
- Perhaps someone might use a camera to record stages of discovery.
- Keep track on graph paper of exactly where on the site finds have been located and illustrate the exact method of digging being used (trench, quadrant—check your class notes for the different types of methods!).
- Be sure to record (draw) each piece as it emerges.
- Maintain a journal of the activity on site.

Bulletin boards provide a forum for students to display what they have learned.

- Identify and describe. Prepare written copies and graphs—all records of your process.
- Reconstruct and preserve. As archaeologists, your job is to reconstruct and preserve the item(s). Hang on to your sketches and the item pieces. (Put broken bits back together, if possible.)

Now That the Dig Is Over, This Is Your Job. Hopefully you have kept careful records of everything you accomplished and what you found as it happened. You have been maintaining a complete record of the dig as it progressed for next week's presentation to the museum curator (that's me!)—the sponsor of the dig. As part of the presentation, your team will be sharing the methods and procedures your team chose to use; you will be telling the story of your dig and showing the physical results. (Remember, notes and quick sketches made on site can be tidied up before the presentations.) During the next few days (and any time you and your team members arrange to meet together), work on your curator (teacher!) presentation, which is due next week. Other noted archaeologists (your classmates) will observe. We're excited to see what you have to share! As part of your presentation, your team will:

- Share the methods and procedures your team chose to follow.
- Tell the story of your dig and show the results. (Remember, sketchy notes and drawings made on site can be tidied up before the presentations.)

The Content of Your Presentation

- Decide who will report what.
- As a team, explain the find and the process you followed. Remember, the final job of an archaeologist is to report findings.
- Organize your information so that it will tell the story of your experiences (remember the Howard Carter and King Tut video we saw). Unfold the facts gradually. Tell about the methods you used and why you chose them. Take the rest of the class through each step as you share graphs and/or posters with us.
- Show us the reconstructed item (glue is fine). Describe it carefully; tell us what you know.
- Do some research: Can you date the item? Where did it probably come from? What was it used for? Get us excited!
- You could mount sketches and photos on posterboard so we can see everything as you present. Perhaps you have a better, more creative idea for presenting (Video? Computers?). Remember to keep quality in mind. Don't be sloppy in your presentation, or the curator may not hire you next time!
- Finally, hand in an official half-page summary on the curator conclusion form. The whole team should have contributed to this, and names of all team members should appear on the sheet. What are your conclusions?

(Hey, even Indiana Jones had to start this way!)

Summary

Your textbooks and other programs can furnish you with existing plans. It would be exhausting for you to attempt to develop all your own lessons and units. In some instances, however—for example, in developing local studies—you will need to make your own lesson plans. In either case, you should perceive an underlying rationale designed to expand students' knowledge (content), ideas (concepts), investigative skills (processes), and attitudes and beliefs (values).

ACTIVITIES

1. Examine a teacher's edition of an elementary social studies textbook and try to find at least five suggested activities that you think would lend an added dimension to social studies lesson plans. Share those ideas in a small-group discussion of effective planning.
2. It has been suggested that teachers often fail to teach concepts or ideas in social studies. Why do you think that this might be the case? What can you suggest to improve the conceptual aspect of lesson planning?
3. Some teachers might argue that planning takes away from the more creative aspects of teaching, that it inhibits spontaneity in learning. What are the arguments for and against planning social studies lessons? What is your position on planning?
4. Develop a one- or two-page lesson plan on the topic of the importance of reading biographies of key people in American history. Include an excerpt or two from actual biographies as part of the material for your lesson plan. Share your plan with several others who have attempted this same activity. What did you learn from them? What did they learn from you?

NOTES

1. Robert Marzano and Daisy Arredondo, *Tactics for Thinking* (Aurora, CO: Mid-Continent Regional Laboratory, 1986).
2. Edwin Fenton, *The New Social Studies* (New York: Holt, Rinehart and Winston, 1965).
3. Thanks to Shirley Riley for her contributions to the archaeology unit.

SUGGESTED READINGS

Eggen, P., and Kauchak, D. (1996). *Strategies for Teachers: Teaching Content and Thinking Skills*. Boston: Allyn and Bacon.

Ellis, A. (2001). *Teaching, Learning, & Assessment Together: The Reflective Classroom*. Larchmont, NY: Eye on Education.

Gardner, H. (2000). *The Disciplined Mind*. New York: Penguin.

Joyce, B., Weil, M., and Calhoun, E. (1998). *Models of Teaching* (6th ed.). Boston: Allyn and Bacon.

Kinnucan-Weisch, K. (1999). "Strategic Teaching and Strategic Learning in First Grade." *Reading Horizons, 40:* 3–21.

Olson, K., and Kovalik, S. (1999). *Integrated Thematic Instruction: Classroom Stages of Implementation*. New York: Classroom Books for Education.

Rose, M. (2000). "Lessons: Social Studies/Math, Millenium Mastery." *Instructor, 109:* 14.

Ryan, K., and Cooper, J. (2000). *Those Who Can, Teach*. Boston: Houghton Mifflin.

Sternberg, R. (1999). *Thinking Styles*. Cambridge: Cambridge University Press.

Wasley, P. (1999). "Developing a Repertoire." *Childhood Education, 75:* 276–279.

Yelon, S. (1996). *Powerful Principles of Instruction*. New York: Longman.

Teaching and Learning Strategies

This chapter is devoted to the practical application of ideas developed in earlier chapters. Theories of experiential learning, motivation, multiple intelligences, learner differences, child development, stage theories, the zone of proximal development, and other considerations of how children learn come to life when they are built into lessons, activities, and shared experiences. Research in effective teaching has shown that the use of a variety of learning experiences is far superior to repetitive, highly predictable, paper-and-pencil–oriented lessons. We learn best by doing.

Teaching and learning strategies can be divided into two broad and related categories: direct teaching and indirect teaching. Both are necessary. Proper balance is the key. The strategies included in this chapter are:

- Direct teaching strategies
  Teacher presentation
  Whole-class discussion
  Demonstration
- Indirect teaching strategies
  Role-play and dramatic play
  Interest centers and stations
  Group investigation and
    presentation
  Independent study and
    presentation
  Reflective thinking

  Creative expression
  Content analysis/critical
    thinking
  Differentiated assignments
  Jigsaw/peer teaching
  Games and simulations

To see a child learn is to see a miracle unfold.
—Anna Rosewell

S ocial studies is an area of the curriculum that demands alternatives not only in terms of the content learned by students but, more important, also in terms of *how* students go about learning. Some evidence exists that social studies is one of the least-liked subjects in the curriculum.[1] It is especially important, then, that students be motivated by a variety of experiences in social studies, and that those experiences be designed to reach students whose interests and needs vary—not only from student to student but from day to day as well.

The alternatives presented here are not meant to be an exhaustive list of the possibilities inherent in teaching social studies. Rather, they are designed to serve as models. In the pages that follow, each learning alternative is explained and accompanied by examples. Some examples are primary-school oriented; others are oriented to intermediate school-age students.

Student Perceptions of Social Studies

A number of studies have been conducted over the years in which students are given an opportunity to voice their opinions about social studies. Two of them are particularly worth noting. A study by Mark Schug[2] explored the question of how students thought social studies teaching and learning might be improved. The following is a list, in order of preference, of the students' ideas:

- Group projects
- Field trips
- Less reading
- Role-play and simulations
- Class activities
- Independent work
- Class discussion
- Student planning
- Less lecture
- Challenging learning experiences
- Clear examples

Another study, conducted by Jeffrey Fouts,[3] used a questionnaire/survey of students to determine their perceptions of what creates a positive attitude toward social studies. Fouts characterized the findings under positive and negative attitudes. The results are shown in Table 7.1.

The obvious and very compelling message from students is that they wish to be actively involved, they want to work with others, and they would appreciate a certain amount of variety. The evidence is clear that *how* we teach does make a difference. Every now and then, research and common sense come together.

Variety in Teaching

Research in effective teaching supports the use of a variety of teaching strategies. It is useful to use variety in how you teach social studies for two reasons. First, students respond differently to various ways of learning. One student learns effectively through silent reading, but another does not. One student benefits from direct instruction, but another seems to learn more from inquiry methods. Of course, learners should not be typecast and exposed to only one strategy; you indicate a degree of sensitivity when you provide for a wide range of learning styles.

The second reason is for the sake of variety itself. Just as people prefer to vary their diets and other routines, they benefit from variety in instruction. A class is more interesting and appealing when students can look forward to

TABLE 7.1

Classroom Characteristics Related to Student Attitudes toward Social Studies

More Positive Attitudes	More Negative Attitudes
A variety of teaching strategies used; classroom routines often vary	Heavy reliance on a few teaching strategies; classroom routines seldom vary
Teacher involved with students; knows students personally; perceived as having caring attitude	Teacher perceived as aloof and noninvolved with students; perceived as noncaring by students
Classroom rules and expectations are fair, clear, and equitable; consistent enforcement of expectations by the teacher	Classroom rules and expectations are arbitrary and unclear; poor communication and possible favoritism by the teacher
Students are activively involved in diverse learning activities; structure of the class and assignments requires high student active participation	Students are in passive learning roles; students are simply recipients of information and content
Positive and frequent student-student interaction; high student support and cooperation with one another	Very limited student-student interaction; students usually working in a competitive environment
Teacher continually striving to show relevance of subject matter and content; teacher creates interest in subject by various strategies	Teacher relies on "innate" importance of subject matter; makes little attempt to show relevance or to develop interest

discussions, hands-on projects, games, demonstrations, role-plays, and other strategies. A monotonous, predictable routine reduces both motivation and the retention of ideas.

Direct Instruction

Direct instruction, or expository learning, is defined as the transmission of knowledge from a source to a receiver. The sources of information vary widely. They can include teachers, textbooks, films, lectures, records, tapes, trade books, and encyclopedias. The receivers, of course, are the students. Although direct instruction is generally associated in social studies with the transmission of content information about events, eras, regions, families, tribal groups, cities, governments, and so forth, it can also be used to impart skills or offer explanations, such as how to read a map or how to write an information-seeking letter.

Proponents of inquiry and student-involvement approaches to social studies learning are often mistakenly thought to take the position that expository learning is outdated and a poor use of learners' time. In fact, such criticisms are generally leveled at those who use direct instruction as a teaching strategy to the exclusion of other approaches. In those cases where students assign a low rating to social studies, no doubt a heavy measure of direct instruction is involved.

Viewed as one of the viable alternatives, however, direct instruction can be an effective and stimulating way to learn. Perhaps its greatest strength (as well as its

Freedom of movement and expression are fundamental experiences in childhood.

greatest potential weakness, if overdone) is its efficiency as a learning strategy. Because expository learning provides students with information, they are spared the inconvenience of having to discover it. None of us would be very far along in our academic development if we were forced to discover everything we needed to learn.

We'll examine three direct instruction strategies: lecture, or teacher presentation, class discussion, and demonstration. In each instance, the teacher is directly in charge of the instructional process and the students are challenged to acquire information.

Teacher Presentation

The idea of lecturing or presenting directly to young children may at first seem preposterous, particularly in light of what we have learned from the constructivist movement. Of course, long, didactic presentations are inappropriate. However, the idea of a well-constructed teacher presentation, used in concert with other more involving strategies, can make a lot of sense.

For example, primary students who were investigating the safety of a crosswalk near the school and who had been involved in a number of experiential activities were perfectly willing to listen as the teacher told them how professional traffic personnel do similar investigations. Intermediate students who were producing a product to sell needed to hear their teacher tell them about supply and demand, inventory, advertising, profit and loss, and other economic concepts. These presentations were given in meaningful contexts to students who were able to apply the information. Students who were to prepare a Mexican meal in the context of their study of that country were quite eager to hear their teacher present to them a talk on Mexican geography, agriculture, and customs. A felt need to learn on the part of students makes all the difference in the world.

Presentations should be reasonably brief, well thought out on your part, and focused on key ideas or concepts. It is important to use numerous examples of the concepts you stress, and to make as many real-world applications as you can. Stories also make presentations more appealing to children and adults alike. You should encourage active listening by having students take notes if they can. It also helps to have a listening partner with whom students can discuss information as you pause from time to time in your presentation. Figure 7.1 provides 12 concrete suggestions for making your presentations successful. Study it carefully and try to use it when you plan presentation lessons.

Class Discussion

Class discussion can be a meaningful social studies teaching/learning strategy. It is a direct teaching strategy because the teacher is responsible for structuring the flow of the interaction and for directing the students' involvement and participa-

---

FIGURE 7.1

Suggestions for Successful Teacher Presentations

1. *Remember who your audience is.* These are children of elementary school age. Their attention spans are short. Try to make your presentation appealing and contextual.
2. *Prepare an outline.* Have just a few key points. Keep in mind the idea that less is more.
3. *Use examples.* Illustrations help people understand and remember. Use multiple examples to make a key point.
4. *Speak clearly.* Pronounce your words clearly, speak at a moderate to slow speed, and be sure that you can be heard in the back of the room.
5. *Provide an introduction.* Begin with a brief preview of what you plan to say. Build a frame of reference—especially try to relate the topic to previous learning.
6. *Emphasize concepts and generalizations.* These are what you really want to teach and what you want your students to remember. Show how the concepts relate to one another as you proceed.
7. *Pause.* Give your students time to think, to write, or to discuss with a partner.
8. *Be enthusiastic.* Communicate with your attitude that you think this material is well worth learning.
9. *Use props.* Models, transparencies, pictures, diagrams, and so on will bring your presentation to life. These visuals provide variety and reach out to different learning styles.
10. *Provide change.* Move around the room. Ask for questions or comments. Pose a question or two. Have students draw an illustration of what they have learned to this point.
11. *Summarize.* Remember the adage, "Tell them what you are going to tell them, tell them, then tell them what you have told them." It really works.
12. *Assess.* Give the students an opportunity to discuss with a partner what they have learned. Have them draw or write about the topic. With older children, you may even want to give a brief quiz.

*Whole-class discussion is an example
of direct instruction.*

tion. The secret to effective class discussion is organization. A well-organized discussion has four basic components: a base of information, a central focus, effective questions, and a supportive classroom environment.

Information is essential to a purposeful exchange of ideas and points of view—you should get that point across to your students. Even good questions will not rescue a discussion floundering because you didn't give students sufficient information on which to build answers. Related to this is the idea of a *central focus* of discussion. In a whole-class discussion, you should ensure that questions keep coming back to the key issues. You can facilitate this by writing out your questions in advance and gently reminding students that extraneous information, while often interesting, is not useful in the process of examining ideas in depth.

The issues of *effective questions* and a *supportive environment* are complex. As you develop questions for discussion, use Bloom's *Taxonomy* to ensure that your questions include knowledge and understanding of the issue and allow for applications to the real world. You also need to include higher-level questions that ask students to analyze, synthesize, and evaluate. The level of the questions you ask sets the tone for the level of thinking by the students. The pacing of your questions is also important. Casual observation in elementary classrooms leads to the obvious conclusion that teachers are trying to teach students to be impulsive in their answers. Seldom does one encounter a classroom discussion in which the wait-time between a teacher's questions and students' answers exceeds a few seconds.

Demonstration

A demonstration lesson represents a direct teaching strategy in which the teacher models the behaviors of presentation, analysis, and synthesis. The student's role is observer and recorder of information and/or skills. Demonstrations, often wrongly called experiments, are in fact carefully rehearsed situations in which the teacher knows the outcome. Demonstrations are most effective when followed by a corresponding student activity. Thus, a teacher demonstrating a measuring technique for determining distances on maps would expect the class to use the same technique in a follow-up activity. Or, if the class were going to conduct an experiment in product testing, the teacher might demonstrate the appropriate techniques for testing a given product.

Application is the key to a demonstration's worth. If something is worth demonstrating to students, it is also worth the teacher's time to engage students in a direct application of the skill or activity. Demonstration is an efficient strategy because it allows the teacher to illustrate procedures and to communicate information at the same time. The danger of the demonstration strategy lies with the passive role of the students, who may or may not understand the concept or skill the teacher is demonstrating. The solution is to accompany the demonstration with application by the class. Ideally, the students will perform exactly the same activity the teacher has demonstrated in much the same way he or she demonstrated it. In some cases, however, that is not possible. For example, you might demonstrate the working of a volcano, and the student follow-up might consist of completing a diagram or drawing of a volcano. Or, using a chart, you may have demonstrated the flow of wealth in the U.S. economic system. The follow-up might consist of students keeping records of the money they spend.

Observations on Direct Instruction

To summarize thoughts about these direct instructional strategies, we can make the following observations:

1. Direct instruction usually involves whole-class instruction. Basically, the teacher is the presenter or explainer, and the students are the receivers of information.
2. Direct instruction need not be passive learning. It is best to have students involved through questions, note taking, drawing, constructing, and so on, either as accompaniment or follow-up to a teacher presentation.
3. You don't have to do all the talking. Even though a high teacher profile is basic to direct instruction, remember that a textbook, film, filmstrip, video, or guest speaker can also deliver information.
4. Timing and pacing are crucial to the success of direct instruction. Children can learn more from you when you lecture or present to them for a brief time period than when you take a longer time to tell them the same thing. If you have too much information, break it up into two presentations.
5. Direct instruction works best in social studies when you use other teaching/learning strategies as well. Too much of anything is not good. What are some of those other strategies that you ought to consider in addition to direct instruction? Let's explore them right now.

Indirect Instruction

Indirect instruction is an approach that reorganizes classroom activities in such a way that students take responsibility for much of their own learning. Indirect instruction has been called "democratic learning" because it emphasizes such experiences as student leadership and initiative, group interdependence, shared decision making, and reflective thinking. In his book *Democracy and Education*,[4] educational philosopher John Dewey presented his vision of a classroom as a miniature democracy where children participate actively and purposefully. His vision seems even more crucial today.

The teacher's role in indirect instruction is that of facilitator of learning. He or she often works behind the scenes to prepare the intellectual, social, and moral environment. One goal is the development of a classroom environment where children feel free to express themselves, to explore actively, and to work together. The teacher ensures that the needed materials and strategies are in place. He or she expects the individual student or the class, depending on the nature of the activity, to assume ownership and responsibility for learning. The teacher questions, suggests, and mediates. A teacher who is accustomed to being the center of attention, direction giver, or autocratic leader often finds this role very difficult.

The student's role is that of active learner. Students are expected to inquire, discover, discuss, plan, act on, and evaluate ideas. The ratio of student-to-student interaction is much higher in classes where indirect instruction takes place. Students seldom sit in straight rows for their work, simply because this configuration is not conducive to working together. Thus, students find themselves playing the role of people who are responsible—morally, intellectually, and socially—for their own learning and that of their fellow students. Table 7.2 shows certain contrasts between direct and indirect instruction.

Now let's turn to 10 different indirect instruction strategies: role-play, interest centers, group investigation, independent study, reflective thinking, creative expression, content analysis, differentiated assignments, jigsaw/peer teaching, and simulations. In each strategy, the teacher plays the role of facilitator of learning, the process of learning is emphasized, and students are actively engaged in learning.

Role-Play

Role-play is an exceptionally versatile strategy. It is used in drama, simulation, play, games, and, of course, counseling. Essentially, role-play is a projective technique wherein the role-player either "becomes" someone else or pretends to be performing a task that is different from what he or she usually does. An example of the former could be a student role-playing Martin Luther King Jr. or Harriet Tubman. An

TABLE 7.2

Contrasts between Direct and Indirect Instruction

Direct	Indirect
Passive student role	Active student role
Teacher as director	Teacher as facilitator
Student receives knowledge	Student generalizes knowledge
Answers to questions are predetermined	Answers to questions are discovered by students
Promotes convergent thinking	Promotes divergent thinking
Learning consists chiefly of recall and explanation	Learning consists chiefly of analysis, synthesis, and judgment

example of the latter could be a student pretending to be a nurse, fire fighter, or store clerk.

Role-play comes naturally to children, who do it without ever having heard the term. They use it intuitively as a means of learning. It is a part of their exploratory nature. A young child becomes a truck driver in a sand box. Several children play house on a Saturday afternoon. Children pretend to be famous movie stars or popular entertainers. They become traders and bankers in games they play. However, with the exception of the few who try out for the high school play, role-play is often sadly left behind with early childhood. This is unfortunate, because role-play is a viable way to teach and to learn. It helps a child get beneath the surface of learning and begin to explore moods, feelings, and values.

Harlan Hansen (a nationally known specialist in early childhood education) and I once had a grant that enabled us to develop a curriculum for children in kindergarten through second grade. We used an interest-centers approach to learning, and one of the centers that Harlan installed in a first-grade classroom was a shoe shop. It wasn't much on the surface—just a countertop in a corner of the room with a sign saying "Shoe Shop" and a bunch of donated, mostly worn-out shoes. But what was special about that shop was the role-playing the girls and boys did there. The children took turns being the proprietor or a customer. Here is a typical exchange at the Shoe Shop:

Clerk: Hello, may I help you?
Customer: Yes, I'd like to buy a pair of shoes.
Clerk: Oh, what kind of shoes would you like?
Customer: Well, I would like some brown shoes.
Clerk: Brown shoes? Yes, we have some. Here, would you like to try these on?
Customer: Okay. (*Child puts on the shoes with assistance from the clerk.*)
Clerk: How do they feel?
Customer: They're fine. I'll take them.
Clerk: Okay. That will be ten dollars.
Customer: Here is your money.
Clerk: Thank you.
Customer: Good-bye.
Clerk: Good-bye.

The politeness and civility of this exchange are remarkable, yet it is typical of the role-play children are capable of when they are given the chance. Don't underestimate the power of role-play or consign it to the dustbin of "child's play." Language development and a sense of others' perspectives are two of the consistent outcomes of role-play. This strategy can be meaningfully integrated into your social studies program, as the example in the next paragraph illustrates.

The poster reproduction included here, advertising farmland for sale in Illinois in the 1860s, suggests a role-play activity related to the study of the Westward Movement. In the activity, students are assigned the roles of various family members who live on a farm in the eastern United States during the days of the expansion of the country to the West. The father in the family is excited about the opportunities for a new chance out West (Illinois, in this case)—things haven't been so good on the present farm. Other members of the family react to the proposed move in several

133
Strategies

An artifact such as this poster provides a springboard for student role-play. The poster advertises Illinois farmland in the 1860s.

different ways. The mother isn't sure; she would have to give up a great deal. A sickly daughter fears the move. An older son thinks it would be a great opportunity.

I have used this role-play activity a number of times. The dynamics are fascinating. What emerges are the feelings, hopes, and fears that the pioneers must have known. In other words, the activity humanizes history because the role-players (and audience, if there is one) begin to think about actual lives and how people

Students can take an active role in learning history by donning costumes from the period.

were affected by such changes. Of course, the role-play works best when knowledge of the Westward Movement is applied. Role-play furnishes the social studies teacher with a perfect intersection of cognition and affect.

One last thought about role-play: You should model it to your class occasionally. Try teaching your students about George Washington or astronaut Sally Ride by dressing up like the person and talking to your students as though that is who you are. You have to do a little background reading about your character, of course, but I think you'll be pleased with the effect your little performance will have on your class. It's fun, and social studies ought to be fun. Don't you agree?

Interest Centers

The interest-centers approach to teaching and learning social studies is primarily a child-centered, exploratory way to get children involved in self-directed, autonomous behavior. Interest centers are not dependent on such well-known phrases as "All right, class, take out your books and turn to page 59." Your students will be doing different activities of their own choosing.

The key to successful interest centers is to make them meaningful, appealing, and self-sustaining. In order for centers to be meaningful, they should reflect the purposes of your social studies program. Ask yourself: What am I trying to teach my students that they could learn essentially on their own at a center? To make your centers appealing, try to put yourself in a child's position. Games, maps, puzzles, activities, videos, and so on are highly attractive to a child, especially when organized in an attractive way. For example, it doesn't take much to make a reading center appealing—a small rug, some beautiful posters, a table covered with wonderful books, and you're ready to go. The children's imaginations will supply the rest of what your center needs. To be self-sustaining, a center must be a place where a child can function successfully and independently. If your presence is constantly needed at a center, it is probably too difficult or ambiguous for the students to understand. Remember: One of the reasons for having centers is to give students a sense of autonomy and not a sense of dependence. The key concept in the interest-centers approach is freedom of choice.

A teacher who uses interest centers is dedicated to the idea that in an attractive, purposeful environment, students will make meaningful use of their time based on the pursuit of knowledge and ideas of their own choosing. Thus, the teacher does much behind-the-scenes work, establishing the centers and providing resources and other types of materials. During center time, the teacher moves about the room and is available to the children. The role of the teacher is that of support person, sympathetic listener, mediator of ideas, and arranger of possibilities.

The teacher assumes a low profile, being careful not to talk too much, not to give too many directions, and not to tell the children how to do things unless it's absolutely necessary. The term *facilitator* is appropriate in this context of the teacher's role. A good facilitator is someone who works behind the scenes to make things function as smoothly as possible. The main "problem" with being a good facilitator is that it makes his or her work look so easy. Have you ever watched a really accomplished talk-show host do his or her job? The better the host is, the more people like us are apt to think, "I could do that; it looks so easy." Well, facilitating is not so easy.

The role of students in learning-centers instruction is that of active explorers. The students are decision makers who choose freely among an array of attractive ways of spending time. They are learning and expressing a great variety of content and concepts in a variety of ways, and they are enjoying their learning.

Group Investigation or Projects

Imagine a group of students who, with their teacher's guidance and support, decided to do something about the environment where they lived. Imagine further that these students took up the challenge of asking the school board to ban the use of styrofoam cups and other containers by the schools in their district. This is exactly what happened in Victoria, British Columbia, when some sixth- and seventh-grade students at James Bay School decided to seek such a ban.

Cross-age tutoring experiences are rewarding for both younger and older students.

The work of these students first came to my attention one fall morning as I drove along the interstate listening to a Canadian radio station. The announcer mentioned the work the James Bay students were trying to accomplish, and I was quite impressed that young people would take up such a challenge. I decided to write them a letter, seeking more information about the project. Their reply appears as Figure 7.2.

There is something very compelling about positive social action mounted by a group of concerned citizens. It seems to address the very heart of democracy. This is especially true when those citizens are young people who are still in the process of learning how democracy works. The efforts of the students to ban styrofoam use were successful, by the way, but they had to do a considerable amount of work in order to achieve their goal. I'm sure they learned that one has to present evidence and do background work in order to present one's case clearly and persuasively to elected officials.

The James Bay project exemplifies the spirit of group investigation. A group project is an effort by a class—or a whole school—to make a difference in their world. The exciting thing about group investigation is that issues abound in every locality in democratic societies such as Canada and the United States. The teacher just needs to be sensitive to the issues and willing to do the work it takes to keep the students' effort going, ensuring that it is a positive, purposeful effort.

Students of any age can conduct group investigations. I've seen first-graders investigate a potentially dangerous crosswalk near the school and make it safer, possibly saving a life. I've seen third-graders investigate the playground equipment at their school and make it safer and more creative. I've also seen intermediate-grade students make their school cafeteria a more appealing, saner place to eat lunch. You ought to try the approach—it works!

The role of the teacher in group investigation is complex. He or she must facilitate group processes, keep the focus on the problem to be solved, ensure that *all* students are involved actively, help the students locate appropriate resources and information, and evaluate the group's progress as it conducts its investigation. Some teachers find this overwhelming and fall back on traditional seat work assignments. Admittedly, it does take a lot of energy to guide a group of children through an investigation, but the rewards of seeing students grow and learn to work effectively with each other are considerable.

Independent Study and Presentation

It goes without saying that children need to learn to work together, but they also need to find out what they can do largely on their own. Children learn interdependence when they collaborate as well as when they work alone. In life we need both. Independent study can be conducted as a solo investigation or as a piece of a larger group investigation. It is ideal for invoking the Doctrine of Interest, which states that students should study what they are personally interested in.

When a student studies something he or she is curious about or wants to learn more about, or simply chooses for whatever reason(s) to study something, a powerful energy is already in place. That something is called *motivation.* When teenagers get to take driving lessons, we typically do not have to worry about their motivation to learn. They bring that commodity along with them. When a young

FIGURE 7.2

*Correspondence
Concerning a
Group Project*

JAMES BAY
COMMUNITY SCHOOL

140 Oswego Street
Victoria, B.C.
V8V 2B1

384-7184

Dr. Arthur K. Ellis, Professor
Seattle Pacific University
Seattle, Washington

Dear Dr. Arthur Ellis:

Your letter about the styrofoam project arrived at James Bay Community
School on November 14. We want you to know that it was grade 6/7 students
that were working on the project not grade 5/6. We got started when the
question "How does dumping garbage affect our environment?" was raised.
We decided we had the power to change our environment. Our first step was
to write letters. We wrote to places like grocery stores and the B.C.
Ferry Corporation. Later on we talked about writing to government
officials and the school board.

Our first response was from the school board who wanted a
presentation. In our presentation we talked about what styrofoam is doing
to our environment. We also talked about the recycling program that we
started in our school and and asked if they would recycle papers in the
school district. In the end they passed both motions. We did not know that
a spokesman from C FAX radio station was sitting silently at another table
taking in bits of our presentation.

The B.C. Ferry Corporation then responded by buying a new type of
styrofoam cups with out the Chloro Fluoro Carbons

A student in our class came up with the name S.P.O.E.—Students
Protecting Our Environment. Some of us are still carrying on with the
project.

The news media asked us if they could get a picture of S.P.O.E. for an
article in a magazine.

Thank you for your interest in Students Protecting Our Environment.

Sincerely,
Grade 6/7 class of
J.B.C.S.

Warren Walbaum
K R
Zach Whitmarsh
Corrine Wilson

child asks a parent if he or she can bake some cookies, we know that motivation is already in place. And when a child learns to ride a bicycle, painful as it is, the child typically won't stop until he or she can do it no matter how long it takes. The motivation is there.

So, what I am saying to you is, let students decide for themselves some of the things they want to study. Here are some examples. In a primary class, the teacher asked the students what seasons, games, and activities interested them the most. The students volunteered their ideas while the teacher wrote them on the board. When the board was filled with ideas, the teacher talked with the class about ways in which students could learn more about the topic of their choice. The teacher gave each student three tasks to carry out: (1) each child was to talk with his or her parent(s) about the topic, and the parent was to help write down some of the things they discussed; (2) each child was to draw a picture showing something he or she learned or enjoyed about the topic; and (3) each child was expected to tell the class about his or her findings. This assignment involved the home. It asked the child to inquire on his or her own. It asked the child to express himself or herself artistically. And it gave each child an experience with presentation skills. As simple as this independent study is, consider that it involved choosing freely, carrying out a task, talking to an adult, and presenting before an audience.

In an intermediate-level class that was studying Native Americans, the teacher showed the class a large map that illustrated the locations of various nations on the North American continent. The teacher spent a little time telling the class about various tribal groups, their customs, habits, food, and shelter. The teacher stressed the idea that each Nation had its own unique identity and way of life. The independent study flowing from this overview/introduction was challenging each student to make a booklet and accompanying display on one of the Native American Nations. Each student chose a different Nation and did research, including writing letters to the Nation to learn of modern-day life, reading accounts of tribal life in the past, and learning as much as possible in order to become an "expert." As the study progressed, the room began to fill up with maps, pictures, drawings, artifacts, stories, letters, and so on. Each student reported his or her findings to the class during a culminating activity, and a number of students taught a "lesson" on their chosen Nation to a class of younger students in the school.

In both of these cases, the teacher played the role of facilitator, helping students with sources of information and guidance when they needed it. But in both cases, the ultimate responsibility was with the individual student.

Reflective Thinking

Reflective thinking is designed to give learners the opportunity to be philosophical —to consider, discuss, and argue issues. Reflective thinking sessions are often used to help students analyze certain tasks they have performed. This strategy is also involved in situations in which the teacher wants students to do some speculating on how a certain chain of events might take place under certain conditions.

Reflective thinking and inquiry share the idea of active student involvement in problems and questions. They differ as learning strategies in that inquiry learning is predicated on the notion that sufficient data will enable a student to answer a question or solve a problem, whereas reflective thinking often deals with questions that cannot be answered solely by data. The following questions provide a simple contrast:

1. *Inquiry question:* How do messages flow in our school?
2. *Reflective-thinking question:* What are the advantages of written versus oral messages?

The first question can be answered on the basis of data gathered, whereas the second may be a matter of opinion.

➤ *Example: Settlement of the United States*

One example of an effective teaching strategy that uses reflective thinking is the Question of the Week. On Monday morning, the teacher posts a question and tells the students that on Friday approximately 15 minutes will be spent discussing it. This gives students a chance to ask others (e.g., parents, teachers) about the question as well as to do some reading and thinking before the discussion. Following is a sample question of the week. Space is provided for your answer. Compare your answer to those developed by a fifth-grade class that discussed this same question.

In what ways would this country be different if it had been settled west to east instead of east to west?

_____

_____

_____

_____

_____

_____

_____

_____

_____

_____

_____

Following are answers developed by fifth-graders:

- "We'd have a different language. Maybe Chinese."
- "People would have come mainly from Asia."
- "The capital city would probably be in the West."
- "We'd have easterns instead of westerns on TV."
- "We probably wouldn't be here."
- "The western areas would probably have a larger population."
- "The high mountains of the West would have been a barrier to early expansion."
- "There might be several countries where Canada and the U.S. are today."

▶▶ *Example: An Incident in Human Behavior*

A teacher told a third-grade class the following story:

> Mary, a third-grader, checked a book out of the library. When school was over, she took the book home to read. On the way home, Mary's friends asked her to play outside. So Mary ran into her house, changed into play clothes, left the book on a chair in the living room, and went outside to play. Her brother Tim, who was 3 years old, found the book and colored the pages with crayons. The book was ruined.

The teacher then asked the class this question: "How many people could we name who *might* be responsible?" The class listed Mary, her mother, her father, Tim, Mary's teacher, and the librarian. The teacher did not ask the students to reach conclusions about responsibility at this point. She told the students to think about it, and they would discuss it the next day.

During a discussion period the next day, the teacher asked the students to tell who they thought was responsible. Here are some responses:

- "Mary is responsible. She shouldn't have left the book where her little brother could get it."
- "Her brother is three. He shouldn't be coloring in books. A two-year-old might."
- "Her mother didn't watch her little brother very carefully."
- "The teacher shouldn't let kids take books home."

Some students took issue with certain responses. Others supported their classmates' reasonings. Others had asked their parents and gave their parents' opinions. The teacher then asked, "How do we know the right answer?" One student said, "Some families are different, so it might not be the same for everyone."

The teacher asked another question: "What should be done now that the book is ruined?" Some students had ready answers, while others made such suggestions as "We could ask the librarian what she thinks about it."

▶▶ *Example: Looking Forward and Looking Back*

The Roman god Janus (for whom the month of January is named) could look forward into the future and back to the past. So can we, at least to an extent. Many learners (not just children) tend to be impulsive when it comes to carrying out an assignment. Reflective thought can improve one's work substantially. Let's say that you want your students to make a map of the school and play area. Prior to the activity itself, allow your students to meet in groups of two or three to think and plan about the qualities of a good map. Depending on the age of the pupils, you may want to list some key terms on the board, including *scale, key, cardinal directions, color, perspective, accuracy*, and so on. Following the activity of making the maps, give your students an opportunity to talk about the assignment, including such issues as: What was difficult about it? What did you learn? What would you tell someone who was going to make such a map? Before-and-after sessions like this raise students' levels of consciousness about their work. In doing so, they practice metacognition, or thinking about thinking. It's time consuming but eminently worthwhile.

One proven method for tapping into the creativity of a group is the brainstorming strategy. It is particularly useful at those times when the teacher wants to give students an opportunity to think expansively about a problem, activity, project, or the like. Brainstorming in problem solving, for example, typically is done early in the process. If your class was studying economics and the children decided to manufacture a product that they will then market, you might begin with a brainstorming session in which you allow students to think of as many possibilities as they can. Eventually, you and the children will decide on a single product to manufacture, but for now, you want to let the creative potential of the students flower.

There are three essential elements of brainstorming, and you must honor all three for the process to work effectively. First, there is the rule of *quantity over quality*. This means that you want the children to come up with as many possibilities as they can; the more, the merrier. The second rule is *no judgments*. There will be plenty of time later to decide if an idea is practical, achievable, whatever. For now, refrain from judging; to do otherwise kills creative instincts. The third rule is *inclusion*. Everyone in the class needs to feel welcome to take part, not just the more vocal or more opinionated.

There are two alternative grouping possibilities available, and I suggest you use them both from time to time. First, there is the whole-class group with the teacher at the chalkboard. Students simply speak up while you record their ideas. Generally speaking, you will have no trouble filling an entire board with suggestions. A follow-up session can be devoted to discussing the feasibility of the various suggestions. The second procedure is to put students in small groups of three or four and allow them to brainstorm. Each group will need a recorder or some way of keeping track of ideas. The class then comes back together for a time of sharing.

The last thing to keep in mind is how much you want to structure the process. Free-form brainstorming allows people to speak up spontaneously. Its advantage is obvious—the spontaneous nature of the process. Its disadvantage is that more vocal, outgoing types will dominate, while others will be reluctant to compete. Structured brainstorming is a process whereby a group (class or small group) actually gives each person a turn either to make a suggestion or to "pass." The great advantage is equal opportunity to participate; the disadvantage is some slight loss of spontaneity. Try both approaches.

Creative Expression

Social studies offers great potential for students to express themselves creatively in a variety of ways. Although consuming knowledge, inquiring into problems, and discussing ideas are important uses of students' time in social studies, it is also important that they be given opportunities to build, act, draw, paint, and photograph as a means of involving themselves in learning and sharing (see Figure 7.3). Here are some examples of creative expression by students.

- A second-grade class presented a slide show to the PTA, illustrating their work on improving the safety of a crosswalk near the school.
- A sixth-grade class constructed a diorama in the school showcase, illustrating life on a medieval manor during their study of a unit on life in the Middle Ages.

FIGURE 7.3

Keys to Creativity: 15 Things You Can Do

The teacher's behavior is crucial in establishing conditions conducive to creativity. The following suggestions are designed to help you establish a creative climate in your classroom:

- Give freedom and space.
- Promote discovery learning.
- Create a playful atmosphere.
- Encourage projects.
- Allow students to make choices.
- Bring interesting things to class.
- Be a good listener and sounding board.
- Give open-ended assignments.
- Encourage students to help each other.
- Encourage fresh perspectives on ordinary things.
- Model and encourage trust and respect.
- Encourage student initiative and risk taking.
- Have a sense of humor.
- Give unusual assignments.
- Encourage good literature and the arts.
- Relax and enjoy your work.

- A student constructed a model of the school playground and presented his recommendations for improving its use during recess periods.
- A group of fifth-grade students made puppets and presented shows to kindergarten and first-grade classes on the topic of school safety.
- A third-grade class put together a directory of mini-field trips in the local area that students could take with their parents.
- Some sixth-graders developed and constructed a simple game designed to teach cardinal directions. They mass-produced the game and made copies available to children in the lower grades.

The student products listed here are often associated with creative expression in social studies:

poems	murals	drawings
stories	paintings	booklets
models	puppet shows	games
plays	dioramas	radio programs
photographs	skits	television programs

▶ *Example: Nursery Rhyme Newspaper Stories*

One way to support children's creative instincts is to let them write newspaper stories about nursery rhymes. Give each child a nursery rhyme (there will be nursery rhyme books in your school or branch library) and ask him or her to write a newspaper article about the story. Here is an example of how one child wrote up the story of Jack and Jill:

143

Strategies

> Jack and Jill went up the hill,
> to fetch a pail of water.
> Jack fell down and broke his crown,
> and Jill came tumbling after.
> Now up Jack got and home did trot,
> as fast as he could caper.
> He went to bed and covered his head
> with vinegar and brown paper.

"YOUNGSTERS HURT IN TRAGIC FALL"
by
Shandra, Room 17

Jack and Jill, both aged ten, were injured today when they fell while running down the hill from the town well. Witnesses said they tripped over each other in their hurry to bring the pail of water back to the Old Washerwoman. Jack apparently broke his crown. He ran home and covered his head with vinegar and brown paper, and is expected to make a full recovery. Jill needed no treatment. Safety Officer Billy Bones said that children should *never* run down the hill because it is too steep. Concerned citizens will meet at Town Hall on Friday night to discuss this important safety issue. Officer Bones will lead the opening flag salute. Both Jack and Jill said this sure has been a lesson to them, and from now on they will walk down the hill. The Old Washerwoman said in an interview that maybe she had been working the children too hard, and that is why they fell. No charges are expected to be filed in the case.

Content Analysis

Because so much of what people learn and know is information received from secondary sources, it is important to develop the skill of content analysis. Content analysis is a means of examining content more closely than if one merely wanted to know what it stated. Content analysis raises such questions as interpretation of meaning, significance of material, and even its accuracy or bias. It is also a way for students to take information presented globally and break it into categories that are more manageable.

The content that students can analyze can come from any source: film, story, textbook, newspaper, and so forth. Practice at content analysis should make students more critical thinkers and critical readers. The interpretive activities involved in content analysis enable students to construct meaning as they read, view, or listen to information. Take some time to consider the following examples.

▶ *Example: The Zuni Culture*

The following example of content analysis gives students an opportunity to learn about another culture and to compare and contrast it with their own. The topic of the lesson is the Zuni Native American culture. After students have read the following narrative about the Zuni and have had a chance to study the accompanying picture in Figure 7.4, ask them to consider the concepts list that follows. First, the

FIGURE 7.4

Source: Price Stern Sloan, Incorporated. Reprinted by permission.

students are to decide how the Zuni observe the concepts. Second, the students are to decide how they themselves observe the concepts.

Zuni

In the fine craftsmanship of their turquoise and silver jewelry, in the fabulous designs of their dance masks and in their wealth of ceremonial observances, the Zuni Indians have displayed a creative spirit which has brought great beauty to their desert home.

The Zuni now occupy an area along the Zuni River, south of Gallup, New Mexico. Their old home was a terraced, stone and adobe pueblo on a hill overlooking the river. Originally they lived primarily by agriculture, raising corn, beans, squash and chiles.

During the last hundred years, or so, Zuni Indians developed skills as jewelry-makers—and are now famous for this work.

Zuni use a variety of jewelry designs—deer, butterflies, eagles, dance figures in flat relief and more—in which turquoise stones are individually set or arranged in mosaics. Different colors of stone, shell and coral pieces, delicately elaborate designs and silverware trim often distinguish Zuni creations. Jewelry-making has joined agriculture as their important economic activities.

The artistry expressed by the jewelry-makers was traditionally found in the fertile imagery of the abundant religious dances and ceremonials of the Zuni. Kiva groups, priesthoods, fraternities and medicine societies played important roles in preserving sacred traditions and observances. For it was through proper attention to ritual and prayer that rain, fertility and a joyful life were granted by the gods.

Religious dances were not diversions from a rigorous life, but a highly important unifying element in the Zuni harmony with life. Dances were held often throughout the year, except during the crucial planting and harvest seasons.

Masks became a vital element in these dances. The Zuni were renowned for the skill in construction, imagination in design and the sheer variety of their masks. They were bizarre, often grotesque creations, symbolically painted and, at times, impressively large. The masks used for the Shalako festival after the harvest were as much as three meters (nine feet) high and enclosed the men who danced within them.

The Zuni sun priest set the dates for the dances. In the summer, rain dances were held. In winter, members of the Wood Fraternity—men and women—performed the dances of the sword swallowers. With great dexterity they combined dancing with swallowing red-colored swords made of juniper and decorated with feathers. Their rites lasted for several days. The medicinal powers of the Wood Fraternity were said to have been most useful for treating sore throats.

The climax of the year was the Shalako ceremonial, held in November or December. This was a symbolic representation of the Zuni's creation and migration to their homeland. Dancers completely enveloped in huge, awe-inspiring masks personified the Shalako, divine messengers from the rain gods who devoted prayers to the happiness and fruitful life of the Zuni.

Preparations for this festival went on throughout the year. Participants honored special rites to prepare themselves for their roles. As the great time approached, special houses built for the Shalako were decorated, great amounts of bread baked and meals readied. Finally a masked, nude youth painted black with red, yellow, blue and white spots, representing the fire-god, appeared carrying a burning cedar brand. He was followed by a Council of Gods and finally, by the six Shalako. These figures were striking, enormous masks with eagle-feather headdresses, turquoise faces with rolling, bulging eyes, clacking beaks, and accents of long black hair and ravens' feathers. These marvels were received in their houses where they danced through the night. Truly, the gods seemed to be among their people.

The Zuni have preserved much of their heritage to this day. Many of their dances survive. (Price Stern Sloan, Incorporated. Reprinted by permission.)

Culture Concepts	How the Zuni Observe Them	How I Observe Them
Food	_____	_____
	_____	_____
Shelter	_____	_____
	_____	_____

Seasons	_____	_____
	_____	_____
Religion	_____	_____
	_____	_____
Festivals	_____	_____
	_____	_____
Ceremonies	_____	_____
	_____	_____
Heritage	_____	_____
	_____	_____
Artistry	_____	_____
	_____	_____

▶ *Example: Nursery Rhymes*

Nursery rhymes have potential for content analysis at several levels. In that respect, they are appropriate content at both primary and intermediate levels. At the primary level, you might focus on the sequence of events within a nursery rhyme. After memorizing "Humpty Dumpty," for example, you might ask the children to draw a series of pictures showing what actually happened. Figure 9.1 on page 179 illustrates a young child's sequence content analysis of the nursery rhyme.

At intermediate levels, you can use the same content to get at different things. Here are two possibilities:

1. Write about what you think the "message" really is in the story of "Humpty Dumpty." The literal meaning is obvious: He fell off the wall; but is there a moral to the story?
2. "Humpty Dumpty" was written in a historical context. Investigate the origins of this nursery rhyme. Does it portray an actual king? What were the conditions that led to his fall? What were the consequences?

▶ *Example: Textbooks*

All textbooks, by definition, contain content. A very useful exercise in content analysis for a team of intermediate-level researchers is to take two social studies textbooks designed for their particular grade level and to compare and contrast them. A good place to start is the tables of contents and the indexes. Ask the students to focus on these questions: To what extent are the two books alike in coverage and different? How difficult and how interesting is the writing? How do the illustrations compare? How complete and how fair is the coverage given to certain culture groups? To women? To minorities? Which of the two texts do you prefer?

Nursery rhymes, with their repetition of sounds, provide one of the best avenues of language expression for young learners.

Differentiated Assignments

Often, assignments are given to a whole class as though all students had the same needs and the same learning styles. In fact, they do not. If you provide choices for children, they have an opportunity to practice decision making and to fulfill your requirements along the lines of their own interests. Of course, not every assignment need be differentiated, but many should be, if only to provide variety.

➤➤ *Example: The Pioneer Treks*

The idea of a differentiated assignment is to give students choices. The teacher has a goal, which, in the case of the following example, is for students to learn about the westward expansion of the United States across the Great Plains and on to the territories of California and Oregon. In a true differentiated assignment, there are a number of ways in which students might achieve this goal. Learning styles, interest, and motivation are factors that will guide students' choices of activities.

In most cases, a differentiated assignment will take several days for the students to complete because of the research, construction, drama, and other activities involved. Time should also be allowed for class presentations, because much additional learning will take place as the children share what they have learned. As you examine the following assignment options,[5] keep in mind Howard Gardner's multiple intelligence theory as well as what you know about student learning styles.

1. Find a book that has a picture of a covered wagon in it. Sketch a copy of the covered wagon.
2. As the covered wagon trains moved along the trail, they would stop for the night. Find a picture of a covered wagon encampment and draw a sketch of it.
3. Using craft sticks, cloth, glue, and other materials, make a model of a covered wagon.

4. Most families that traveled west had to leave many of their possessions behind. Prepare a list of the things you think a family might have had to leave behind and a list of things a family would need to take with them on the trail.

5. Write a fictional story about a family and their decision to leave the eastern United States and move west.

6. Draw a map that illustrates the Oregon Trail, the California Trail, and the Mormon Trek.

7. The Westward Movement of the pioneers must have seemed strange from the perspective of the various tribes through whose territory they traveled. Write a story explaining the Westward Movement from a Native American point of view.

8. Read the book *The Children of the Covered Wagon* by Elizabeth Carr. Present a brief oral report to the class on the life of children in a wagon train.

9. Pretend you are a child journeying west on a wagon train. Write a letter to a friend who stayed behind and tell him or her about life on a wagon train.

10. Some people who went west went to the gold fields of California and Colorado. Draw a sketch of a gold-mining camp.

11. Write a song about life along the trail.

12. What job would you have liked to have on a wagon train? Wagon master? Scout? Write a paragraph telling what job you would have liked and why.

13. Look through the index of a book on the Westward Movement. Find a topic that looks interesting to you and research it.

14. Find a play at the library about pioneer days or the Westward Movement. Round up enough students to put it on and present it to a primary class in your building.

15. Make a salt/flour map of the Westward Movement. Show the major trails, forts, and other important features.

16. Find out which songs were sung along the trail by pioneers. Learn a song and teach it to the class.

17. How fair do you think the Westward Movement was to the Native Americans? Do some research into this question and report to the class.

18. What was the typical diet along the trail? Find out and (with the teacher's help) prepare a meal for the class to eat.

19. Where will pioneers go in the future? Under the oceans? To the Antarctic? To outer space? Do some research and write a report on future pioneer efforts.

20. Look through the district's film catalog for a good film on the Westward Movement. Ask your teacher to order the film. Preview it so that you can introduce it to the class for showing.

▶▶ *Example: A Differentiated Assignment*
Using Three Modes of Learning:
Verbal, Activity, and Production

One way to ensure that you reach children with a variety of learning styles and preferences is to use the differentiated assignment strategy. You should keep in mind that the type of differentiated assignment strategy illustrated here is really a template that you can use for any unit or area of instruction. You merely change the focus of the assignments to whatever content you are teaching.

Archaeology Unit: Differentiated Assignment. Choose *any two* assignments from *each* list. You must do a total of *six* assignments:

List A: Verbal
- Read any one of the books on our Unit Resource List.
- Write a letter to a museum and ask how the curators do their work.
- Read an article on archaeology from *National Geographic* or *Smithsonian* magazine and write a report on it.
- Write an essay on archaeology. Be sure to include at least three references.
- View a video on archaeology (select one from the video list) and write a report on it.
- Write a short play or skit about an actual archaeological expedition.
- Write a story about a fictional archaeological expedition.

List B: Activities
- Make a model of an ancient dwelling.
- Construct a diorama of life in an ancient setting.
- Draw a series of pictures that illustrate an archaeological dig.
- Use clay and sticks to make a model of an ancient city.
- Make a reproduction of an artifact from ancient times.
- Draw sketches of several ancient tools.
- Make a collage from magazine pictures of an archaeological expedition.
- Make a time capsule filled with artifacts from our culture.
- Tour a local museum and draw pictures of the exhibits.

List C: Production
- Help stage a play about an archaeological expedition.
- Do a role-play in which you become an actual archaeologist who tells about his or her work.
- Prepare and present a group presentation on an actual archaeological expedition.
- Prepare and teach a lesson on archaeology to another class.
- Have a discussion on archaeology at home with your family members.
- Be an archaeologist. Carry out your own expedition using artifacts from your home or neighborhood.
- Visit a garage sale or yard sale. Pretend you are an archaeologist and the items for sale are artifacts.

Jigsaw/Peer Teaching

The jigsaw strategy, developed by Elliot Aronson, is an interesting combination of cooperative learning with an individualistic goal structure. The idea of this teaching/learning strategy is that each student in a cooperative learning group of, say, three students is responsible for peer teaching his or her companions a portion of the material that they all need to learn. Thus, each student teaches one-third of the information, skills, or whatever, and is taught two-thirds of the content. It is important that students do their best to teach their compatriots well, because all the members of the group are depending on each other. This truly creates a "we're in this together" mentality.

A sample jigsaw is included here (see Figure 7.5) because I'm convinced that peer teaching is one of the best ways for children to learn. Jean Piaget noted that children are more effective than most adults realize in teaching each other, especially if teachers provide some structure and support. This is so, he claimed, because of a language issue—namely, greater syntactic compatibility is found within

---

FIGURE 7.5

Keys to Cooperative Learning

The jigsaw strategy is illustrative of the broader idea of cooperative learning. Cooperative learning is dedicated to the idea of civil conversation and working together in an atmosphere of mutual interest and collaboration. Cooperative learning is based on the idea of shared goals. If you and I want the same thing, why don't we work together to achieve it? The work of such theorists as Vygotsky, Piaget, and Bruner points to the need for children to express themselves civilly in social situations in order for language and thought to codevelop. Johnson and Johnson, pioneers in this area, cite cumulative research findings that support cooperative learning.

- Higher achievement, better retention
- Growth in moral and cognitive reasoning
- Enhanced motivation to learn
- Improved attitude toward school and school subjects
- Improved attitude toward teachers
- Enhanced self-esteem
- Greater liking toward one another

Cooperative learning is based on a six-fold foundation:

- Positive interdependence
- Small groups (2 or 3)
- Face-to-face interaction
- Individual accountability
- Development of small-group skills
- Time for reflection and analysis

The teacher's role is to act as a consultant, mediator, and facilitator in order to keep the process going forward. The teacher becomes a strategist who carefully considers who should work with whom. He or she teaches the skills needed to work together, helping students know when to listen, when to talk, how to be supportive, how to ensure participation by all, and so on. The teacher creates an atmosphere in which students are able to construct knowledge, reflect on what they are learning, practice good citizenship, and build one another up in an academically and socially supportive atmosphere.

The student's role is to work with others to achieve common goals. Many students today come from small families where there is little of the give and take that occurs with brothers and sisters. They need to learn to share, give, listen, care, and experience the transcendent moments of life that come only when people are part of something larger than themselves. When students come to learn the skills of cooperation, projects, productions, committee work, and other experiences found at the heart of social studies are greatly facilitated.

Source: Adapted from D. Johnson and R. Johnson, *Circles of Learning* (Edina, MN: Interaction Book Company, 1998).

the peer group than exists when, for example, adults talk to children. What this means in simple terms is that adult language is far more complex than children's language; therefore, a child talking to another child does not take linguistic short-cuts, use sophisticated terminology, or assume years of experience. John Dewey noted that one of the biggest problems in teaching is the false assumption by teachers of experience on the part of students. All of this in no way diminishes the importance of your role as a teacher; it does, however, shift the center of gravity from you to the students, making your job one of organizer and facilitator of learning rather than lecturer or presenter.

➤➤ *Example: The American Revolution*

Three events that took place leading up to the American Revolution were the Boston Tea Party, the Battle of Lexington, and Paul Revere's ride. Each student group of three is assigned the responsibility of learning about all three events. Using the jigsaw strategy, each student within a group takes one of the events and studies it thoroughly. After each child has had an opportunity to study his or her respective event, the small groups are convened, and each student takes turns teaching his or her peers. You will need to coach your students in techniques for making the information they present interesting, significant, and involving. With practice, the students will improve their teaching, especially if they have learned a variety of teaching strategies that you have modeled.

Simulations

Simulations are an attempt to represent and model social systems, often through the medium of a game. Those social systems may be economic, political, spatial, or cultural, or they may be some sort of combination of systems. *Reality* is a key word in simulation activities. If students are to learn how a market system or a governing system works through their involvement in a simulation, then it is important that they not only play the roles and use the processes but also that those roles and processes accurately reflect the reality of the system they are intended to represent.

Of course, in all simulations some compromise must be reached between an attempt to represent the reality of a system and the limitations imposed by such factors as the age and maturity of the students, the resources available, the size of the classroom, and the constraints of time. Oversimplifying processes and interactions in order to make a simulation more exciting or easier can be dangerous. The key to developing effective simulation lies in the wise choice of exactly which elements of reality need to be included in order to make the activities valid, and which elements can be factored out as extraneous to the fundamental processes involved.

Thus, in any social system you choose to model—or in any simulations you select for use in social studies—it is crucial that you determine whether the elements included accurately represent the ideas you think children should learn about that system. One way to ensure that this happens is to determine exactly what your learning and valuing objectives are and to choose or develop a simulation on that basis.

▶▶ *Example: The Bicycle Path Simulation*

This simulation is not tied to any particular textbook or unit of study. Its rules are as follows:

1. A bicycle path will be built from the Lower Town to the Little Red School House (see Figure 7.6). The proposed path will enable the children who live in Lower Town to ride their bikes to school.

FIGURE 7.6

*Gameboard for
Bicycle Path
Simulation*

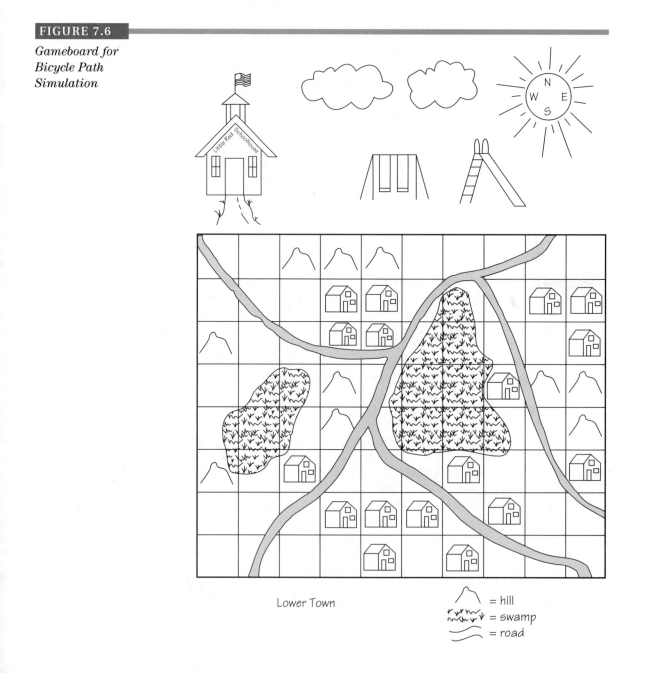

Lower Town

⌢ = hill
〰 = swamp
〰 = road

2. The problem is that several obstacles lie along the way from Lower Town to the school. Those obstacles are hills, swamps, roads, and houses.

3. City engineers do not want to build the path over hills because doing so raises construction costs. The Wildlife League does not want the path built through swamps because it might harm animal habitats. The Safety Commission does not want the path to cross streets because that would be dangerous to young bikers. The Housing Commission does not want the path built through people's homes and yards.

4. Each student is assigned one of the four roles listed above: city engineer, Wildlife League member, Safety Commissioner, or Housing Commissioner.

5. The object of the game is for each player to draw a path from *any* of the southernmost squares to any of the northernmost squares. For each square a player's path goes through, he or she must add 5 points to the total. In addition, players are penalized 5 points per square for each square they enter that causes problems for their particular role. For example, an engineer must add 5 points for every square with hills; a wildlife person must add 5 points for every square with swamps, a Safety Commissioner must add 5 points for every square with streets, and a Housing Commissioner must add 5 points for every square with houses. Thus, for an engineer, a square with hills in it costs 10 points—5 for the square and 5 for the hill.

▶ *Example: Starpower*

Starpower has been used extensively in age groups ranging from third grade to college graduates and business personnel. It is designed to set up a three-level, low-mobility socioeconomic society in which the low group remains low in power and the high group remains high in power and ultimately is allowed to make the rules for continuing the game. The wealthy power group generally makes rules that maintain its own wealth and power rather than benefit the poorer groups. The parallels with real-life society are startling and dramatic and are missed by few participants. Participation and interest are reliably high, with most participants becoming highly emotionally involved.

Although recommended for 18 to 35 participants, Starpower has been successfully used with groups as small as 13 and as large as 70 or 80. The use and abuse of power demonstrated by the game is particularly appropriate to a number of factions in today's society. Discussion during the debriefing of the highly stimulating activity is frequently intense and heated, even for young fifth- and sixth-graders. Although the facilitator's guide recommends a 50-minute period for playing Starpower, experience dictates that a 3-hour time block should be allowed, excluding preparation time of about 30 minutes. At least one hour should be allowed for debriefing and discussion, since emotionally charged topics often occur and should be dealt with thoroughly during the course of the debriefing.

During the game, interaction among the participants is spirited, is basically cooperative within each of the three groups, and is allowed to occur naturally with little or no outside control on what is said or what roles are portrayed. The roles of the three groups are allowed to develop naturally along the lines dictated by the power structure involved. Overall, this is an excellent simulation that would be highly recommended for fourth grade or higher. For information, contact Simile II, 1155 Silverado, La Jolla, CA 92037.

▶▶ *Example: Bafá Bafá*

In this simulation, participants are divided into two groups. Each group is taught certain rules and develops its own culture. Then visitors are exchanged to experience the foreign culture instituted by the other group. The game helps students understand the meaning of the term *culture* in graphic and physical ways, understand how cultural misunderstandings and miscommunications occur, and how stereotypes and cultural prejudice evolve.

Although the simulation seems complex at first to participants, after a few minutes of practice at their given culture, participants find the simulation enjoyable, exciting, and interesting. The cultural exchange and subsequent debriefing provide many opportunities for the eliciting of cultural stereotypes and misunderstandings and provide for an emotional understanding of what it is like to be a visitor to another culture. Bafá Bafá also helps illustrate that values are culture laden, and that neither culture is necessarily better, but merely different. This understanding is an important one for increasing world harmony in a modern technological society. This is an excellent cross-cultural simulation that has been used successfully with Peace Corps volunteers, teachers, legislators, and students; it is highly beneficial to understanding cultural attitudes and cultural norms. For information on Bafá Bafá, contact Simile II, 1150 Silverado, La Jolla, CA 92037.

Computer Simulations. Simulations have taken a great leap forward with the advent of videodiscs, games, and the whole theory of computers as learning environments in thems5elves. The early days of so-called drill-and-kill computer programs have come and gone; they have been replaced by exciting ways to access and interact with stored knowledge. The videodisc encyclopedia is a good example. A child reading about the origins of World War II can virtually watch and listen to President Franklin Roosevelt's speech to the nation following the attack on Pearl Harbor in 1941. Or a child using videodisc technology can suddenly find himself or herself on the banks of the Zambesi River in Africa, surveying the landscape.

At a heightened interactive level, computer simulations allow learners to take part in making decisions, solving problems, and otherwise applying their knowledge and skills to situations where they have consequences. Computer simulations range from those suitable for one or two students at a time to whole-class simulations. At their best, they represent situations much like those that students will encounter in real life. One of the first computer simulations to achieve widespread popularity was *Oregon Trail.* It is perhaps primitive by the standards of the new generation of simulations, but it remains no doubt one of the most played school-related simulation. Students take on roles of pioneers traveling west and must make decisions regarding food supplies, safety, health, and various other issues all along the trail. The idea is to survive and reach the Oregon Territory. Three of the most widely used and successful computer simulations of recent times are *Where in the World is Carmen Sandiego?*, *Sim City*, and *Science 2000* (see Figure 7.7).

Where in the World is Carmen Sandiego? begins with the whole class playing the game, which is projected from the computer onto a large monitor or screen. The students practice observation, note taking, and other skills needed to capture the wily criminal, Carmen Sandiego. The teacher guides the class at first, teaching students to use reference materials that they will need for tracking and apprehending the criminal. Because Carmen Sandiego travels all over the world, geographic

FIGURE 7.7

Screen Shot and Text from **Where in the World is Carmen Sandiego?**

Welcome to the

DISCOVER Carmen Sandiego, where the chase first began in popular computer software games by Brøderbund Software.

LEARN about countries and cultures as you search for the elusive Carmen in beautiful locations, rich with history, culture and music. Software, educational television shows and other Carmen products are available worldwide.

Where in the World is Carmen Sandiego? A PBS television game show for kids that builds knowledge of geography; on air for 5 seasons; nominated for 7 Emmys and won in 1995 and 1996; airs in local languages in four countries.

As kids chase Carmen Sandiego and her gang through countries around the globe, or through all 50 United States and Washington DC, kids learn about *geography and cultures*. Carmen has also been known to challenge kids to learn more about history, music, and the solar system.

Carmen Sandiego began her career in 1985 as an original character in an innovative detective software game that broadened kids' knowledge of geography and cultures. Carmen products have been translated into three languages and over 5 million copies have been sold into schools and homes worldwide. Carmen is one of the ongoing success stories of Brøderbund Software, that has worked to spark the imaginations of children and adults for over 15 years.

knowledge builds as the game proceeds. In time, students work in pairs to solve the problem and to prepare a report about the state or region they have researched.

Sim City (and a related simulation, *Sim Earth*) places students in the roles of planners and builders of cities. They must take into account the systems upon which cities depend, including transportation, water, industry, communications, recreation, and residences. Problems occur along the way that must be solved, whether they be traffic congestion, water supply, inadequate residential zoning, or whatever. The complexities introduced in *Sim City* give students a far more sophisticated sense of urban planning, development, and maintenance than they could obtain in less interactive ways.

Science 2000 is a thematic curriculum that uses hypertext databases connected to videodiscs. Students encounter problems found in real life, including pollution, fragile ecosystems, water supplies, soil conditions, climate factors, and so on. The approach is based on cooperative group learning in which students take on roles ranging from farmers, developers, elected officials, and law enforcement personnel, to naturalists and representatives of the Environmental Protection Agency. The rich databases enable the students to access information useful in representing their positions and reaching decisions made in the best interests of society.

Observations on Indirect Instruction

The strengths of the indirect instructional strategies are exemplified by the contrasts between direct and indirect instruction. Although the contrasts seem on the surface to be heavily weighted in favor of indirect instruction as a way to learn, keep in mind that it is not practical for students to use any one strategy exclusively. Knowledge of events, eras, and places and explanations of spatial, cultural, and economic systems, which are certainly major objectives of a social studies program, are often better suited to direct teaching. Perhaps the major contribution of indirect learning is that it gives students opportunities to become involved in the processes used in the formation of knowledge. Such intimate contact with knowledge formation gives learners an important perspective as they read, see, and hear what others have to show and tell them about human beings through books, films, lectures, and other sources of information. But when the subject lends itself to indirect learning, the rewards of this democratic learning strategy are great for both the facilitator/teacher and for the active, independent learners.

Summary

This chapter defined and illustrated a wide range of ways that you might teach and students might learn social studies. Two categories, direct and indirect instruction—each with numerous permutations—were developed. The search for curricular balance in teaching and learning is particularly important. Keep in mind as you combine lessons into units that students need a certain amount of meaningful reception learning balanced with a certain amount of construction of knowledge and meaning on their own part. It is also helpful to keep in mind the social aspects of social studies. Whenever possible, students should learn and work together. A final thought is that yet another kind of balance should be sought: one that ensures that students learn through verbal modes, through construction and related activities, and through productions and presentations that they carry out themselves.

ACTIVITIES

1. Analyze a unit in a teacher's guide. How many teaching/learning alternatives does it suggest? How could you enhance the unit or otherwise improve on it using the suggestions found in this chapter?

2. Choose a key idea or concept from one of the social sciences. For example, you might choose the concept of *culture* from anthropology. Briefly describe at least five different strategies you could employ in order to teach the concept. Try to achieve balance in your choice of strategies.

3. Try teaching one or more of the example lessons or activities illustrated in this chapter.

4. Discuss with a partner, a small group, or your class the issue of how a teacher decides how much time to devote to particular strategies in teaching social studies.

5. Return for a moment to Figure 7.1. Discuss with several other people the educational implications of the suggestions listed.

NOTES

1. See John Goodlad, *A Place Called School* (New York: McGraw-Hill, 1983).
2. Mark Schug et al., "Why Don't Kids Like Social Studies?" *Social Education, 48* (1984): 382–387.
3. Jeffrey Fouts, "Classroom Environments and Student Views of Social Studies: A Replication Study," *Theory and Research in Social Education* (Spring 1989): 136–147.
4. John Dewey, *Democracy and Education* (New York: Macmillan, 1916).
5. Thanks to Anne DeGallier for many of the suggestions for the Westward Movement differentiated assignment.

SUGGESTED READINGS

Bolen, J. (1999). "Taking Students Seriously." *Social Studies and the Young Learner, 11* (Jan./Feb.): 6–8.

Lederer, J. (2000). "Reciprocal Teaching of Social Studies in Inclusive Classrooms." *Journal of Learning Disabilities, 33* (Jan./Feb.): 91–106.

Marzano, R. (2000). "20th Century Advances in Instruction," In R. Brandt, ed., *Education in a New Era* (pp. 67–96). Washington, DC: Association for Supervision and Curriculum Development.

Matthews, D. (1999). "What We Are Learning about How Children Learn, and What This Means for Teachers." *Education Canada, 39* (Spring): 35–37.

Szepkouski, G. (1999). "The Minisociety Classroom." *Teaching Exceptional Children, 32*: 34–37.

Assessing
Student Progress

The role of assessment, even its very meaning, has changed considerably in recent years. The nation-wide standards movement and the identifying of standards at state and district levels have created a much clearer sense of the goal structure of social studies and other subjects in the school curriculum. Accompanying the implementation of standards has been the development of performance assessment criteria. As a result, the relationship between stated goals and measured outcomes is more tightly coupled than it was in the past.

Meaningful assessment is a logical extension of effective planning and teaching. Still, a problem exists at the level of childhood education because it is never easy to determine what young children know using either traditional or innovative measures. We know that their thinking abilities typically transcend their abilities to read and write. This chapter addresses that very issue. The major focus is upon authentic, integrated assessment strategies. In that sense, many of the techniques I will propose are themselves activities for teachers and students in the spirit of teaching, learning, and assessment as seamless whole. The following topics are addressed:

- 20 Integrated authentic assessment strategies

"I learned" statements	Record keeping
Key idea identification	Self-reporting
The week in review	Circle meetings
Pyramid discussion	Question authoring
I can teach	Journal entries
Parents on board	Learning illustrated
Search for meaning	Thinking aloud
Thank you	Displays
Clear and unclear windows	Spot-check inventories
Choices and feelings	

- Performance assessment
    Teachers and parents as partners
    Types of formal assessment
    Portfolios

I guess I lost track of the time.

—A child's assessment of why she came back late from recess.

159

Assessing

Assessment is best perceived as a natural and logical part of the teaching/learning process. Try not to think of it as something set apart or as a kind of "outside event." Perceptions of assessment as integrated into the routine of school life are not easily held, given the experiences we've all had with tests through the years. Let's consider three key questions about assessment. *Why* should we assess? *What* should we assess? *How* should we assess?

Assessment: An Overview

Why Assess?

Many people feel that nothing takes the joy out of learning more than a test. There is some merit to this sentiment, especially where young children are concerned. Children are often not test-wise and may not understand school assessment purposes in general. They tend to see the world as a whole, and only gradually do they begin to perceive that there are activities and there are tests. As this unfortunate dualism becomes a reality, some children, often high achievers, fall prey to learning not for its own sake but for getting good grades. Others find assessment interventions as traumatic, worrisome, or lacking in meaning.

Of course, there is another side to this argument. There are compelling reasons why we do assess student progress. First of all, individuals need to know how they are doing. Their parents need and want to know as well. And you need to know to what extent your students are learning important ideas, skills, and content. Your own concerns will range from the professional to the personal as you consider your students' progress. Finally, there is the role of assessment as a means of getting your students to take learning seriously, to realize that accountability is a fact of life.

What Should Be Assessed?

The question of what to assess is not as simple as it may seem at first glance. You can't assess everything. This argues for strategic use of assessment. In social studies, we can start with the standards as our long-term goal structure. From there, we consider the age level and the specific course of study at a particular grade. Within that structure lie the various units you will teach during the year. And finally, we come to the day-to-day experiences. So when we arrive at the place where you and your students are involved concretely in reading, discussing, writing, constructing, and otherwise performing in some meaningful manner, we can reflect on the idea that goals, plans, activities, and assessment make up our social studies curriculum. Further, we can reflect on tile idea that each of these separate pieces must be joined together in ways that make sense. The flow looks something like this:

How Should We Assess?

Let's say, for example, that one of your unit teaching objectives is: "Students will develop a sense of chronology or time order." This objective fits NCSS Standard II, "Time, Continuity, and Change" (see Chapter 3). Obviously, your plans will call for activities that give your students opportunities to develop their sense of time. Such activities might include having students make time lines of their lives to date with speculation about their lives into the future, or family trees showing parents, grandparents, and other relatives. Another activity might include a whole-class project on the history of the community and how local history fits into state, national, and world history. Assessments might include writing or otherwise explaining how time lines or family trees work. The point is that goals, objectives, plans, activities, and assessments should be aligned.

So when you think of how you should assess, think of how you should teach, how your students should learn, and keep the assessment procedures in line with experiences. A balanced curriculum will contain a balance of experience, including reading, writing, listening, speaking, constructing, inquiring, and performing. In addition, keep in mind that some experiences are individualistic and some are collaborative. A balanced curriculum leads naturally to balanced assessment.

CHECK-UP

Mr. Hayward, a fourth-grade teacher, brought a large number of Brazilian artifacts to class one day. He placed them on a display table in a corner of the room. The students eagerly examined the artifacts and asked their teacher many questions. He said he would rather let them guess about them for a while. On the next day, Mr. Hayward gave two artifacts each to small groups of four and asked the groups to consider the following questions: (1) How are the two artifacts alike and different? (2) Who might use them? (3) What uses might they have? (4) How many uses can you suggest for them? On the third day, he told the name and use of each artifact and explained that the items were from Brazil. He told the class that they would be involved in a unit on Brazil and he just wanted them to be inquirers. He said he was pleased with their guesses and their active involvement.

To evaluate the outcome of this experience, Mr. Hayward gave the class a test in which he selected 20 of the artifacts, numbered them, and asked the students to write the name and use of each artifact beside its number on a sheet of paper.

How fair was this test to the learners? Choose one of the following responses and defend your choice in the space provided.

1. This test was fair to the learners.
2. The test was somewhat fair to the learner.
3. The test was unfair to the learners.

_____

_____

_____

_____

I choose Response 2. Mr. Hayward was not totally fair because he tested only for the third day's experience. Before that, he had the students hypothesizing, probing relationships, communicating in groups, and making inferences. After they engaged in these high-level activities, he tested the students only on their ability to recall. If you chose Response 3, I can certainly sympathize with you. If you chose Response 1, as Mr. Hayward obviously did, I think you made a very common error—you defended an assessment strategy that is attractive because the test is easily developed, is easily scored, and provides an objective progress check. Unfortunately, the students deserved more in this case.

This check-up example illustrates an essentially invalid test. For an assessment to be valid, it must be <u>a representative measure of the material that was taught</u>. Mr. Hayward had three days of instruction, but his test measured only the learning that took place during a portion of that time. He used an <u>inquiry-teaching strategy</u> but not an inquiry-testing strategy.

What could Mr. Hayward have done to make his assessment strategy valid? He overlooked a simple procedure, which, if followed, helps ensure that assessments provide accurate reflections of potential learning outcomes. Objectives, activities, and assessment must parallel one another. Take a moment to study Figure 8.1.

For a portion of the inquiry activity, Mr. Hayward might have stated the following objective: "Students will be able to state ways in which two artifacts are alike and different." The statement of such an objective, clearly present in the activity in which the students were involved, would have helped focus the assessment. Obviously, another objective was the following: "Students will be able to list the name and use of each artifact." As we saw, the teacher taught toward that objective and tested for it.

teaching testing strategies need to line up.

FIGURE 8.1

Relationship of Objectives, Activities, and Assessment

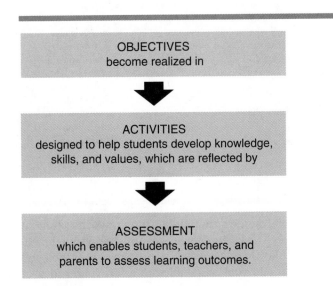

OBJECTIVES
become realized in

ACTIVITIES
designed to help students develop knowledge,
skills, and values, which are reflected by

ASSESSMENT
which enables students, teachers, and
parents to assess learning outcomes.

Following are a sample objective, some activities, and a test item that Mr. Hayward might have used to assess learning outcomes other than recall of information.

- *Objective.* Students will be able to state ways in which two artifacts are alike and different.
- *Activities.* Students discuss and record similarities and differences between two artifacts in small groups. Student groups share their analyses with the class. The teacher helps students consider the physical properties, form, and potential uses of artifacts.
- *Sample assessment.* The teacher gives groups two new artifacts and asks them to record differences and similarities.

You may be wondering about the propriety of such a group assessment procedure. Remember that the students learned in groups. They should therefore be given some opportunity to illustrate how effective that strategy was. This is not to say that all group activities need to be tested in groups. However, some provision should be made for such a procedure if for no other reason than students should sense that you have confidence in group activities as a way to learn effectively.

CHECK-UP

Let's continue by considering two questions: (1) Should children's learning in social studies be evaluated? and (2) Why or why not? To answer the first question, place a check at the point on the continuum that describes your feelings.

| Elementary students should *never* be assessed in social studies. They should just enjoy it and learn what they will. Tests are evil. | Low-key assessment is okay, but not formal tests. | Some form of assessment is necessary—not always in the form of tests. A wide variety of measures should be used. | Formal tests are necessary, but other measures can be used to supplement assessment by tests. | Elementary students *must* be assessed by formal tests. Letter grades are necessary in order to assess student progress, and only formal assessment procedures can give reliable grades. |

Authentic Assessment Strategies

For the teacher of elementary social studies, authentic, integrated assessment strategies are completely necessary. They accomplish several important teaching/learning goals at once. They enable you to get a clearer picture of how well you are teaching. They provide both you and your students with a far clearer idea of how well you and they are learning. They promote a reflective atmosphere in which you and students begin to become more consciously aware of what is being learned and how meaningful it is. (This is known as *metacognition*, or thinking about thinking.) And they help provide a classroom experience that is itself more integrated and seamless. I can tell you this: If you use these strategies faithfully, two things of great and lasting significance will happen. First of all, student achievement will increase. You will definitely see improvement on standardized tests. Second, the social/moral fabric of life in your classroom will be improved. Your classroom will be a better place for you and your students, and citizenship will be something real, not just an academic study.

"I Learned" Statements

This is a simple and durable strategy and one you should use often. At the end of an activity or lesson, ask your students to write down (or tell you if they are too young) something they learned. When you have your students write down what they learned and turn in the paper, you have given each student the opportunity to think about the experience and to reflect on it. You will also notice that the aggregate of what gets turned in is an excellent measure of what your students thought was significant. Don't be disappointed if the first time you try this, many students don't write or say anything. Why should they? No one ever asked them such a question. They will get the idea in time. Use "I learned" statements a couple of times a week—in other words, often enough to keep the students thinking that you just might ask them following any given experience.

Key Idea Identification

At the close of a lesson or activity, ask your students to explain, preferably in writing if they can, what they think was the key idea. The researcher John Goodlad has faulted teachers for failing to teach ideas. That can't happen if you teach your lessons with a key idea in mind, and you ask your students to identify it. Don't worry if they identify something other than you were looking for or if different students identify different key ideas. That becomes the essence of a good discussion. By using this strategy from time to time, you will raise your own level of consciousness about the importance of ideas in learning while you raise your students' consciousness.

The Week in Review

This is a small-group assessment strategy best done on every Friday afternoon. Place students in groups of two or three and challenge them to look back over the week with the idea of identifying some of the most important things the class did and learned. Each group should submit a written statement or should be asked to explain their findings. When the students know that they always reflect back on the week, they begin to think about what they are doing and learning during the week, especially if you remind them that on Friday, they will do the Week in Review. It makes a great way for you to begin on Monday. You start the week by saying, "Well, here were the big stories from last week. Let's see what happens this week."

Pyramid Discussion

Have you ever thought of class discussion as assessments? Probably not, if for no other reason than that most class discussions involve only the teacher and a handful of more talkative students. But what if you wanted everyone to discuss and reflect? Here's how you can do it. Begin by asking or writing on the board one or two important questions related to what your students should be learning. Place students in groups of two and have them discuss the questions. When the groups of two have had a chance to discuss, place students in groups of four and have them discuss the same questions. Groups of eight come next, discussing the same question. Then we go to the whole class. This accomplishes two things. First of all, everyone has a chance to talk. Second, if the questions are important, then the students should have the chance to consider and reconsider them. By the time you reach whole-class discussion, everyone will have had an opportunity to think through something important.

I Can Teach

We've all heard the expression, "The best way to learn something is to teach it." There is some profound wisdom in the saying, for teaching involves expression and performance, two commodities often sadly lacking in school learning. So, the assignment is for the students to teach an idea, skill, or some content they have learned in social studies to someone else. Typically, you would ask your students to teach one of their parents or a brother or sister. This accomplishes the goal of having your students revisit what you taught them from a different perspective, that of a teacher.

Parents on Board

Social studies is a natural subject area to share with parents. To accomplish this strategy, send a letter home to parents, saying that once a week you would like them to listen while their child tells them about what is being studied at school. It is really very helpful if you are able to suggest an activity that they can do together. For example, if you ask parents to go for a walk with their child and to make a map together, you might be surprised with what you've accomplished as a result.

Search for Meaning

One of the most important assessment strategies you can utilize is to search for meaning in learning. From time to time you need to ask your students to write (or tell) you what they are learning that is meaningful to them. This takes trust on your part and theirs, but I guarantee you that it is rewarding. Ideally, all learning should be meaningful, but we know that is not always the case. However, as a search for meaning becomes a part of the goal structure for you and your students, meaning will begin to develop if for no other reason than that you and they are looking for it.

Thank You

There is a powerful idea known as *serial reciprocity*. Simply put, it means that if someone does something kind, helpful, or thoughtful for you, you need to pass it along. This is different from merely giving back directly to the person who helped you. It goes around and comes around. This is an assessment technique that will in time make your classroom a truly civil place to be. It is based on the notion that in a classroom everyone is a teacher in one way or another. We can all help each other. Make it part of the routine to encourage students to write or draw thank-you notes and notes of appreciation to each other. You might be surprised how many come your way!

Clear and Unclear Windows

Have you ever tried to look through a window that was dusty, dirty, or foggy? You can't see much, can you? Or have you ever noticed a child whose glasses are so smudged that you wonder how he can see anything? Sometimes social studies can be that way for some students. Why not ask your students now and then how "clear" things are? Give them an opportunity to show you by putting some things that they understand in a clear window and things that are hard for them in an unclear window. Here is an example of Sarah's windows.

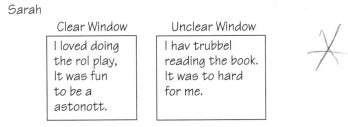

Sarah

Clear Window	Unclear Window
I loved doing the rol play, It was fun to be a astonott.	I hav trubbel reading the book. It was to hard for me.

Choices and Feelings

At the end of a lesson or at the end of a week, give your students a few minutes to reflect on the choices they were able to make in social studies. Did they get to decide anything? What was it? How do they feel about how things are going? Let them express their feelings in a brief note or conversation with you.

Record Keeping

Record keeping uses Skinnerian reinforcement techniques and, at the same time, turns a measure of responsibility over to the student. In order to carry out accurate individualized record keeping, your students will need to record the assignments they have completed, the score or grade they received on each assignment, the pages they have read, the films they have seen, the books they have read, the projects they have participated in, the maps they have made, and so forth. It sounds complicated, doesn't it? It's not, though, if you have your students record each item as soon as they complete it or as soon as you return it to them. I would also encourage you to have your students make a brief notation beside each entry. The notation should include the main idea or most important point of the activity. Here is an example.

Noah M.
Social Studies Record

Date	Assignment	Grade	Note
Mon. 6th	Film on traffic safety		Don't just depend on cars to stop for you.
Tue. 7th	Worksheet on traffic safety	100%	Rights and responsibilities of pedestrians
Wed. 8th	Make map of crosswalks by Oak Point School	A	My map shows what the crosswalks look like, only flat.

I guess every teacher wants to teach his or her students ways of becoming more responsible. Record keeping is a tangible way to do that. It is also a kind of metacognitive strategy, because it enables students to increase their awareness of the work being done in social studies.

Self-Reporting

An obvious but often overlooked assessment strategy is to have students assess their own progress. It's their work after all; why not let them help to assess it? Self-reporting gives students an opportunity to be analytical about their own progress. A good self-report should deal with both the strengths and weaknesses of progress as viewed by the student.

Because self-analysis is rarely encouraged in school settings, you will have to be patient at first. In fact, some students may even consider self-reporting inappropriate. But what, after all, is the purpose of learning if it is not to encourage independence on the part of the learner? I think that in time you will be gratified with the ability students develop in this area. Following is an example of a self-report turned in by a fourth-grade student.

February 10
Mark Goldberg

I liked learning about the feudal economy. I'm glad we don't have it anymore though. The best thing I did was when Jason, Maria, and me made the feudal manor out of cardboard. I really did a lot of work and so did everyone. We showed where the lord of the manor lived and where the serfs were. The poor serfs loved holidays. So do I! Do you know where we got most of our information? We got it out of a book called *Life in Medieval Times*. Part of it was hard to understand.

Circle Meetings

The circle meeting is a very helpful way to gauge the class's feelings and thoughts about how things seem to be going. Everyone's seat, including yours, is arranged in a circle. You begin the meeting by telling about what you have been trying to accomplish and how you think it is going. After your introduction, simply go around the circle and give each child an opportunity either to say something or to "pass" if he or she does not wish to talk. Don't be discouraged if, at your first try, the children do not offer up gems of wisdom and insight. They will, in time, if you are patient and supportive. This technique, which draws on Vygotsky's ideas of social intelligence, is one of the surest ways of getting at the truth of things based on the group's collective perceptions and impressions. Primary school-age children take to this format naturally. By the intermediate grades, some children have become reluctant to speak up in a group setting. Your job is to overcome that unfortunate phenomenon. Circle meetings take anywhere from 10 minutes to an hour, depending on how deeply the class gets into the matters at hand. Once a week is probably a good target for circle meetings.

Question Authoring

This seldom-used strategy can provide brilliant insights to your students' sense of what is important and just how curious they have become about learning. Simply ask the children to write down (orally with young children) any questions they would like to ask about the content and experience in general. This activity provides you with a context for telling the class about higher-level questions. In time, if you are patient, you will see a tremendous improvement in the nature of children's questions. Also, many of the questions they raise will help you with your teaching because the children are, in effect, acting as diagnosticians for you.

Journal Entries

One of the greatest improvements in teaching and learning in the past few years has been the idea of student journals. Although journals serve a variety of purposes, they are quite useful as an assessment tool. Encourage students to make entries about the subject matter they are studying, including their feelings about it as well as their thoughts and ideas. Their entries provide them with an ongoing record of their perceptions of social studies. You should collect student journals periodically and make brief comments of encouragement and support.

Learning Illustrated

At least once a week you should ask your students to draw a picture or make a map of something interesting or important that they have learned recently in social studies. Their drawings and maps make excellent displays, and they should find their way into the students' portfolios in time. It is important to remember that some children who may not be adept verbally are actually learning a lot, and this provides one way for them to show it.

Thinking Aloud

The simple technique of thinking aloud is one of the best ways to prevent the "in one ear and out the other" syndrome that seems to haunt children's learning of social studies (not to mention other subjects!). This should be a 5- to 10-minute activity in which you ask students to talk and listen with a partner about what they are learning. Sometimes you may want to place a question or two on the board for them to discuss. However, if you leave the discussion open, you will find that you get a wider range of student input. It is useful to have a class discussion following the thinking-aloud session in which students can volunteer aspects of their talk together.

Displays

It has been noted that doing schoolwork is like preparing for an athletic event or a drama production that never happens. You just prepare. Imagine spending time rehearsing a play and never putting it on. Doesn't that strike you as strange? But this is what happens with schoolwork all the time. Perhaps this is one reason it seems unreal to some children. You might be surprised at the number of nursing homes, hospitals, clinics, restaurants, shopping malls, stores, and so on that would welcome the chance to display your students' work. Parents and children alike are proud when they see student work put on public display. By the way, it is very good public relations for the school.

Spot-Check Inventories

The spot-check inventory is a simple strategy that allows you to obtain from your students a brief synthesis about what they think they have learned during a particular amount of time. To do a spot-check inventory, merely stop whatever is going on at a given time (class discussion, group work) and ask each student to list several things that he or she has learned during the activity. Be patient and allow students to become better at this metacognitive strategy over time.

Younger children will simply have to tell you what they have learned as you list their thoughts on the board. Older children can write down their own lists to share with the class. A useful alternative to the listing approach is to have students write a paragraph or essay telling what they have learned. The example in Figure 8.2 was written by a Scottish girl, Diane, age 9, after a discussion about life in America.

Assessing Assessment

Perhaps at this point you are thinking something like, "OK, Arthur, those may be good metacognitive strategies for assessing student learning, but where on earth am I supposed to find the time for them?" I have an answer for you. The saying "Less is more" is really quite profound. It has been attributed to Theodore Sizer, a leader in the school restructuring movement. The idea is actually rather an old one, dating back at least to Jean Rousseau, who wrote in the preface to his book *Emile*, "Teachers, teach less and teach well." A so-called coverage mentality is self-defeating. The more you try to cover, the less your students will learn and retain. The strategies I have presented here are time consuming, but they have several advantages.

First, they will facilitate language development, one of the most important goals of teaching. As Piaget, Vygotsky, and others have pointed out, children need to reflect and talk about about what they are learning. Speech and thought co-develop; they are not separate functions. So, by giving children time to talk about, draw about, and reflect in general on what they are learning, you actually create a more efficient system. Second, one the major goals of social studies is to build opportunities for citizenship. The participating citizen is basic to our democratic way of life. The kinds of activities and conversations you focus on during assessment of learning represent

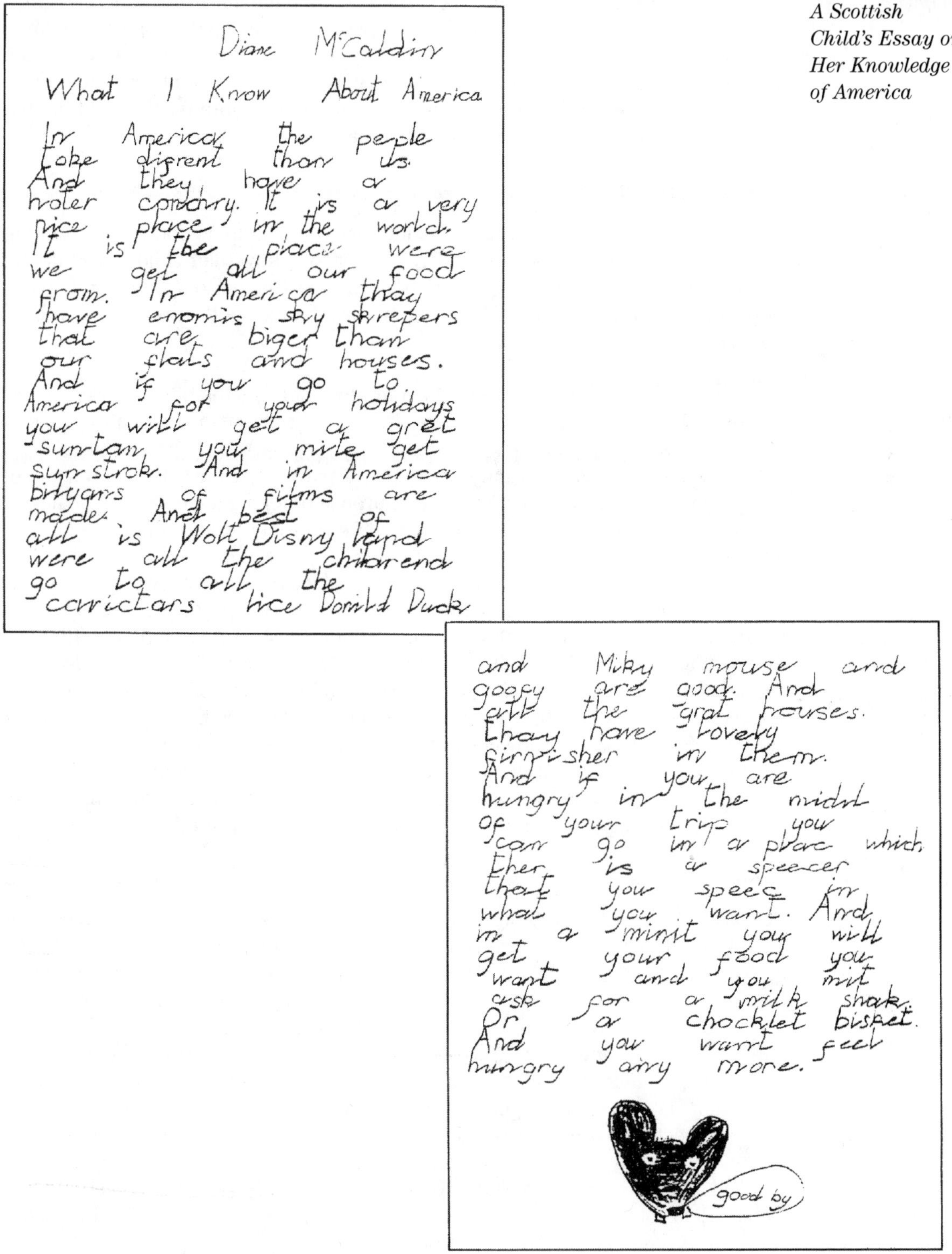

FIGURE 8.2

A Scottish
Child's Essay on
Her Knowledge
of America

Diane M'Calldin

What I Know About America

In America the peple
are diffrent than us.
And they have a
holer condiry. It is a very
nice place in the world.
It is the place were
we get all our food
from. In America thay
have enormis sky skrepers
that are biger than
our flats and houses.
And if you go to
America for your holidays
you will get a grét
suntan. you mite get
sun strok. And in America
billyans of films are
made. And best of
all is Wolt Disny land
were all the chidrend
go to all the
carrictars lice Donald Duck

and Miky mouse and
goofy are good. And
all the grat houses.
Thay have lovery
firnisher in them.
And if you are
hungry in the midst
of your trip you
can go in a place which
ther is a speecer
that you speec in
what you want. And
in a minit you will
get your food you
want and you mit
ask for a milk shak.
Or a chocklet bispcet.
And you want feel
hungry any more.

good by

fundamental practice in speaking one's mind and in publicly expressing oneself. Third, if you are patient, you will begin to see a group intelligence start to emerge— something that simply cannot happen when people are denied the opportunity to reflect on and talk about ideas publicly. So, yes, it does take time. Anything worthwhile takes time. My advice is to take these strategies seriously and integrate them into your teaching. It will mean less talking time for you and more for the children, but since their growth and development is at stake, it is well worth it.

Teachers and Parents as Partners

Parents send their children to you, hoping that you will do a good job of teaching them. In most cases, they are extremely interested in how their children are doing. Report cards give parents a sense of a child's progress, but only a general sense. Here are several strategies you can use to inform parents of the progress their children are making in social studies:

- *Send a note home.* If someone in your class did a nice job on an assignment, worked effectively in a group, or whatever, send a brief note home that explains to the parents what happened.
- *Make a phone call.* You and your students' parents are busy people. But a one-minute phone call in the evening for the purpose of telling a child's parent that he or she is doing very well (it helps to be specific) in social studies doesn't take very much of anyone's time, and it will be appreciated.
- *Have a conference.* In most schools, conferences are used once or twice a year for the purpose of reporting pupil progress. It is important to be prepared for such an important meeting. First, don't sit behind your desk at a conference—it is too threatening and official—rather, sit at a table with the parent. Try to be positive; remember, you are discussing the parent's own child. If you do have some negative comments, be sure that they are specific and that they are not a personal attack against the child. Balance any negative comment with something positive. Perhaps the most important thing at a conference is to have numerous examples of the child's work. Parents are impressed with maps, artwork, and so forth. Above all, express genuine interest in the child. That won't be hard, because you really do care.

Tests

The assessment procedures described to this point are essentially unobtrusive; that is, they are designed not to interrupt the flow of teaching/learning activities. Tests, on the other hand, are generally perceived by students as special events for which they often must prepare and that have an air of finality. If you use formal tests, you should make sincere efforts to reduce the anxiety that many children associate with testing by emphasizing the diagnostic and remediative functions tests can serve. Keep in mind that your success as a teacher depends to a great extent on your students' success in acquiring skills and developing ideas and that this success is only reflected by well-constructed tests. Therefore, good planning and teaching lead quite logically to student success on tests.

There are essentially two types of formal tests: essay tests and objective tests. Robert Ebel lists certain advantages and disadvantages of the two types of tests in his book *Measuring Educational Achievement*.[1]

- An essay test question requires students to plan their own answers and to express them in their own words. An objective test item requires them to choose among several designated alternatives. (p. 84)
- An essay test consists of relatively few, more general questions that call for rather extended answers. An objective test ordinarily consists of many rather specific questions requiring only brief answers. (p. 87)
- Students spend most of their time thinking and writing when taking an essay test. They spend most of their time reading and thinking when taking an objective test. (p. 90)
- An essay examination is relatively easy to prepare but relatively tedious and difficult to score accurately. A good objective examination is relatively tedious and difficult to prepare but relatively easy to score accurately. (p. 92)
- An essay examination affords much freedom for students to express their individuality in the answers they give and much freedom for the scorer to be guided by individual preferences in scoring the answers. An objective examination affords much freedom for the test constructor to express his or her knowledge and values but gives students only the freedom to show, by the proportion of correct answers they give, how much or how little they know or can do. (p. 93)
- An essay test permits, and occasionally encourages, bluffing. An objective test permits, and occasionally encourages, guessing. (p. 93)
- The distribution of numerical scores obtained from an essay test can be controlled to a considerable degree by the grader; that from an objective test is determined almost entirely by the test. (p. 101)

Essay Tests

It is important to keep in mind that you should have at least two purposes in giving students an essay test. You want to gain some idea of how much they know. You also want to help your students learn to present their ideas in a logical and coherent manner. Here are some suggestions that may help you to achieve these two purposes:

1. Essay tests, because they require extended answers to few questions, should focus on main ideas from social studies experiences rather than on specifics. When you prepare for a unit, identify the main idea you wish students to learn. Essay items should parallel those main ideas.

> *poor:* What caused the fight between Peter and James? (This question seeks recall of a specific event.)

> *better:* Peter and James fought over who would take over Bob's paper route. List some reasons such conflicts happen. Tell how you think such conflicts can be avoided. (This question seeks students' understanding of the concept of *conflict*.)

2. Essay tests should be designed to elicit higher-level thinking from students. Such lower levels as recall are more easily tested for by objective tests.

> *poor:* Why were Iroquois longhouses made of wood? (This question seeks lower-level information that could be incorporated into a higher-level question.)

> *better:* Do you think an Iroquois longhouse is more like an apartment building or a one-family house in our culture? Tell why. (This question gives

students the opportunity to choose alternative answers and seeks criteria for the defense of the answer chosen.)

3. Essay test questions should be written in a clear and unambiguous way so children know what is expected of them. One way to ensure that your questions are reasonably clear is to list the criteria you will use in judging students' answers.

> *poor:* Discuss the causes of the American Revolution. (This question invites rambling answers and does not specifically seek alternative perspectives on the issue.)

> *better:* (a) List two reasons the colonists felt they should break away from England. Do you think those were good reasons? Why or why not? (b) List two reasons the English wanted to keep the colonies. Do you think those were good reasons? Why or why not? (Questions are broken down so specific criteria can be applied. Questions guide students toward developing reasons that reflect alternative perspectives.)

Objective Tests

Three types of items for objective tests are: (1) true-false, (2) multiple choice, and (3) matching. These three types of items have certain common characteristics. Tests containing such items are easily scored. A relatively high number of questions can be included on a test, thus ensuring adequate representation of topics and ideas. Elementary students who lack the capability to develop an essay that conveys their true understandings of a topic are often able to demonstrate their understandings by discriminating among alternative answers. Also, objective tests are potentially fairer than essay tests in that they prevent teachers from favoring student responses on the basis of penmanship, personality, or other essentially irrelevant variables.

Perhaps the greatest potential shortcoming of objective tests involves the tendency teachers have to develop questions that seek answers based only on recall or explanation. This is certainly a difficult obstacle to overcome, and a certain number of lower-level questions are acceptable on an objective test. However, if you taught higher-level thinking during a social studies unit, logically you should attempt to assess whether your students profited from that instruction. Let's examine the three types of objective test items and strategies for their effective development.

True-False. Following are some suggestions for developing true-false test items for social studies:

1. Statements should be entirely true or entirely false.

> *poor:* The population of California grew rapidly as settlers moved east during the gold rush of 1849.

> *better:* The population of California grew as settlers moved west during the gold rush of 1849.

2. Include only one idea or thought in a true-false item.

> *poor:* Producers offer both goods and services in our economy, and consumers help regulate supply and demand.

> *better:* Producers offer both goods and services in our economy.

3. Use terms that are clear and unambiguous.

   poor: Trading things is better than buying and selling.

   better: Trading goods and services is more common than using money in our
      country.

Multiple Choice. Multiple-choice tests permit inclusion of a wider range of possible answers to items than do true-false tests. Obviously, a person responding to
multiple-choice items has less chance of surviving questions on the basis of guess-
work. It is important that the test writer attempt to keep all potential responses
plausible and ensure that the stems to each item are parallel.

   poor: Persons everywhere have unlimited wants and limited resources. James
      and Heidi are persons who live in different countries.
   a. James and Heidi have unlimited wants and limited resources.
   b. James lives on the moon and Heidi lives in Switzerland.
   c. Heidi is a young girl.

   better: Persons everywhere have unlimited wants and limited resources. James
      and Heidi are persons who live in different countries.
   a. James and Heidi have unlimited wants and limited resources.
   b. James and Heidi can have all their material wants fulfilled.
   c. James and Heidi must produce all the goods that they consume.

Portfolio Assessment

One of the most promising ideas to come along in recent years is authentic assessment of learning. The term *authentic assessment* implies that the assessment
of student learning should be more reality based. This is not to say that standard
paper-and-pencil tests are of no value; rather, it is to say that the more natural
forms of assessment are not only less threatening to children but also make more
sense to them. Perhaps the best-known approach to authentic assessment is portfolio assessment.

   The idea of children putting together and keeping track of their own portfolios
comes from such professional areas as architecture and art. An architect keeps a
folder or portfolio of his or her sketches, designs, plans, drawings, photographs,
ideas, and so on. The architect will show the work to interested people who will
then decide if they want him or her to do architectural work for them. It is a way
of showing what one has accomplished and is capable of doing.

   For children in social studies classes, the building of a portfolio makes good
sense. A good portfolio will contain a variety of entries that provide a record of
authentic student accomplishments. Here are some suggestions for what a portfolio should contain:

   1. Student daily work samples; ordinary papers that are part of the daily routine
   2. Various data entries—for example, research notes, graphs, and surveys
   3. Student writing samples, such as essays and stories
   4. Rough drafts of work in progress
   5. Finished products, final drafts, and papers turned in for final grading

6. Group or cooperative efforts that illustrate the work of several students
7. Sample journal entries
8. Reflections, such as "I learned" statements
9. Tests, exams, and so on
10. Major projects or pictures of displays
11. Teacher comments and feedback
12. Creative thoughts, ideas, insights, and personal-growth reflections

Figure 8.3 also offers some thoughts on the type of work samples to keep in portfolios.

Each child is responsible for building and maintaining his or her own portfolio. Of course, some teacher guidance and support is necessary, especially with younger children, but it is important that children assume as much responsibility as they can for their portfolio.

Several interesting moral issues arise in connection with the keeping of portfolios. For example, whose property is the portfolio? Should the school keep it and pass it along to next year's teacher? Is it a private possession to be viewed only by the child and the teacher? Who decides what goes into the portfolio? Remember, a portfolio can, at most, hold a mere sample of the child's work. Should only his or her "best" work be included? These are important moral issues for you and your students to discuss.

My own position on ownership is that the portfolio belongs to the child, and it is his or hers to take home at year's end. Does the teacher have the right to examine the portfolio? I think, yes, he or she does, but I hope that the trust level is such in your classroom that the child wants you to see the portfolio. Actually, portfolios are wonderful to share with parents at conference time. As for the last question: What should go into the portfolio? I think it's the child's decision.

Assessing Your Own Effectiveness

When people think of assessment, such things as tests, conferences, and report cards typically come to mind. I've attempted to persuade you in this chapter that there is much more to assessment than that, even though those things are important. I do want to impress on you how meaningful informal assessment strategies can be. I hope that you will use them often.

FIGURE 8.3

Portfolios: Work Samples

- A sample that reflects a problem that was difficult for you
- Work that shows where you started to figure it out
- A sample that shows you reached a solution
- A sample that shows you learned something new
- A sample of incomplete work and where it will lead
- Two items of which you are proud
- An example of something that did not work out well

Let's now take the process of assessment a step further. How do you, the teacher, know whether you are doing an effective job of teaching your subject? I'd like to close this chapter by sharing some strategies that will help you probe deeper than most teachers ever go in assessing the effectiveness of their instruction.

These strategies are metacognitive strategies in that they enable you to think reflectively about your work. I'll pose them as questions for you to answer from time to time. In fact, I guarantee you that if you tape these questions to the top of your desk and read them occasionally, your teaching will improve. Here they are:

- Am I trying to learn more about the content I'm teaching? What books have I read lately?
- Am I talking with the children about how they feel about the material we are studying? Am I genuinely interested in their thoughts about social studies? Do I seek to know their interests?
- Are my lessons organized appropriately? Are we studying ideas in depth, or are we just covering the material?
- Do I attempt to make connections? Do I relate social studies to other areas of the curriculum? Do I attempt to build continuity from one day to the next?
- Am I teaching key ideas and concepts and not just information? What are some of those ideas?
- What values are the students and I exploring? Do we have conversations that take us into depth? When was the last time the children and I really explored feelings?
- Am I developing lessons and activities that allow for many ways to learn? Are my students involved in making things, talking to each other, doing cooperative projects, artwork, music, role-play, drama, and so on?
- Am I getting the students involved in making decisions and participating in democratic processes? Does my class ever get involved in the community?
- Am I making real readers out of my students? Do they read biographies, historical fiction, stories about other lands, and so forth?
- Would I want to be in this classroom if I were a child? Is this room an interesting place to come to every day?

These questions ought to shape your thoughts about social studies teaching. Ask them of yourself often. Take them seriously, but have fun with them as well. Relax and enjoy social studies. After all, as I told you earlier, social studies is about people, so it's a pretty exciting subject to teach.

Summary

Assessment of student learning in some form is necessary. If you are planning social studies experiences that focus on content, concepts, processes, and values, you and your students will certainly want to obtain some measure of their progress. The most effective way to assess student progress is to use a variety of measures.

Perhaps you have strong feelings about formal tests for children. If you feel they are harmful or ineffective, then you will need to depend more heavily on such unobtrusive measures as checklists, observations, and interviews. If you favor the use of formal tests, you will have to justify their use as an effective means of finding out how much learners really know. The balance you achieve among the various assessment measures available to you will be a function of your teaching style and the ages and capabilities of the students you teach.

ACTIVITIES

1. Interview some elementary school students. Discuss their attitudes toward testing and being tested. Is there a relationship between student success and attitude toward tests?
2. Make a list of some things children might do in social studies that cannot really be evaluated. Then figure out ways to evaluate the outcomes of those things.
3. Write an "I learned" statement about something you have learned in this chapter. Share it with someone.
4. Collect student social studies work from a number of classrooms. See what inferences you can make about what is happening in those classrooms.
5. Make a list of 10 different social studies activities. Have children rank-order them from most to least favorite.

NOTE

1. Robert Ebel, *Measuring Educational Achievement* (Englewood Cliffs, NJ: Prentice-Hall, 1965). Quoted in R. F. Biehler, *Psychology Applied to Teaching* (Boston: Houghton Mifflin, 1971), p. 388.

SUGGESTED READINGS

Brown, S., Race, P., and Smith, B. (1996). *500 Tips on Assessment*. London: Kogan Page Limited.

Fenwick, T. (1999). "A Note on Using Portfolios to Assess Learning." *Canadian Social Studies*, *33* (Spring): 90–92.

Glatthorn, A. (1998). *Performance Assessment and Standards-Based Curricula: The Achievement Cycle*. Larchmont, NY: Eye on Education.

Marzano, R. (2000). *Transforming Classroom Grading*. Washington, DC: Association for Supervision and Curriculum Development.

Trice, A. (2000). *A Handbook of Classroom Assessment*. New York: Longman.

Inquiry and Discovery: Children as Researchers

This chapter gives you the background necessary to use several inquiry procedures with your students. Specifically, you will read about and be involved with the following four types of social science inquiry:

- Inquiry and discovery defined
- Historical research
- Descriptive research
- Survey research
- Experimental research

These children can do wondrous things,
if only we would let them.
—Akmed Ahkbar

I In this chapter you will learn about several kinds of inquiry—historical, descriptive, survey, and experimental research—that social scientists use to refine and expand existing knowledge of human behavior. As you consider these ways in which children, too, can be researchers, note carefully the differences and similarities among the four types of research in respect to the following:

Data sources used
Data-gathering techniques
Data processing
Quantification of data
Inferences made from data gathered

Note also the level of active involvement expected of students in these approaches to learning. Consider the role of the learner as well as the role of the teacher. See if you can determine what types of skills and attitudes inquiry-learning experiences will develop in learners.

The inquiry tradition is an ancient one, dating back at least to Aristotle, who emphasized the use of the five senses in learning. In fact, although John Dewey is generally credited with the idea of "learning by doing," Aristotle himself wrote, "It is in doing that we learn best."

Sensory experience is fundamental to discovery learning, and all people employ it, at least in casual fashion, on a daily basis. If, for example, you decide to go for a walk, step outside, and realize you had better go back in the house for a coat, you are using sensory learning. You *felt* the chill or damp, or you *looked* at the sky, *saw* threatening clouds, and predicted rain. Perhaps you *heard* the wind whistling around the buildings or through the trees. Some people say they can *smell* rain in the air. These sensory experiences, of course, are direct encounters with the environment—a hallmark of discovery learning. The teacher who wants to emphasize discovery learning capitalizes on the built-in tendency for people to use their senses to help them learn. The keys to discovery learning in a school setting are twofold: (1) provide your students with sensory experiences and (2) help them develop the skills of systematic inquiry.

Fortunately, children are natural inquirers. They excel at the art. Unfortunately for them, most teachers spend no time on problem finding whatsoever. It is simply overlooked as a skill in school life. On the other hand, from the first day they enter school, children are given problems to solve. These "problems," which are actually exercises, appear in seemingly unlimited quantities in their workbooks and textbooks.

Let's see what we can do to remedy that. I think a good place to start the process of inquiry is with children's stories and nursery rhymes. For example:

> *Humpty Dumpty sat on the wall,*
> *Humpty Dumpty had a great fall.*
> *All the King's horses,*
> *And all the King's men,*
> *Couldn't put Humpty Dumpty*
> *Together again.*

Now, what exactly is the problem here? See if you can state it:

_____

_____

Incidentally, stating a problem does not have to be restricted to only those with writing skills. Figure 9.1 shows a 6-year-old's interpretation of the story of Humpty Dumpty.

Let's try another:

> *Mary had a little lamb*
> *Its fleece was white as snow.*
> *And everywhere that Mary went*
> *The lamb was sure to go.*
> *It followed her to school one day,*

FIGURE 9.1

A 6-Year-Old Child's Interpretation of the Sequence of "Humpty Dumpty"

Humpty Dumpty sat on a wall....

Humpty Dumpty had a great fall.

All the king's horses and all the king's men....

Couldn't put Humpty Dumpty together again.

Which was against the rule.
It made the children laugh and play
To see a lamb at school.

Can you state the problem?

_____

_____

Aesop (620–560 B.C.), a slave who lived in ancient Greece, collected and wrote a large number of animal fables that contained moral problems within them. Consider the story of the moles and porcupine:

> Once a porcupine asked a group of moles if he could live with them in their safe, snug, warm underground tunnels. Feeling sorry for the porcupine, the moles agreed to let him live with them. But the porcupine's quills stuck the moles, making them uncomfortable when they tried to sleep.

What is the problem? _____

Can you offer a solution? _____

_____

179

In the Gospel of Luke, Jesus tells the parable of the good Samaritan:

> A man was going down from Jerusalem to Jericho when he fell into the hands of robbers. They robbed and beat him, leaving him half dead. A priest going down the road saw the hurt man but crossed over to the other side to avoid him. Another man came along, and he too passed by the hurt man. But a Samaritan traveling the road stopped to help the hurt man. He bandaged his wounds, put the man on his donkey, and took him to an inn to take care of him. The next day, he gave the innkeeper two silver coins and asked him to care for the hurt man. He said if there were more expenses, he would pay for them when he returned from his business.

Can you state the problem or key issue in the story? _____

_____

Stories, parables, and nursery rhymes have been used for centuries to help children frame problems, think about right action, and consider moral issues. I encourage you to draw on the wealth of stories that already exist in folklore, fable, myth, and legend to find and solve problems with the children you teach.

Real and Contrived Problems

Now let's look at a few of the characteristics that distinguish *contrived* and *real* problem solving in the inquiry process. A contrived problem may deal effectively with the inquiry process; however, it is imposed on learners by the teacher or the program. A contrived problem does not arise directly from the life experiences of the students. Obviously, textbooks and other social studies programs cannot anticipate and make provision for the real problem issues that may confront a given group of students located in a particular geographic/economic/social setting at a particular time. Proponents of real problem solving point out that because the learners are attempting to deal with an issue that they helped to develop and that is part of their lives, the learning process has more meaning. Proponents of contrived problem solving point out, on the other hand, that many worthwhile issues in historical, economic, and anthropological inquiry might never come to the learners' attention if they had not been guided into them by a creative teacher working with a good program. Rather than take sides in an either/or dichotomy, let's assume that both approaches have their merits. Note the steps of inquiry process in the following two examples.

▶ *Activity: A Contrived Problem*

Before the formal introduction of a unit on Japan, a fourth-grade teacher brought a number of Japanese artifacts to the classroom. He divided the class into "research teams" of five students each. He gave each team three artifacts, which he asked them to spend a few minutes examining and discussing. He then placed the following questions on the board for each team to answer:

1. How would you describe each artifact?
2. How are the artifacts alike and different?

3. Are these artifacts like any tools that we use?
4. What uses would you guess these artifacts might have?
5. Who might use these artifacts?

The small groups of students discussed the questions and recorded their answers. As the discussion progressed, the teacher moved around the room and helped students focus on the analysis of the artifacts. When the discussion groups had completed their tasks, each group was given an opportunity to present its conclusions. When each group made its presentation, students from other groups were allowed to ask questions about the artifacts and their possible uses.

Later, each group developed a chart based on its speculations about the artifacts, and the chart and accompanying artifacts from each group were displayed in various areas of the room. The teacher asked the students to treat the statements on the charts as hypotheses that they would either accept or reject as the unit progressed and more information was acquired.

Thus, in this lesson, students are given a *problem*. The teacher *gathered appropriate data sources*, which the students examined. The students then *processed the data* through oral discussion and the development of their charts. The charts contained the students' *inferences*, which were to be treated as *hypotheses* that could later be verified.

▶ *Activity: A Real Problem*

One morning, members of a second-grade class were excitedly telling their teacher and each other about a near accident that had occurred at a pedestrian crossing next to their school. A primary-age child had nearly been struck by a car as she was crossing the street. The students exclaimed that the intersection was dangerous, especially during the winter months when ice and snow were present. The teacher asked the students if they would like to conduct an investigation of the intersection to see how dangerous it really was and to see if they could suggest ways to make it safer. The class agreed that this would be a worthwhile project.

Problem solving in social studies involves learners in a variety of shared experiences.

The class wrote a *statement of the problem* as follows: "How can our school crossing be made safer?" With the teacher's help, the class decided to use the following *data sources* in their research: a model of the intersection; the intersection itself; other students in the school; school staff members, including teachers, custodians, the principal, and the secretary; local residents; photographs of the intersection; and drivers who use the intersection. Working all together as well as in teams over the course of several weeks, the class *gathered data* through interviews, observation of traffic flow, timing the speed of cars near the intersection, and taking pictures of pedestrian, bicycle, and automobile traffic at peak crossing times before and after school. The students *processed their data* with a photo essay of the intersection, summaries of interviews, drawings of the intersection depicting the various problems they had discovered, and charts showing the volume of foot, bicycle, and auto traffic at peak hours. They *made the following inferences:*

1. The crossing is dangerous, especially for younger children, and a safety awareness campaign is needed.
2. Four safety patrol students should be placed on duty rather than two, the present number.
3. Larger, more visible warning signs should be posted along the streets leading to the intersection.
4. The crosswalk lines should be repainted.

Their report was given to the school principal and to the police department. The students were pleased to see that all four of their recommendations were enacted.

Differences and Similarities

Although these examples of contrived and real inquiry problems were intended as models rather than as exhaustive explanations of the possibilities inherent in each approach, let's take a moment to review their differences and similarities as teaching strategies.

The most obvious point of contrast is that the intersection investigation came directly from the life experiences of the students, whereas the artifact lesson was imposed on students at least partly in order to broaden their life experiences. A second contrast is found in the ways in which the students dealt with the steps in the inquiry process. In the artifact lesson, the statement of the problem, the selection of data sources, the means of gathering and processing data, and the making of inferences were predetermined by the teacher. In the intersection problem, the structure of the inquiry problem was much less obvious. A third contrast involves the outcomes of the students' findings. The intersection investigators were able to effect changes in the community. The artifact investigators were given an opportunity to become actively involved in previewing a forthcoming social studies unit.

The two examples also had similarities. Both used the steps in the inquiry process presented at the beginning of this section. In each case, students moved through a progression from problem statement to inference making. Second, both problems provided for a high degree of student interaction. Third, both problems provided for the development of the following skills: observation, description, problem definition, classifying, decision making, hypothesizing, verifying, and inference making. Fourth, in each lesson the teacher played the role of facilitator, guiding but not dictating to the students. A further similarity is the active involvement of the students. Finally, both lessons had transfer value; that is, they had the potential to be used by learners as models for investigating and solving problems in many situations other than the actual lesson situation. The next section expands on the idea of transfer of learning.

Reflective Thinking as a Follow-Up to Inquiry

Perhaps either of the foregoing inquiry examples could be justified on the grounds of student motivation and active involvement. But it should be emphasized that problems such as these have an inherent potential for helping students make applications of their learning that are generalizable beyond the specific problem. A useful strategy to facilitate learning transfer is a short *reflective thinking session* held either at the conclusion of a given lesson or on the following day before the introduction of new material.

Four Types of Inquiry Research

Historians and archaeologists attempt to reconstruct past events and eras. Anthropologists observe and try to describe cultural aspects of human behavior. Sociologists deal with the behavior of groups. Psychologists conduct experiments with human subjects in an effort to expand our knowledge of human responses and behavior.

What do these investigators have in common? They share a common subject matter: (human beings), a respect for evidence, and a desire to increase the world's knowledge of human behavior. In each case, their investigations represent attempts to answer questions by seeking appropriate sources of data, gathering and processing data, making inferences, and reaching conclusions about human behavior. Differences exist as well. The historian cannot replicate a situation, as a psychologist often can, nor can the historian mail questionnaires to subjects in many cases.

Four types of inquiry research are historical research, descriptive research, survey research, and experimental research. The following sections give many illustrations of ways these inquiry methods can be implemented in the classroom, turning your children into researchers and active learners. As you read about the investigations, try to view them from the dual perspective of teacher and researcher.

Historical Research

Historical research represents an attempt to put together the pieces of the past. Because historical research deals with events that have already happened, it is often difficult to acquire precise reports. Historical researchers cannot control the events they wish to recapture; more often than not, they cannot even find enough documentation to ascertain all the facts of an occurrence, much less all the inferences. Historical events, such as the assassination of Martin Luther King Jr. and the Watergate affair, illustrate the difficulties involved in attempting to reconstruct details of the past. The problems involved in even relatively simple investigations, such as finding out about one's grandparents or reconstructing one's past hairstyles, illustrate the difficult task of the historian. Figure 9.2 illustrates an example

FIGURE 9.2

Rhonda's Essay

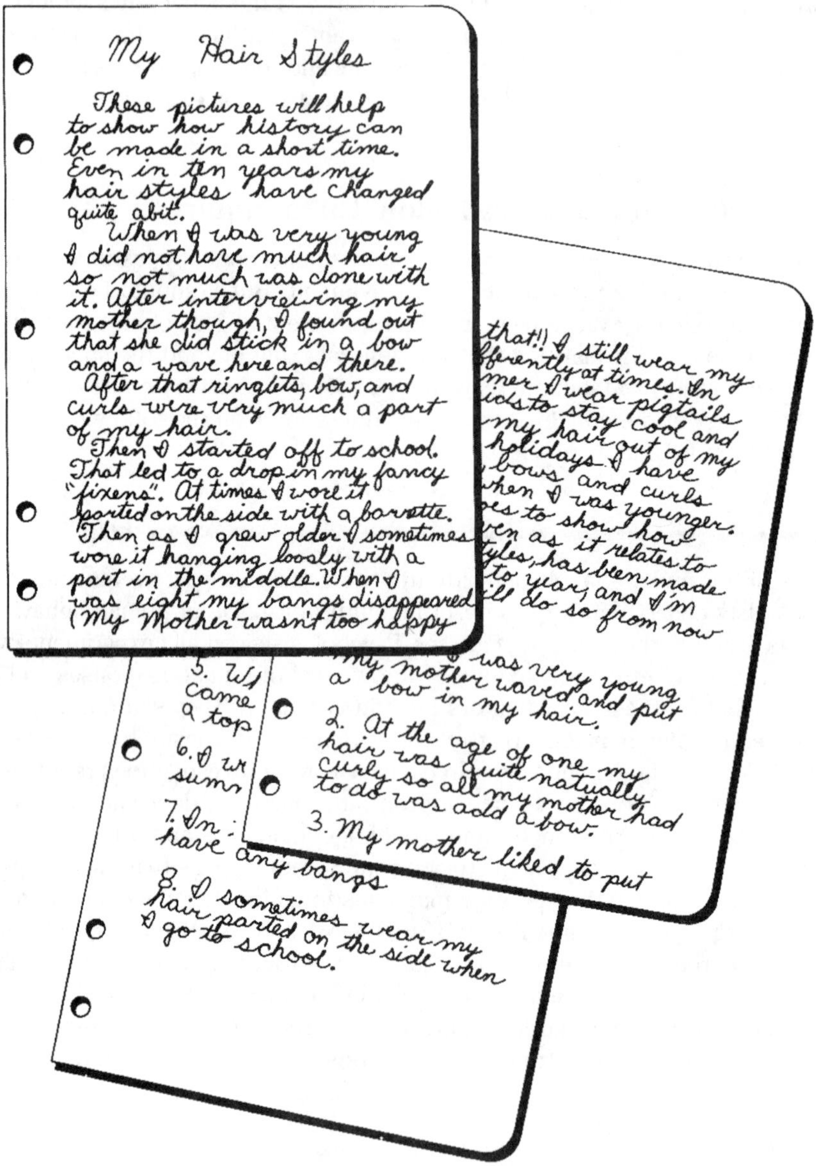

of historical inquiry. Hairstyles, clothing, toys, and so on provide excellent sources of historical data for children's investigations.

Activity: Oral History

This lesson provides an example of oral history. Oral history is particularly suited to younger learners, because it places emphasis on interviewing subjects rather than on letters, documents, and other written records. In this lesson, children

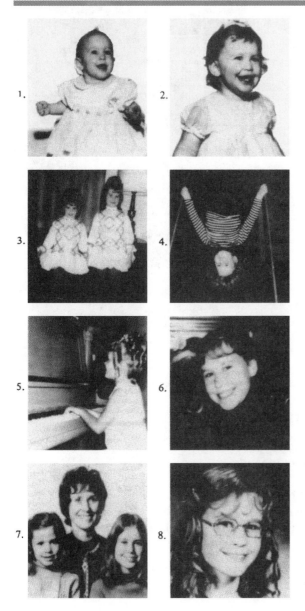

Rhonda illustrated her essay,
"My Hair Styles."

studying family structures try to reconstruct the life of a grandmother when she was their age. The following transcript details the lesson.

> *Teacher:* How many of you know a grandmother? (Students raise hands.) Where was the grandmother born?
> *John:* I don't know.
> *Stephanie:* In Minnesota.
> *Per:* Norway.

*A young historian and his good friend
from another generation.*

Others: Minnesota, Wisconsin, Korea, California, North Dakota, Arkansas, Sweden, New Hampshire.

Teacher: What do you suppose the grandmother studied in school when she was your age?

Alex: She might have had reading.

Mary: She probably had a lot of work.

Kathy: She had math.

Teacher: Let's put these guesses on the board under the heading of School-work. (Teacher lists students' contributions on board.)

Teacher: What kinds of games do you think she played?

Stephanie: Hopscotch.

Mary: Jacks and hide-and-go-seek.

Robert: Baseball and horses.

Sandy: Dolls and house and work.

The teacher proceeded to record the students' guesses (hypotheses) on the board under the heading Games. The class then developed and recorded guesses for the following other categories: Work, Food, Transportation, and Clothes.

Teacher: We've made guesses about schoolwork, games, work, food, clothes, and transportation. How do you think we could find out whether our guesses are right or wrong?

Mary: We could ask our mothers. They might know.

Alex: We could ask our grandmothers.

Teacher: We could learn from both of them.

Teacher: Does anyone know a grandmother who could come to our class so that we could ask her about these things?

A few days later, a grandmother visited the class. The students had questions for her based on the categories the class had established earlier. The grandmother answered the questions on the basis of her recollections of her childhood. The answers she gave were recorded on the board beside the students' guesses. When the students finished the interview, they spent some time comparing their guesses with the answers the grandmother had given. They were pleased with some of their guesses and surprised by some of the answers. In addition, the grandmother spent some time teaching them a game she had often played as a child.

The next day, the teacher asked the students whether all grandmothers would have given the same answers to their questions. They didn't think so. In order to find out, they decided to take home information sheets that would be filled out by parents or grandparents on behalf of the students' grandmothers. Figure 9.3 illustrates a completed information sheet.

Activity: *Origins of Special Days*

Elementary-age children particularly enjoy the various holidays and special observances that dot the calendar. Teachers use these special occasions for everything from parties celebrating Valentine's Day or Halloween to serious teaching about contributors to our heritage such as Martin Luther King Jr. and the Pilgrims of Plymouth Plantation. These days are rich in symbolic and cultural meaning and can become the object of fruitful historical investigations by children.

FIGURE 9.3

A Grandmother Information Sheet

My Grandmother's Name	Wilma Pederson
Her Place of Birth	Grand Rapids, Mich.
Games She Played	Hopscotch, Tag, Run-Sheep-Run, Baseball
Her Schoolwork	Reading, Numbers, Artwork, Writing
Her Chores at Home	Set the Table, Watch Her Brother, Do Errands
Food She Ate	Fruit, Vegetables, Meat, Cereal, Bread, Potatoes, Sweets

Primary-age children can do whole-class investigations in which teacher and students study the origins and history of holidays. Why is there a Valentine's Day? Thanksgiving? Mother's Day? When did a particular holiday begin? How has its observance changed over the years? You can read to the class from key sources. It is especially useful to have the children interview their parents, grandparents, or people in a nearby nursing home about how they celebrated a particular holiday when they were a child. A person of another generation can be invited to come to class to reminisce and answer questions about the activities of a particular holiday he or she remembers from childhood. What games, food, and observances were prominent then? Can a celebration of Independence Day—for example, from 50 years ago—be re-created?

At the intermediate level, children can do independent investigations or small-group research into particular holidays. This can develop into a year-long mini-unit in which holidays are chosen or assigned. Students then present their research just prior to or on a particular holiday. The presentations should include written, pictorial, graphic, oral, and other modes. Skits, displays, bulletin boards, "news" programs, group presentations, and speeches should be encouraged. In some cases, students may wish to explore the origins and traditions of significant, but less prominent, holidays such as April Fools' Day, Oktoberfest, or St. Patrick's Day. The distillation of the various studies could be edited by class members and assembled into a Book of Holidays.

➡ *Activity: Using Original Source Material*

Students desperately need to be exposed to original source materials as they conduct inquiry. Far too often, even university-level students read only textbooks and other secondary interpretations—the academic equivalent of TV dinners. Original source materials, such as the exchange of letters between Thomas Jefferson and Meriwether Lewis (see Figure 9.4) represent rich text, real food for learners. The nonsensical objection that such material is too difficult has led to the "dumbing down" of the curriculum. Perhaps you need to read the letters in Figure 9.4 (preferably in role-play costume) to your students. You may have to walk them through some difficult terms, but that's what real teaching and learning is all about. Don't worry; they can understand the ideas. Trust them. If you don't believe me, go back and reread the quote at the beginning of this chapter. Figure 9.5 shows a sample discussion guide based on material in Figure 9.4.

➡ *Activity: Birthdays*

A challenging historical investigation is one in which students research the particular day they were born. In most cases, local libraries will have copies (or microfilm) of the daily newspaper from the day on which a student was born. Students will enjoy reading the newspaper representing the day they entered the world. Things to look for from that special day include:

Headlines	Want ads
Newsmakers	Movies
Sports stories	Television shows
Comics	Fashions
Advertisements	

FIGURE 9.4

Exchange of Letters between Thomas Jefferson and Meriwether Lewis

While Jefferson used the term "secretary" *for this position, he generally wrote his own letters even when in office and sought rather to have a special assistant to organize meetings, his schedule, and serve as a personal representative.*

relinquish: *From the Latin prefix re-, behind, + linquere, to leave; meaning to abandon or release.*

A Private Secretary
—*Jefferson to Lewis*

Washington, February, 23, 1801

Dear Sir

The appointment to the Presidency of the U.S. has rendered it necessary for me to have a private secretary, and in selecting one I have thought it important to respect not only his capacity to aid in the private concerns of the household, but also to contribute to the mass of information which it is interesting for the administration to acquire. Your knowledge of the Western country, of the army and of all its interest & relations has rendered it desirable for public as well as private purposes that you should be engaged in that office. In point of profit it has little to offer; the salary being only 500. D. which would scarcely be more than an equivalent for your pay & rations, which you would be obliged to relinquish while withdrawn from active service, but retaining your rank & right to rise. But it would be an easier office, would make you know & be known to characters of influence in the affairs of our country, and give you the advantage of their wisdom. You would of course save also the expense of subsistence & lodging as you would be one of my family. If these or any other views which your own reflections may suggest should present the office of my private secretary as worthy of acceptance you will make me happy in accepting it. It has been solicited by several, who will have no answer till I hear from you. Should you accept, it would be necessary that you should wind up whatever affairs you are engaged in as expeditiously as your own & the public interest will admit, & adjourn to this place and that immediately on receipt of this you inform me by letter of your determination.

Source: R. Scheuerman and A. Ellis, *Journeys of Discovery: An Interdisciplinary Curriculum* (Mountain Light Publishing, 2001).

FIGURE 9.4

Continued

It would also be necessary that you wait on General Wilkinson & obtain his approbation, & his aid in making such arrangements as may render your absence as little injurious to the service as may be. I write to him on this subject. Accept assurances of the esteem of Dear Sir your friend & servant.

Th. Jefferson

—*[Lewis to Jefferson]*

Pittsburg, March 10, 1801

Dear Sir,

Not until too late on Friday last to answer by that day's mail did I receive your much esteemed favor of the 23rd Ult. In it you have thought proper so far to honor me with your confidence, as to express a wish that I should accept the office, nor were further motives necessary to induce my compliance, than that you Sir should conceive that in the discharge of the duties of that office, I could be serviceable to my country, or useful to yourself Permit me here, sir, to do further justice to my feelings by expressing the lively sensibility with which I received this mark of your confidence and esteem.

I did not reach this place on my return from Detroit until late on the night of the 5th instant, five days after the departure of General Wilkinson. My report therefore on the subject of your letter was immediately made to Colonel Hamtramck, the commanding officer at this place. Not a moment has been lost in making the necessary arrangements in order to get forward to the City of Washington with all possible despatch. Rest assured I shall not relax in my exertions. Receive I pray you, sir, the most undisassembled assurance of the attachment and friendship of your most obedient, & very humble servant,

Meriwether Lewis

Ult. *is the abbreviation for ultimo which means in or of the preceding month.*

James Wilkinson *(1757–1825) was commanding general of the U.S. Army in 1801 and later served as governor of the Territory of Louisiana.*

"knowledge of the Western country"

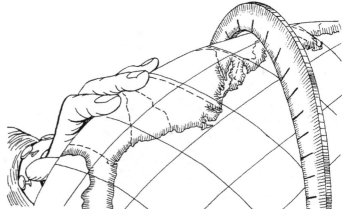

FIGURE 9.5

Discussion Guide Based on Exchange of Letters between Thomas Jefferson and Meriwether Lewis

Discussion Guide

Directions: Please check each statement that you can support and be prepared to cite your evidence from your reading and experience.

Definitions and Knowledge:

_______ 1. President Jefferson invited Meriwether Lewis to be his private, presidential secretary.

_______ 2. President Jefferson liked Lewis's knowledge of the western country and the army.

_______ 3. Jefferson pointed out that Lewis could serve his country and also get to know important people.

_______ 4. Jefferson offered to make Lewis a member of his family, which meant Lewis would receive both food and lodging.

_______ 5. Lewis retained his rank in the army.

_______ 6. Lewis accepted Jefferson's invitation to become his private secretary.

_______ 7. Lewis had to travel from Pittsburgh, Pennsylvania, to Washington, DC, to accept the position.

Comprehension (Relate and Apply Knowledge to Experiences and Concepts):

_______ 1. Jefferson was a good judge of character and loyalty.

_______ 2. Lewis was honored to serve his country.

_______ 3. Salary was not an important factor in Lewis's decision to take the job.

_______ 4. Lewis gave up his opportunity to advance his rank within the militia.

_______ 5. It took 15 days for Jefferson's letter to reach Lewis in Pittsburgh.

_______ 6. Lewis was a humble servant.

Evaluation (Judgments about the Value of Ideas, Objects, and Actions):

_______ 1. He profits most who serves best. (Arthur Sheldon—Rotary International)

_______ 2. Honor lies in honest toil. (Grover Cleveland)

_______ 3. Nothing endures but personal qualities—nothing. (Walt Whitman)

Thanks to Jim Worthington, Ph.D., for the discussion statements.

Activity: Time Lines

The concept of chronology is difficult for many children to acquire in a meaningful sense. Time lines provide a graphic aid that enables the students to think of the passage of time in a more concrete fashion. A useful assignment is to ask each child to prepare a personal time line with one or two events from each year of his or her life (see Figure 9.6).

FIGURE 9.6

Student's Time Line

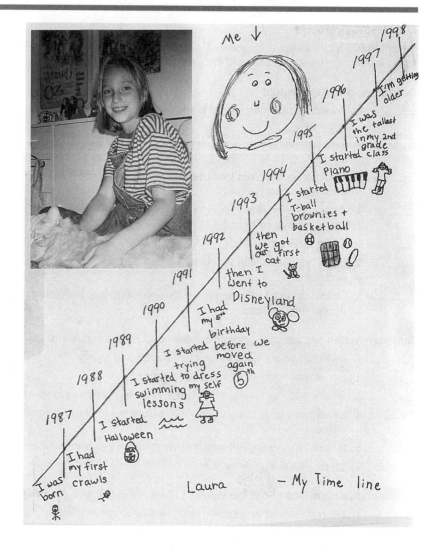

On a different scale, students should be encouraged to make time lines of people and events from history. Possible topics for time lines include:

Women in American History   Famous American Presidents
Voyages of Discovery   Scientists and Inventors
Great African Americans   Authors and Artists

▶ *Activity: Autobiographies*

Every child has a history, and every child's history is interesting and worth probing. I suggest that from time to time you have your students write autobiographical sketches. In time, these sketches can be put together to form a personal history. The data gathering, interviewing of parents, personal insights, and self-reflection that occur as a result of this process will have the effect of making historians out of your students. Don't be surprised if they start lifelong habits of keeping personal diaries. You never know what your influence may lead to. Figure 9.7 illustrates a page from a third-grade child's autobiography.

Activity: Replicating Ancient Inquiry

The ancient Greek mathematician and philosopher Thales (sixth century B.C.) once journeyed to Egypt where it is said he used his knowledge of geometry to measure the height of the Great Pyramid and other structures. He also is said to have been able to calculate the distance from shore to nearby ships at sea.

FIGURE 9.7

An Autobiography

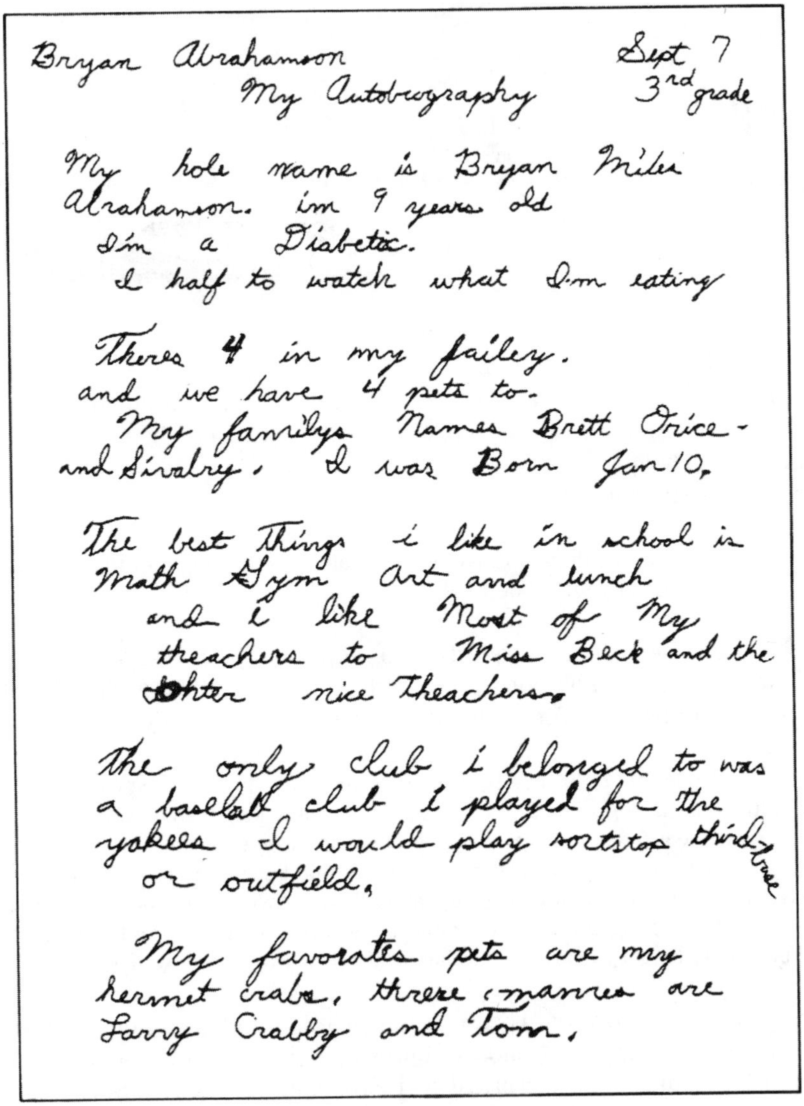

Bryan Abrahamson Sept 7
My Autobiography 3rd grade

My hole name is Bryan Miles Abrahamson. im 9 years old I'm a Diabetic. I half to watch what I'm eating

Theres 4 in my failey. and we have 4 pets to. My familys Names Brett Orice - and Sivalry. I was Born Jan 10.

The best Things i like in school is Math Gym Art and lunch and i like Most of My theachers to Miss Beck and the ohter nice theachers.

the only club i belonged to was a baslall club I played for the yakees I would play sortstop third base or outfield.

My favorates pets are my hermet crabs. threre names are Larry Crabby and Tom.

Thales was able to calculate the height of the Great Pyramid or any other object using simple methods. All he needed was sunshine to cast shadows and a knowledge of his own height.

The question for students is:

With this much information, do you think you can calculate the height of the flagpole or some other structure at your school?

This problem can be posed as a question to be put on the board on Monday morning with discussion and solutions presented later in the week. Or, it can be posed as a *think-aloud* problem for students to solve in pairs.

Here is how Thales is said to have solved the problem. He stood near the Great Pyramid and waited until his own shadow was exactly the same length as he was tall. For example, if someone is 5 feet tall and has a 5-foot shadow, then it is merely a matter of measuring the length of the shadow of the Great Pyramid because that is how tall the Pyramid is. Of course, you wouldn't have to wait until your own shadow is exactly your height. You could use proportions. For example, if your shadow is half your height, then the structure whose height you are calculating would also have a shadow half its height.

Using Primary Sources. Most of what children learn at school about history comes from what are known as secondary sources: textbooks, workbooks, encyclopedias, even biographies and historical works of fact and fiction. Secondary

Young historians replicate Thales' experiment by calculating the height of the flagpole on the school grounds.

sources are fine, to a point. Their limitation is found primarily in the fact that someone else does most of the thinking for the reader, presenting him or her with conclusions. Primary sources, on the other hand, are filled with potential but not with conclusions. The reader, not the writer, must analyze, synthesize, and come to conclusions. In that sense, the learning equation is turned around, and the reader becomes not a recipient but an investigator. Consider the following example.

Abraham Lincoln gave the most famous speech in American history in 1863 on the battlefield at Gettysburg, Pennsylvania, where months before that great armed conflict between the Union and the Confederacy had taken place. No television cameras were present, no tape recordings were made, and conflicting reports of the speech itself and how it was received were filed by different newsmen. Figure 9.8 presents what is thought to be the most accurate version.

The speech is only 10 sentences long; it contains only 271 words. It is hardly the length of an essay a child of 10 or 12 years old might write. Most of the words are simple words. What makes it so powerful? What ideas are found in it? What values does it contain? Lincoln's speech can form an example of whole-class inquiry in which the teacher leads the class through the investigation. For starters, students can illustrate, on the basis of their research, each of the 10 sentences. Some can memorize it and deliver it as a role-play. Others can look up difficult words and report their meanings. Still others can investigate the context of the time Lincoln spent before and after the speech. Of course, you will want to have a class discussion or two devoted to the meaning of the speech.

The phrase "of the people, by the people, for the people" is the best-known part of the speech. In 1930, Lincoln scholar William Barton found some prior uses of those or similar words. Here are some:

- "a government of all the people, by all the people, for all the people."—Theodore Parker, at an antislavery convention in Boston, May 20, 1850
- "the people's government, made for the people, made by the people, and answerable to the people."—Daniel Webster, January 26, 1830

FIGURE 9.8

Four score and seven years ago our fathers brought forth on this continent a new nation, conceived in Liberty, and dedicated to the proposition that all men are created equal.

Now we are engaged in a great civil war, testing whether that nation or any nation so conceived and so dedicated, can long endure. We are met on a great battle-field of that war. We have come to dedicate a portion of that field, as a final resting place for those who here gave their lives that that nation might live. It is altogether fitting and proper that we should do this.

But, in a larger sense, we can not dedicate—we can not consecrate—we can not hallow—this ground. The brave men, living and dead, who struggled here, have consecrated it, far above our poor power to add or detract. The world will little note, nor long remember what we say here, but it can never forget what they did here. It is for us the living, rather, to be dedicated here to the unfinished work which they who fought here have thus far so nobly advanced. It is rather for us to be here dedicated to the great task remaining before us—that from these honored dead we take increased devotion to that cause for which they gave the last full measure of devotion—that we here highly resolve that these dead shall not have died in vain— that this nation, under God, shall have a new birth of freedom—and that government of the people, by the people, for the people, shall not perish from the earth.

Abraham Lincoln

- "a government made by ourselves, for themselves, and conducted by them-selves."—John Adams, 1798
- "I am in favor of democracy . . . that shall be of the people, by the people, for the people."—attributed to Cleon, 420 B.C.

▶▶ *Activity: A Riddle from the Past*

The following story deals with the possibility that the Chinese may have sailed to America centuries before the arrival of Columbus (see Figure 9.9). After you have read it, develop questions at the various levels of the taxonomy that follows it. A sample question is provided for each level.

Try the following investigation with your students as an exercise in developing a hypothesis. At the conclusion of their inquiry into the question, Did the Chinese really discover America? students should be encouraged to share their hypotheses with each other. Even though the students have spent a considerable amount of time dealing with the question, their conclusions should be treated as hypotheses in this case because of the slight amount of evidence presented.

FIGURE 9.9

197

Researchers

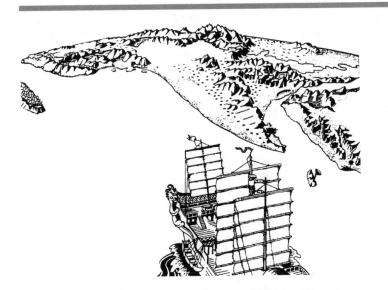

Did the Chinese Sail to America Long before Columbus? We Do Know They Made Great Voyages to Africa, as Depicted in This Illustration.

After the students have read the story and studied a map showing the directional flow of the Japan Current, ask them to make preliminary hypotheses by indicating on this continuum their feelings at this point.

Impossible, couldn't have happened	Might have happened	Probably happened	I'm sure it happened

Now divide the students into small groups. Ask each group to build a database from which to refine or revise their earlier hypotheses using the data shown in Figure 9.10.

Did the Chinese Discover America in 458 A.D.?

In 458 A.D., five men supposedly set sail from China. Following the Japan Current, they traveled twenty thousand li eastward. Twenty thousand li equals about seven thousand miles. [Students refer to a map of the Japan Current in an encyclopedia, atlas, or geography book.]

Sometime during the same year, the five travelers reached a land which they called Fusang. It is where Mexico can be found today. They are supposed to have stayed there for forty years. In 499 A.D. they returned to China.

When they returned, one of them, Hwui Shan, told the emperor about their adventures in the New World. A servant of the emperor wrote down Hwui Shan's story. We still have that story. Some scholars who have read it believe it can be used to prove that Hwui Shan and his friends discovered the New World in 458 A.D.—more than one thousand years before Columbus.[1]

As you read part of Hwui Shan's story, ask yourself if you agree with those scholars. Try to decide whether it was possible or probable that the Chinese reached America before the Vikings or Columbus.

FIGURE 9.10 *Evidence That Can Be Used to Consider Whether the Chinese May Have Sailed to and Landed in America*

Hwui Shan's Claims	Archeological Evidence
1. Hwui Shan said he traveled east 20,000 li from China.	1,000 li = about 333 miles 20,000 li = about 7,000 miles Mexico via the Japan Current is about 7,000 miles from China.
2. The Land of Marked Bodies was 7,000 li from Japan.	Marked women lived at Point Barrow, Alaska, about 2,400 miles from Japan.
3. Fusang has copper but no iron. The people there also have a system of writing.	Archeologists have found that Mexican Indians used copper by 400 A.D. Spanish explorers discovered iron in Mexico after 1500 A.D. By 400 A.D., some Indians in Mexico had a system of writing.
4. The people of Fusang use large cattle horns as containers.	Scholars knew that Montezuma, the Aztec chief of Mexico, showed Cortez, the Spanish explorer, some large bison horns after 1500 A.D.
5. The Land of Women is 1,000 li beyond Fusang.	Central American monkeys live about 300 miles south of Mexico. These monkeys are shy, chattering, and hairy.
6. The Land of Fusang is named after the Fusang trees, which have reddish, pearlike fruit. Sprouts of the Fusang trees look like bamboo.	Mexico means land of the century plant. The century plant's sprouts look like bamboo. Some people call it a tree. The Mexican century plant grows to a height of about thirty feet. The plant does not have reddish, pearlike fruit. The prickly pear or cactus apple is reddish and grows on a cactus, which looks like a century plant.
7. Fusang people make thread and paper from Fusang trees.	Archeologists have found that Mexican Indians made thread from century plants, and a form of paper can also be made from them.
8. Fusang has no forts or armies.	Archeologists have found that around 400 A.D., the Mexican Indians were at peace.
9. Hwui Shan gave the emperor of China a mirror-like object from Fusang.	Archeologists have found that some Mexican Indians used mirrors made of polished stone.
10. Fusang has carts pulled by horses, cattle, and reindeer.	Archeologists have found that the Mexican Indians put wheels on their toys. There is no evidence as yet to show that Indian adults made use of the wheel. Spaniards brought the first horses and cattle to the Americas after 1500 A.D. The reindeer nearest to Mexico are found in Norway and Siberia. Hwui Shan probably stopped over in Siberia.

Source: Adapted from W. R. Fielder, *Inquiring about American History* (pp. 23–27) (New York: Holt, Rinehart and Winston, 1972).

Hwui Shan's Story

Fusang is located twenty thousand li east of the country of Ta Han in China. The Land of Marked Bodies is seven thousand li northwest of Japan. Its people have marks or stripes on their bodies like wild animals. In front they have three marks. If the marks are large and straight, they belong to the upper class, but if the marks are small and crooked, they belong to the lower class.

The land of Fusang has many Fusang trees, which give it its name. The Fusang tree's leaves look like those of the T'ung tree in China. Its first sprouts are like bamboo shoots. The people of the country eat these sprouts. Their fruit is like a pear but reddish.

The people also spin thread from the bark. They use the thread to make coarse cloth from which they make their clothing. They also make a finer fabric from this thread. The wood of the Fusang tree is used to build houses, and the bark is used to make paper.

The people of Fusang have a system of writing. But they have no forts or walled cities, no military weapons or soldiers. They do not wage war.

Their ground has no iron, but it has copper. They have large cattle horns which they use as containers. The largest horns hold about five gallons. They have carts drawn by horses, cattle, and deer.[2]

The Land of Women

The Land of Women is about one thousand li beyond the Land of Fusang. Its women are completely covered with hair. They walk standing up straight, and chatter a lot among themselves. They are shy when they see ordinary people. Their babies are able to walk when they are one hundred days old, and they are fully grown in three or four years.

(Hwui Shan also gave the Chinese emperor a kind of stone which was almost transparent. It was about a foot around and made in the form of a mirror.)

Knowledge

1. Where were the explorers in the story from?

2. _____

3. _____

Comprehension

1. Give a brief summary of the story.

2. _____

3. _____

Application

1. Can you give the names and circumstances of other explorers who might have "discovered" America?

2. _____

3. _____

Analysis

1. Why don't all historians reach the same decision after they've seen the same evidence?

2. _____

3. _____

Synthesis

1. What are some reasons either for or against accepting this story?

2. _____

3. _____

Evaluation

1. Some people have said that even if this story is true, Columbus's voyage to America was more important. How do you feel about this statement?

2. _____

3. _____

Descriptive Research

Descriptive research, as the term implies, has as its purpose the description of human behavior, primarily through observation. Groups and/or individuals are the descriptive researchers' data sources. For example, it has been common practice for anthropologists to live among tribal groups in order to make direct observations of their behavior. Such a method of investigation is known as *participant observation* because the investigator plays the dual role of participant in the daily life of a group and observer of that group.

Another form of descriptive research is *direct observation*. One can observe without actually becoming involved in a situation. Although participation puts the observed at greater ease and thus produces a more "natural" situation, it may make the observer less objective because of personal involvement in the activities of a group.

Another type of descriptive research is *indirect observation*. This often involves the use of such data as pictures, artifacts, written accounts, books, and

A young inquirer makes a careful descriptive study of the Sacajewea dollar coin.

A young sociologist conducts survey research.

maps. Of course, someone engaged in direct or participant observation might also use such tools as the camera, tape recorder, and field notes as aids to ensure the accuracy and permanence of his or her record keeping.

Another means of gathering information for use in descriptive research is the technique of *interviewing informants*. Members of a group often are a valuable source of data. In addition to observing their behavior, an investigator can obtain information by interviewing them—asking individuals questions about leadership, customs, rapport, and so on within the group.

As an illustration, let's see how the four descriptive research techniques of participant observation, direct observation, indirect observation, and interviewing informants might be used in investigating the activities and behavior of a Cub Scout pack. As a participant observer, you would "join" the Cub Scout pack, attend meetings, and take part in the rituals and activities. You would, in effect, become one of the group. As a direct observer, you would watch the pack at its meetings but refrain from taking part. In addition to keeping notes, you might photograph and tape record events. As an indirect observer, you might examine crafts made by members of the pack. You might also examine minutes of meetings, the *Cub Scout Handbook*, and other relevant artifacts. As an investigator interviewing informants, you would seek out one or more members of the pack and ask such questions as: How do you usually spend your time in meetings? and Who do you think are some leading members of the group?

Obviously, to do a thorough study of the scout pack, it would be advisable to use all the foregoing techniques, because (1) to use all four would provide a greater and more varied base of information and (2) the different approaches might provide cross-checks on the validity of the information obtained.

As is the case with all social science research, descriptive research attempts to answer questions or solve problems by gathering and processing data and making inferences from those data. The following examples illustrate various techniques students might use in doing descriptive research.

Young social scientists observe artifacts and record their findings.

▶ *Activity: The Observation Game*

The observation game can take many forms and should be played as often as it takes to see real improvement in the children's ability to observe systematically, a very valuable skill. Here is one example. Take the class out to the playground or to some interesting scene near the school. Each student should have a pencil and a sketch pad. The idea is to let the students look at the scene for a couple of minutes or so. Then ask them to turn around and sketch or map what they saw. A variation on this theme is to ask students to write down a description of what they saw. Older students, of course, can and should do both. After students have finished their "descriptions," ask them to turn around and check their work against what they see. How accurate was it?

A participant-observer plays tetherball while studying habits of childhood.

Another example of this form of descriptive research is to have students make a drawing of an object such as a vase, a toy, or whatever. The brain begins to function elaborately in such a situation. The concentration, the careful observation, and the attempt to render what you see brings out subtleties that are too easily overlooked in casual observation. I suggest that you put on a tape or compact disk of Mozart or Haydn when you do this activity. I think you'll find the students will like it. Finally, another variation is to describe the music. See the activity called The Five Senses Game for other possibilities.

Activity: The Interview

The interview as a descriptive research tool provides investigators with an informant's perspective on a group or event. Obviously, investigators could add validity to their research by interviewing more than one group member. Also, it is important that investigators consider a member's status within a group. For example, the perspective of the president of a club is likely to be different from that of a member with lower status who attends meetings only occasionally. When an interview is expanded to include larger numbers of respondents, it becomes a questionnaire. Figure 9.11 illustrates an interview situation in which a third-grade investigator questioned a 4-year-old about her membership in a YMCA group.

To summarize, the task of the descriptive researcher is to pose a question or problem about human behavior and to attempt to answer that question by gathering data through observation and/or interview. Thus, descriptive researchers add to the existing base of knowledge of human behavior through their investigations.

FIGURE 9.11

The Interview Guide

I talked to Robyn. Age 4.

She belonged to YMCA. She goes there 2 times a week. This is how she feels about it. ______. Her favorite things to do at YMCA are swimming and gym. I asked her if she thought other 4 year olds would like to be in YMCA. She said Yes.

Comments. She likes to go there.

▶▶ *Activity: Community Study*

The community study descriptive investigation can become a whole-class project. The object of the study is to describe the community around the school. Students can work in teams to develop their descriptions. Among the descriptive research tools they might use are drawings, maps, photographs, and interviews. The following elements of the community would be worth describing:

Types of trees	Streets
Parks	Churches/temples
Houses/apartments/condominiums	Vacant lots
Businesses	Playgrounds

▶▶ *Activity: The Five Senses Game*

The Five Senses Game, which takes on many variations, can be played as often as you like. It takes its cues from the work of Francis Bacon, and before that, from Aristotle, who were both convinced that sensory learning was the foundation of scientific inquiry. I would recommend that you try the game with your class as a whole, at least for starters. If you have a primary class, you may have to do most of the note taking. Older children can do their own.

The key idea of this game is the ability to *describe*. It is useful to isolate one of the senses each time you play the game. If you decide to emphasize the sense of touch, you can take your students outside and ask them to identify various objects in the environment they would like to touch—for example, a leaf, a mud puddle, a worm, grass, bark, the air, the side of the building, and so on. The idea is to draw out of your students descriptive terms related to texture, feel, and touch. You can do the same for the other senses: sight, hearing, smell, and taste. (You may want to elicit taste descriptions in the classroom using some things to eat that you have brought.)

▶▶ *Activity: Map Making*

Map making begins with observation and description. In fact, a map is a spatial (as opposed to verbal) description of a place. Make sure everyone has a notebook or sketch pad and a pencil and ruler, and take your class outdoors. If you can find one, choose an elevated spot, such as a hillside, and put the children to work sketching what they see. Don't be too concerned with some of the details at first. Things like which way is north and how does one draw to scale can come along gradually. The key is to observe and describe, not in words, but using a spatial approach (drawing) to description. I guarantee that you will gain some new insights regarding students' abilities. Some of the children who don't shine verbally will surprise you with their spatial abilities.

Survey Research

Surveys are a means of gaining information about groups of persons. Often, an investigator will be interested in discovering the attitudes, preferences, or opinions held by large numbers of people concerning particular ideas or issues. This precludes the possibility of mere observation because of the difficulties posed by such factors as time and distance. Assume, for example, that a student investigator at Washington Elementary School wishes to assess the attitudes of the students at the school toward some newly installed playground equipment. Although it might prove instructive to observe who uses it, it could be difficult to provide observation coverage during the many recess periods throughout the school day. Additionally, an observer would probably see only students who chose to use the equipment, thus failing to tap the attitudes of nonusers who might have a preference for different kinds of equipment. Thus, the survey offers an alternative to the observation/descriptive approach.

Three important considerations for the student researcher to bear in mind when conducting surveys are (1) what to measure, (2) how to measure, and (3) whom to measure.[4]

The question of *what* to measure needs to be defined with precision. For example, a surveyor who wishes to determine how students feel about school assemblies must decide exactly what it is about student attitude toward the assemblies it is important to know. Consider the following two questions:

1. What do you think of school assemblies?
2. Are you in favor of school assemblies?　　yes　　no

Although Question 1 may provoke interesting responses, it is a vague question and thus it may be difficult to quantify the responses. Question 2 is more precisely defined, and it allows one to quantify the responses given to it. Figure 9.12 illustrates the processed data for Question 2.

The question of *how* to measure involves the idea of sampling. A survey researcher need not ask all the students at the school whether they favor school assemblies in order to make valid inferences about the opinions of students at the school. Rather, an effective method is to *sample* student responses from the school's population. These are three different sampling techniques:

1. *Simple random selection.* If our school has a student population of 500 and we wish to sample 10 percent, or 50 students, we need only ensure that the 50 we choose are selected on the basis of pure chance.
2. *Stratified random selection.* Because we might wish to ensure equal numbers of primary and intermediate students, we could take room lists and randomly select three students from each room in the school.

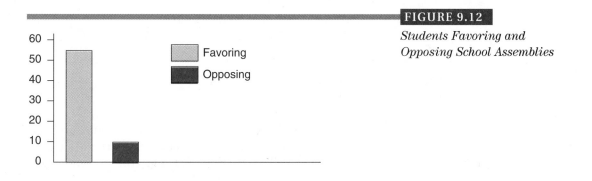

FIGURE 9.12

Students Favoring and Opposing School Assemblies

3. *Stratified selection.* To do a stratified sampling, a researcher would take, for example, every tenth name from room lists. This might be useful if we wished to ensure equal boy/girl representation, in which case we would use separate boy/girl lists.

All three procedures provide "fairness" in the selection of samples and allow investigators to make inferences about a population without interviewing every person in that population.

The question of *whom* to measure is important because survey researchers need to ensure that their samples adequately represent the various types of groups and/or individuals found in the population. Thus, in a student preference poll it may be crucial to ensure that primary-age as well as intermediate-age students are given an opportunity to respond and that teachers, clerks, custodians, and cooks are not included.

Let's consider two examples of surveys done by elementary classes. The first, a playground equipment survey, was conducted by a second-grade class. The second, a Halloween survey, was conducted by a fifth-grade class.

▶▶ *Activity: A Playground Investigation*

Students in a second-grade class had experienced a number of problems with the use of the playground equipment at their school. They wondered if students in other classrooms were having similar difficulties. Among the problems the class listed were the following:

1. Some things are too crowded and we don't get to use them.
2. People get hurt on some of the equipment.
3. We would like to have some new equipment.

The students randomly chose five students from each room in the school and asked them the following questions:

1. Have you ever been hurt while using playground equipment at school?

    yes   no

    If so, on which piece of equipment? _____

2. Do you ever have to wait to use playground equipment?

    never   sometimes   often

3. Would you like to have some new playground equipment?

    yes   no

    If so, give the name of the new equipment._____

4. Are you a boy or a girl?_____

5. What grade are you in? _____

The results of the survey indicated that few children had ever been hurt using the playground equipment. However, 83 out of 110 students indicated that they often had to wait to use equipment. The most asked-for piece of new equipment was a tetherball pole. Two such poles were installed at the principal's request after he had reviewed the students' findings.

▶▶ *Activity: Halloween Study*

Students in a fifth-grade class were interested in the question of who trick-or-treats. To investigate the question for their school's population, they devised the questionnaire shown in Figure 9.13.

The class decided to try each of the three sampling procedures previously described to see if different results would be obtained. The three charts in Figure 9.14 illustrate the data received from the three sampling procedures.

In addition, the father of one of the students agreed to gather age and sex data from the trick-or-treaters who came to his house that Halloween. (The student would have done this, but she was busy trick-or-treating.) Figure 9.15 illustrates these data.

On the basis of their survey work, the class made the following inferences.

1. Trick-or-treating is popular among all age groups at our school.
2. Between 6:00 and 7:30 are peak trick-or-treating times.
3. There doesn't seem to be much difference between boys and girls in trick-or-treating.

FIGURE 9.13

A Survey Form

Trick or Treat Survey Form

_____ Boy _____ Girl _____ Age

Do you plan to trick-or-treat on Halloween this year?

_____ Yes _____ No

FIGURE 9.14

Analyzing the Halloween Survey

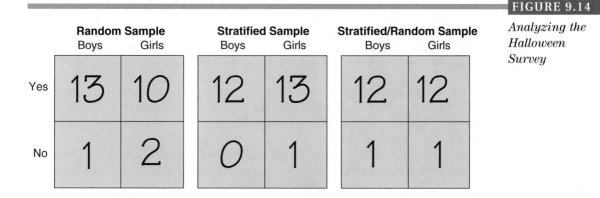

	Random Sample		Stratified Sample		Stratified/Random Sample	
	Boys	Girls	Boys	Girls	Boys	Girls
Yes	13	10	12	13	12	12
No	1	2	0	1	1	1

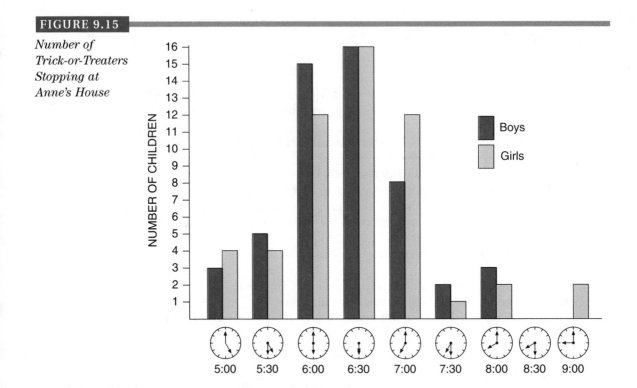

FIGURE 9.15

Number of Trick-or-Treaters Stopping at Anne's House

▶ *Activity: Consumerism*

An example of a child researcher using survey techniques can be found in Evelyn Kaye's book *Family Guide to Children's Television.*[5] An 11-year-old girl named Dawn Ann Kurth from Melbourne, Florida, became interested in advertising to children because of her younger sister:

> My sister Martha, who is seven, had asked my mother to buy a box of Post Raisin Bran so that she could get a free record that was on the back of the box. It had been advertised several times on Saturday morning cartoon shows. My mother bought the cereal, and we all (there are four children in our family) helped Martha eat it so she could get the record.
>
> It was after the cereal was eaten and she had the record that the crisis occurred. There was no way the record would work.
>
> Martha was very upset and began crying and I was angry too. It just didn't seem right to me that something could be shown on TV that worked fine and people were listening and dancing to the record and when you bought the cereal, instead of laughing and dancing, we were crying and angry.

Dawn had been chosen with 35 other students at Meadowlane Elementary School to do a project in any field they wanted. She decided to find out how other children felt about deceptive advertising. She began by watching television one Saturday morning. She clocked 25 commercial messages during one hour, 8:00 to 9:00, not counting ads for shows coming up or public service announcements. She also discovered that during shows her parents liked to watch there were only 10 to 12 commercials each hour, which surprised her.

Dawn devised a questionnaire and asked 1,538 children the following questions (answer these questions yourself):

1. Do you ask your mother to buy products you see advertised on TV?

    yes   no

2. Did you ever buy a product to get the free bonus gift inside?

    yes   no

3. Were you satisfied?

    yes   no

4. Write down an example.

    _____

    _____

5. Do you believe that certain products you see advertised on TV make you happier or have more friends?

    yes   no

6. Please write an example.

    _____

    _____

7. Did you ever feel out of it because your mother wouldn't buy a certain product?

    yes   no

8. Did you ever feel your mother was mean because she wouldn't buy the product you wanted?

    yes   no

Dawn got the following responses to her questionnaire: (1) yes 1,203; no 330. (2) yes 1,120; no 413. (3) yes 668; no 873. (5) yes 1,113; no 420. (7) yes 802; no 735. (8) yes 918; no 620.

Dawn's teacher sent the results of Dawn's work to a local paper, the kind known as an advertising shopper that carries a few stories of local interest. To their surprise, Dawn was invited to testify before a U.S. Senate committee that was investigating the effects of advertising on children. In her testimony, she explained her concerns and how she conducted her research. Her work is now part of the *Congressional Record.*

▶▶ *Activity: Gender Roles*

Figure 9.16 illustrates a cartoonist's view of the changing role of women in our society. This cartoon could be used as a vehicle for surveying awareness and attitudes of boys and girls of elementary age. The following survey questions might be asked:

1. What does this cartoon tell you?
2. Could a girl become owner of a ranch?
3. Should girls think about becoming ranch owners?
4. Why do you think so many ranch owners are men?

FIGURE 9.16

Cartoon
Illustrating
Changing Sex
Roles

Little Bo Peep had lost her sheep
and couldn't tell where to find them—
So when she grew up and had her
own ranch, she hired someone
to take care of lost sheep for her.

Illustration by Allen Glenn; prose by Arthur K. Ellis.

Activity: Weather Stations Survey

An effective method for developing such survey skills as data gathering, recording, and graphing data is a weather stations survey. Assign each child in class the task of recording the high temperature and low temperature in a major U.S. city for two weeks. The temperatures are given in most daily papers every day, so you need to be certain the class has access to the weather page. One child takes Seattle, another Phoenix, another Houston, another Cleveland, and so on. When they are finished, the graphs make an impressive display in your classroom.

Of course, an additional outcome of the weather stations survey is the introduction of geographic concepts and how geography affects weather and climate. Here are some questions you will want to consider with the class:

- How does latitude affect temperature?
- Does closeness to large bodies of water have an effect on temperature (Seattle vs. Minneapolis, for example)?
- How do mountains affect temperature?

With younger students, you may wish to do the project together, selecting only four or five cities. With older students, you may wish to include international temperatures.

➡ *Activity: A Critical Issues Survey*

A survey can serve more of a purpose than mere information gathering. Sometimes the results of a survey can help people take positive action. If you send your surveyors (your students) out around the school environment to look for potential problems, they can no doubt come up with a list of them: litter, vandalism, faulty playground equipment, pollution, noise, dangerous intersections, and the like. Thus, your students' survey can serve as the basis of a list of concerns that they can survey the whole school about. Then they can determine the rank order of the student body's concerns and try to involve the whole school in taking positive action to remedy the situation.

Getting a whole elementary school mobilized to study and correct a pressing problem is a wonderful experience. It allows for cross-age grouping, coaching of students by each other, discussions by children in different grade levels, and much more.

Experimental Research

In social science, experimentation involves the manipulation of variables to determine whether a particular treatment has an effect. In its simplest form, this generally means that subjects are placed in control and experimental groups and an assessment is made at the end of the experiment to see which group receives a higher average score on a test or performs better according to some other criterion. Commonly, the experimental group is given a special or "experimental" treatment, whereas the control group is given "other" (perhaps traditional) treatment. Experimental treatments often involve a special group of lessons or a special way of teaching those lessons. For example, an experimenter might wish to know whether learning pioneer history through stories (the experimental treatment) is as effective as learning history from the textbook (the control treatment).

➡ *Activity: The Great Paper-Towel Experiment*

Here is an example you can try with a class of students. It's an experiment I've done many times with children, and I can tell you they do a remarkably good job. Begin the session by asking the class if anyone has ever bought a product that he or she thought was very good. Perhaps students will tell about bicycles, toys, or video games. Give them plenty of time to tell about what makes a product good. Then ask them if they have ever had a product that was not so good. Let the children reflect on what makes a product not so good.

Tell the class that they are going to become experimenters who do research on products. Of course, their scientific work may take several days, and they will want to be very careful that they do a good job. The first product they will examine is paper towels. You need to get three rolls of paper towels, each a different brand. You will need a little bit of equipment: rulers, water, oil, containers, and calculators.

Place the students in groups of three, and have them begin their plans for how they will conduct their research. Be sure to tell them that their challenge is to determine which of the towels is the best buy, second best, and third best. When the groups are ready to proceed, let them go ahead and begin their testing. (Your job is that of coach, to make sure the students are considering how good their tests are.)

When the tests are completed and each group has its ranking of the towels, you can put your data on the board to see how the groups' results compare. This will be a time of discussion as each group reports to the class.

Of course, there are many other products to test. You and the class may decide to test brands of popcorn, orange juice, crayons, peanut butter, or other products the children may suggest. Your research may lead to letter writing, analyses of advertising, or even suggestions for improvements in various products.

⏩ *Activity: Analysis of an Experiment*

In the following activity, experimental research is combined with role-play to help children examine a hypothetical argument between Tiffany and her grandmother. Ask for volunteers to play the roles of Tiffany and Grandmother. The rest of the class will be researchers who attempt to describe and make inferences about the experimental conditions you have established.

> *Grandmother:* Tiffany, it's 9:00 and time for you to go to bed.
>
> *Tiffany:* Oh, gee, Grandma, my favorite TV program is just starting.
>
> *Grandmother:* Well, that's too bad. Anyway, you'd say that no matter what time it was.
>
> *Tiffany:* No, I wouldn't! Mom and Dad wouldn't make me go to bed if they were home.
>
> *Grandmother:* Well, they're not here, and I'm in charge tonight. So off to bed with you!
>
> *Tiffany:* Please, Grandma, let me stay up for just a little while. Then I'll go to bed.
>
> *Grandmother:* When your father was your age, he was in bed every school night by 8:00. He'd come home from school, do his chores, eat his dinner, do his homework, and go to bed.
>
> *Tiffany:* It's just not the same. Things are sure different now that you are living with us. I wish that you'd never come to stay here. Good night!

After the class has watched the role-play, you can begin your group analysis. Each child will meet briefly with a partner to describe the situation. The class will consider the following questions:

1. How would you describe Tiffany's behavior?
2. How would you describe Grandmother's behavior?
3. Why do you think they quarreled?
4. What are some reasons that people disagree?
5. Could the situation have been different? How?

Now ask the class to pair up once more and write a different possible script about the same situation. A discussion should follow in which students share their insights. Encourage students to role-play their different scripts.

➤➤ *Activity: Experiments in Schoolwork*

One way to allow your students to practice metacognition is to allow them to reflect on their own learning. Here are some examples of experiments you and your students can conduct together in order to test attitudes and achievement.

Earlier in this chapter, on descriptive research, I described the Observation Game. There are several experiments you can conduct using it. One investigation can be done comparing how effectively students observe on their own versus how well they observe with a partner. Allowing the same amount of time for each observation, say 5 minutes, one day ask students to observe a painting alone. After the 5-minute observation, remove the painting and ask the students to (1) draw a picture of it and (2) write down everything they can recall about it. The next day, using a different painting, again allow five minutes for observing but have partners observe and discuss together what they see. Test them again (individually) to see how different the results are. You cannot generalize too much from two brief episodes; however, you could continue this exercise and reach firmer conclusions.

Does listening to classical music help a person think better as he or she studies? Some experts think it does; others think there is not enough evidence to warrant such a conclusion. Try something like spelling lessons each day for a week accompanied by a Mozart or Haydn piece. Then give the spelling test. The next week, study without music. Are the results any different? By the way, this is a good time to teach your students how to compute an average score for the class. One week's average can be compared with another. You might also want to compare attitudes. Did the students have a preference? Do they all agree? What might be some weaknesses in this study?

➤➤ *Activity: Health-Drink Design*

This problem-solving experiment challenges students to invent and advertise a new health drink. Working in small groups of about five, students will need to test various formulas, figure ways to keep costs down, and plan a promotional campaign for their product. You will need to supply such raw materials as fruit, juices, and kitchen measuring instruments.

Summary

The purpose of this chapter was to illustrate a number of ways in which children could themselves become social science researchers. All too often, children are exposed only to the results and conclusions of the research of others. They therefore gain little insight into the processes of producing knowledge. By allowing them to conduct historical, descriptive, survey, and experimental research, you give your students the opportunity to move toward the forefront of knowledge. A student who has helped to develop new knowledge is in a far better position to consume knowledge because he or she understands what is involved in gathering the original ideas from which conclusions are made.

No school-age child is too young or immature to conduct research of the kind described in this chapter. Allowances must be made for students' abilities to work independently of the teacher as they mature. Younger students often profit from whole-class investigations supervised by the teacher. So, whether your students are primary or intermediate, or perhaps older than that, get them involved as inquiring, curious researchers.

ACTIVITIES

To review what you have just read about the use of social science research methods in elementary social studies, take the following quiz:

1. Indicate whether you think each of the following research problems would best lend itself to historical, descriptive, survey, or experimental methods.

   a. _____ A study of the previous uses of the land presently occupied by our school.

   b. _____ A study to determine which of two ways of studying our spelling words produces higher average test scores.

   c. _____ A study in which investigators observe the flow of the school lunch lines in order to determine whether improvements could be made.

   d. _____ A study to determine local residents' preferences concerning topics the P.T.A. might present at its monthly meetings during the school year.

   Problem (a) is historical. The study deals with the past. Investigators might do some interviewing of local residents (oral history). Also, they would quite likely want to review such data sources as maps, photographs, and village or city records.

   Problem (b) is experimental. Investigators could randomly assign students in the classroom (or classrooms) to two groups, each of which would study the same spelling list in a different fashion for a certain time period—perhaps 15 minutes per day for four days. Both groups would then be tested on the fifth day to determine which received the higher average score.

   Problem (c) is descriptive. Observing, photographing, mapping, and drawing the flow of traffic through the lunch lines in order to recommend improved procedures would make this a descriptive study. However, you might have thought of experimenting with alternate flow routes, staggered serving times, and so on. Also, investigators could certainly survey students, teachers, and lunchroom personnel to see if they had ideas for improving the lunch line service.

   Problem (d) is survey. Students could make a valuable contribution to the P.T.A. or other parent group by consulting with the group's leadership about potential offerings for that year and then surveying community interest in proposed topics.

2. Explain the differences among the following types of sample selection: simple random selection, stratified random selection, stratified selection.

3. Choose any one of the four methods of research presented in this chapter and develop a possible investigation at a grade or age level of interest to you. Use the following form to outline your proposed study.

   Topic:_____

   Problem or question to be investigated:_____

   _____

   Data sources:_____

   _____

Procedures: _____

_____

Means of gathering data: _____

_____

Means of processing data: _____

_____

Possible inferences to be made: _____

_____

_____

NOTES

1. Adapted from W. R. Fielder, ed., *Inquiring about American History* (New York: Holt, Rinehart and Winston, 1972), pp. 23–27.
2. Ibid.
3. Ibid.
4. S. J. Devlin and A. E. Freeney, *The Design of Surveys and Samples* (Newton, MA: Education Development Center, 1973).
5. Evelyn Kaye, *The Family Guide to Children's Television* (New York: Random House, 1974).

SUGGESTED READINGS

Benson, J. (1998). "Using an Inquiry Approach with Preservice Teachers to Explain the Process of Facts, Concept, and Generalization." *Social Studies* (Sept./Oct.): 227–231.

Brown, R. (1998). "Outdoor Learning Centers: Realistic Social Studies Experiences for K-6 Students." *Social Studies* (Sept./Oct.): 199–204.

Freese, J. (1998). "Using the National Geography Standards to Integrate Children's Social Studies." *Social Studies and the Young Learner* (Nov./Dec.): 10–13.

Howard, J. (1999). "Using a Social Studies Theme to Conceptualize a Problem." *Social Studies* (July/Aug.): 171–176.

Murphey, C. (1998). "Using the Five Themes of Geography to Explore a School Site." *Social Studies Review* (Spring/Summer): 45–48.

Penyak, L. (1999). "Oral History and Problematic Questions Promote Issues-Centered Education. *Social Studies* (Mar./Apr.): 68–71.

Riley, J. (1999). " 'Did They Really Believe This?' Authentic Medical Documents as Window on the Past." *Social Studies and the Young Learner* (Jan./Feb.): 2–5.

Soto, B. (1998). "Walking on the Wild Side: Geographic Field Study for Fifth Graders." *Social Studies* (Sept./Oct.): 236–238.

Whiting, N. (1998). "Archaeology and Intercultural Education in the Elementary Grades: An Example from Minnesota." *Social Studies* (Nov./Dec.): 254–259.

Zarnowski, M. (1997). "Interpreting Critical Issues: Comparing Past and Modern Plagues." *Social Studies and the Young Learner* (Nov./Dec.): 10–13.

chapter 10

Teaching and Learning Responsible Citizenship

This chapter examines the role of citizenship education in social studies. What conditions are needed in order to provide students with the opportunities to become good citizens? The focus in not on conformity without thought but rather on active, meaningful participation. The following ideas are addressed:

- The roles of the informed citizen
- Citizenship and community service
- A conflict model of citizenship
- Decision making
- The research base for citizenship education
- The meaning of citizenship in a democracy

We have physiocrats, geometricians, chemists,
astronomers, poets, musicians, and painters aplenty,
but we have no longer a citizen among us.

—Jean Jacques Rousseau

Citizenship is at the heart of the social studies curriculum. Nearly two centuries after Rousseau lamented that "we have no longer a citizen among us," Adlai Stevenson wrote that "as a citizen of this democracy, you are the rulers and the ruled, the lawgivers and the law-abiding, the beginning and the end." It is a beautiful thought, and it represents a great challenge to the teacher of elementary social studies.

What does citizenship mean to a child? How can children grasp this seemingly abstract concept? The answer is found in experience. Always remember that children learn what they live. If your classroom is a miniature democracy, where students are expected to participate in decisions, work and play together, share their thoughts and dreams, and become involved in school and community, I think they will begin to understand what it means to be a citizen.

If a citizen is the "beginning and the end," the alpha and the omega, then citizenship education is a necessity, not a luxury we can do without. Each of us, as cit-

Two young Americans display their Good Citizenship Awards.

izens of the United States of America, Canada, or any other democracy for that matter, has certain *rights* and *responsibilities*. This is what is meant by the beginning and the end: Our rights are the beginning and our responsibilities are the end. You cannot have one without the other if democratic citizenship is to have meaning. Just imagine what a position of trust this places you in.

What Are the Roles of the Citizen in American Democracy?

It is always useful to approach teaching and learning as problem solving. The organizing question posed as the heading to this portion of the chapter serves as a problem for you and your students to solve. Don't worry if you don't solve it completely. It takes a lifetime of learning to be a good citizen. Your job is to get children started in the right direction. Figure 10.1 illustrates the spiraling effect of a single important question. Notice that the question remains the same throughout the entire school experience, but the response deepens over time. The examples change. The experiences take on greater sophistication as students move from elementary to middle to senior high school. The young child learns about individual responsibility by helping to make classroom rules and learning to follow them. The young child learns that we must take responsibility for our actions. These early experiences serve as a foundation for increasingly sophisticated experiences throughout the succeeding school years.

The Role of Social Knowledge

At its best, a school is a community of learners. This implies that the children and teachers, administrators, and support staff who go there will find themselves in a communal setting. A true community is a relational place where people work together, play together, and share their thoughts, feelings, and dreams. School is a

FIGURE 10.1   *The Roles of the Citizen*

K–4	5–8	9–12
What Are the Roles of the Citizen in American Democracy?	**What Are the Roles of the Citizen in American Democracy?**	**What Are the Roles of the Citizen in American Democracy?**
The meaning of citizenship	The meaning of citizenship	The meaning of citizenship in the United States
Becoming a citizen	Becoming a citizen	Becoming a citizen
Rights of individuals	Personal rights	Personal rights
Responsibilities of individuals	Political rights	Political rights
Dispositions that enhance citizen effectiveness and promote the healthy functioning of American democracy	Economic rights	Economic rights
	Scope and limits of rights	Relationships among personal, political, and economic rights
	Personal responsibilities	Scope and limits of rights
Forms of participation	Civic responsibilities	Personal responsibilities
Political leadership and public service	Dispositions that enhance citizen effectiveness and promote the healthy functioning of American constitutional democracy	Civic responsibilities
Selecting leaders		Dispositions that lead the citizen to be an independent member of society
	Participation in civic and political life and the attainment of individual and public goals	Dispositions that foster respect for individual worth and human dignity
		Dispositions that incline the citizen to public affairs
	The difference between political and social participation	Dispositions that facilitate thoughtful and effective participation in public affairs
	Forms of political participation	The relationship between politics and the attainment of individual and public goals
	Political leadership and public service	The difference between political and social participation
	Knowledge and participation	Forms of political participation
		Political leadership and careers in public service
		Knowledge and participation

Source: National Standard for Civics and Government (Calabasas, CA: Center for Civic Education, 1997).

socially contrived environment. This means that society has determined that academic learning should take place in social settings.

The term *public school* originally meant that students learned in each other's company rather than privately from a tutor. In the first century A.D., the Roman orator Quintilian advocated public schools over private instruction because, he argued, in public settings, children have the benefit of friendships, examples, and associations. In other words, Quintilian felt that the school environment would make children better Roman citizens. Like Plato before him, Quintilian thought that group play was especially productive for children. Games, activities, and free play put children in situations where moral issues, differences of opinion, camaraderie, sharing, and give-and-take inevitably arise.

In more recent times, such theorists as Jean Piaget and Lev Vygotsky have addressed the idea of social knowledge. Social knowledge arises from shared group experience. When children and teachers play and work together on projects, activities, and other aspects of school life, they become bonded through their commonly held knowledge and collective memory. This leads to a sense of community, a sense of belonging—the beginning of citizenship. Just how this happens is captured by Don Rowe, who writes:

> Schools are highly complex communities [with] value systems linked to their purpose and role, power structures, and rules enforced by a justice system. The "citizens" (or "subjects") of school communities can exhibit widely differing degrees of loyalty to the community. Pupils who feel disregarded by a school (or at odds with its aims) will have little reason to feel a sense of obligation to uphold its values or rules.[1]

The power of the school's social system to make a child feel part of things (or alienated) is enormous. Therefore, the social studies teacher's role is crucial. You must take seriously the social aspects of the school curriculum. How a child feels about being included or excluded will go a long way toward determining his or her lifelong view of the value of participating in society. Oh, the responsibilities of an elementary teacher are never ending! But it's worth it, because you have the opportunity to do such important work. Just imagine: Your job is about improving people's lives. What could be more significant?

Citizenship and Community Service

To be a citizen means many things. We are citizens of the world, citizens of our country, citizens of our state or province, citizens of our school and classroom, and citizens of our family. One of the arenas of citizenship that children need to experience is citizenship in the local community. The community affords opportunities for participation at many levels; children can be helpful citizens by picking up litter, planting trees, helping elderly people, and undertaking service projects.

One group of primary school children studied a crosswalk near their school with the idea of making it safer. Their work was very important because it probably prevented injuries or loss of life. A class of middle school children were successful in having chlorofluorocarbon-containing styrofoam cups removed from the school district's purchasing list. A third-grade class studied their school's playground equipment and were successful in having dangerous equipment replaced. An intermediate-level class decided to "adopt" a retirement home near their school; they were successful in making ties and friendships between themselves and the elderly. As Martin Luther King Jr. once said, "Everyone can be great, because everyone can serve."

Anderson and associates[2] report on a community service program implemented in the Springfield, Massachusetts, schools. They describe a program built around the following components:

1. Establish a schoolwide service-learning theme.
2. Determine the objectives.

3. Meet with community representatives.
4. Build a repertoire of activities.
5. Develop learning experiences.
6. Establish a time line.
7. Reflect on the experience.
8. Celebrate.

One of the Springfield schools, Lincoln School, adopted a citizenship theme to help develop a sense of community within the school. The guiding idea was, "If children are exposed in their formative years to the values of participation in the community, they will internalize those values. . . . The climate of the school is orderly, friendly, open and warm. Negative behavior is rare, and children routinely choose to be helpful, kind, and caring."[3]

Children live what they learn. If you give your students love, kindness, fairness, consideration, politeness, and warmth, they will reflect it. I can remember in my own elementary teaching experience that I routinely thanked a child every time he or she handed me a paper. It became a matter of course that students would always thank me or others when we handed out papers. Courtesy, in an age where drivers show extreme anger toward one another on the streets of our cities and rudeness is displayed in a dozen different ways, is something that must become "natural behavior" when a child is young.

▶▶ *Effective Citizenship: An Interview with JoAnne Buggey*

JoAnne Buggey is a nationally recognized authority on social studies and citizenship education. Her work represents some of the best text material on the subject available today. She is known by her students and by the educational community to be an outstanding educator. Following is an interview with Buggey concerning citizenship education.[4]

What are the implications of citizenship education for children?

Effective citizenship education has been a major concern of educators in the United States throughout our history. All that occurs in our schools each day can be broadly interpreted as citizenship education. In addition, it is a central focus of the social studies. The role of citizenship education in the elementary school is to prepare students for their roles as responsible decision makers and concerned citizens. The focus is on setting the stage for a life of meaningful participation for each and every learner.

What can teachers and children do to bring citizenship education to life?

Social studies textbooks continue to provide the firm foundation for meaningful citizenship education in most classrooms. Children's literature provides a valuable resource for building on the textbook. Extending activities beyond the classroom and into the community is the ultimate goal. In order for this to happen, a total community-involvement program must be developed. The teacher/school and parent/community must interact in a planned and meaningful way for citizenship education to come alive for students.

Can you cite some examples of classes or schools that are doing a good job of citizenship education?

It is most effective when a school adopts *citizenship education* as its school theme. However, there are individual classrooms where citizenship is also a meaningful focus. The following are only a few examples:

Kindergarten classes and the forestry department worked together during the year on a community reforestation project. Pictures were taken of each tree being planted. Students continued to observe the trees throughout their grade-school experience.

The parents and their first-graders organized a community clean-up campaign as a result of student interest in pollution. Teams worked several Saturdays cleaning up areas of their community. Posters were displayed to try to get others interested in keeping the community clean.

Second-graders worked with the local police department on a bicycle safety program. The culmination of the program was a Bicycle Safety Day.

Third-graders took a survey of the community regarding the installation of street lights at an intersection near the school. Students devised the survey, and teams of students and parents collected the information. Results were sent to the city council.

Fourth-graders subscribed to the local newspaper and several news magazines. They worked in teams, each of which focused on one problem. Once a month, they produced a class newspaper in which each group summarized its special problem area. They distributed the paper to each class in the school.

Fifth-graders belonged to the Birthday Club at a nearby senior citizen residence. Each month, those students who had a birthday attended the party at the senior residence. Students participated in the entertainment and made cards for their birthday friends.

Sixth-graders were in charge of organizing a mock election for the school. The election took place in November in conjunction with the local election. Everyone had a chance to vote. Students made posters and gave campaign speeches. Election results were reported and compared to local election results.

What are the key concepts of citizenship education?

There are many key concepts relating to effective citizenship education. The following are only a few: patriotism, government, participation, caring, rights and responsibilities, and rules and laws. Figure 10.2 illustrates the relationships between a citizen's *rights* and *responsibilities*.

A Conflict Model of Citizenship

Don Rowe[5] describes a conflict model of citizenship education designed in Britain. The model is designed to stimulate critical and reflective thought built around key questions such as the following:

- What rules are needed for people to live together?
- Why do people break rules, and what should happen to them?
- What makes a rule or a law fair?

FIGURE 10.2

Our Rights and Responsibilities Are Like Two Sides of a Single Coin. Rights Have Little Meaning without Responsibilities. Each Gives Meaning to the Other.

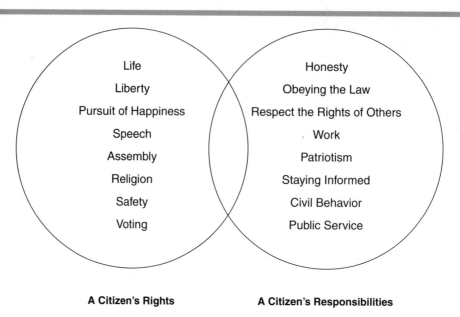

A Citizen's Rights	A Citizen's Responsibilities
Life	Honesty
Liberty	Obeying the Law
Pursuit of Happiness	Respect the Rights of Others
Speech	Work
Assembly	Patriotism
Religion	Staying Informed
Safety	Civil Behavior
Voting	Public Service

- Who has rights, and what are they?
- What responsibilities arise from these rights?
- What happens when our rights conflict with the rights of others?
- Who can tell you what to do and on what basis?
- What makes a good or fair leader?
- What is meant by fairness or justice?

These questions, to have meaning, must be considered in context and posed in appropriate ways for children of different ages; nevertheless, they are at the very heart of what it means to be a citizen. Teachers can apply these questions to the ordinary routines of schoolwork and play. As Rowe notes, "Posed at an appropriate level, these questions are as interesting and relevant to pupils of seven as they are to moral and political philosophers."[6]

The appealing thing about a conflict model of citizenship is that it addresses the points of tension that arise naturally when people work and play together. To deny that conflicts exist in the lives of children is to limit their moral horizon. Conflict resolution is an ongoing process in a democratic society. Children need to learn at an early age that they can talk about their feelings, share their points of view, and learn to appreciate the fact that others may see things differently from time to time. It's part of a functional, healthy social environment to have a certain amount of conflict.

I would go so far as to say that you should set time aside each day for you and your class to talk about classroom and playground life. Your young citizens should be given ample opportunity to express themselves in an open forum. This is the essence of democracy: to hear and to be heard. If you take this idea seriously and stay with it, you will see considerable advance in your students' insights, openness,

FIGURE 10.3

223
Citizenship

A Child's Essay
on Citizenship

What is a good citizen?

I think a good citizen is a person who does what he or she is asked to do and obeys the rules. Another thing a good citizen does is when he or she is nice to one another and helps someone out if somebody is hurt or needs help with schoolwork. That's what I think a good citizen is.

Lauren Griffin
Mr. Johnson's class Grade 5

reflective thinking, and willingness to participate in the fundamental processes of daily life. Note a child's attempt to articulate the meaning of citizenship, as illustrated in Figure 10.3.

Knowledge versus Information

Much of what children are taught in school consists of information. They are told or they read about places, names, events, and dates. This is exactly what information is: unconnected bits and pieces that the learner is supposed to make sense of. Some children see or make their own connections, but most do not. Social studies especially, with its bewildering array of facts, is difficult to understand and appreciate. The problem is quite simple: information overload. The solution is even simpler: Create meaningful experiences. But in spite of how easy it is to identify both problem and solution, few teachers seem to grasp the obvious.

For citizenship education to be effective, we must lead our students beyond the horizon of information. One can have information about the three branches of the government and not be a particularly good citizen. One can know that the United States consumes something close to 40 percent of the world's natural resources and do nothing about it. One can be aware about poverty in one's neighborhood and not try to help. Information in learning is like a spectator sport; watching tennis on television won't make you physically fit or even sweaty.

Jean Piaget once noted that verbal knowledge is not real knowledge. By that, he meant that there are differences between information and knowledge. John Dewey noted that the abstract nature of the curriculum prevented it from having intellectual potential. Dewey explained that most of what children are taught is merely abstract information from books or lectures. The constructivity principle states that activity or experience must precede analysis. The point of all this is that you must seek ways to actively involve your students in learning, particularly in learning about what it means to be a citizen in a democratic society.

Let me give you an example of learning about citizenship through experience. An elementary school in Kingston, Washington, recently decided to study the Asian-Pacific Economic Cooperation (APEC) group of nations. The United States and Canada are member nations of APEC, as are Japan, China, South Korea, Australia, New Zealand, Singapore, Taiwan, and a few others. Led by the school principal, every teacher and student in the school studied about APEC. It was very much a hands-on study, with emphasis on letter writing, performances, speeches, maps, drawings, and construction. This is very different from merely studying these countries from a text. The two basic differences between this experience and traditional instruction are (1) the study took place around a theme (APEC) involving the whole school and (2) the learning was active and experiential.

For a child to learn to be a good citizen, the child must work with others, become actively involved, and somehow see himself or herself as contributing to knowledge as opposed to taking in information. The beneficial outcome of such an approach is that students enjoy learning more, they retain more knowledge, and they get to practice being a participating citizen.

Experiences in democracy should be an integral part of school life.

Effective citizenship education has been a major concern of educators in the United States throughout its history. Much of what occurs in our schools each day, including the teaching of the three Rs, can be interpreted as preparation of our citizens. James Madison identified the importance of citizenship education when he stated, "A people who mean to be their own governors must arm themselves with the power which knowledge gives." More than a hundred years ago, Herbert Spencer restated the importance of citizenship education when he wrote, "The need to function as effective citizens called for familiar school subjects: history, civics, economics, and politics. These subjects should stress practical application." Citizenship education was clearly to be a central focus of the social studies.

Whether citizenship education continues to be a central focus of social studies has been asked many times in the twentieth century; however, this question has recently gained renewed emphasis. Current societal problems, a stress on back to basics, and an increased concern for patriotism and global education have all worked to renew interest in citizenship education. Figure 10.4 shows an illustration drawn by a child in Lithuania who corresponds by letters with children in the United States, an example of global education.

Decision Making: Classroom Civics Lessons

In a democratic society, it is expected that citizens will participate as fully as possible in the decision-making process. A citizen entering a voting booth keeps alive and passes on a centuries-old tradition of right and privilege.

Yet, one wonders how people learn (or are taught) to make wise and good decisions. Even though it is important to focus on political decision making, don't forget that people make hundreds of personal decisions every day. Those decisions range from whether to wear blue socks or white socks, whether to cook dinner or grab some hamburgers, whether to play outside or watch television, and so on, depending on the circumstances. Of course, if the person has only a pair of blue socks, little money, and no television, the choices are narrowed.

Decision making, therefore, is a function of the alternatives available to the individual. In a country offering only one political slate of candidates, no decision making is necessary. In a classroom in which the teacher makes all decisions, students have no opportunity to develop the skill. I argue that you should provide numerous opportunities for your students to make decisions and, at least in some cases, those decisions should be real and not merely part of a case study or a contrived activity.

Free Time: An Experiment

In an educational experiment I helped conduct, a class of first-graders was given a half hour of free time each day. The children were told they could do whatever they chose during the free time. A few rules were agreed on, such as no leaving the room except by permission and being fairly quiet. There were two reasons for giving the students this free time. One was to give them the opportunity to make real decisions about something important—their time and how to use it. The other reason

225

FIGURE 10.4

Illustration of the Statue of Liberty Drawn by a Lithuanian Child Involved in an Exchange of Letters with American Students

was to see if the children could put the time to constructive use. The teacher was instructed to develop a rich classroom environment with games, interest centers, a small library, art materials, and science materials. The teacher was also instructed to interact with the students, not by telling them what to do, but by talking personally to individuals, helping them with various tasks, and reviewing the free-time use with the students.

The outcome was very gratifying. The children showed that they could make wise decisions about their use of free time. In fact, they invariably chose productive activities that permitted cooperative learning, language development, sharing, taking turns, peer teaching, and exploration. The free time provided a wonderful opportunity for growth in such areas as responsibility, organization, reflection, and planning. The experiment lasted the entire year and received many parental compliments.

Today's students must prepare to be citizens of the world's "global village."

The Research Base

As Kathleen Cotton has so correctly pointed out, "Nearly all writers on the subject of citizenship education agree that it is essential for preserving America's democratic way of life."[7] Cotton reviewed some 93 articles and reports on citizenship education and developed a profile of the good citizen as a person who is informed, autonomous, respectful, participating, mindful of the common good, and committed to democratic values and principles.[8] Sadly, there is little evidence that social studies teachers take these attributes seriously in terms of the day-to-day experiences in classrooms. In fact, there is some reason to think that the way citizenship education is typically taught, mainly through textbooks, that those attributes are in fact not a high curricular priority.

I've laid out the problem pretty clearly: As teachers, you and I need to do a better job of educating for citizenship. I don't feel very good about giving you such bad news, but you are the country's best hope for turning things around. What can you do to improve the situation? To begin, take a few minutes to study Figure 10.5, which lists six attributes of a well-prepared citizen. As you study it, keep in mind that these are desired outcomes of the entire school experience, grades K–12. Thus, the attributes listed in Figure 10.5 represent the profile we hope to produce over time, not overnight. Using the basic premise of the spiral curriculum—identifying important concepts and teaching them each year at increasing levels of sophistication—we can imagine that primary students can learn these attributes through simpler experiences that have meaning in their lives, and intermediate students will continue the journey.

FIGURE 10.5

Attributes of a Prepared Citizen

- *Democratic values.* Prepared citizens understand and are committed to the values inherent in the U.S. Constitution and Bill of Rights: justice, freedom, equality, diversity, authority, privacy, due process, property, participation, truth, patriotism, human rights, rule of law, tolerance, mutual assistance, personal and civic responsibility, self-restraint, and self-respect.

- *The common good.* Citizens need to act from respect for the common good; that is, they need to be willing to deliberate about the nature of the public good and how to achieve it. They also need to possess compassion, ethical commitment, social responsibility, and a sense of interdependence among people and between people and their environment. They need to express their commitment to the common good through their actions, such as voting, volunteering, serving on juries, petitioning the government for change, and so on.

- *Knowledge.* Effective civic education results in knowledge and understanding of our nation's founding documents, the structure of government, the political process, and the global context in which the United States functions.

- *Thinking skills.* Competent citizens require skills in higher-level thinking processes—critical reasoning, problem solving, decision making, perspective taking, divergent thinking—constructing hypotheses, and evaluating evidence.

- *Social process skills.* Social skills identified as critical for high-functioning citizens include communication, conflict management, consensus building, and working in cooperative endeavors.

- *Student attitudes.* Effective civic education influences students in such a way that they believe in the efficacy of civic participation, are interested in participating, and have a feeling of obligation to participate.

Source: Adapted from Kathleen Cotton, *Educating for Citizenship* (Portland, OR: Northwest Regional Laboratory, 1996), pp. 6–7.

Researchers and writers in the area of citizenship education have given us a clear picture of how schools can contribute to the goal of producing good citizens. They point to such factors as school and classroom climate, teaching practices, student experiences, and the content and materials taught and learned.

John Dewey's dream of school as a miniature democracy represents a school and classroom ideal. In fact, there are a number of ways in which a school cannot be a democracy; but it can be a place where certain democratic values can be lived and learned. For example, you can allow your students to participate in decisions that affect school and classroom life. For instance, it is easy for adults to overlook how meaningful it is for a child to choose among alternative possibilities in carrying out an assignment. Students can and should be encouraged to make classroom rules. They should have class government with elected officers. They should take responsibility for helping to decorate and keep the room orderly.

Beyond these matters, a more subtle issue of class climate emerges. It has to do with how open your classroom is. According to Angell's[9] review of the research, an open classroom is characterized by democratic leadership behaviors, positive teacher verbal behaviors, respect for students, peer interaction, open discussion, student participation, and cooperation. Interestingly, another factor related to openness is the use by students of source materials other than textbooks. According to researcher Torney-Purta,[10] allowing students to express their opinions freely is the most positive contribution a teacher can make toward the acquisition of democratic values.

Teachers who are committed to citizenship education realize that good citizenship is an active role, and therefore the classroom must be a place dedicated to active learning. A great deal of support has already been given to active learning for other pedagogical reasons, so this only strengthens the case. Passively learning facts about citizenship will not do. Children must experience active learning in order to practice doing what involved citizens do. Nothing does this better than group projects that involve teamwork, decisions, investigation, and production.

A number of learning strategies[11] are recommended to facilitate citizenship education. Each of them is addressed in one chapter or another of this text. I've included them in Figure 10.6 for your closer examination. Those strategies include practice in class discussion, the use of open-ended and higher-level questions by teachers, research by children using sources other than textbooks, writing projects (including letter writing), cooperative group projects, brainstorming, role-play, simulations, field trips and on-site investigations, observation, class meetings, class and school government, community service projects, and interaction with guest speakers. Of particular importance is the much needed component of reflective thinking. The strategies enumerated in this paragraph have much deeper implications for learning and for application to life experiences when students are given ample opportunity to discuss, reflect, seek meaning, and employ a range of metacognitive techniques.

Community service projects deserve additional mention here because they truly are at the heart of what it means to be a giving, participating person in one's school, neighborhood, larger community, and so on. To quote Berman, "Community service efforts build self-esteem and allow students to experience themselves as part of the larger network of people who are helping to create a better world."[12] A review of the writing and research on community service projects indicates that several variables, when present, enhance the effectiveness of such experiences.

Community service projects should address real needs. Elementary school children are perfectly well equipped to take the age-old "Community Helpers" study to deeper levels by becoming community helpers themselves. Among the projects that work well are such involvements as an ongoing relationship with a nursing home near the school where the children touch the lives of elderly people, many of whom are lonely and whose days tend to be tedious; projects such as cleaning up a stream, pond, or field near the school; assembling published local histories and geographies in conjunction with the local historical society, museum, or library; the production of dramas or pageants to which community people are invited; volunteer efforts by older elementary-age students who are willing to read to young children; and even the old school carnival experience, if the children can be meaningfully involved, is an excellent means of bringing community people to the school and creating a positive image. Take a moment to consider this child's experience as she reflected on her visits to a nearby nursing home:

> When our class went there first I didn't know what to think. The people were old and it smelled funy. But everyone was nice they were happy when we gave them the pictures. My frend Helen put my picture of my dog on her wall. His name is Tykey. Now

FIGURE 10.6 *Civic Ideals and Practices*

Social studies programs should include experiences that provide for the study of *the ideals, principles, and practices of citizenship in a democratic republic,* so that the learner can:

Early Grades	**Middle Grades**
a. identify key ideals of the United States' democratic republican form of government, such as individual human dignity, liberty, justice, equality, and the rule of law, and discuss their application in specific situations;	a. examine the origins and continuing influence of key ideals of the democratic republican form of government, such as individual human dignity, liberty, justice. equality, and the rule of law;
b. identify examples of rights and responsibilities of citizens;	b. identify and interpret sources and examples of the rights and responsibilities of citizens;
c. locate, access, organize, and apply information about an issue of public concern from multiple points of view;	c. locate, access, analyze, organize, and apply information about selected public issues—recognizing and explaining multiple points of view;
d. identify and practice selected forms of civic discussion and participation consistent with the ideals of citizens in a democratic republic;	d. practice forms of civic discussion and participation consistent with the ideals of citizens in a democratic republic;
e. explain actions citizens can take to influence public policy decisions;	e. explain and analyze various forms of citizen action that influence public policy decisions;
f. recognize that a variety of formal and informal actors influence and shape public policy;	f. identify and explain the roles of formal and informal political actors in influencing and shaping public policy and decision-making;
g. examine the influence of public opinion on personal decision-making and government policy on public issues;	g. analyze the influence of diverse forms of public opinion on the development of public policy and decision-making;
h. explain how public policies and citizen behaviors may or may nor reflect the stated ideals of a democratic republican form of government;	h. analyze the effectiveness of selected public policies and citizen behaviors in realizing the stated ideals of a democratic republican form of government;
i. describe how public policies are used to address issues of public concern;	i. explain the relationship between policy statements and action plans used to address issues of public concern;
j. recognize and interpret how the "common good" can be strengthened through various forms of citizen action.	j. examine strategies designed to strengthen the "common good," which consider a range of options for citizen action.

Source: Expectations of Excellence: Curriculum Standards for Social Studies (p. 44), Bulletin 89, Fall 1994, Washington, DC: NCSS. © National Council for the Social Studies. Reprinted by permission.

she asks me about Tykey and I told her he took some meat off the table when my mom went outside. The we started lafing. Helen is hapy to see me I love her. Some of the people ded there to. Mrs Lowe tokked to us about it.

Among the other research-based recommendations[13] for community service projects are that they should (1) incorporate academic skills, (2) provide opportunities for young people to be depended on, (3) encourage collaborative work, (4) give students responsibility for organizing and following through, and (5) produce a tangible product or evidence of accomplishment.

The Meaning of Citizenship

A Multicultural Perspective

In our democratic society, the freedom, rights, and responsibilities of the individual are prized above all else. We are a pluralistic society composed of a multitude of racial and ethnic groups and backgrounds. We have different heritages, but we share a common dream. We are truly in this together. The richness of a multicultural society is something to be celebrated and appreciated. As children experience their formative years, the school can contribute toward broader understandings of the complex workings of a pluralistic society.

⏩ *An Interview with Patricia Hammill*

Patricia Hammill is my colleague in elementary social studies education. She is a recognized authority in multicultural education and teaches courses in that area. Following is an interview with Hammill concerning multicultural education.[14]

What is multicultural education?

Most theorists agree that there are several major aspects of multicultural education, but that three things in particular stand out. Multicultural education is an idea or concept, an educational reform movement, and a process. It is the *idea* that all students—regardless of social class, gender, ethnic, racial, cultural characteristics, or exceptionality—should have equal opportunities to learn in school. In addition, it is the idea that some institutional characteristics of schools inhibit the progress of some groups of students, while others have better chances to achieve academically. Therefore, an important thrust of multicultural education is to *reform* the schools and other educational institutions so that all students have equal access to knowledge. Reform involves the total school or educational environment, not just the curriculum. Multicultural education should therefore be viewed as an ongoing *process,* with educational equality as an ideal toward which we can continue to strive.

What do you see as the relationship between multicultural education and being a good citizen?

At the core of multicultural education is the idea of equality, which has also been a key concept in the development of our country. The idea of equality or "unalienable rights" of the human being had a very limited meaning at the time that the Declaration of Independence was written in 1776. However, this powerful idea has been used throughout our history by victimized and excluded groups to justify their struggles for equity. A knowledge of the key concepts of multicultural education, as well as an increased awareness of and empathy for struggling groups, can assist us in making wise decisions as informed citizens. In extension, multicultural education helps us understand the nature of, and the need for, individual and social reform and action.

Is this just one more special-interest group seeking
a place in an already crowded curriculum?

No. Multicultural education is not a "tack-on" to the school curriculum, nor is it the outgrowth of a particular interest group. It is also not a "subject" to be taught at a particular point in the school day or year and then put aside. Multicultural education is infused throughout the educational process as reflected in instructional strategies, selection of content for inclusion in the curriculum, the attitudes and actions of school staff and students, and the total culture, or ecosystem, of the school.

What are some positive outcomes of multicultural education?

In my opinion, multicultural education has benefits for all aspects of the educational enterprise. Teachers benefit by the training they receive in multicultural education in enhanced teaching skills; the development of a broad range of teaching strategies that assist them in meeting the needs of a diverse student population; a broadened understanding of culture; and an awareness of how such elements as world view, ethnic identity, and social class can influence the ways in which their students process information and learn. Teachers also gain skills in choosing appropriate content by learning how to recognize bias in materials and by making adjustments or in countering bias through class discussion.

Students benefit from multicultural education through increased access to knowledge and from expanded opportunities for achievement in school. As teachers incorporate techniques such as cooperative learning strategies, students experience opportunities to engage in collaborative group work, which has been shown to enhance attitudes toward school and toward peers from varying racial and ethnic backgrounds. Excellence in education is a positive outcome for all students in our pluralistic society. As a result of excellent teaching and systematic program reform, learners are offered an increased range of options through which they can achieve their educational goals.

How would you respond to the criticism that multicultural
education is an attempt to downplay our Western heritage?

Controversy over the field of multicultural education has increased in the last few years. However, I would argue that a goal of multicultural education is to help teachers and students to understand their own culture(s) as well as others. Only when one has an understanding of one's own culture can one attempt to understand other cultures. One way to do this is to look at culture as a survival program . . . the way in which a social group promotes the survival of its members. A social group's program consists of knowledge that is public, that is shared by most members of the group. Values are an extremely important component of a cultural program. By examining the underlying values of our own culture as well as others, we can develop a more sophisticated understanding of the nature of a pluralistic society. In addition, by studying cultural universals such as verbal and nonverbal behavior, socialization, aesthetics, and myth, we can build on the idea that all human groups have similar needs that are met in very specific and unique ways. If we couple our study of culture with the notion of cooperative pluralism, we can promote the idea that while cultures do have unique forms, all peoples are interdependent in a pluralistic society. By better understanding the struggles of various groups to survive, we can assist each other in the continuous formation of our common shared ideal, that of participatory democracy.

At what age should multicultural education begin?

In my opinion, very young children can benefit from being introduced to the basic concepts of multicultural education. Indeed, there is increasing evidence that children develop an awareness of racial differences at a very young age. Skills of cooperation and conflict resolution can be taught early in the primary years. The attitudes and behavior modeled by classroom teachers can go a long way in promoting tolerance and acceptance of differences. In addition, by offering children a wide range of educational opportunities that also promote cross-cultural understanding, educators can lay the groundwork for the development of attitudes and skills necessary for cooperative pluralism.

What are some of the key ideas or concepts of multicultural education?

Equity is the major concept of multicultural education. A closely related concept is that of educational excellence. Other concepts or ideas that form the basis of multicultural education are reform (as a continuous process), culture, change, conflict and conflict resolution, pluralism, cooperation, empathy, and tolerance.

A Global Perspective

As our world grows increasingly interdependent, the global village described by Marshall MacLuhan has come to pass. A nuclear power plant leakage and near meltdown sent shockwaves around the world. Thor Heyerdahl reports seeing pollution and debris constantly as he crosses the ocean by raft. Hostage situations highlight tension in the Middle East. Shifts in the balance of power occur as nations such as the United States and China enter into major trade agreements. East and West Germany have reunited, and demands for local rule press *perestroika* in Russia toward democratization. And fewer than 5 percent of the teachers in the United States have studied comparative or international education.

➤➤ *An Interview with John J. Cogan*

John J. Cogan is my colleague in elementary social studies education. He is widely known as an expert on global education. Following is an interview with Cogan concerning global education.[15] Learning strategies to facilitate teaching global awareness may be found in Figure 10.7.

What is global education?

It is a way of viewing the world. Simply stated, global education is a systematic effort to communicate the awareness that the planet Earth and the people who live on it are increasingly *interdependent*—that is, we are all citizens of the world as well as of our respective nations. It is a way of viewing and thinking about the world that is quite different from traditional models. What one nation does today greatly affects other nations. The day when each nation "does its own thing" is no longer applicable, if indeed, it ever was.

FIGURE 10.7 *Global Connections*

Social studies programs should include experiences that provide for the study of *global connections and interdependence,* so that the learner can:

Early Grades

a. explore ways that language, art, music, belief systems, and other cultural elements may facilitate global understanding or lead to misunderstanding

b. give examples of conflict, cooperation, and interdependence among individuals, groups, and nations;

c. examine the effects of changing technologies on the global community;

d. explore causes, consequences, and possible solutions to persistent, contemporary, and emerging global issues, such as pollution and endangered species;

e. examine the relationships and tensions between personal wants and needs and various global concerns, such as use of imported oil, land use, and environmental protection;

f. investigate concerns, issues, standards, and conflicts related to universal human rights, such as the treatment of children, religious groups, and effects of war.

Middle Grades

a. describe instances in which language, art, music, belief systems, and other cultural elements can facilitate global understanding or cause misunderstanding;

b. analyze examples of conflict, cooperation, and interdependence among groups, societies, and nations;

c. describe and analyze the effects of changing technologies on the global community;

d. explore the causes, consequences, and possible solutions to persistent, contemporary, and emerging global issues, such as health, security, resource allocation, economic development, and environmental quality;

e. describe and explain the relationships and tensions between national sovereignty and global interests, in such matters as territory, natural resources, trade, use of technology, and welfare of people;

f. demonstrate understanding of concerns, standards, issues, and conflicts related to universal human rights,

g. identify and describe the roles of international and multinational organizations.

Source: Expectations of Excellence: Curriculum Standards for Social Studies (p. 45), Bulletin 89, Fall 1994, Washington, DC: NCSS. © National Council for the Social Studies. Reprinted by permission.

Is this just one more special-interest group seeking a place in the curriculum?

No. People supportive of global education come from all walks of life. Although some see global education as the sole province of the social studies, most supporters believe strongly that global education should permeate *all* areas of the curriculum—that is, science, math, language, music, art, and so on. What is not needed is another course added to an already overcrowded curriculum. Rather, a global perspective should be woven into the very fabric of the elementary curriculum. We need to help in-service and prospective teachers see how they can highlight a global perspective in existing programs. This necessitates making them personally aware of just how interdependent the world in which they live is—for example, just bringing to their attention how many of the many products they use during any given day are from another country, or where products raised or manufactured in their communities are sent internationally. This is easy enough to do and yet doesn't overwhelm the teacher. If teachers begin slowly and do a little at a time, the overall picture will begin to develop.

What are some positive outcomes of global education?

This, of course, rests in part on how one interprets *positive.* I would interpret it as "furthering the development of the human condition." In this context, there are several hoped-for outcomes as a result of global education programs:

- An increased ability to perceive the world in a more systematic manner.
- An increased awareness of the world as an ecosystem with finite resources that must be carefully managed.
- An increased ability to perceive alternative choices to problems and issues that face all humankind.
- An increased empathy for the worth, dignity, and uniqueness of all members of the human species. We really need to work very hard at breaking down ethnocentric attitudes that become major barriers to understanding one another— break down stereotyping.
- An increased recognition that *all* human beings contribute to the "world bank of culture."
- An increased recognition of the interdependent nature of the planet Earth.
- An increased awareness of one's own values and beliefs in relation to others.

What criticisms are typically leveled at global education?

There are several criticisms often leveled at global education. They clearly reflect the value orientation of the individual and/or movement with whom they are associated.

1. One has already been referred to in your question about whether or not this was just a special-interest group trying to get space in the curriculum. Some educators believe that in spite of statements regarding the need to integrate a global perspective into the entire curriculum, what will really happen is that another new course will emerge. They cite their recent experiences with career education, environmental education, ethnic studies, and law education as examples. It's up to us to demonstrate *how* to integrate concepts into ongoing programs to dispel these fears.
2. Some educators, parents, and pressure groups view the achievements of the United States as demonstration of the fact that "we know best" and thus the rest of the world ought to be modeling us. They fear "basic American values" will be undermined or compromised via a global perspective.
3. Some people with fundamentalist religious backgrounds view development of a global perspective as a direct contradiction to Biblical teachings.
4. Some people in the business community view the development of a global perspective as a direct threat upon the free enterprise system.

I believe the key factor in all of these criticisms is fear. What people don't understand scares them and thus they reject it. These are not "bad" people. Indeed, most are very well-meaning. I think we have failed to communicate adequately the need for a global perspective, given the realities of the modern, technological world in which we live. This is a major task confronting proponents of global education.

At what age should global education begin?

One major obstacle to introducing global education content into the school curriculum is the belief that young children are not capable of learning the concepts of interdependence, change, and systems. However, available research indicates just the opposite—the primary and middle school years are perhaps the optimal time for introducing these concepts.

An extensive review of research by Judith Torney-Purta strongly suggests that the years of middle childhood, roughly the ages seven to twelve, may be the ideal period for developing a global perspective. Preconceptions about the world have not yet been formed, and the child may be more receptive to a broader international view than in the later years of schooling. During these early years of primary schooling, the child is moving from what Piaget terms "egocentric" thought, in which actions and attitudes are judged more in terms of the possible personal impact, to more "sociocentric" thought, in which the child considers the broader consequences, not only personally but also for others as well; the child becomes able to understand perspectives other than personal ones.

Torney-Purta summarizes the critical nature of the primary school years in the development of a global perspective:

> These five years, then, are unique. They come *before* too many stereotypic attitudes dominate the child's view of the world, and are *concurrent* with the period in which the child's cognitive development is sufficiently advanced to accept a diversity of viewpoints. This is the time in which learning about the larger world from a global vantage should begin.[16]

There are no national frontiers to learning.— Japanese proverb

Copyright 1984, USA TODAY. Reprinted with permission.

What are some of the key concepts of global education?

Interdependence is the key concept in global education. This concept of mutual dependence stresses the interrelatedness of and the connections, consequences, and vulnerabilities among natural and social systems; it underlies all other concepts. Other closely related major concepts include change, systems, conflict, cooperation, tolerance, problem solving, cultural diversity, adaptation, modification, responsibility, distribution, pluralisms, and technology.

What would be missing from childhood education if children did not study global education?

Students in schools today will live their adult lives in the twenty-first century in an increasingly complex and interrelated world. Preparing them to live as effective, responsible citizens has traditionally been a major goal of the social studies. This goal has become even more complex as new developments in scientific technology produce an expanding amount of data and problems, while at the same time developments in the areas of transportation and communication make the world smaller and smaller almost daily. The quality of life these students will experience, possibly their survival on this planet, will depend on the extent to which they develop the abilities to think, feel, and act from a global perspective. In addition to their roles as citizens in their local communities and nations, they will need to assume responsibilities at the global level.

CHECK-UP

Consider the characteristics necessary to describe a good citizen. Now make a list of 10 activities you would expect to see in an elementary school that is trying to help its students meet the goals of citizenship education.

_____

_____

_____

_____

_____

_____

_____

_____

_____

_____

Summary

A child is a citizen of the family, classroom, school, community, state, country, and the world. Inevitably, our citizenship takes place within diverse and pluralistic environments. The abiding concepts of rights and responsibilities are found within this framework. The classroom and the school offer wonderful possibilities for participation, cooperation, team building, and esprit de corps. These are the building blocks of citizenship education.

Citizenship education is a part of every school activity, but it is especially central to the social studies experience. Elementary social studies stresses its importance at each grade level. Students learn the ideas of citizenship best when they are given the opportunities to experience it in the classroom, the school, and the community.

A classroom should be a miniature community, democratic in structure and experience, in which students participate actively and reflectively in decision-making processes and where they learn what it truly means to work and play together. As they mature, their horizons continue to expand and their sense of rights and responsibility deepens.

Here is a closing thought for your consideration. The philosopher Mortimer Adler has written that only in a democracy can a person be considered a citizen. In an autocracy, a person is not a citizen but a subject. Without freedom and the duties attendant to freedom, there is no citizenship in its deeper meaning. With that thought in mind, I challenge you to make your classroom a place of opportunity rather than one of restraint. I challenge you to make your classroom a place where children are truly citizens.

ACTIVITIES

1. Describe at least three ways in which a classroom can become a place where students truly experience citizenship.
2. What are some examples of community activities in which teachers can involve their students in order to promote a sense of citizenship?
3. Voting is considered both a right and a responsibility of the citizen. Why do you think the percentage of people who vote in U.S. elections is often so low?
4. What are the key differences and similarities between primary and intermediate experiences in citizenship you would implement as classroom activities?

NOTES

1. Don T. Rowe, "A Conflict Model of Citizenship Education," *Curriculum* (Winter 1992).
2. C. Anderson, "The Context of Civic Competence and Education," *Social Education* (April 1993): 160–164.
3. Ibid., p. 162.
4. Printed with permission of Dr. L. Joanne Buggey.
5. Rowe, "A Conflict Model."
6. Ibid.

7. Kathleen Cotton, *Educating for Citizenship* (Portland, OR: Northwest Regional Educational Laboratory, 1996), p. 1.

8. Ibid.

9. A. V. Angell, "Democratic Climates in Elementary Classrooms: A Review of Theory and Research." *Theory and Research in Social Education* (Summer 1991): 241–266. Quoted in Cotton, *Educating for Citizenship.*

10. J. Torney-Purta, "Psychological Perspectives on Enhancing Civic Education through the Education of Teachers," *Journal of Teacher Education* (Nov.–Dec. 1983): 30–34.

11. Cotton, *Educating for Citizenship.*

12. S. Berman, "Educating for Social Responsibility," *Educational Leadership* (Nov. 1990): 75–80.

13. Cotton, *Educating for Citizenship.*

14. Printed with permission of Patricia Hammill.

15. Printed with permission of John J. Cogan.

16. J. Torney-Purta, "Global Awareness Survey: Implications for Teacher Education," *Theory into Practice* (Summer 1982): 200–205.

SUGGESTED READINGS

Blanchard, R., et al. (1999). "The Organic Social Studies Curriculum and the 1994 NCSS Standards: A Model for Linking the Community and the World." *Social Studies, 90* (Mar./Apr.): 63–67.

Bolen, J. (1999). "Taking Student Government Seriously." *Social Studies and the Young Learner, 11* (Jan./Feb.): 6–8.

De la Cruz, R., et al. (2000). "Let's Play Mancala and Sungka! Learning Math and Social Skills through Ancient Multicultural Games." *Teaching Exceptional Children, 32:* 38–42.

National Standards for Civics and Government. (1994). Calabasas, CA: Center for Civic Education.

Sanders, S. (1999). "Get Your Students Involved in Civics." *Social Education, 63* (May/June): 228–232.

Schmidt, J., et al. (1999). "Human Rights Education: A Framework for Social Study from the Interpersonal to the Global." *Social Studies and the Young Learner, 11* (Jan./Feb.): 1–4.

Wetherly, R. (1999). "Resources for Multicultural Awareness and Social Action." *Social Studies and the Young Learner, 11* (Jan./Feb.): 31–32.

11

Teaching Values, Character Education, and Moral Development

All aspects of a social studies curriculum have their foundation in values, character, and moral issues. Regardless of how you teach, you convey your values, your character, and your moral judgment to your students. There is truth in the old expression that values are more often caught than taught. In recent years, a number of options have become available to teachers who are interested in teaching and exploring values issues with children. This chapter is designed to help your understanding of those issues and to present you with different models for teaching and learning in this sensitive area. Specific topics include the following:

- The social context
- The moral life of schools
- Strategies for teaching and learning
- Character education
- Values realization
- Moral development

We passed the School, where Children strove
at Recess—in the Ring.
—Emily Dickinson

Questions of value are among the most basic of social studies issues. Use of such inquiry procedures as data gathering and inference making to determine relationships and provide descriptions and explanations of human behavior is itself indicative of a values position—a position that favors the use of empirical evidence to answer questions. Even these activities do not or cannot always lead people to similar judgments on given issues. One can, for example, investigate which attributes combine to make the best teachers. A survey can help determine which attributes are most often favored, but the results—no matter how clearly they favor certain attributes—do not necessarily make teachers who have those attributes the best. *Best* is a matter of individual judgment and thus a question of value.

Values issues include the moral development of children and the teaching and modeling of human relationships. Where you stand on these issues is largely determined by your own individual moral attitudes, and you should be aware of how influential those attitudes are in the classroom.

Let's look at some social studies curriculum issues. Place an I beside those statements that could be answered by inquiry processes and a V beside those that are statements of value.

_____ 1. It would be more appropriate for primary students to study Japanese families rather than Hopi families.

_____ 2. Students prefer geography over spelling.

_____ 3. Students should spend much of their social studies time working in small groups.

_____ 4. Students should decide for themselves what they should study in social studies.

_____ 5. An inductive approach to a primary geography unit results in more effective learning than a deductive approach to the same unit.

_____ 6. Students' attitudes toward other cultures change as a result of a unit on cultures of different lands.

_____ 7. The behavioral sciences of anthropology and sociology should receive more emphasis than history and geography in elementary social studies.

_____ 8. Emphasis on not always knowing the "right" answer to social studies questions makes children insecure.

I put an I beside numbers 2, 5, 6, and 8. Number 2 could be answered by taking a survey; number 5 could be tested with an experimental study; and numbers 6 and 8 could be answered by administering attitude scales to children who had been exposed to such social studies experience.

I put a V next to numbers 1, 3, 4, and 7. These are issues that data will not necessarily resolve. Take number 7 as an example—one must admit that effective (or ineffective) learning outcomes in terms of achievement could result from an emphasis on either the behavioral sciences or the more traditional history and geography. Additionally, one could note that a recent trend is to give increased emphasis to the behavioral sciences. However, neither of these observations answers the question, which is essentially one of preference.

Considering the Social Context

Values represent both the ideal and real dimension of our feelings as individuals and as a culture. Every individual possesses a set of values, and, except in extreme cases, those values are primarily mirrored at a larger level by the culture as a whole, and by its history. Our ideal values are represented by our beliefs, our real values by our actions. For individuals to function successfully within their societal context, they must recognize and abide by the values of the larger society. That, of course, is why society has laws, and, on occasion, hermits. Laws and rules are subject to change over time. Not too many years ago, persons of color were required by certain local laws to sit in the back of buses. Not too many years ago, cars were allowed to travel at 70 miles per hour on interstate highways. By changing the first law, we made it possible for a whole group of U.S. citizens to begin a long overdue march toward equality. By changing the second law, we have saved billions of gallons of gasoline and an estimated 6,000 lives per year through reduced speed limits. Now, however, speed laws have been raised again, representing yet another change in values.

A wide range of thought and activity can exist within the framework of the law. This fact leads to two values you will probably want to emphasize in teaching social studies to children: diversity and the respect for the rights of the individual. Democratic societies such as those in the United States and Canada place great value on the uniqueness of the individual and on personal freedom to pursue a path of self-determination in life.

Nowhere should these primary values be more in evidence than in your classroom. The children you teach will vary greatly, perhaps with respect to race, ethnic background, religion, and/or social or economic status, intelligence, and self-concept. You will have diversity within your classroom because classrooms are microcosms of society. To what extent will you tolerate, appreciate, and celebrate these differences? Will you show as much respect for the poor child as you show for the well-to-do child? Will you be as tolerant toward the slow learner as you are toward the student who catches on quickly to everything you assign? Will the child whose behavior is often less than socially desirable be welcome in your classroom, or will that child have to find compassion elsewhere? These are real values you must resolve every day of your teaching career.

Researcher Lawrence Kohlberg[1] suggested that a just classroom environment is a remarkable medium for enhancing the moral development of students. The classroom, with its potential to mirror democracy, is the perfect place in which to resolve the great and abiding issues of the tensions between rights and responsibilities.

What Really Matters?

Few questions are more basic in life than questions of value. At some point, all people ask themselves: What really matters? The fact that you are a teacher is a major statement of your values. You have chosen a profession of service. You have said, in effect, that you want to work with children and to help them grow. Economist E. F. Schumacher spoke to the values issue in his book *Small Is Beautiful* when he

A Golden Rule Test

The happiest people are those who help others. Is that true of people you know? Psychologist Bernard Rimland, at the Institute for Child Behavior Research in San Diego, has published a simple test. The test reads as follows:

Make a list of the ten persons whom you know the best. After each name, write H (for happy) or N (for unhappy). Go down the list again, this time writing S (for selfish) or U (for unselfish) after each name. Once you have completed your list, draw a table like the one below, count each category, and place the numbers in the appropriate block.

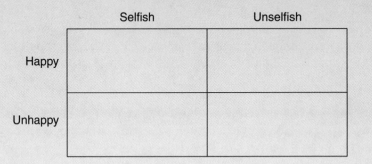

When Rimland added up the cases of 1,988 people rated by 216 students in six college classes, he found that the happy/selfish block was almost empty (only 78 cases), whereas 827 cases fell into the happy/unselfish block. A paradox exists in that selfish people are by definition "devoted to one's time and resources to one's own interests and welfare—an unwillingness to inconvenience oneself for others." In other words, selfish people are devoted to bringing themselves happiness. When judged by others, they seemed to be less successful than people who work at bringing happiness to others.

Conclusion: Do unto others as you would have them do unto you.

Source: Adapted from *Psychology Today*, December 1982, p. 78.

said that nothing is more important than education because it answers the question of what to do with our lives.[2]

The classroom has the potential for being a powerful forum for values. The proof of that statement is made by the occasional great teacher you and I have had along the way. A great teacher always lives and teaches a set of positive values. Think about your own best teachers. They taught you much more than content. They taught you about lasting ideas—integrity, compassion, self-discipline, and dignity—and they managed to do it without your knowing it at the time. They did it through a process of modeling the high-level, abstract concepts just mentioned.

You bring your own values to the classroom every day. You are on display. Young children will be your witnesses. Occasionally, they will wonder why you are the way you are, but mostly, they will accept your behavior as natural for a teacher. In their naive and unsophisticated way, they may characterize you to parents and friends as being "nice," or "mean," or "friendly." To a greater extent than perhaps you and they know, your students will be internalizing or rejecting your values as you model them. The students, of course, bring their own values to the classroom. Interest inventories provide a useful way for students to reflect on and share their own values.

CHECK-UP

List five important qualities of a good teacher. Why do you believe they are important? What you say will provide an initial look at your system of values. When you have completed your list and have given your reasons, join a group of others who have done the same thing and share your thoughts.

Some Important Qualities of a Good Teacher

    Quality   *Why It Is Important*

1. _____   _____

2. _____   _____

3. _____   _____

4. _____   _____

5. _____   _____

The Moral Life of Schools

In an important book titled *The Moral Life of Schools*, Philip Jackson and his colleagues make a contribution to one's knowledge of the social/moral fabric of school life. Using an ethnographic approach in their research, they furnish readers with unusually helpful glimpses of everyday life in classrooms and schools. They have analyzed a range of events that take place in the routines of school life, including interaction between teachers and their students, how students spend their time, the content and procedures of the school curriculum, attempts by teachers to instruct students in matters of morality, and the general social/moral ethos of the school. As a result of their exhaustive fieldwork, these researchers identified eight categories of "moral activity" that take place at school. The first five categories represent deliberate attempts by the school to promote moral consciousness and to encourage positive behavior. The last three categories consist of "activities that embody the moral," and are hence considerably more subtle. I will give a brief account of each of the eight categories with the hope that you will reflect on them in such a way as to deepen your own awareness of the implications of this important topic for bettering the lives of children.

■ The first category is *moral instruction* as a course in the curriculum. Japanese schools have such a course, and it is considered to be a basic curricular offering. In the United States, such separate courses are found more commonly in private schools, especially schools operated by particular church denominations. The course may take the form of attending chapel, or it may be a course in religion or perhaps character education. Public schools rarely offer such a course.

■ The second category is *intervention programs*. These are special offerings that teach to a specific point of moral choice and behavior, generally about a topic of great societal concern. Often, they are taught by resource people, and students receive a certificate upon completion of the course. The most prominent of these programs in recent times has been the DARE program, a special course aimed at children in fifth grade. DARE is a drug awareness course, often taught by a representative of the local police department. Children pledge to refuse to become involved with drugs as a result of their heightened awareness. Other programs focus on such topics as sex education, smoking and alcohol, and even self-esteem. These programs have been questioned as to their actual effects, but it does seem that the public looks increasingly to the schools to solve these troubling problems.

■ The third category is *moral instruction within the curriculum.* Here, teachers make conscious use of examples from literature, biographies, music, art, stories, history, science, civics, and so on to draw out acts of courage, loyalty, perseverance, dedication, helping behaviors, and determination. These virtues are abundantly found in good source material and many teachers make it a point to build discussions and lessons around them.

■ The fourth category is *rituals and ceremonies*. School is a place filled with rituals that would interest any anthropologist. Most of them are simply taken for granted and go unquestioned. Rituals and routines give a kind of rhythm and punctuation to the day or school year. Included in this category are the pledge of allegiance to the flag, patriotic music and songs, show and tell, celebrations including holidays such as Thanksgiving or Martin Luther King Jr.'s birthday, pageants, heritage celebrations, seasonal festivals, ethnic celebrations, assemblies, school elections, and attempts to create community at school. Adults sometimes overlook how important these rituals and routines are in the life of a child. Children look forward to many of them with great anticipation and wonder, and they find security in the patterns and routines that recur day in and day out, lending a sense of predictability to their lives.

■ The fifth category is *visual displays with moral content*. Foreign visitors are often surprised at the sheer number of flags on display in an American elementary school, from the school yard, to the gym, to nearly every classroom. The flag is the single-most visible symbol in American schools, and in the function of symbols, it is a nonverbal communication tool serving to remind us that we are united as a people. Other visual displays include portraits of famous Americans, exhibits, showcases with trophies, and so forth. Other displays are more subtle, but they are nonetheless reminders that this is a school, not anything else. Examples of these include the clock on the wall (you know, the one that never seemed to move when you were a kid) and the ever-present alphabet above the chalkboard.

These first five categories are rather obvious, and they stand out in sharp relief to the observer. The next three are more elusive, but the careful investigator will find them.

■ The sixth category is *spontaneous moral commentary into everyday activity.* In the social fabric of school life with its crowded conditions and problematic contexts, untoward things as well as delightful things will happen from time to time. Sensitive teachers use these examples from school life in order to draw out and develop ideas of morality. Fights, acts of cruelty, cheating, tattling, bullying, vandalism, and other antisocial behaviors inevitably manifest themselves, but they need not occur totally in vain. A teacher may use such situations to great advantage if he or she can lead the students to deeper insights to human behavior. Of course, good things happen as well. To recognize situations where children have behaved with honesty, kindness, or helpfulness is a wonderful thing for a teacher to do.

■ The seventh category is *classroom rules and regulations.* A classroom is a small, often crowded society that needs to function as smoothly and purposefully as possible. Every classroom has rules and norms designed to make it work. This is the realm of fairness, justice, and freedom put to the test. To the extent that the children themselves can be included in making and reviewing rules, they become participants in a democratic society.

■ The eighth category is *the morality of the curriculum.* The textbooks and other materials, the experiences themselves, the exams, the opportunities to work together, and the assignments—all speak to a moral point. How good are they? How purposeful? Who gains from the experience? Of course, there is a published and obvious curriculum, but this category addresses a far more subtle level of life in classrooms, that of the hidden curriculum. It doesn't say very much to learn that fourth-graders are studying regions in their social studies class. It is with the quality of the experience that teachers must be ultimately concerned.

Jackson and colleagues have given us a framework within which to reflect on the fabric of school life. A teacher has great discretionary power to make life challenging, purposeful, engaging, rewarding, and socially and morally uplifting. Your room needs to be one of those places where children genuinely desire to come and for all the right reasons.

Citizenship education encompasses a wide range of activities from ritual to community involvement.

What Is Teachable?

What is teachable and what is learnable have long been a matter of debate. As mentioned before, no teacher teaches anything in a vacuum. Students bring with them to every situation certain abilities, interests, aptitudes, readiness, and outside support from parents and other sources. Therefore, teaching anything is always more complex than the content itself might suggest. This is particularly true of attempts to teach values to students.

Teaching values presents several problems. First, whose values will you teach? In an integrated, homogeneous society, we might have little trouble agreeing on a list of important values. In a diverse, pluralistic society, the task becomes more difficult. Second, how will you teach values: by indoctrination? by example? with a workbook? Third, why bother when so many other value-laden forces, such as the home, street, and peer groups, might contradict your efforts?

To answer the first question, ask yourself this question: Is our society so pluralistic that people cannot agree on any values? I think we can find areas of common value. I'll show you a list in a moment. The answer to the second question is that you should provide an example of certain values, and you should also provide some formal instruction in them. Third, a teacher's job will always be influenced by outside forces, but you still need to be optimistic that you can make a difference.

Let's look at some values I think you ought to teach. I'll say more about how to teach them in due course.

Participation. Society needs participants for it to function. The town meeting, the voting booth, the PTA, and the many public and private organizations are symbols of this participation. At the classroom level, students must be given the opportunity to participate in active learning, developing rules, group functions, and anything else you can think of to get them off the sidelines. Active participation encourages feelings of affiliation and serves to combat apathy.

Cooperation. A classroom is a crowded place. Why not encourage your students to share it in an atmosphere of cooperation? People need each other and can come to be freely interdependent in a classroom that fosters group projects, helping, and common goals.

Self-Discipline. True discipline comes from within; it is self-directed. It is a powerful idea that sets people free to learn on their own, to get along without being forced to get along. Self-discipline is a good topic to bring up from time to time with your students.

Pluralism. It is one thing to have a different set of values from your neighbor. It's another thing to respect your neighbor's right to personal values. Tolerance and appreciation for people who are different is fundamental to the maintenance of a free society.

Responsibility. Aristotle pointed out that virtuous habits are best learned in childhood. This way, they become patterns of behavior. The child who has learned responsibility has acquired one of life's most important skills.

247

Dignity. Every child's sense of dignity is a precious commodity. It is easily destroyed by sarcastic comments, by embarrassment, and by humiliation. It is enhanced when you show respect for each student and when you expect your students to show respect for each other.

Freedom. Above all, a classroom ought to be a place where minds are set free. Ironically, this is seldom the case. Yet one expects students who are given little or no freedom to understand freedom and to take their places somehow in a democratic society. Risk taking, curiosity, creativity, and outlandish ideas are integral components of a classroom in which freedom is being taught.

Excellence. Why expect less? Children quickly come to respect a teacher who cares enough to ask great things of them (in effect, "I know your abilities differ greatly, but I want your personal best from each of you").

Integrity. The dictionary lists several synonyms for the word *integrity:* honesty, sincerity, wholeness, completeness. You could develop an entire curriculum from those values. You need to tell the children that integrity includes "trying my best," "becoming a person and not just a number," and "reaching toward my unique potential."

Joy. We need more joy in our classrooms. Childhood is a brief season. Why not celebrate it? Let's rejoice when a student learns something. Let's laugh when something is funny. Let's set free, not destroy, the natural spirit of the young.

There are other values, but I hope you get the idea from this sampling. These are not controversial values. They are building blocks of a free society. Refuse to acknowledge them, or tear them down, and society becomes the poorer for it. Discuss them, build them up, and model them, and all of us will gain from your efforts.

Strategies for Teaching Values

There is much you can do to actively teach a set of positive values to your students. The extent to which your students embrace those values is difficult to predict when one takes into account the many variables in any given child's life. The influences are many, and they are often far from positive. Some children are given moral and spiritual training at home, and some are not. Some are the products of homes where generosity and compassion are practiced on a daily basis, and some are the products of homes where looking out for yourself and doing anything you want in order to get ahead are modeled. Sadly, many of the children you will teach over the years are neglected in the most fundamental sense of the word. They may really believe that no one cares about them. But when these children end up in your classroom, it's time to be positive and to take positive action. Following are some things you can do to raise the moral tone of your classroom.

1. Hold regularly scheduled class meetings in which students are free to share their feelings in a supportive atmosphere. If you are willing to do this and to be consistent about it, you will harvest a treasure. Once your students realize that they

can trust you and that they are free to speak their thoughts during these meetings, they will begin to open up.

2. Be sure that each of the children you teach understands that you care. Call each student by name. Try to find time to talk with each child privately at some point during the week. Let the child know that you've been thinking about him or her. Ask the child if there is anything you can do to help with schoolwork or other matters.

3. Provide opportunities for students to practice cooperative learning and shared responsibility in day-to-day assignments. Individual accountability is important and you will have to ensure that it occurs in your class, but, after all, there are so many things students can and should do together. Working together builds a sense of esprit de corps. Children need to learn early in life that people need each other and that they can help each other.

4. Invite guests of other racial, ethnic, or national origins to your classroom and allow them to share their insights and experiences with your students. Prejudice and stereotyping of others are often a result of wrong ideas and lack of familiarity with the unknown. Responsible role models are very influential; you can play a key role by bringing in business people, artists, and others who represent varying ethnicities or racial backgrounds. If you are near a college or university, you might want to contact its foreign student association to see who is available to visit your class.

5. Allow your students to help you develop a few simple rules of classroom and school conduct and see that they are enforced. Dewey thought of the ideal classroom

Values such as participation, freedom, and excellence are best learned through experience.

as a miniature democracy in which students actually became involved in the processes of citizenship. You need to begin to develop a democratic flavor in your class by inviting the students to help you govern it.

6. Expect a lot from all your students. High expectations communicate a caring, believing attitude on your part. Students respond when they know that you expect the best from them. You need to convince each of your students that you believe in his or her ability to work productively. Once they see you are sincere, the students will help you with this.

7. Give your students opportunities to make decisions, take risks with ideas, and experiment with learning. Don't force everyone to respond to every assignment in the same way. There are so many ways to show that you are learning. The best social studies experiences begin to happen when students find themselves in a stimulating environment where multiple options exist. Getting to choose is a liberating experience, and it is especially instructive when you help a child to think reflectively about choices.

8. Model the behaviors you seek from your students: openness, courtesy, tolerance, kindness, curiosity, scholarship. As you model these crucial attributes, be sure to discuss them with your students. They need to have these values laid on the table for exploration and thoughtful analysis. They need to hear stories about people who have set a positive example for others. But, above all, your students will profit from the daily encounter with you as you model desirable behaviors.

9. Use good children's literature to explore positive values. Stories from *Aesop's Fables* is a great place to begin. Each fable explores a virtue without being too heavy-handed, and the stories are timeless in their ability to fascinate both children and adults. Other books such as *The Clown of God* by Tomie de Paola, *Little House in the Big Woods* by Laura Ingalls Wilder, and *Just Enough Is Plenty: A Hanukkah Tale* by Barbara Diamond Goldin are excellent books to read to young children. For middle-graders, I would recommend books such as *The Chronicles of Narnia* by C. S. Lewis, *Good Morning, Miss Dove* by Francis Gray Patton, *Sounder* by W. H. Armstrong, and *The Secret Garden* by Frances Hodgson Burnett as a place to begin exploring values. Read them aloud to the class, and spend time talking about the lasting values presented so eloquently by these authors.

Using Moral Dilemmas

Let's look at three moral dilemmas that children could ponder. The first is one suggested by Jean Piaget. In this dilemma, two boys acted quite differently with similar results. Following the story are the responses I got from three children to whom I told the story. I should mention that I interviewed each child separately.

> This is a story about two boys, Larry and Henry. First I'll tell you about Larry. Then I'll tell you about Henry. Once when Larry's mother was out of the kitchen, Larry decided he would help clean up. As he was taking some plates from the table to be washed, he dropped them and five plates broke. Now I'll tell you about Henry. Once when Henry's mother was out of the kitchen, Henry decided he would sneak a cookie. When Henry reached for a cookie, he knocked a plate off the shelf and it broke. Which boy do you think was naughtier?

A child's self-image is a fragile thing that must be given love and kindness in order to blossom.

John (age 5): Larry was.
Me: Why?
John: Because he broke five plates and Henry only broke one.
Me: Does it matter what they were trying to do?
John: Five plates made a big mess.

Kenny (age 7): They both were.
Me: Why?
Kenny: Because they both should have been more careful, that's why.
Me: Does it matter what they were trying to do?
Kenny: Yes, but neither one was very careful.

Julie (age 8): Henry was.
Me: Why?
Julie: Well, Larry was trying to help. And Henry was trying to sneak a cookie.
It was an accident, but one boy was trying to help.

You can see in the responses of these three children noticeable progression in moral development, particularly from John, the 5-year-old, to Julie, the 8-year-old. For John, the issue was the number of plates that were broken. Perhaps he has a point if you have to clean them up or if you have to set the table that evening and there aren't enough plates to go around. For Julie, the matter is more complex. She takes into account the two boys' motivation. In other words, she considers the extenuating circumstances before she reaches a decision. Thus, on the basis of intent, she decides that Henry's action was naughtier. In fact, she gives us no hint that Larry's action was naughty at all: "Larry was trying to help." Kenny, the 7-year-old, appears to be in a stage of transition and refuses to give a decision. In a way, his

A List of Values

Linda and Richard Eyre have written a very practical book titled *Teaching Your Children Values*. The book is designed to be used by parents with their children, but it is filled with useful suggestions that could benefit social studies teachers. One thing the Eyres did was to make a list of core values with brief explanations of each value. They have separated values into two categories: values of being and values of giving. The list is presented here.

Values of Being

Honesty . . . with other individuals, with institutions, with society, with self . . . the inner strength and confidence that is bred by exacting truthfulness, trustworthiness, and integrity

Courage . . . daring to attempt difficult things that are good . . . strength *not* to follow the crowd, to say *no* and mean it and influence others by it . . . being true to convictions and following good impulses, even when they are unpopular or inconvenient . . . boldness to be outgoing and friendly

Peaceability . . . calmness, peacefulness, serenity . . . the tendency to try to accommodate rather than argue . . . the understanding that differences are seldom resolved through conflict and that meanness in others is an indication of their problem or insecurity and thus of their need for your understanding . . . the ability to understand how others feel rather than simply reacting to them . . . control of temper

Self-Reliance and Potential . . . individuality . . . awareness and development of gifts and uniqueness . . . taking responsibility for own actions . . . overcoming the tendency to blame others for difficulties . . . commitment to personal excellence

Self-Discipline and Moderation . . . physical, mental, financial self-discipline . . . moderation in speaking, in eating, in exercising . . . the controlling and bridling of one's own appetites . . . understanding the limits of body and mind . . . avoiding the dangers of extreme, unbalanced viewpoints . . . the ability to balance self-discipline with spontaneity

Fidelity and Chastity . . . the value and security of fidelity within marriage and of restraint and limits before marriage . . . the commitments that go with marriage and that should go with sex . . . a grasp of the long-range (and widespread) consequences that can result from sexual amorality and infidelity

Values of Giving

Loyalty and Dependability . . . to family, to employers, to country, church, schools, and other organizations and institutions to which commitments are made . . . support, service, contribution . . . reliability and consistency in doing what you say you will do

Respect . . . for life, for property, for parents, for elders, for nature, and for the beliefs and rights of others . . . courtesy, politeness, and manners . . . self-respect and the avoidance of self-criticism

Love . . . individual and personal caring that goes both beneath and beyond loyalty and respect . . . love for friends, neighbors, even adversaries . . . and a prioritized, lifelong commitment of love for family

Unselfishness and Sensitivity . . . becoming more extra-centered and less self-centered . . . learning to feel with and for others . . . empathy, tolerance, brotherhood, sensitivity to needs in people and situations

Kindness and Friendliness . . . awareness that being kind and considerate is more admirable than being tough or strong . . . the tendency to understand rather than confront . . . gentleness, particularly toward those who are younger or weaker . . . the ability to make and keep friends . . . helpfulness, cheerfulness

Justice and Mercy . . . obedience to law, fairness in work and play . . . an understanding of natural consequences and the law of the harvest . . . a grasp of mercy and forgiveness and an understanding of the futility (and bitter poison) of carrying a grudge

Source: Adapted from Linda Eyre and Richard Eyre, *Teaching Your Children Values* (New York: Simon and Schuster, 1993).

judgment is the most puzzling of all. But these were real kids, and this is what they told me in answer to the problem.

Think about the possibilities for fruitful discussions with children using moral dilemmas. Many children never get the opportunity to discuss such issues. As a result, their judgment is impaired. Most dilemmas have elements of complexity about them, and the best way to gain insight to those complexities is to discuss the relevant issues with others.

The teacher's role here is crucial. A good teacher will probe, suggest alternate decisions and reasons for decisions, listen, and help children think about the consequences of decisions. Kohlberg warns about attempts to "speed up" the process by getting children to agree to solutions that are beyond their understanding. Keep in mind that your modeling of appropriate moral behavior will always be more powerful than your exhortations.

Another moral dilemma for your consideration is one that deals with a topic familiar to many children: shoplifting.

> Pat and Morgan go shopping. While they are shopping, Pat takes an item of jewelry and slips it into a pocket. Morgan sees Pat take the item. What should Morgan do? I asked a boy named Ian what he would do in such a situation.

Ian: I'd probably tell my friend I saw him take it.
Me: Do you have any other choices?
Ian: Yeah. I could tell the manager and get him in trouble.
Me: What else could you do?
Ian: I could just tell him to put it back before he gets in trouble.
Me: What if he refuses?
Ian: I could just ignore it. I didn't take anything.
Me: Do you feel you have any responsibility in this situation?
Ian: No, I mean, maybe if he's my friend I do.

In this case, we have a child thinking about a serious but hypothetical issue: stealing. The job of the questioner is to mediate the child's thinking by posing questions that reveal the complexity of the issue. It is tempting to tell the child what to do, but what has he or she learned if you do that? By asking probing questions, you can help the child search through the many dimensions of such a situation.

Students can help each other probe issues through role-play in which one person is given a script of questions while the other is left to think through and express his or her answers. This is typical of the kind of analytical thinking session in which students can be of help to each other. A group discussion fosters the opportunity for a variety of viewpoints and insights to flower. Again, the teacher must exercise patience and tolerance and allow students to speak their thoughts. Even in a whole-class or group discussion, the teacher's role remains that of questioner and mediator.

Let's examine one more moral dilemma. It involves a number of complex issues.

> Queens High School, a private institution located in an urban setting, has a stadium with a football field and running track on its campus. The facility is enclosed by fences, and there are several gates by which people can enter.
>
> The relationship between the school and the surrounding community is a good one, and the school has always allowed people from the community to use the track for

A Values Issue: Who Ought to Teach What?

All of us can agree that children learn from a variety of sources: the home, school, neighborhood, religious organizations, and clubs, for example. But can everyone agree about who ought to teach what? Examine the accompanying list of topics and sort each into one of two groups: "Best Taught by the Schools" or "Best Taught outside the Schools." After you have sorted the topics, join a small group of interested persons to discuss points of agreement and disagreement.

Drug awareness	AIDS education
Personal values	Handwriting
Sex education	Map skills
Mathematics	Healthful diets
World religions	Grammar
Grooming habits	Inquiry skills
Holiday celebrations	Spelling

Best Taught by the Schools   *Best Taught outside the Schools*

_____   _____

_____   _____

_____   _____

_____   _____

_____   _____

_____   _____

_____   _____

_____   _____

_____   _____

jogging and walking. Certain entrances are typically left unlocked year around to accommodate them.

Recently, the school posted new signs at the entrances that listed the rules for using the track. In general, the rules are typical of those found at any track, but a recently added rule states that dogs are prohibited from the grounds. In the past, people often brought their dogs to run there, but the school board decided to post the ban because a number of joggers had complained of being attacked or bothered by dogs and because some senior citizens from a nearby retirement home mentioned that the dogs intimidated them when they used the track for walking.

People living in the area in apartments and in houses with small yards have complained that they have nowhere else to run their dogs. One person said that her dog would not bite anyone. Others have made the case that they have small dogs, friendly dogs, dogs kept on a leash, dogs that have been trained to obey, and so on.

Some dog owners have refused to obey the rule banning dogs from the track.

1. How would you state the nature of the conflict?
2. What questions would you ask about this issue?
3. Identify at least two possible solutions to the problem.
4. What do you think is the best solution to the problem? Why?

One last point is in order: The teacher needs to stand for something. Children desperately need positive role models. But the difference between standing up for your values and attempting to shove them down children's throats is a great and significant one. Students will want to know what you think, and you ought to feel free to tell them. But the process of discussion and reflection in a free, open, and supportive environment is crucial to the moral development of young people.

CHECK-UP

The following statements represent values positions on how a social studies classroom should be operated. Circle the response that more closely approximates your attitude toward each statement.

1. I think such values as patriotism and loyalty are best taught by exposing children to examples set by great national leaders.   Yes   No
2. I think an important reason for studying other cultures is to expose children to alternative value systems and to teach children that one culture's values are not necessarily better than another's, even though they may be quite different.   Yes   No
3. I think children need to learn how our democratic system works so they will be able to use it effectively as citizens.
4. I think a teacher needs to provide opportunities for children to clarify their values and a teacher must accept children's values positions, no matter how divergent they might seem.   Yes   No
5. I think a high priority should be placed on developing children's skills of critical thinking and investigation, because a primary purpose of education is the development of effective decision makers.   Yes   No
6. I think history and literature can make an important contribution in social studies, because they can give children a sense of the time-honored human values.   Yes   No
7. I think that there is no one right set of values that children should learn in school and that "right" is a matter of perspective.   Yes   No
8. I think a teacher should operate as a facilitator rather than as a truth giver and students must learn to develop their own ideas of right and wrong.   Yes   No

9. I think environmental education is a top priority in social studies, because it is necessary for the survival of the human race.   Yes   No
10. I think that for children to become effective thinkers they must conduct their own investigations by posing questions and gathering and sorting evidence.   Yes   No

Now go back to the statements to which you responded yes and rank them in terms of your priorities. Place a 1 beside the yes statement you think is most important, a 2 beside the next most important, and so on.

Having done this, you have begun to articulate a values position for your social studies teaching. I will refrain from trying to tell you whether your answers were right or wrong because I do not feel that I am in a position to dispense the truth for you—*which I guess is* my *values position.*

Let's now turn our attention to three different models: (1) character education, (2) values realization, and (3) moral development. All of them have something to offer, and although you may find one most to your liking, you need to be aware of the nature and purpose of each. No doubt, you find attractive elements in each model.

Character Education

Character education, sometimes called *character training*, is focused on traditional values. These values are sometimes known as virtues or character traits. When someone notes that a person is of good character, it is of these virtues that he or she speaks. The greatly increased interest in character education on the part of professionals and the lay public alike can no doubt be traced to the many problems besetting society, including drug use, teen pregnancies, declining respect for authority, and so on. Of the three models presented here, character education is clearly the most dominant in schools today (see Figure 11.1).

Character education is based on a simple premise that can be traced back in time to such different sources as the Bible, Aristotle's *Ethics*, and the *Analects* of Confucius. The guiding premise is that young children need to acquire virtuous habits and behaviors even before they have reached an ability to rationally examine the full meaning and implications of these habits. To wait until a person has reached the age of reason, say character educators, is too late. Thus, those who instruct the young (parents, teachers, clergy, etc.) are faced with the paradox of trying to teach children to be good before they can understand why. Of course, there are many such paradoxes in life. Adults teach children not to run into the street, to brush their teeth, and to pick up their toys. These become habits. One could say much the same about such character traits as honesty, respect for others, kindness, willingness to work, and others. To train young children in this manner strikes some people as manipulative, whereas others applaud, saying it is about time that adults assumed their responsibility to the young. In fact, however, recent brain re-

FIGURE 11.1

257
Morals

A PORTRAIT OF CHIEF JOSEPH

search indicates that most life character patterns are set by about age 11, offering a powerful argument for training young children in virtuous habits.

Character education places great responsibility in the teacher's hands. Serious proponents of character training would say that the most fundamental responsibilities are with the home, but the familiar question inevitably arises: What if the home is negligent? Regardless of the home situation, everyone would agree that the school experience plays a key role in the shaping of children. In school-based character education, the center of gravity lies with the teacher; it is his or her responsibility to model and teach virtuous habits. Teachers who take character education seriously know that they must first serve as a model for the character traits they wish to instill in the young. The guiding idea is that children will respond positively to kindness, honesty, courtesy, fairness, the work ethic, and other virtues when they see them lived by a respected authority figure in the form of their teacher.

With regard to instruction and curriculum in character education, the most common methods employed are exhortation, the reading of stories, and discussions. William Bennett's best-seller *Book of Virtues* is perhaps the best-known character education resource. It is filled with essays, stories, poems, fables, object lessons, and parables for the teacher to read to students. Generally, after a reading, a teacher-led discussion follows. The discussion is focused on the moral of the story, for example, courage, loyalty, compassion, or some other virtue. *The Book of Virtues* is also available as a video series using an animated cartoon format that is quite appealing to children.

A host of character education organizations have sprung up in recent times, most notably the Center for the Advancement of Ethics and Character (605 Commonwealth Ave., Boston, MA 02215); the Character Counts Coalition (4640 Admiralty Way, Marina del Ray, CA 90292); and the Character Education Partnership (1250 N. Pitt St., Alexandria, VA 22315). Each of these organizations is an extremely valuable source of materials, ideas, and support for those teachers who would like to include character education in their curriculum. Figure 11.2 is also an effective teaching aid to stimulate classroom discussion about different forms of the Golden Rule.

FIGURE 11.2

Forms of the Golden Rule

Baha'i	He should not wish for others that which he doth not wish for himself. —*From writings of Baha u'llah 1870 CE*
Christianity	Treat others as you would like them to treat you. —*From Luke: Revised Standard Version of the New Testament c 90 CE*
Confucianism	Do not do to others what you would not like for yourself. —*From The Analects of Confucius c 500 BCE*
Epictetus	What you would avoid suffering yourself, seek not to impose on others. —*The Greek philosopher, Epictetus c 90 CE*
Hinduism	This is the sum of duty: Do naught to others which, if done to thee, could cause thee pain. —*From The Mahabharata c 150 BCE*
Islam	None of you "truly" believe, until he wishes for his brothers what he wishes for himself. —*A saying of Prophet Muhammad recorded by accepted narrators al-Bukari and Muslim 7th century CE*
Jainism	He should treat all beings as he himself should be treated. The essence of right conduct is not to injure anyone. —*From the Sutra Kritanga c 550 BCE*
Judaism	What is harmful to yourself do not to your fellow men. That is the whole of the law and the remainder is but commentary. —*From Hillel: The Talmud c 10 CE*
Sikhism	As thou deemest thyself, so deem others. —*From Guru Granth Sahib 1604 CE* Treat others as thou wouldst be treated thyself. —*Adi Granth*
Taoism	Regard your neighbour's gain as your own gain and your neighbour's loss as your own loss. —*T'ai Shang Kan Ying P'ien*
The Buddha	I will act towards others exactly as I would act towards myself. —*From The Siglo-Vada Sutta c 500 BCE*
Zoroastrianism	Do not unto others all that is not well for oneself. —*Shayast-na-shayast*

Source: Adapted from Alex Rodger, *Developing Moral Community in a Pluralist School Setting* (Aberdeen, Scotland: Gordon Cook Foundation, 1996).

Is character education at all controversial? Indeed, it is. First of all, there are those who are bothered, as previously mentioned, by the inculcating process of teaching virtues to young children who do not really understand what they are being taught. That argument aside, however, more serious objections are raised by those who find it difficult to agree on a set of virtues to be taught and by those who question whether the school is the appropriate setting for such instruction. Both of these objections are reminders of the diverse, pluralistic nature of our society. For example, some may feel that punctuality is a virtue; others may not. The work ethic is seen by some as the foundation of our society, whereas others view it as based in greed, guilt, and material desire. Does wearing a baseball cap (turned backwards) indoors constitute rebellion against authority, or is it merely a harmless fad? It is easier than we think to confuse virtues with certain cultural norms that are intrinsically neither virtuous nor lacking in virtue. Still, when it comes to such core virtues as honesty, respect for others, and kindness, there does seem to be rather widespread agreement. Figure 11.3 is an interesting commentary on the search for universal values.

Given the perception of the need to do something, the question remains: Does character education work?—that is, Do children's behaviors change in a positive direction as a direct result of instruction? Actually, there is very little empirical evidence showing that it does. Although character education is experiencing a revival, it is not new. Studies by Hartshorne and May in the 1920s showed no evidence then that it produced better behaviors than were exhibited by children who did not receive it. In its current revival, too little work has been done to warrant any vast conclusions. What does this mean to teachers who are conscientiously looking for ways to improve the individual and social lives of the children they teach? I would remind you that teaching is primarily about *trying*. We try to do our best. We want to do what is right. We are caring people. Many children have little to count on when it comes to finding a caring, responsible adult in their lives who wants to point them in the right direction. I think it's worth the try.

FIGURE 11.3

The Tao: The Search for Universal Values

Is there such a thing as a universal set of values that ought to guide all human experience, regardless of culture? Is there a set of values based on natural law in somewhat the same way that natural laws of physics—for example, gravity or motion—exist? Cambridge University professor and noted writer C. S. Lewis set out in search of just such a thing. He reasoned that if certain laws of right conduct were found in all or nearly all cultures, that would strengthen the claim that those laws are indeed universal. Lewis found that certain values were indeed universal, and he called these values *Natural Law,* or *the Tao.* Lewis noted that he was not trying to prove the validity of the Tao as universal, even on the basis of common consent. As he said, its validity cannot be deduced. Nevertheless, the fact that the values found in the Tao are universally subscribed to by serious thinkers in all cultures does represent a significant finding for those who would teach traditional values to the young.

Among the universal values Lewis found were beneficence or kindness toward others; duties to parents and elders; duties to children and posterity; justice; truthfulness and sincerity; mercy or compassion; and magnanimity or forgiveness. All major religions and world views have taught these values as guides to right conduct. Perhaps this list developed by Lewis is a place to start.

Values realization, formerly known as *values clarification*, was a very popular phenomenon in U.S. education during the 1970s. Leaders in the movement such as Sidney Simon and Howard Kirschenbaum were in great demand as workshop leaders, writers, and gurus. Like many educational innovations, it swept the country by storm, disappearing almost as quickly amidst a raging controversy over its perceived harmful effects. What is values realization, and why does it have such numbers of advocates and detractors?

The guiding premise of the values realization model is that each individual has vague feelings about what is right, what he or she might become, how to relate to others, and so on, but that these feelings are seldom clear. Much of the reason for this, advocates maintain, is because too few forums exist in which people might express themselves and listen reciprocally to others. Thus, the values realization model is one in which discussion and activities are employed to draw out feelings and thoughts on various important issues.

The teacher's role in values realization is to facilitate a child's quest for clarification by supporting, questioning (though not in an aggressive way), and listening. A typical activity is to present a situation involving moral judgment and then ask students how they feel about it. This is not a model based on traditional values or virtues, although it is not necessarily opposed to them; rather, the equation is turned around in that one starts with what an individual thinks instead of with the weight of authority and tradition. So, if a story is about shoplifting, the moral is not necessarily "Honesty is the best policy," but the question is asked, "What would you have done in similar circumstances?" Students are encouraged to speak their real opinions, while the teacher attempts to remain neutral and to facilitate any discussion. The center of gravity lies with the student, and it is incumbent on the teacher to allow a student to say what he or she really feels.

The obvious criticism is: How will children learn what is right in life if responsible adults do not point the way? The answer given by advocates of values realization has been that adults should tell children what they think is right (as opposed to what is right), but should leave room for dissenting opinions. Further, say supporters, a young person may have an opinion on a matter that is at odds with what you think is appropriate, and wouldn't you rather know that than to remain ignorant of it?

Not all aspects of values realization are so controversial. Much of the time spent focuses on goal setting, social skills, and decision making. Goal setting enables a young person to think about his or her future and what he or she wants to make of it, to consider alternatives, and to choose from a range of possibilities. Social skills are necessary in order for people to get along, to work together, and to tolerate and appreciate others. In recent times, much emphasis has been placed on the social skills basic to conflict resolution in a day when some children do not seem to realize options other than force or withdrawal when differences arise. Decision-making skills enable young people to set priorities, develop strategies, and make the necessary links between thought and action in leading productive lives.

A key concept in values realization is that of self-esteem. Teachers who use values realization strategies will often comment that they consider it one of their most important duties to enhance the self-esteem of every child. A wide range of self-esteem programs are available, and most of them focus on learning to accept one-self, to prize oneself, and to feel worthy. As Kirschenbaum writes,

> The connection of self-esteem with values education and moral education may initially not be apparent, but it is important. The lower a person's self-esteem, the less worthy a person feels, and therefore, the less likely a person will be to take charge of his life, set appropriate goals, or get out of an abusive situation. If we devalue ourselves, the less likely we will be to realize our values and find satisfaction and meaning in our lives.[3]

Do values realization programs work? Apparently enough people thought they did to become upset with their use in the 1970s. However, there is not much empirical evidence of their effectiveness one way or the other. One of the problems with values realization, unlike the other two models examined in these pages, is that it lacks a solid theoretical framework. Thus, it falls into a category that people either like or dislike, based more on intuition than anything else. I do find it necessary to say that in its more extreme instances, for example, The Lifeboat Activity, where students are asked to decide which members of an overcrowded lifeboat should get to live, it is counterproductive, to say the least, and possibly even dangerous to ask young people to determine the value of one life over another. On the other hand, where teachers have the common sense to use activities that draw out a child's dream, that teach children to listen peaceably to and value others' comments, that enable them to predict from an array of alternative decisions the consequences of each, then it seems to me to be something needed in a teacher's repertoire.

Moral Development

Moral development is based on concepts of justice, ethical behavior, and fairness. This model, which has much of its foundation in law, represents an attempt to lead students to think rationally about what is right and wrong. While character education

Children need examples of moral leadership.

is based on adult authority and the teaching of right and wrong to the young, and values realization is based primarily on affective and experiential considerations, moral development takes a reasoned, analytical approach to exploring beliefs, rules, and values.

Of course, any time one encounters the word *development* in connection with teaching learning, one can be quite sure that it involves stage theory. Stage theory implies that people progress through a hierarchical set of levels from more concrete to the abstract. Prominent among stage theories of moral development is that of Lawrence Kohlberg, who based his ideas that people progress through developmental stages of moral reasoning on the prior work of Jean Piaget.

How does a child's moral sense develop? How capable are elementary-age children of reasoning about questions of morality? To what extent does a child's ability to reason through an issue affect his or her receptivity to adult values of right and wrong? Piaget writes,

> Most of the moral rules which the child learns to respect he receives from adults, which means that he receives them after they have been fully elaborated, and often elaborated, not in relation to him as they are needed, but once and for all and through an uninterrupted succession of earlier adult generations.[4]

This statement furnishes a clue to the source of children's values, but one must look further to determine how and when values are acquired. The development of a person's moral sense is something that has intrigued a number of philosophers and researchers over the years. Jean Rousseau developed a stage theory in the eighteenth century, one that led him to the conclusion that children should not be coerced into behaving as though they were miniature adults. John Dewey was convinced that childhood is marked by stages of development, and, of course, Jean Piaget, that most famous of stage theorists, wrote at length on the moral judgment of the child.

Psychologist Lawrence Kohlberg has developed the most widely studied and used stage theory of moral development. His research began nearly half a century ago with a longitudinal study of a cohort group of boys whom he subsequently studied into their adult years. Kohlberg's research resulted in a hierarchical model of levels of moral development. He concluded that the levels and the stages within levels through which a person passes are sequentially ordered, from stage one, a kind of primitive level of moral development based in rewards and punishments, to stage six, a rarified level of universal ethical-principle orientation. A synopsis of Kohlberg's model is presented on the following pages.

Children's Values

Preconventional Level

At the preconventional level of Kohlberg's hierarchy, the child is responsive to such rules and labels as *good* or *bad* and *right* or *wrong*. He or she interprets these labels in purely physical or hedonistic terms: if the child is bad, he or she is punished; if the child is good, he or she is rewarded. The child also interprets the labels in terms of the physical power of those who enunciate them—parents, teachers, and other adults. The level comprises two stages.

Stage One: Punishment and Obedience Orientation. The physical consequences of an action determine its goodness or badness, regardless of the human meaning or value of these consequences. Avoidance of punishment and unquestioning deference to power are valued in their own right, not in terms of respect for an underlying moral order supported by punishment and authority (the latter being Stage Four).

Stage Two: Instrumental Relativist Orientation. Right action consists of actions that instrumentally satisfy one's own needs and occasionally the needs of others. Human relations are viewed in terms similar to those of the marketplace. Elements of fairness, reciprocity, and equal sharing are present, but they are always interpreted in a pragmatic way. Reciprocity is a matter of "You scratch my back and I'll scratch yours," not of loyalty, gratitude, or justice.

Conventional Level

At this level, maintaining the expectations of the individual's family, group, or nation is perceived as valuable in its own right, regardless of immediate and obvious consequences. The attitude is one not only of conforming to the social order but also of being loyal to it; of actively maintaining, supporting, and justifying the order; and of identifying with the persons or group involved in it. This level comprises the following two stages.

Stage Three: Interpersonal Concordance or "Good Boy–Nice Girl" Orientation. Good behavior is behavior that pleases or helps others and is approved by them. There is much conformity to stereotypical images of what is majority or "natural" behavior. Behavior is frequently judged by intention: "He means well" becomes important, and one earns approval by "being nice."

Stage Four: "Law and Order" Orientation. Authority, fixed rules, and the maintenance of the social order are valued. Right behavior consists of doing one's duty, showing respect for authority, and maintaining the social order for its own sake.

Postconventional Level

At the postconventional level, there is a clear effort to reach a personal definition of moral values—to define principles that have validity and application apart from the authority of groups or persons and apart from the individual's own identification with these groups. This level has two stages.

Stage Five: Social-Contract Legalistic Orientation. Generally, this stage has utilitarian overtones. Right action tends to be defined in terms of general individual rights and in terms of standards that have been critically examined and agreed on by the whole society. There is a clear awareness of the importance of personal values and opinions and a corresponding emphasis on procedural rules for reaching

Goals of Moral Development during the Elementary School Years

Children receive a multitude of messages from society, some of which are uplifting and some of which are less so. Your role as their teacher is crucial to their positive moral development. The following goal structure is suggested for you and your students to pursue:

1. Children must be led away from their egocentric tendencies toward a sense of others.
2. Children must be given opportunities to act on moral principles. Mere knowledge of what is right is not enough.
3. Classrooms and schools must become communities where right moral principles and actions become a part of everyday life.

Specifically, teachers must share with parents and others responsibility for developing the following character traits in children:

1. Moral judgment, a sense of what is right and what is just
2. Participation in the life of the school community, its day-to-day activities and routines
3. Responsibility for one's actions with an accompanying sense of duty toward others
4. Opportunities for self-development and self-realization, a sense of efficacy
5. Practice with democracy: opportunities for self-expression and learning to listen, to communicate, to solve problems cooperatively
6. Learning to trust others, to be given opportunities to share with and to believe in others

consensus. Other than what is constitutionally and democratically agreed on, right is a matter of personal values and opinion. The result is an emphasis on procedural rules for reaching consensus. Outside the legal realm, free agreement is the binding element of obligation. This is the "official" morality of the U.S. Government and the Constitution.

Stage Six: Universal Ethical-Principle Orientation. Right is defined by the conscience in accord with self-chosen ethical principles, which in turn are based on logical comprehensiveness, universality, and consistency. These principles are abstract and ethical (the golden rule, the categorical imperative); they are not concrete moral rules like the Ten Commandments. At heart, these are universal principles of justice, of the reciprocity and equality of human rights, and of respect for the dignity of human beings as individual persons. (Kohlberg eventually dropped Stage Six because no one in his sample of respondents reached it.)

> Given that moral development passes through a set of six distinct stages, what can the educator do to foster it in his students?
>
> First, and fundamentally, if you want to develop morality or a sense of justice in kids, you have to create a just school, a just classroom environment and atmosphere that you establish in your classroom—your *hidden curriculum*.
>
> In setting up a moral educational environment, the teacher does not relinquish his authority. Rather, the source of that authority is changed: instead of deriving from the role of teacher and being backed up by threat, punishment, reward and sanctions, the authority comes from being a mediator in the conflicts between children. A teacher using this approach would say, "Look, you're not going to solve your conflicts by force or trickery. You're going to solve them by talking—by trying to agree on something you and the other kids consider fair." Moral development, we have found, is facilitated in open, informal classrooms where there is a great deal of interaction among children and where the teacher is concerned with developing patterns of cooperation among the children.[5]

Of course, the question of how and at what level you treat values issues with elementary students persists. How you deal with values issues (or refuse to deal with them) is something you have to come to grips with for yourself—it is a philosophical matter you alone can decide.

The levels of moral development of students within a classroom will vary; although they are to some extent age related, they are not necessarily age determined. Evidence exists that parents are a powerful factor in their children's moral development, and, as Paul Brandwein suggests, not all children choose their parents wisely. Your own observation of students' comments as you deal with moral dilemmas can help to determine their levels of moral development. Kohlberg's research indicates that moral messages aimed at more than one stage above a child are seldom understood and that messages aimed at too low a level are demeaning to students.

To what extent does the moral development of a child influence receptivity to adult ideas about good and bad, right and wrong?

Gender and Moral Development

The work of Harvard psychologist Carol Gilligan offers several contrasts to Kohlberg's theory. She challenges the idea that Kohlberg's sequence of stages is fixed and universal. Kohlberg's claim that his stages are universal is undermined, Gilligan points out, if for no other reason than that the original research sample on which the stages were based was composed exclusively of boys. Gilligan hypothesizes that females conceive of morality in interpersonal terms. Thus, for many females, moral goodness is conceived in terms of helping others and working cooperatively with others.

Gilligan suggests that a higher stage of morality exists than that postulated by Kohlberg. She calls this advanced level of moral development a "love ethic." The love ethic is based on the assumption that meeting mutual needs, loving meaningfully, and being willing to make sacrifices for others are the fabric of advanced morality. Gilligan also notes that early in life, females learn to play nurturing roles, while males learn to be competitive and aggressive. This, of course, represents sexrole typing because these characteristics are learned by expectation and example. Young boys could just as well be taught to be more cooperative and supportive of the feelings and needs of others.

Not everyone agrees with Gilligan's assessment of the differences between boys and girls. Christina Hoff Sommers (2000) has been particularly critical of Gilligan's conclusions as well as her research. Sommers has concluded that differences in moral reasoning and judgment between boys and girls are greatly exaggerated. She cites a number of studies that point to no significant differences in moral reasoning. Further, she notes that the so-called achievement gap between boys and girls, if indeed it does exist, actually favors girls, who not only receive higher school grades but who also continue on to higher education in greater numbers than boys.

Gilligan has called for fundamental changes in child-rearing practices that would develop the more sensitive, feminine side of boys' behavior. She has concluded that the very nature of childhood must be changed in order to keep boys more closely bonded with their mothers. Doing so would, she thinks, promote a more nurturing, caring, and supportive nature in boys than they typically exhibit. The debate continues.

Summary

The exploration of values is an integral part of the elementary social studies curriculum. The manner in which content, concepts, and processes are taught is itself a question of value. Your own values position is something you need to consider seriously, because your work with children in this sensitive area will serve little purpose until you have clarified your values. Whatever values position(s) you assume as a teacher of children, your actions will speak more loudly and clearly than your words.

Posing and discussing moral dilemmas is one strategy for actively exploring values in the classroom. Discussion of controversial issues should not be avoided, although the stage of moral development that your students are in will affect your values teaching.

ACTIVITIES

1. Select an elementary social studies textbook and try to determine what values the authors of that book are trying to promote.
2. The elementary social studies program *Man: A Course of Study* became controversial over questions of value. Research the arguments on both sides and decide where you stand.
3. It has often been said that no teacher can escape teaching values to his or her students. Do you agree? Why or why not?
4. Make a list of 20 ideas or things that you value highly. Ask yourself: What effect will these priorities have on the children I teach?

NOTES

1. Lawrence Kohlberg, *The Psychology of Moral Development* (New York: Harper and Row, 1983).
2. E. F. Schumacher, *Small Is Beautiful* (New York: Harper and Row, 1973).
3. Howard Kirschenbaum, *100 Ways to Enhance Values and Morality in Schools and Youth Settings* (Boston: Allyn and Bacon, 1996).
4. Jean Piaget, *The Moral Development of the Child* (New York: The Free Press, 1965).
5. Lawrence Kohlberg and Phillip Whitten, "Understanding the Hidden Curriculum," *Learning* (Dec. 1972): 14.

SUGGESTED READINGS

Forsyth, S., and Gilligan, C. (1998). *Girls Seen and Heard: Lessons for Our Daughters.* New York: The Ms. Foundation for Women.

Gilligan, C. (1982). *In a Different Voice: Psychological Theory and Women's Development.* Cambridge, MA: Harvard University Press.

Heidel, J., et al. (1998). *Character Education: Grades K–6.* Incentive Publications.

Jackson, P., Boostrom, R., and Hansen, D. (1993). *The Moral Life of Schools.* San Francisco: Jossey-Bass.

Kilpatarick, W. (1992). *Why Johnny Can't Tell Right from Wrong.* New York: Simon and Schuster.

Kirschenbaum, H. (1995). *100 Ways to Enhance Morality in Schools and Youth Settings.* Boston: Allyn and Bacon.

Lewis, C. S. (1947). *The Abolition of Man: How Education Develops Man's Sense of Morality.* New York: Collier Books.

McCombs, B., and Whisler, J. (1997). *The Learner-Centered Classroom and School.* San Francisco: Jossey-Bass.

Rest, J., et al. (1998). *Postconventional Moral Thinking: A Neo-Kohlbergian Approach.* New York: Lawrence Erlbaum.

Sheindlin, J. (2000). *Win or Lose by How You Choose.* New York: HarperCollins.

Sizer, T., and Sizer, N. (2000). *The Students Are Watching: Schools and the Moral Contract.* New York: Beacon Press.

Sommers, C. (2000). *The War Against Boys: How Misguided Feminism Is Harming Our Young Men.* New York: Simon and Schuster.

Wadsworth, B. (1996). *Piaget's Theory of Cognitive and Affective Development.* New York: Longman.

Making and Interpreting Maps

A map is a spatial essay. It conveys information primarily in graphic and symbolic terms. Don't be surprised if some of your best mapmakers and map readers are children who may not do so well with typical reading/writing activities. Images of space are qualitatively different from words on a page. Different children have different gifts. It has been noted that children who play a great deal with Lego blocks or other building materials often will develop spatial reasoning abilities to a remarkable extent. This should be a reminder to all teachers that concrete activities are especially important for elementary-age children. In this chapter, I will take a developmental approach, suggesting that students need to make maps, models, and drawings of the environment if they are to understand the often abstract nature of maps found in texts and atlases. Strategies will include the following:

- Visualizing the local environment
- Mental maps
- Traverse maps
- Finding your way
- Changing map scale
- Simulating aerial photographs
- Base maps from aerial photographs
- Visualizing space
- Considering variables
- Conceptualizing a common traverse
- Perspective taking
- Four-color map theory
- Estimating distances

Geography is about maps.
—Edwin Bentley

aps are a universal means of expression in the social sciences. They provide to the geographer, historian, political scientist, and anthropologist a graphic portrayal of great economy. In the social sciences, maps are intended as selective and abstracted representations of reality. In contrast to a photograph, which is nonselective (a photograph shows everything seen by the camera's eye), a good map portrays only what is central to the message of the researcher—such as cities and states, reconstructed battle lines from military engagements, results of voting by states in a presidential election, or hunting and gathering territory of a tribal group—and factors out details not essential to the researcher's message.

A map, then, is a basic communication tool that represents reality in an arbitrary and selective way. Keep this idea in mind when you are working with students of elementary school age. The selectivity that makes a map a powerful means of communicating spatial relationships renders that same map potentially confusing to the child, who has not had experience in making a developmental transition from real and pictorial representations to abstract representations. This chapter, rather than attempting to be a traditional remedial map handbook, is devoted to strategies designed to make mapmaking and map interpretation an involvement-centered and developmental part of elementary students' social studies curriculum.

Strategies for Making and Interpreting Maps

A child's ability to conceptualize space develops with age and experience. Figure 12.1 shows a bedroom map drawn by a 6-year-old; the bedroom map in Figure 12.2 was drawn by an 11-year-old. What differences can you see in the older child's conception of space?

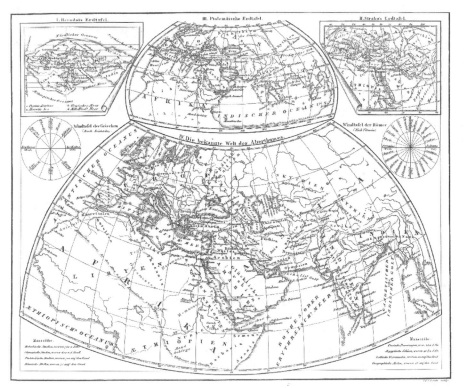

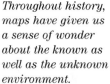

Throughout history, maps have given us a sense of wonder about the known as well as the unknown environment.

FIGURE 12.1

*Map of Bedroom
Drawn by a
6-Year-Old*

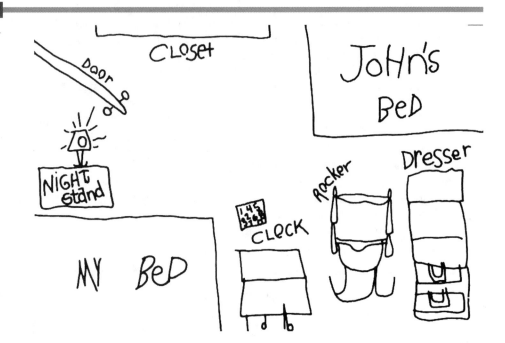

In the area of map interpretation especially, experiential approaches to teaching the concepts and skills are much more effective than are textbook and lecture approaches. The younger the children, the more hands-on (and feet-on!) experiences are needed to allow the children to make the connection between physical features and graphic representation.

The globe-making activity pictured in the illustration on page 284 is one example of a way to help children understand mapping and geography. More than a dozen other strategies for making and interpreting maps are detailed throughout this chapter.

Visualizing the Local Environment

To help students participate in the transition from reality to abstraction in representing space, you might involve them in the following progression:

1. On a walking tour of the area surrounding the school, note various landmarks, such as the school, businesses, houses, streets, parks, and so forth.
2. With only a camera and a roll of film, you and the students can put together a "slide tour" of the area surrounding the school in which various landmarks are portrayed.
3. View the school area from some elevated perspective, such as a hill or a tall building. Take some pictures and review them in class.
4. Have the class or several small groups do murals depicting the school and the surrounding area.

FIGURE 12.2 *Map of Bedroom Drawn by an 11-Year-Old*

5. Make a model of the area from cardboard, wooden blocks, and paper. Again, this can be done by the class or in small groups.
6. Borrow an aerial photograph of the area around the school from the local office of the U.S. Department of Agriculture. Pick up a map of your city or area. Let the students compare the aerial photograph with the map.
7. Make an enlargement of the portion of a road map that shows the area around the school and give each student a copy. Compare this map to the aerial photograph, the model, the map mural, and the slides.
8. Take another walk around the area. Have each student take a copy of the map in step 7. As landmarks are sighted, have students point to them on the map.

These eight activities take students from the concrete experience of walking through and observing an area to its eventual abstract representation through a series of developmental steps. The activities could be used in a daily sequence of eight lessons or scattered over a longer time period.

271

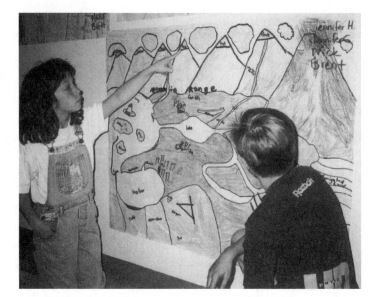

Spatial perspectives emerge as students become mapmakers.

Mental Maps

People carry images, or mental maps, of space and place in their heads. Mental maps are more or less accurate, depending on how often someone goes from one place to another and/or how important it is for someone to know how to get somewhere. For example, even very young children have pretty good mental maps of the rooms in their houses or apartments. They typically have little trouble navigating from one area to another. But if a very young child lives in a house with a basement into which the child never or seldom ventures, then the mental map may be quite inaccurate. On a different scale, the mental map of western North America for many years contained about as much fiction as fact. In fact, Thomas Jefferson sent Lewis and Clark from the Missouri River to the Pacific Ocean across North America in the early nineteenth-century for the purpose of finding the so-called Northwest Passage, a water route from the Great Plains to the Pacific. Many maps of the day already showed the Northwest Passage in one location or another. The only trouble is that it never existed except in people's imaginations.

An individual has literally dozens of mental maps stored in his or her mind. Many of them are so accurate that the person navigates flawlessly, perhaps from his or her residence to the shopping mall, or to the grocery store, or to Aunt Margaret's house. Certain other maps may be a bit on the hazy side, especially if the person is the type to get lost occasionally. Some mental maps cover small distances, and others may cover great distances. We are all mapmakers and navigators, some of us better than others.

Generally, a mental map is "retrieved" only when the person needs it to go somewhere; in that sense, mental maps are quite functional. However, there are other uses for them as well. Sometimes people just like to think about places that they've been to and even places they've never visited. Other times someone may ask another for directions, as in, "How do you get from here to the aquarium?" or whatever.

Allow your students to get their mental maps "out of their heads" and onto paper. Here is how this activity works. Ask each of your students to think about a place, not far from home, that he or she enjoys visiting. For each student it may be a different place—that's good because you will have more variety when the children put their maps up for display. On the other hand, if you want to start with a place in common, have the students make a mental map of the playground or how to get from their room to the principal's office. Step 1 in creating a mental map is to make a list of landmarks along the way—things that stand out in one's mind. Younger children can tell you what landmarks they intend to include when they draw their maps, and older children can make a written list. Step 2 is to draw the map as one "sees" it in the mind. Step 3 is the process of verification, a very important skill that children need to learn. The verification stage involves checking the map for accuracy. Step 4 is making a new map based on the knowledge gained in the verification process. This is a good time to reflect with the students on the idea of errors, because their first maps may have contained some. You need to draw out the idea that errors are not bad, as some children and adults think, but merely items to be corrected. Error analysis is used a great deal in problem solving, especially in the form of a technique called *reverse engineering*, where one takes a look at some product one has constructed, and works backwards to see what needs to be improved.

Traverse Maps

A traverse map has a line through an area. Usually, the "line" is an obvious one, such as a street, a lakeshore, a river, or a boundary of some sort. Actually, a traverse creates a spatial sample of an area. Traverse maps are very easy to make, and I would encourage you to have even the youngest children construct them. To do a traverse, you begin with observation and recording, the two most basic skills of the investigator. For example, if you wish to follow a creek for, say, 200 feet, then merely walk along the side of the creek and record the significant things (trees, docks, bridges, houses, etc.) that you see along the way. This is called *fieldwork*. When your fieldwork is completed, you are ready to make your traverse map. Figure 12.3 shows the development of a child's traverse map.

Finding Your Way

Obviously, one of the main purposes of a map is to help a person find his or her way from one place to another. Children benefit greatly from little practice games in which they are challenged to tell how they would go from point A to point B. For example, on the map of Lancaster shown in Figure 12.4, how would you explain to someone how to go from St. Peters Cathedral to the Maritime Museum? from Town Hall to Grand Theatre? from City Library to the Roman Bath House? from the Police Station to the Sports Centre?

Changing the Scale of a Map

There are three basic techniques for changing the scale of a map: mechanical, optical, and mathematical. Each method is described here.

FIGURE 12.3

*A Child's Traverse Map of the
Fremont Neighborhood*

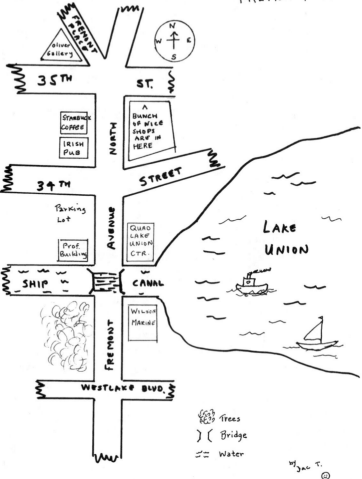

FREMONT, U.S.A.

Mechanical Method. The mechanical method uses a pantograph, which is an inexpensive instrument in the shape of a parallelogram. A pantograph, which may be set to various scale changes, will make a very accurate enlargement or reduction of an existing map. It has the advantage of letting junior cartographers decide exactly what change of scale they want to make. You can order a pantograph from any school-supply store.

Optical Method. The elementary school counterpart of the precision optical instruments available in certain cartography laboratories is the opaque projector. By placing a map in the projector and projecting it on a wall, it is possible to trace the enlarged map outline onto a sheet of paper taped to the wall. Although it is probably the most commonly used scale-change instrument, it is the least satisfactory. It is not possible to reduce maps with an opaque projector. Second, students using this

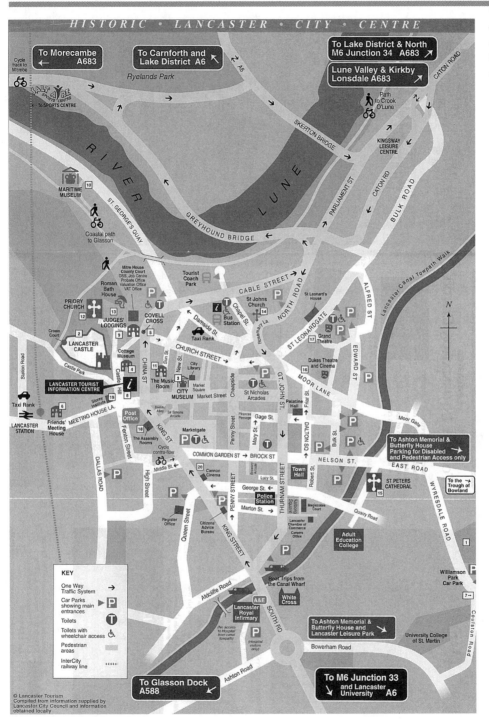

FIGURE 12.4

*A Map of
Historic Sites
in Lancaster,
England*

method do not really know what the change of scale is; they only know that the new map is larger. Third, distortions often occur because a book page does not lie flat in the projector or because the instrument is projecting at a slight angle to the wall.

Mathematical Method. The mathematical method, which is also called the method of similar squares, is useful for both enlargements and reductions. After plotting points on a grid of larger or smaller dimensions than a grid superimposed on an existing map, a student can then connect the points into a line in order to construct a new outline. Points for cities, mountains, and other features can also be plotted. Figure 12.5 illustrates this method.

Simulating Aerial Photographs

To give younger students some insight into the overhead vertical perspective generally portrayed by maps, let them use a camera to take pictures of a terrain model or a set of blocks laid out to simulate a village. By standing directly over the model while photographing it, a student achieves the physical perspective of the mapmaker.

Constructing Base Maps from Aerial Photographs

Students can produce original and very accurate large-scale maps by placing tracing paper over an aerial photograph and tracing roads, cities, waterforms, wooded areas, farmland, and so on. The product is an interpreted form of the photograph in which the child makes decisions about what to portray and what to leave out. Figures 12.6A and 12.6B illustrate the translation of an aerial photograph into a base map.

FIGURE 12.5   *Illustration of Mathematical Model for Changing the Scale of a Map*

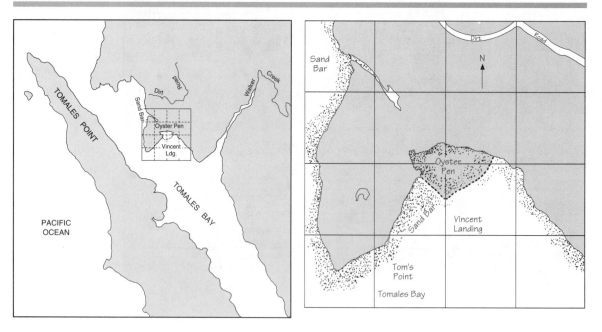

FIGURE 12.6A

FIGURE 12.6B

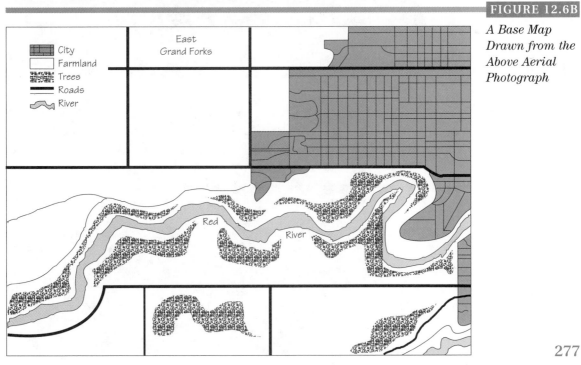

A Base Map Drawn from the Above Aerial Photograph

City
Farmland
Trees
Roads
River

East Grand Forks

Red River

Studying Land Use Change

Figure 12.7 shows two aerial photographs of basically the same site. The photographs were taken about 30 years apart. Ask students to study the two photos by observing and mapping them. When they have done this, challenge them to document as many changes in the landscape as they can. While it is acceptable to use the two photos shown here, it is far better if you are able to obtain two such photos of your school site or of the landscape in your local community. Aerial photographs are available from the Department of Agriculture and perhaps from local real estate agencies.

FIGURE 12.7

Aerial Photograph of a Site Taken 30 Years Apart

Origami Paper Folding: Japanese Peace Cranes

Perhaps you're wondering: Why origami in a chapter on maps? The answer has to do with what is called *developmentally appropriate practice*. Spatial logic and per-

ceptions are developmental aspects of map reading and map making. In other words, we need strategies to help children make sense of space. Art forms such as origami, or Japanese paper folding, help young learners to articulate spatial proportions while they experience the joys of creating.

The Japanese crane inhabits parts of China, Japan, Korea, and Siberia. Artistically, it symbolizes peace, happiness, and longevity. In recent times, these beautiful birds have become an endangered species. In Japan, the cranes are considered a special natural monument. Using thin, stiff paper, children can construct peace cranes by following the spatial directions illustrated in Figure 12.8.

Visualizing Space

Visualizing space is a useful, intellectual exercise for children. At the primary level, you can challenge students by asking them to verbalize the directions for getting from their homes to school. At the intermediate level, you might want to assign students the tasks of giving directions for getting from the school to certain landmarks, such as the city center, airport, zoo, parks, or athletic stadiums.

Children also enjoy visualizing imaginary space. Figure 12.9 shows yet another way for children to portray their ideas in spatial form. This map, drawn by a child

---

FIGURE 12.8 *Origami Paper Folding: Japanese Peace Cranes*

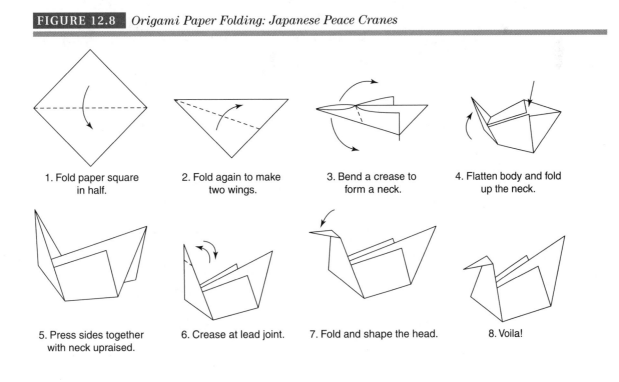

1. Fold paper square in half.

2. Fold again to make two wings.

3. Bend a crease to form a neck.

4. Flatten body and fold up the neck.

5. Press sides together with neck upraised.

6. Crease at lead joint.

7. Fold and shape the head.

8. Voila!

named Ted, illustrates his conception of a map of Narnia after he read the book, *The Lion, the Witch, and the Wardrobe.* For many children, such a project is a welcome relief from the usual book-report format.

Mapping Directions. This activity is designed to help students visualize oral or written information spatially. Any story or written information that includes directions for traveling around a given space will do. Here is an example. You and your students can develop others. Read your students the following story and have them draw a map of the places involved. One such map is shown in Figure 12.10.

> One morning, Little Red Riding Hood decided to visit her sick grandmother. After she left her house, she went to the muffin man's for some muffins for her grandmother. Then she went to the flower lady's for some nice fresh flowers to take to her grandmother. Next, Little Red Riding Hood entered the south entrance to the woods and walked along the path toward the woodcutter's house, which was west of her house. When she reached the woodcutter's house, she stopped for a drink of water. She then walked north to feed some squirrels, and from there, she went by the most direct path to her grandmother's house.

FIGURE 12.10

The Road to Grandmother's House

NORTH

Grandmother's
House

Woodcutter's
House

Deer
crossing

WEST   EAST

Flower
Lady

Muffin
Man's

Little Red
Ridinghood's
House

SOUTH

Considering Variables in Finding Your Way

People spend much of their time going from one place to another. They go on foot, sometimes by bicycle, sometimes by bus or car. Rarely is there only one way to get from one place to another. When a person decides to go from point A to point B, he or she usually considers the purpose of the trip, how much time he or she has, the means of transportation, and so on. These things that are considered are called *variables*. Thus, a child walking to school must consider several variables: time, safety, friends, and, perhaps, scenery.

To carry out this map activity, have your students select any two points in the local environment and illustrate on a map how they would travel from one point to another. You might have them show three routes between the two points: the quickest route, the safest route, and the most scenic route. Figure 12.11 shows a typical response to this activity.

Conceptualizing a Common Traverse

Constructing a map of the route from home to school affords children an excellent opportunity to conceptualize a common spatial traverse. It's more complicated, of course, if students ride a bus to school over some distance than if they live a block or two away. The assignment progresses like this:

1. For several days, have the children observe carefully as they walk or ride to and from school. They should notice the street names and other important

---

FIGURE 12.11

*Child's Map
Showing
Alternate Routes*

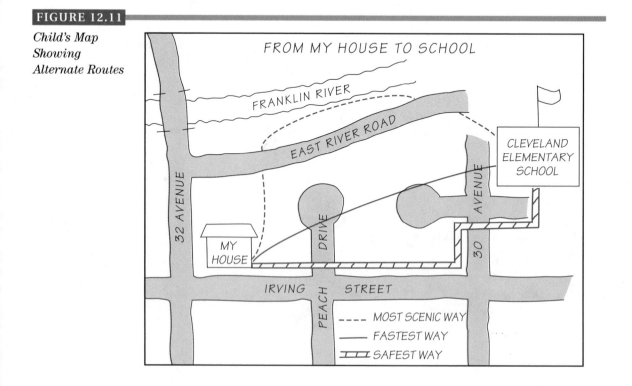

landmarks. This period of incubation and reflection about the landscape is cru-cial. Don't hurry the children into making a finished product. Instead, at this point, stress the skills of observation and mental recording.

2. Older children should be encouraged to learn the particular cardinal directions they travel. For example, a child might walk two blocks south before turning east, and so on.
3. Have the children begin taking field notes. They should write down street names, draw rough sketches, and so forth.
4. Have the students use their field notes to draw maps during class time. Be sure that there are several city maps available so that they can refer to them as they construct their own maps.
5. Have the students give brief oral reports in which they show the class their maps and verbalize the way they come to school.
6. Display the maps on the wall of the classroom. Encourage the students to study them and make comparisons of the various routes used to get to school.

Perspective Taking

There is nothing like a map to teach children the concept of perspective taking. The best way to use maps, of course, is developmentally. By that, I mean lessons should come from direct experience, which is then thoughtfully considered and discussed. For example, to teach perspective taking for the first time, try the following two activities.

Bird's-Eye View. Find a picture of a bird in flight (a magazine photograph, for ex-ample). Ask the students to tell what the bird sees from its vantage point in the sky. Perhaps students who have flown in an airplane can describe the perspective as they recall it.

Now tell the students that they are going to draw maps using a bird's-eye view. To do it, have each student create a model of a small village from construction paper, complete with stream, forest, roads, houses, and so on. When the villages are done, ask each student to place his or her village on the floor right beside the desk, so that he or she can look straight down on it. Then ask the students to draw a sketch, or map, of what they see. Following this activity (perhaps the next day), take the class outside to an elevated place (if there is one) on the playground. Have them draw maps of what they see. Now you are ready to have a good discussion of the differences in perspective between an aerial view and a view from the ground.

Map Projections. I am convinced that it is difficult for most children to under-stand that maps are, in fact, *projections* of the earth's curved surface onto a flat piece of paper (see Figure 12.12). For that reason, it is completely necessary to do the previous activities and others like them. If you don't, the readiness will not exist for children to comprehend the somewhat abstract nature of mapping. That is why the constructivity principle, which states that activity must precede analysis—is so crucial—why *drawing* maps should come before *studying* maps, especially maps drawn by someone other than the child herself.

A World Globe Activity

The figure below contains the six settled continents of the world. The continental landforms shown here can be used in an activity designed to help children understand the relative size and location of the continents on the globe. Simply make copies of the figure and give them to children to cut out and glue onto a blue balloon. Be sure to remind students to study the actual location of the continents before gluing them to the balloon's surface.

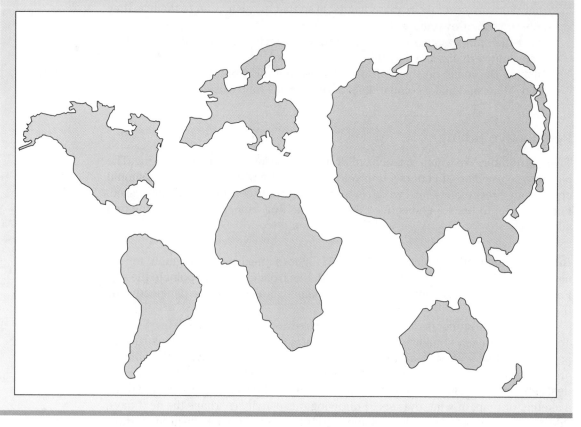

The map in Figure 12.13 is a good example of perspective taking. Notice that the centerpiece of the map is the North Pole; therefore, this map is called a *polar projection*. The space shown on the map is projected out from the North Pole. In this case, the horizon of the map is the Equator, so we are looking at half the world's surface. It becomes apparent that the vast majority of the earth's land surface is in the Northern Hemisphere.

Make copies of this map, and have the students cut it out along the Equator. Then ask them to rotate the map and examine it from Africa, Asia, North America, and so on. Ask them to express their thoughts about how the earth appears from these various vantage points. Ask them if they have ever considered looking at North America from such a perspective.

FIGURE 12.12

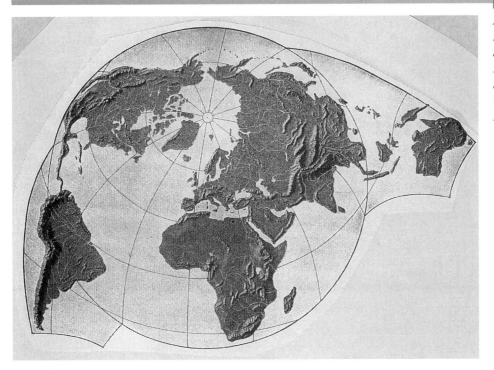

*Attempts to
Portray a
Sphere (the
Earth) on a Flat
Surface Are
Called Map
Projections*

Now have each student draw the map. This enables them to let the perspective sink in. North America may appear to be "upside down" in their drawing, but that is only because they are used to a different perspective (Figure 12.14). Of course, the concept of perspective is pervasive. Even the perspective on a lesson is different for a child sitting in the back versus the front of the class, or near a window.

Any attempt to portray a sphere (the earth) onto a flat surface meets with difficulty. Nevertheless, it is necessary to do so, simply because one can't use a globe as efficiently as flat maps on the wall or bound up in books. A map can portray details and show particular regions using different scales. When the round earth is portrayed on flat paper, the result is called a *map projection*. This is because the sphere is projected onto a flat surface. There are many map projections of the earth, but they all have one thing in common: Inevitably, they distort something. The most well-recognized case of distortion is the case of Greenland. Many children (and some adults) assume that Greenland is larger than it is. In fact, Greenland is about one-seventh the size of South America. The most common source of distortion arises from the attempt to portray lines of longitude and the space between them. As you know, lines of longitude converge at the poles; they have to, since the earth is shaped like a ball, not like a table top. But when they are shown on a flat map, the lines of longitude are often shown as straight vertical lines running from the North Pole to the South Pole, thereby creating the distorted size of land masses in the far north and south.

285

FIGURE 12.13

Polar Projection Map of the Northern Hemisphere

The three most common projections of the round earth onto a flat surface are (1) the cylindrical projection, (2) the conic projection, and (3) the plane-surface projection. These three projections are illustrated in Figure 12.15. I suggest that you demonstrate them to your students and let them practice the activity as well. It's a hands-on way of experiencing the difficulties of showing a sphere on a flat surface.

In Figure 12.16 (page 289), we see the different results of attempts to *project* the globe onto flat surfaces. In each case, something is sacrificed. Notice that the three main distortions are size, shape, and our sense of what the map "really" should look like.

Four-Color Mapping Theory

An interesting and useful technique used by cartographers is four-color mapping. Intermediate-age children can quickly learn the idea and use it in their own map-

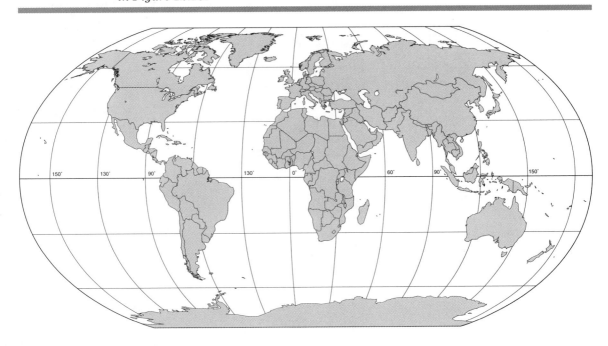

making. Four-color map theory is based on the fact that, by using just four colors, one can color a map of the United States (or anyplace else, for that matter) such as the one illustrated in Figure 12.17 (page 270) without ever duplicating colors along any given border. Of course, that's easy to see in the case of our big western states because of their geometric shapes. By the way, there are two reasons they have such regular shapes: (1) there are fewer major rivers to create natural boundaries, although there are exceptions such as the Columbia River, which forms the Washington-Oregon boundary; and (2) the boundaries were created much later by mapmakers sitting in offices in Washington, DC, who seemed to love drawing long, straight lines such as you find in Wyoming, Colorado, and Utah.

Just notice the squiggly lines created by the Mississippi and Ohio Rivers! These two mighty bodies of water account for the boundary lines between more than a dozen states. The Mississippi creates a natural boundary all the way from Minnesota to Louisiana, where the river meets the Gulf of Mexico. Trace it with your finger from north to south. Notice how the Ohio River forms the entire northern boundary of Kentucky. Trace the Ohio from its origins in Pennsylvania, where it begins at the junction of the Allegheny and Monongahela Rivers, all the way to where it joins the Mississippi in southern Illinois. Activities such as this are powerful conceptual ways of anchoring ideas of space and place in the minds of children. A map begins to take meaningful form, it begins to make sense, and it takes its place in the memory when a person engages in activities such as these.

The four-color theory is really put to the test by such states as Tennessee and Kentucky. Just count their neighbors! But still, it works. Maine has only one

FIGURE 12.15

The Round Earth on Flat Paper

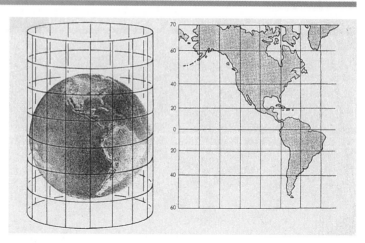

A cylindrical projection is based upon the projection of the globe onto a cylinder.

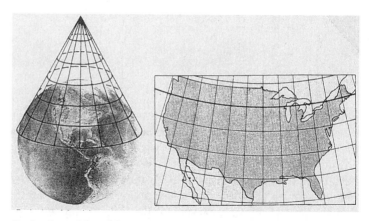

Projection of the globe onto a cone becomes a conic projection.

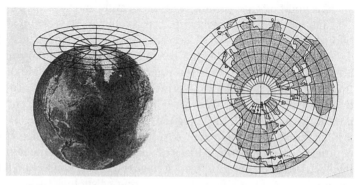

Plane-surface projection is based upon the projection of the globe onto a disc.

FIGURE 12.16

Portrayals of Globe

289

Maps

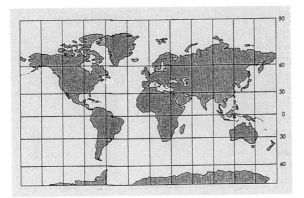

When the globe is portrayed as a rectangle, the correct shapes are shown, but notice how large Greenland and Antarctica appear to be.

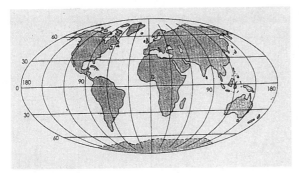

When the globe is portrayed as an oval, the sizes are shown correctly, but the shapes are distorted.

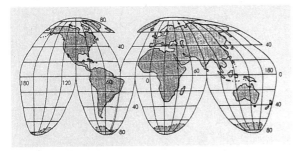

When the globe is portrayed as an orange peel, both size and shape are accurate, but notice what happens to Antarctica.

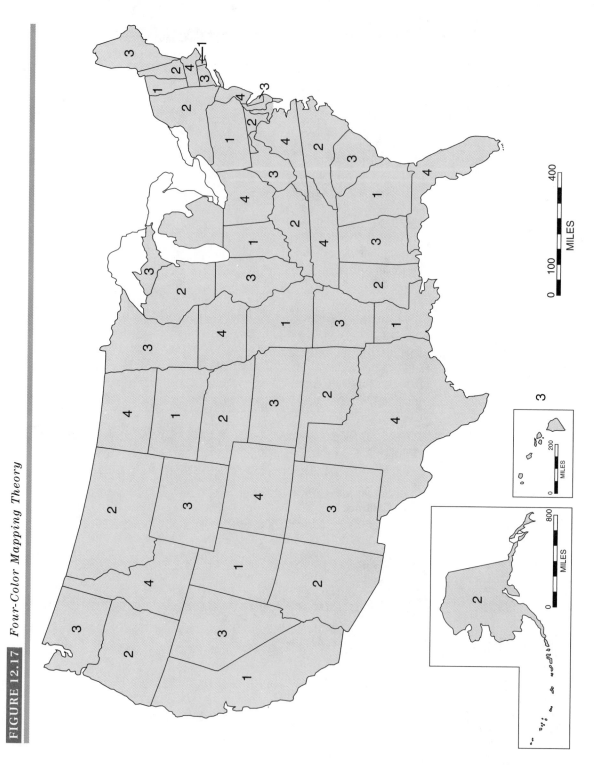

FIGURE 12.17   *Four-Color Mapping Theory*

neighbor, so it's easy. I would suggest you create an inductive lesson for your students. Give them each an outline map of the United States (if you copy the one from Figure 12.17, remove the numbers first), and challenge them to color the map using only four colors, without ever duplicating colors along any state boundary line. With you as their teacher, they're sure to be successful, but have a few extra maps just in case the trial-and-error process doesn't work at first.

Estimating Distances

The ability to estimate distance is a very valuable skill (e.g., in driving). The National Council of Teachers of Mathematics (NCTM) lists *estimation* as one of its 10 goal statements for learning mathematics. There are several things you can do to develop this skill; here are two suggestions:

1. Take the class out on the playground (or to a long hallway) and set two markers a certain distance apart. Have everyone write down or tell their best guess about the distance between the markers. Then measure the distance between the two markers with a tape measure like the kind used for measuring distances in track meets. (Your school probably has one.) Measuring is an important skill, and in this instance, it allows your students to employ yet another skill, that of verifying their guesses. With repeated practice, students will become quite skilled at estimating distances.

2. Have your students work in cooperative groups of two using yardsticks or metersticks to measure each other's typical stride. The best thing to do is to work in a little math here. If you measure your stride, say, five times, you can add up the total of all five strides and divide the total by 5 to derive the average or mean stride.

These young mapmakers are estimating, measuring, and recording distances on the playground.

Once a child knows the approximate distance of his or her stride, he or she can use it to pace off distances. This becomes a built-in tool for estimating, measuring, and verifying distances anywhere.

Summary

Maps are abstract representations of the surface of the earth or some other sphere that help people see certain spatial relationships. Aerial and satellite photographs can help students view the earth's surface features more concretely. Maps are particularly useful to social scientists as a means of illustrating spatial data, such as political boundaries, population distributions, the relative locations of goods and services, and the distribution of land and water forms. The interpretation and development of maps by elementary-age students give them a clearer picture of spatial phenomena.

The ability to interpret and develop maps is most effectively taught through experiential approaches. This chapter described a wide range of strategies and activities to help students learn map concepts and skills.

ACTIVITIES

1. Make a model of your neighborhood with cardboard and Monopoly™ houses. Ask some elementary-age students to help you.
2. Ask the weather bureau or your local television station for satellite photographs. Make a map from one of the photographs.
3. Using a road map of your locality, make an enlargement of your neighborhood.
4. Take some students to the top of a hill or a tall building. Photograph and sketch what you see. Talk about the spatial relationships of natural and human-made phenomena.

SUGGESTED READINGS

Dill, B. (1994). *Teaching the Five Themes of Geography.* New York: Frank Schaffer Publications.

Haas, M. (2000). "A Street through Time Used with Powerful Instructional Strategies." *Social Studies and the Young Learner, 13* (Nov./Dec.): 20–23.

Kirman, J. (1999). "Radarsat Satellite Images: A New Geography Tool for Upper Elementary Classrooms." *Social Education, 63* (Apr.): 167–169.

Murphey, C. (1998). "Using the Five Themes of Geography to Explore a School Site." *Social Studies Review* (Spring/Summer): 45–48.

Pearson, J., and Wright, D. (1994). "First Maps." *Childhood Education* (May): 31–38.

Triifinoff, K. (1995). "Going Beyond Location: Thematic Maps in the Elementary Grades." *Journal of Geography* (Mar./Apr.): 368–374.

Social Studies and Curriculum Integration: Projects and Themes for Learning

In his insightful book, *The Schools Our Children Deserve*, Alfie Kohn writes that often he will ask teachers which of two fractions is larger: 4/11 or 5/13? He writes that nearly everyone he asks gives the wrong answer, especially mathematics teachers. The right answer, according to Kohn is, "Who cares?" His point is that isolated facts and skills are not particularly important in the greater scheme of things. This brings us quickly to a deeply imbedded problem in the school experience. The problem is that bits and pieces of information are all too often taught to children outside of any meaningful frame of reference or context. The stuff literally goes in one ear and out the other. All of us were taught at some point in our school days (probably around fifth or sixth grade) how to compare the size of fractions by dividing the numerator by the denominator. It isn't difficult, so why don't we remember that particular skill or others? I'll let you answer that.

Integrated studies represent a kind of "seamless whole" in learning. Children see the world as a whole. They don't think in terms of separate disciplines—incidentally, so do great philosophers and other profound thinkers. Leo Tolstoy, the author of *War and Peace* and other great novels, was himself deeply interested in childhood education. He even started his own school for poor children. Tolstoy observed that children, unlike most adults, are drawn to and enjoy complex themes. He also noted that unfortunately most teachers are not drawn to complex themes; they prefer the oversimplified world of textbooks, separate subjects, facts, skills, and so on. Of course, the secret is to see the world as children see it. The purpose of this chapter is to stimulate your thoughts about the possibilities inherent in integrated teaching and learning. We will address the following topics:

- The nature of integrated studies
- Kinds of integrated studies projects
- A sample integrated studies project
- Themes for integration

I ntegrated studies in the form of great projects have an energizing quality about them. At their best, they are what psychologists call *flow* experiences. When people are "in the flow," they tend to lose track of time, want to keep going, and feel engaged in something personally meaningful and rewarding. You'll know your kids are in a flow activity when they say, "Can't we just work on this a little longer?" or something to that effect.

Psychologists today say that human beings are "wired" to do projects. Some have gone so far as to say that projects are the single, most purely human activity. I think there is much to this; for example, how often do people think, "One of these days I've got to spend a day getting all my stuff in order" or "Let's plan a trip to the mountains" or "Maybe we can organize a neighborhood cleanup campaign." Actually, something as simple as a trip to the grocery store is, in fact, a project. We may not call it that, but that's what it is. Some projects, of course, are greater than others.

Projects, whether they are ours alone or something we try with a class or even a whole school, have several interesting characteristics. First of all, a good project is a defining activity. If a project is about reconstructing Native American life in your area from 200 years ago, then it is clear what you are doing. You are not studying history or anthropology; rather, you are using both to help you complete your project.

The second characteristic of good projects is that they are interdisciplinary. A project on "Activities of the Night" will use music, art, mathematics, language, science, and, most of all, social studies. Projects have what can be called syntactic complexity. A project really is more complex than reading a text and answering questions. One truly needs all the help one can get from the various areas of the curriculum. The difference is that textbooks and questions are contributors to, not controllers of, the curriculum.

A third characteristic of good projects is that they allow a person the luxury of setting boundaries. Projects have a beginning, a middle, and an end. If students in your class decide to create an art museum, then they must go through the stages of purpose, planning, development, exhibition, and evaluation. That's pretty straightforward compared to the seemingly endless voyage through a textbook. Most projects have a definite time frame; otherwise, students couldn't accomplish their goals.

The fourth, and perhaps most significant, characteristic of projects is that they have an outcome. A good project is undertaken with a clear purpose of achieving something. If your class decides to build a greenbelt along the edge of the school grounds, then you all know what needs to be done. You may not initially know *how* to do it, or even what it will look like, but you know you are heading toward a culminating event, that of a finished greenbelt. An outcome is important, because it addresses the much-needed aspect of reality in learning and gives one a sense of closure.

For starters, consider the fact that projects can be done alone or with others; indeed, this is true of all learning. My position on working together or alone is that students must learn to do both. But in social studies, let's not forget, most of what a class does should be *social*, and that argues for group projects whenever possible. People need to cooperate with each other in life for a variety of reasons. One of those reasons is that many of the worthwhile things in life (a play or pageant, for example) are simply too complex and demanding to orchestrate alone. Another reason for working together on projects is that it gives children a chance to actually practice citizenship. So, a few projects can and should be done alone, but most projects should be group enterprises.

Individual Projects

Here is a list of projects that could be done by children working alone:

- Role-playing a famous person in history
- Constructing a model of a ship, clothing, or village from another time or culture—specifically, its acrchitecture, food, festivals, etc.
- Reporting on another culture—specifically, its architecture, food, festivals, etc.
- Conducting an investigation or neighborhood survey
- Building a kite after the fashion of Japanese kites
- Making a musical instrument from another culture

Of course, these projects could also be done by children working together, depending on one's educational purpose.

Group Projects

Here is a list of possible group projects:

- Putting on a pageant of pioneer or Native American life
- Creating a museum in the classroom
- Investigating different brands of the same product
- Producing a weekly "radio" news program to be broadcast over the school intercom
- Conducting a schoolwide effort to improve safety conditions
- Creating displays or exhibits of schoolwork
- Issuing a class challenge to read a certain number of books
- Putting on a schoolwide social studies fair
- Mapping the local environment

The advantages to group projects are that they allow children to experience the give-and-take of community life and that they create a much more process-centered learning environment. The first advantage is pretty straightforward; working together comes closer to mirroring real life in a democracy than does working alone. The second advantage takes some explaining. To miss the underlying point is to miss something extremely important in learning theory.

When learners work together, a more complex learning environment is established. This is so because there is less opportunity for teacher control of intellectual and social forces. Although this may seem a drawback at first glance, it is actually a step in the right direction. Learning becomes more process centered simply because students get to share their thoughts and feelings with each other. More conversation means more complexity; more complexity means more opportunity for language development, for perspective taking, and for moral development.

The best way for language development to proceed for children is to put them into social situations with their peers and allow them to solve problems together. They learn to express themselves, to find their own voices, to listen to others, and to decide things together. Thus, the social and intellectual aspects of learning become intertwined rather than separated.

The ability to see something from more than one perspective is useful whether one is viewing the Grand Canyon (it looks rather different from the top of the canyon than it does from the bottom) or ways to solve a problem. Weighing different perspectives on an issue is something one can learn from practice. Group projects afford children the opportunity to see things from another point of view. For example, if children want to build a greenbelt on the school grounds, they need to learn that their own viewpoint may be somewhat different from that of the school board or even from that of students in other classrooms.

The richly textured environments that arise when children work together on projects are filled with opportunities for the thoughtful examination of moral issues. For example, children working together will have more disagreements than children working alone, but this is good in an atmosphere where people are free to express their thoughts and feelings. Such conditions help students confront real moral issues, such as sharing, reaching consensus, doing one's fair share, and learning through experience that different people have different innate gifts in life. In short, group work makes it clear that people need each other and that there is no room for condescension toward another if anything is to be accomplished.

Kinds of Projects

Four distinctly different kinds of projects will be discussed here: service projects, production projects, problem-solving projects, and schoolwide projects.

Service Projects

Service projects, as the name implies, are about contributing to community, school, and family life. The purpose of a service project is to provide services or goods to others who can benefit from your work. An example of this would be a project where children become involved with the residents of a retirement home, attempting to include them in their lives. Many teachers have commented on the beneficial effects of such a service project, both to the children and to the residents of the retirement home. The singing, artwork, plays, and reports bring joy to the residents and fulfillment to the children.

One service project done by elementary school children that especially impressed me was at a school that had a considerable turnover of enrollment. New children were continually enrolling in the school. The students entered into a service project that involved making "Welcome to Our School" kits, which were given to a child when he or she enrolled during the school year. The kits were shoe boxes that contained names of friendly children to meet, a map of the school, a letter from the principal, a free lunch ticket, and activities and puzzles. The students who did that project learned about moral development and caring for others who might be scared, anxious, or just plain feeling alone, and that was worth a lot more than some abstract discussion of fairness, caring, and other virtues. But, more than that, when teachers get the children involved in such service projects, they have concrete experience to enhance the discussions.

Many children today do not even know elderly people. They are denied the wisdom and the comfort that older people can share with the young. Others may never have considered what it would be like to be a new student in an unknown environment. The beautiful thing about service projects is that they are truly win/win situations in which it is difficult to know who gains the most.

Production Projects

Anyone who has ever been in a play, helped to set up a school carnival, or participated in any equally ambitious project knows how much fun and how much work they can be. The key to production projects is that the focus is on *producing* something. The event itself represents only the outcome. It's what happens along the way that is so great: the rehearsals, the late-night hammering and sawing, the camaraderie, the worry over whether things will ever come together, and so on.

One of the best tests of school experience comes when one looks back from a perspective of time. In fact, Aristotle noted that such things as happiness are best defined in retrospect. Some of the great memories of school experience are created by production projects. To this day, one of my clearest, best memories of school comes from third grade (in my case, about a million years ago), when our class did a production of the play *The Shoemaker and the Elves*, which was broadcast over a local radio station. What a great teacher Mrs. Knott was to do that with us. Another great production that I recall was in fourth grade, when our class made a huge wrap-around-the-room mural of life in ancient Egypt, Greece, and Rome. Thanks to Mrs. Emery for making social studies come alive. Oh, what vision teachers have who get their students involved in group productions!

Problem-Solving Projects

Solving problems using the project approach is great because it gets you and the students into the business of *applying* ideas and skills rather than merely learning them for their own sake. Problem-solving projects are best organized around an empirical question, one that can be answered by gathering information and reaching a solution on the basis of an analysis and synthesis of the information. Problem-solving projects use methods and ideas from every discipline, combining mathematics, language, science, music, art, social studies, and anything else that might be helpful.

Problem-solving projects are experiences with real problems with real solutions. For example, if your class wants to improve communication in the school, you might begin with the question: How can we improve communication in our school? Once the question is framed to everyone's satisfaction, you are ready to go. The class will have to do surveys, experiments, and whatever it takes to solve the problem. Other examples of questions that can result in problem-solving projects are:

How can we make the pedestrian crossing near our school safer?
How can we determine which of several brands of a product is the best buy?
How can we establish ways for kids of different grades/ages in this school to work together?
How can we find out about different ways to learn?
How can we create a schoolwide celebration of Arbor Day?
How can we redesign our classroom to make it a better place to learn?
How can we get a schoolwide literacy campaign going?

Schoolwide Projects

It is great to involve all the students in a classroom, or even all the students at a grade level, in projects of one kind or another, but schoolwide projects are wonderful because they have the potential to bring the whole student body, faculty, and staff together to focus on a common topic. It takes energy and leadership to mobilize a whole school, but when it is done well, a different ethos will prevail. Schoolwide projects create an esprit de corps that you can't achieve any other way. It is indeed heartwarming to see children of different ages working together, sharing, teaching, and learning from each other. School assemblies take on new meaning as the entire K–6 student body gathers to hear the outcome of a school project on helping the homeless, the elderly, or the needy; to present the culminating activities of a schoolwide fitness and nutrition project; or to present awards and certificates to the children who have taken part in a literacy campaign.

A Sample Project: Constructing a Greenbelt

Many school environments are dominated by pavement and noise. In recent years, greenbelt theory, first developed in England and Australia by urban geographers, has led to ecologically sound, aesthetically pleasing, and economically feasible ways to bring about positive change in even the most paved-over, congested areas. People around the globe have responded to the need to maintain places of beauty, animal habitats, and areas to play and relax.

People have developed the capacity to dominate most plant and animal species. For better or worse, human beings have become the main stewards of the planet. We need to teach our children positive stewardship in order to ensure a productive ecological balance of nature.

In the Greenbelt Design Project,[1] students are challenged to explore the possibilities of designing and developing a greenbelt. The students take part in all facets of the project, from gathering information, doing feasibility studies, creating models, planning, and convincing others of the need, to the final stage, the actual construction of a greenbelt.

The purpose is clear: to design and construct a functional and beautiful greenbelt at the school. The greenbelt, no matter how small or large, must be something the children can themselves produce. The design considerations are beauty, cost, animal habitat, plant choice, safety, and low maintenance. The students will need to take into account ecological factors, such as growing conditions, soil, climate, and so on. This will demand a good deal of research. They will also need to study elements of design, architecture, and safety. Here is how one primary teacher approached the project with her class (see Figure 13.1):

In creating our greenbelt, it was important for us to know all the basic needs of the plants we wanted in our little park, and how we could supply those needs. It was a small, bare lifeless corner of the school yard. What a challenge we faced if we wanted it to be beautiful! We learned all about the plants and animals (everything from dogs and rabbits to earthworms and bugs) that might inhabit the area. We learned how to test soil and how to enrich it. We studied the weather and climate patterns. Each day, we took temperature readings, checked sun angles, shade, and so on. We measured the rainfall faithfully. We took pictures, we drew maps, we interviewed kids, citizens, and experts. We watched films about parks and greenbelts, looking for ideas. We even figured out fund-raising ideas to pay for the plants and other work related to planting. We made design, drew pictures, built models, had landscapers come to class—whatever it took!

Every day, committees met. They discussed, they argued, they listened to experts—they were becoming experts themselves. I was really proud of the kids. At *long* last, we presented our model to the school board, complete with drawings, sketches, and even cost estimates. They were surprised when we told them we had developed a budget and had raised the money to pay for the project. I wish you could have been there on the beautiful spring morning when we dedicated the greenbelt. What a crowd! And such beautiful music and dancing. Everyone was excited. I just watched from the side while the kids gave speeches and graciously accepted the praises of the Parks Commissioner, the principal, and the chairman of the school board. Those kids and I know what it means to be a citizen!

Project Outline

So, here we are in the midst of some innovative curriculum construction. Our common task is to develop a block or unit on the topic of "Building an Urban Greenbelt." Let's look at some ideas for format:

1. *Setting the task.* You need to be as clear as possible about what students will be doing and about the purpose of the experience.
2. *Common experiences.* As you begin the challenge, you will need to ensure that the whole class has a set of common experiences. This will enable the groups that emerge to share a knowledge base so that communication is meaningful.
3. *Greenbelt theory.* One of the problems in curriculum development is that developers give undue emphasis to process and little emphasis to content. You want to be able to say at the conclusion of the project that your students have a body of knowledge, as well as an array of skills and values. So, what are the key ideas of greenbelt theory?

FIGURE 13.1   *Constructing a Greenbelt*

Constructing a Greenbelt

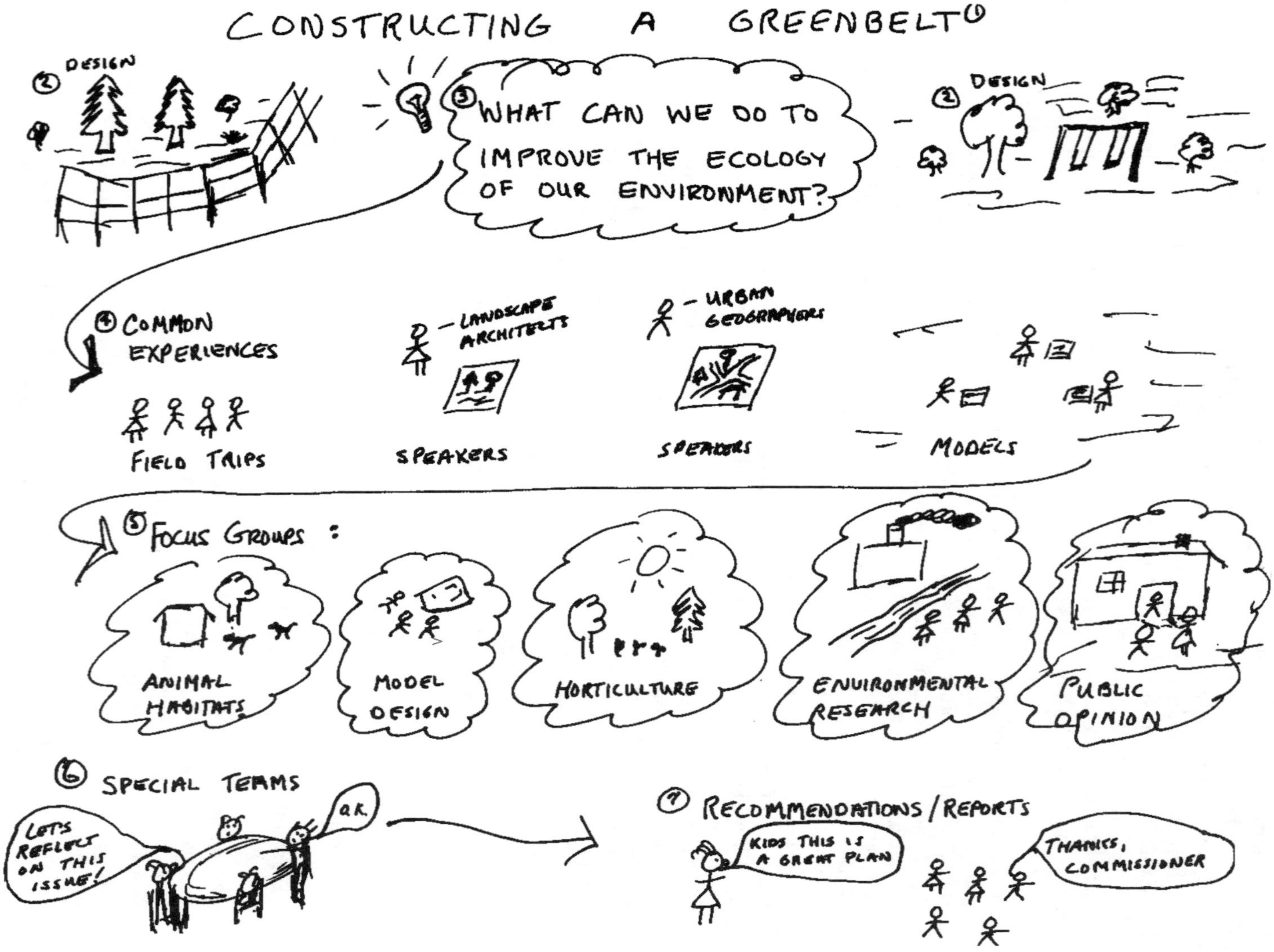

4. *Focus groups.* Once you have established a common body of knowledge, you are ready to move ahead with smaller groups that will work on subchallenges of the larger challenge. Assume that you will have three or four groups, and identify specifically what each group will be doing.

5. *Seminars, class meetings.* The groups will need to keep each other informed. You will need some kind of checkpoint to ensure that this happens.

6. *Presentation.* Once the groups have completed their work and the efforts have been synthesized, you will need to make a presentation to parents, the principal, the school board, or whatever interested parties. A second presentation will come when the students have actually built their greenbelt.

7. *Reflection.* Some ways of providing both formative and summative reflective thinking must be built into the process. Journals and informal assessment strategies seem to work best.

8. *Connections.* A legitimate criticism of schoolwork is that it is often unconnected. Identify connections with literature (specific titles), science, geography, history, language, the arts, mechanical drawing, or landscape architecture.

9. *Skills.* What specific skills will be employed, and where?

10. *Concepts.* What key ideas or generalizations should students learn?

11. *Flowchart or webbing.* You need some sort of diagram to show how the unit works. The webbing shown in Figure 13.2 is an example of how you might proceed.

Significant Themes for Integration

The search for significant common themes is at the heart of integrated studies. Once established, themes become the rallying point of the curriculum, the place to go when you want to be sure that the pursuit is meaningful and excellent. Themes

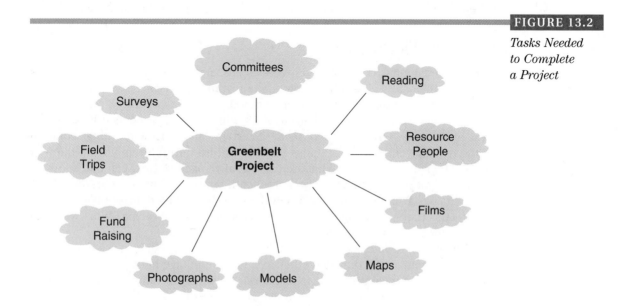

FIGURE 13.2

Tasks Needed to Complete a Project

provide a means for the various contributing disciplines to be different, showcasing their unique properties, yet at the same time carrying out a similarity of conceptual purpose. The liberating sense of a carefully chosen, content-enriching theme is that it is supportive of connected, integrated experiences across the disciplines, and it prohibits a superficial tyranny of integration for its own sake from taking over the curriculum.

Of course, there are many significant themes that teachers and children might pursue. I will suggest here eight broad themes that have the potential to be encountered and reencountered in spiral fashion at gradually increasing levels of sophistication and complexity. The themes, in order to qualify, must meet several important tests. First, are the themes truly conceptual—that is, are they representative of ideas that transcend place and time? If so, they have the potential for transfer and utility beyond the bounds of specific subject matter. Second, do the themes lend themselves to all three knowledge modes—that is, knowledge received, knowledge discovered, and knowledge constructed? If so, then the themes are suited to knowledge acquisition, cultural literacy, problem solving, experiential learning, and constructivist thinking and doing. Third, are the themes fundamentally worth pursuing in each of the separate content areas—that is, social studies, science, arts, humanities, mathematics? If so, then the integrity of the curriculum can be ensured. After all, if a theme cannot be pursued within any given discipline, then it is not actually interdisciplinary but in fact peculiar to certain subject matter. Fourth, do the themes have the potential to enrich the curriculum and therefore the lives of students and teachers? If so, then the themes are useful, they are beautiful, they are truthful, and they address an underlying sense of moral goodness.

There are many interesting and possibly worthwhile themes from which one could begin to integrate the curriculum. By applying this fourfold test, one is able to reduce the list to manageable, meaningful proportions. I do not mean to suggest that I have developed the one magic list; other themes no doubt could be readily added. The following themes, however, will do for purposes of illustration.

Cause and Effect

Children and adults, amateurs and professionals, and young and old notice effects all around them. Any given effect assumes one or more causes. Leaves fall from the trees in October. Someone is in a happy mood. War breaks out in a region of the world. People speak the same language but with different accents. These are all outcomes—that is, they are the effects of certain causes. How do things come to be the way they are? Why do things sometimes turn out differently from the way one had hoped they would? What are the causative agents? How can one know? It seems to be in people's nature to want to identify the cause or causes of the effects they perceive. What were the causes of the Civil War? Why did the cake taste differently this time when you thought you followed the same recipe? What were the lasting effects of Lewis and Clark's epic trek to the West?

Sometimes people use rational explanations to determine cause and effect relationships; sometimes they use other means. The linkage between cause and effect is always explanation. An explanation, however, is only as good as one's information, and one's information is only as good as one's ability to apply insight to it; otherwise, it's just information. Investigation, experience, and reflection are among the most useful tools in the search for explanation. History, science, literature, religion, the arts, myth, and folk wisdom all take their place as explainers in the search for cause and effect. It is seldom a simple process. More often than not, causes are both multiple and complex, especially about worthwhile issues. Just as causes are usually multiple, so are effects. Often, one effect causes another to happen. At some point, teachers and students must acquire a high tolerance for ambiguity. Effects, like causes, are not necessarily what they appear to be. The role of individual or group perception looms large in this business. Astronomy started out as a serious cause and effect "science." The idea held by the ancients (and by many who take astrology seriously today) was that the movement and placement of the stars has serious effects on our daily lives and fortunes. So the next time you're walking down the sidewalk, watch out for that crack, because who knows what effect stepping on it might cause!

Commonality and Diversity

One of the hallmarks of investigation is the attempt to document similarities and differences. People ask themselves how they are like their parents and how they are different from them. They explore the similarities and differences between the travels of Marco Polo and those of Francis Drake. They wonder if reading and writing are both branches of language arts and therefore similar, how, then, are they different? They contemplate how students studying such similar material at school can be so different in their learning preferences and learning styles. They ask how history and historical fiction are as different as a factual and make-believe account of something, yet at the same time both can move one nearer to the truth about the past.

Three of the most basic processes of the arts and sciences are at the heart of an exploration of commonality and diversity. Observation, description, and classification are excellent points of departure. Young children notice differences and similarities in the patterns and shapes of leaves. Flowers are alike and different, beginning with simple and composite blossoms. Foods fit into different groups. Paintings can be classified by schools, time periods, and means of expression. Separate subjects or disciplines arose over time because enough perceived difference developed between and among them. Interdisciplinary teaching and learning turns the equation around and asks: What are the similarities?

People observe how things are alike and different. They begin to describe those properties through drawings, maps, words, diagrams, equations, and other means. Classifications emerge on the basis of observations and descriptions. In time, taxonomies are built. In the eighteenth century, Swedish scientist Linneaus developed whole taxonomies for plants and animals based on differences and similarities. He began with a binomial classification that sorted living things into the kingdoms of plants and animals. From there, the classifications were refined into phylums, families, orders, varieties, and so on. Such a taxonomy allows one to categorize a humming bird and a bumble bee as being both alike and different. Also, people tend to classify paintings according to such different schools as realism, impressionism, cubism, surrealism, and so on. Thus, Leonardo da Vinci's *Mona Lisa* and Pablo Picasso's *Guernica* are alike yet different.

Systems and Patterns

Children learn early in their lives to think and feel in terms of the patterns of holidays, birthdays, and special events in their lives. They intuitively perceive a system of special days and times of the year that take on a rhythm. The start of school in the fall, Halloween, Thanksgiving, Christmas, New Year's Day, Valentine's Day, spring break, and summer vacation all are touch points in the elaborate culture of childhood. As students grow older, many of them relate to the patterns of the sports calendar of the school: football, followed by basketball, followed by baseball, and so on. For teachers, the system is often divided into reporting periods of three or four per school year. Units of study begin and culminate following a pattern. The school itself is a complex social/academic system complete with roles, expectations, rules, checkpoints, diplomas, and so on.

Part of the solar system, Earth is itself a system of water, land, creatures, plants, and atmosphere. Earth's system has an established pattern of seasons, with a time to sow and a time to harvest, a time to work and a time to rest. Within families, patterns of behavior and traditions are established complete with histories and mythologies. People search for patterns in their ancestry. Geneticists look for patterns in the work of such scientific undertakings as the human genome project, an intricate mapping of the the DNA structure of human beings. Each atom of each element is itself a system with certain valences that place it in a family of similar elements.

Patterns of courage and decency, love and war, emerge from the pages of literature and history. Art and music are the continuous assembling and reassembling of pigment or notes into new or varied patterns of expression. When a pattern is broken, a whole new field of expression emerges; for example, in the nineteenth century, a shift occurred away from landscape and portrait painting to impressionism.

Paradigm shifts in science represent fundamental reappraisals of systems. Isaac Newton showed that gravitational pull is a universal force; that is, gravity exists everywhere. In so doing, he altered people's sense of why an object in space behaves as it does. When Copernicus "removed" the Earth from the center of the cosmos, he caused people to change their patterns of thought about the Earth's (and therefore humans') place in the universe. Today, in the midst of the electronic revolution, changing patterns of how people communicate abound in the form of the Internet, faxes, e-mail, and so on.

Cycles and Change

The life cycle of the monarch butterfly illustrates four major changes in the growth and development of that beautiful creature: from egg, to larva, to pupa, to adult. The idea of a cycle is that of an interval of time during which a sequence of a recurring succession of events or phenomena is completed. Thus, the life cycle of the monarch butterfly has a sense of predictability in terms of time and form. Cycles not only have a theme of recurrence but also a theme of circularity that makes them different from a pattern of linear development. The classic Greek sense of time and history was cyclical—that is, no beginning and no end—as opposed to the Hebrew sense of time and history, which was set more to a vector with a beginning point (creation), direction, and end time (judgment). Cycles vary greatly in scale so that some are more immediately distinguishable as cycles—for instance, the cycle of day and night or of the seasons. Others—for example, the recurrence of ice ages that appear at least to have some cyclical pattern—are known only on the basis of serious scientific investigation. Comet Halley, which will reappear in the skies in the year 2061, has a cycle of 76 years, so some people are able to see the recurrence of the cycle in their lifetimes.

In astronomy, a period of time required to bring about the recurrence of certain relative positions (for example, Earth to Sun) or aspects of the heavenly bodies is known as a cycle. The earth orbits the sun every 365+ days, completing a cycle that takes it through its four seasons. In literature, a group of prose or poetic narratives, usually of different authorship, centering on a legendary hero and his or her associates is known as a cycle. Thus, there is the Arthurian cycle chronicling the noble deeds of King Arthur and his Knights of the Round Table. The Arthurian cycle is often referred to in medieval romance as the "matter of Britain." The term *cyclic poems* was first used in late classical times to refer to the independent poems that appeared after Homer to supplement his account of the Trojan War and the homecomings of the heroes.

In music, any compositional form characterized by repetition from an earlier movement in order to unify the structure is called a cycle. The familiar children's tune "Row, Row, Row Your Boat" is a simple example. The need for cyclic devices became crucial during the times of Mozart and Haydn, when the romantic novel took the place of classical drama and narrative poems as the basic model for instrumental music. Thus, the idea of the cycle in music took on somewhat new meaning as changes in forms of expression happened in literature and other arts. The relationship between cycles and change, then, can also be seen between and among different art forms.

Historians search the events of the past in an attempt to identify cyclical patterns, often with little result. American historian Arthur Schlessinger Jr. wrote a book in which his thesis was that American political leadership in the twentieth century proceeds in cyclic form from conservative to liberal and back again. These cycles, according to Schlessinger, provide a kind of equilibrium, giving Americans a conservative president for a while followed by a more liberal administration.

Economists document cycles of prosperity and hard times in the country's financial/industrial/commercial system. They point to panics, depressions, and recessions, followed by booms, expansion, and good times. Nations try, more or less, depending on the form of government, to intervene with programs during difficult economic times in order to control the cycles artificially, but no one seems to know for sure what causes these cycles even though the effects are evident to the most casual observer.

The rate of change and therefore the recurring patterns of certain cycles vary greatly. Weather changes often within minutes from fair to foul. A person's mood may change abruptly on the basis of some new information. A rousing speech or sermon can change people's opinions in the space of an hour, although the long-term effects may be different. A child watching a pot on the stove wonders if the water will ever boil. Iron rusts quickly in a rain forest environment but slowly in desert conditions. People change: They grow and develop quickly in childhood, more slowly in adulthood, and ultimately decline in old age.

Maps change when an empire such as the Soviet Union collapses. The changed map, with its new and unfamiliar borders, confuses people as they try to learn different place names. However, the changed map is merely symbolic of the change after change brought about so rapidly when a seemingly invincible empire dissolves, not on the basis of outside attack, but from decay within. Futurist Alvin Toffler calls too much change in too short a time "future shock." The people of eastern Europe and Russia have seen vast changes in business and commerce, in the availability of consumer goods, and in the breakdown of an existing order in the space of just a few years.

Anyone who contemplates buying a personal computer understands the rapidity with which change occurs on the frontiers of technology. A great fear felt by ordinary people (like me!) is that whatever computer they buy, it will no doubt be obsolete by the time they get it set up at home and learn how to use it. Merchandisers play to these fears by exhorting would-be consumers not to be left behind in the wake of new "breakthroughs." Perhaps one of the most worthwhile pursuits for young learners is to study change and to learn to think about it and act on it responsibly and rationally.

One of the obvious lines of inquiry in a theme-driven curriculum is how exploration and investigation change the world. The Lewis and Clark expedition changed the very idea of the United States in terms of its size, its grasp of a continent, and its place in the world as an ocean-to-ocean country in the making. Within a scant 50 years of the epic trek, the United States sent a seagoing expedition to Japan, a foreshadowing of Americans' perception of themselves as a global presence, and the beginning of a tenuous, sometimes difficult, relationship with that great nation.

The travels of Captain James Cook in the late eighteenth century set in place not only the vast holdings of the British Empire but also a secure niche for navigational and astronomical science in the realms of exploration. Children who compare the voyages of Captain Cook with those of Christopher Columbus will become more fully aware of the rapid development of science and technology that took place in the intervening three centuries.

The travels of Italian teenager Marco Polo and of the more sophisticated African traveler Ibn Batuta, in the late Middle Ages, on the cusp of the Renaissance, brought about a sense of Eurasia as opposed to a separate Europe and Asia. Coming from the east, the Mongol invasion of Russia and eastern Europe also changed people's sense of distance, space, and time.

Some things change slowly, almost glacially, such as the weathering away of the earth's surface resulting in bizarre rock formations. Some changes appear to be isolated and not susceptible to repetition, and others appear to be perhaps cyclical as the warming and cooling of the earth's atmosphere seems to suggest. Some changes are peaceful and tranquil, such as gently falling snow on soft green grass, the maturing of a rosebud, or the rising of the moon on a summer night; other changes, such as earthquakes, tornadoes, and volcanic eruptions, showcase nature's violent side. Certain changes are inevitable, and others are ours to control.

Scale and Symmetry

Human beings are bilaterally symmetrical; that is, one side of the body is nearly a mirror image of the other if one were to draw an axis from the top of the head to the place between the two feet. A hen's egg is bilaterally symmetrical if an axis were drawn on it longitudinally, but not if it were drawn around the middle of the egg as if the line were an equator. A circle, no matter where one draws a line from one side to the other through the center, is biradially symmetrical. Forms of symmetry, more or less, are found everywhere in nature and in the constructed environment. One finds forms of symmetry in a daffodil; in the Parthenon of ancient Athens; in the shell of a chambered nautilus; in Jane Austen's book *Pride and Prejudice;* in the yin and yang of Eastern philosophy; and in Beethoven's symphonies. One also finds a certain symmetry in the seasons, in day and night, and in the configuration of the solar system. Symmetry is found in the leaves of a tree, in the three branches of U.S. government, in the design of the space shuttle, in the balance a teacher brings to the curriculum, in the need for both work and play, and in the graceful contours of a Grecian urn.

The converse of symmetry, asymmetry, also exists in the world. The external symmetry of the human is not necessarily found in the placement of the internal organs. No such symmetry can be found in the placement of heart, liver, appendix, and so on, although one does find symmetry in the placement of lungs and kidneys. Certain animals, notably sponges and ameboid protozoans, are asymmetrical in their design. Their shapes are irregular, different for each individual, or constantly changing. In the constructed environment, asymmetry is often sought by the designer, either for aesthetic purposes or because it suits a certain function.

In cartography, scale is represented by the ratio between distances on a map and distances on the earth's surface. A scale drawing showing the floor plan of a classroom is an attempt to illustrate the relative size and distances of objects from each other as they exist in the actual classroom. The more closely the size of features on a map or sketch approaches actual size, the larger is the scale. Thus, a map showing the whole earth is considered small scale, whereas a map showing a backyard would probably be considered large scale.

In music, scale is any series of tones arranged in rising or falling order of pitch, or vibrations (cycles) per second. The fewer the vibrations per second, the lower the note; the more vibrations per second, the higher the note. On a familiar instrument such as the piano, the white keys represent the diatonic scale of seven notes, five of which are whole tones and two of which are half-tones. The cycle begins anew with each succeeding octave. This repeating seven-note scale can be assembled by a composer in a seemingly infinite variety of combinations to make the many tunes, melodies, and so forth that have been written over the years. Of course, the black keys, or sharp notes, each of which is a half-step between two given white keys, add to the possibility for variety. Other scales are also possible as shown in Hindu and Arabian music.

Athletic fields and gymnasiums are built to certain scales and symmetries. A football field must be built to an exact size, as must a tennis court; but a baseball field or a basketball court can vary in size. A basketball court must be a true rectangle even though it may be somewhat different in size from one court to another. A baseball field, on the other hand, must be regular only in its infield proportions (i.e., from one base to another). The outfield may be allowed to vary so that distances from home plate to the right-, center-, and left-field walls are quite different within a given park as well as from park to park. Thus, a baseball field has qualities of symmetry as well as of asymmetry.

Children, by nature, are marvelous sketch artists and mapmakers. As they begin to learn about scale and symmetry, they need to be encouraged to observe, draw, sketch, map, chart, talk, and sing and dance about what they see. Observing and recording are the two most basic skills of science; both social and natural. When a child begins to observe carefully and to record in some way what he or she sees, subtleties begin to emerge. Elements of color, line, texture, size, distance, symmetry, and scale become clearer, and the child's sense of consciousness is heightened. The doors leading to a world of real learning begin to open.

Interaction and Relationships

In a classroom of 25 people, the number of paired person-to-person combinations is 300! Assuming you and your fellow teacher's classes were 25 students apiece for a total of 50, the three-to-a-group combinations of students the two of you could put together numbers 19,600! Just imagine the possibilities you have to allow your students to really get to know each other. Of course, people interact not only with people but also with nature, the built environment, texts, films, and so on. A child's relationship with others is very different in a classroom where each student works alone at his or her desk versus a room where group projects and collaborative learning are emphasized. A child's relationship with the teacher is very different in a warm, supportive, caring, challenging environment verses an autocratic, aloof, and unfair environment.

School subjects can themselves be related and allowed to interact or they can be isolated, unrelated, and unconnected. Whether there is interaction among people or school subjects in the teaching/learning equation is a fundamental pedagogical question. Where school life is dominated by what German philosopher Jurgen Habermas calls *technical interests*, then predictability and control become paramount pedagogical concerns. The technical interest focuses primarily on means-ends questions. Examples of this are the use of behavioral objectives and the tightly scripted lesson plan. In other words, any attempt to predict and therefore control the behavior of students toward a predetermined outcome is indicative of the technical interest at work. The result of such a preoccupation is a socially, morally, and intellectually simplified syntax of classroom life.

Habermas also identifies the *practical interest*, which, in school life, calls for students and teachers to search for understanding and meaning in what is being learned. The practical interest encourages relationships and relational learning, conversation, working and getting along together, and a sense of integration of people and their experiences. The practical interest is at work when students and teachers engage in project learning, in shared activities, and in the constructivist enterprise. The constructivity principle, that experience precedes analysis, is basic to the practical interest.

Habermas identifies a third interest, one that calls on powers of *reflection* and *insight*. Here, the questions for a thoughtful consideration of school life take one to deeper levels. These reflective issues are developed in the patterns of classroom life through such recurring questions of utility (Is this useful?), aesthetics (Is this beautiful?), truth (Is this meaningful?), and morality (Is this right?). When those who join the teaching/learning enterprise begin to carry out a process of reflection around these key questions, a different sense of curriculum comes forth; hope emerges. This is an empowering curriculum.

Time and Space

History and literature provide insights to time. Geography, art, and geometry illustrate space. Studied in integrated fashion, these disciplines bring time and space together as powerful themes for orienting oneself to one's place in the world. To a child, an hour can seem a long time. Adults often think in terms of projects of several years. Nineteenth-century pioneer Marcus Whitman, who, together with his wife Narcissa, founded a mission settlement near present-day Walla Walla, Washington, once wrote, "My plans require time and distance." Today, someone flies from New York to San Francisco in a matter of hours. Although modern conveniences such as jet planes, telephones, fax machines, and the Internet are wonderful devices, they tend to distort one's sense of time and space. In this limited sense, the people of the past had a deeper understanding of these concepts than the people of today. For instance, if you've walked or hiked somewhere, you have a different sense of time and space than you do if you're going to the same place in an air-conditioned car.

In modern life, things take on a sense of immediacy. A friend of mine once told me of his nightmarish experience on an overseas trip of being cooped up in a plane on a runway for six hours (with no food), being taken off the plane, being bused into the city and put into a hotel for two hours of sleep, and then being taken back to the airport for takeoff at 3:00 in the morning, only to wait until after 9:00 A.M., again with no meal served, to take off. Sounds awful, doesn't it? Relative to most airplane flights, it really was a tough experience and one my friend does not wish to repeat. Mainly, however, it was an inconvenience. He still made it from Tokyo to Seattle in a time frame measured in hours, not days or weeks. Just imagine the "inconveniences" experienced by Marco Polo, the pioneers of the Oregon Trail, James Cook, and other travelers of the past.

Today's students are on the receiving end of these distortions of the realities of time and space. Somehow, the curricular experience must transcend these limitations. This is not a plea to return to those thrilling days of yesteryear. We live in this day and age, and that is our reality. The fact is, however, that most students today have little knowledge of the backcloth of their own existence. In other words, they apparently know little of history, literary portrayals of life in the past, the emergence of artistic and musical forms, and so on. Even the brief history of the United States is a blank slate to many students. Sadly, this can be said of some teachers as well.

Your job as an elementary social studies teacher, among other things, must represent an attempt to recapture with your students a sense of space and time and place. One of the great wonders of childhood is a child's sense of wonder. It's easy for a teacher to forget that very simple thought in the rush to "cover" all the things that need to be taught in school. For a student to join in, to become a participant on a journey of discovery is far more than an academic study of some epic voyage taken by some heroes from the distant past. It is a coming together of a young person's desire to learn about his or her world with a participatory engagement in the journey itself.

Time and space are crucial to the musician. Not merely the musical sounds themselves, but the space between the sounds and the timing of the sounds contribute to a symphony. The composer Hadyn, for example, made remarkable use of the empty space between notes, giving his music a nearly unequaled lightness. Space is also precious to the artist and sculptor. The painter decides how to arrange pigment on the space of a canvas. The sculptor decides how to chip and chisel away space from a block of stone in order to arrive at a finished work. Thus, one creates through addition of color while the other creates through the subtraction of stone.

To the mapmaker, lines organize space. Lines form the boundaries and points of demarcation that separate or denote one area from another. The beauty of a good map lies not only in its accuracy but also in its elegance as a portrayal of space and place. A child discovers that she can create a lake on a piece of paper by drawing an enclosed line. The child looks at it and decides the lake should be colored blue. The child thinks there should be a road leading to the lake and some mountains in the distance. These lines, drawn by the child, organize and give meaningful shape to space. By drawing a modern-looking boat on the lake, the child also orients the reader to a certain time period. The child's teacher asks the child to tell about the map. The child, referring to the map she created, cheerfully explains her thoughts.

Equilibrium and Order

When disequilibrium occurs—for example, in war or in family problems—disorder follows close behind. When feelings, thoughts, and actions are harmonious, equilibrium and order result. Young people desperately need balance (equilibrium) and predictability (order) in their lives. Teachers know this better than anyone. They work daily with students who bring with them equilibrium and order as well as its converse.

The idea of equilibrium applies well to systems theory. For instance, a traffic system maintains much of its equilibrium by balancing the rate and flow of traffic with a network of lights, signs, patrols, and the like. When the system is in a state of equilibrium and good order, traffic flows smoothly. Untoward events (e.g., a rush-hour pile up), however, can quickly throw the smoothest system out of balance. In the balance of nature, disequilibrium can occur in an ecosystem when previously outside elements are introduced. An example of this is the introduction of rabbits to the Australian ecosystem. The system, in its more natural state of balance, was not equipped to accommodate the influx of the fast-breeding and wide-ranging animals. Many attempts have been made to restore balance to the system, with mainly limited results.

In the Pacific Northwest of the United States, the building of several large dams (Grand Coulee, Bonneville, and others) has made the Columbia River system far more orderly and therefore more predictable than it was in its natural state. For purposes of flood control, hydroelectricity, irrigation, and recreation, the system of dams has been a considerable success. On the other hand, the equilibrium of elements of the system has been thrown into disorder. Two examples of this are the greatly diminished salmon run on the Columbia and the displaced river-dwelling Native Americans who, for centuries, had caught fish at such sites as Celilo Falls, now submerged beneath the waters of the reservoir created by one of the dams. Other more subtle changes may not be accurately assessed for years to come.

The warming and cooling cycles of the earth's atmosphere have a long-term scale of order and an equilibrium not easily determined in the short run. Recent scientific evidence points to a warming effect and a diminishment of the ozone layer. Whether this is part of a long-term change of equilibrium is not known. The earth, as part of the solar system, is situated at a point of delicate balance in its distance from the sun. This balance is necessary in order to maintain temperature conditions conducive to life forms as we know them. When the quality of the earth's atmosphere changes because of increased cattle grazing and increased automobile exhaust, the system is altered. The system's ability to restore itself is problematic.

It took human beings thousands of years to discern the order of the seasons and the attendant implications to the point that they could make the change from hunting and gathering to agriculture. Once systems of agriculture were established in place of systems of hunting and gathering, the need for order in architecture, laws, roads, and the many shared functions of permanently settled people emerged.

Each of the foregoing themes is connected to the others in ways that make the continual revisiting of them all necessary. Thus, the content may change from unit to unit and from year to year in the curriculum, but the themes remain as conceptual points of reference. The themes have the power of ideas, and ideas are the mortar that hold together the curricular building blocks of knowledge, insight, and wisdom.

Summary

The project approach to social studies is an effective way to create an integrated studies learning model. Projects have a real-world flavor to them, and that makes them appealing to children. They also have a beginning and end point, which allows students and teachers a better sense of what they are accomplishing. Projects offer splendid opportunities for children to work together, experiencing the give-and-take, shared decision making, and camaraderie that happens only in group activity.

There are four different, but related, kinds of social studies projects: (1) service projects, (2) production projects, (3) problem-solving projects, and (4) school-wide projects. Each is necessary along the road to childhood growth and development. Group projects put the "social" back in social studies, and they provide the syntactic complexities needed to enhance moral development, language development, perspective taking, problem-solving ability, and citizenship.

ACTIVITIES

1. Engage a friend in a conversation comparing classroom life when a project is taking place with classroom life when children do traditional schoolwork.
2. Classroom life is more rich and complex when children are doing projects. Do you agree with this statement? Why or why not?
3. Make two lists of projects students could do—one for primary students and one for intermediate-level students.
4. Some people feel that social studies becomes "watered down" when it is incorporated into interdisciplinary teaching and learning. Do you agree? Why or why not?

5. How are service projects beneficial? production projects? problem-solving projects? What are the essential differences?

6. Recall a project from your elementary school days. Describe it to someone who, like you, is interested in elementary social studies.

NOTE

1. Robin Sharp and Arthur Ellis, "Greenbelt Design." Unpublished paper, Project 2061, American Association for the Advancement of Science, 1994.

SUGGESTED READINGS

Ellis, A. (2001). *Teaching, Learning, & Assessment Together: The Reflective Classroom.* Larchmont, NY: Eye on Education.

Johnson, D., and Johnson, R. (1999). *Learning Together and Alone.* Boston: Allyn and Bacon.

Katz, L., and Chand, S. (1999). *Engaging Children's Minds: The Project Approach.* Norwood, NJ: Ablex.

Kohn, A. (1999). *The Schools Our Children Deserve: Moving Beyond Traditional Classrooms and "Tougher Standards."* Boston: Houghton Mifflin.

Social Studies and Literacy

Reading and writing are fundamental elements of social studies learning—to be able to read and write is to be set free as a learner. Literacy leads to empowerment. No teacher can or should be able to teach a child everything he or she needs to learn about any subject. But a caring teacher can guide a child into reading and writing habits that will lead to a lifetime path of adventure and understanding. Reading and writing remain the two most powerful learning tools that can be put into the hands of a child. Today, traditional forms of literacy are joined by new forms created by the electronic revolution, thus creating even more exciting possibilities for readers, writers, and discoverers. Topics in this chapter include the following:

- Reading and classroom life
- Becoming a reader
- Emphasis in the primary grades
- Reading and democracy
- Writing and literacy
- Social studies and language development
- The spoken word
- Electronic literacy

There is an art of reading, as well as an art of thinking and an art of writing.
—Isaac D'Israeli

In recent years, people have witnessed a phenomenon characterized by two divergent outcomes. On the one hand, the amount of good literature related to social studies topics for children has reached an all-time high. Each year, *Social Education*, the official journal of the National Council for the Social Studies, publishes an annotated list of new books that have great promise. On the other hand, teachers report that many students are less and less interested in reading and writing.

The corresponding decline in literacy is to the point where U.S. government figures show that nearly half of adult Americans are functionally illiterate (see Figure 14.1). The term *functionally illiterate* means that people cannot read the label on a medicine bottle or they cannot write a coherent paragraph describing even the most basic things. The term has nothing to say about who reads the classics or who writes timeless essays. A rather new term, *aliterate*, has emerged to describe a related problem; an aliterate person is someone who *can* read but doesn't. There is, in fact, evidence to suggest that literacy rates today are actually lower in some cases than they were in the Middle Ages.[1]

Reading and writing are related pursuits. They support each other. They supply energy to each other. In this chapter we will search for ways to increase both the amount and quality of students' efforts in these two very important areas of learning.

FIGURE 14.1 *According to the United States Department of Education, only 47 Percent of Adult Americans Can Function at Even the Lowest Literacy Level (Level 1)*

Lagging literacy rates

The National Adult Literacy Survey tested 26,000 adults 16 or older in three skill areas. Few excelled. Many did poorly.

Examples (level 1):	Examples (level 3):	Examples (level 5):
Find a country in a short newspaper article; sign your name; total a bank deposit.	Find an interpretive sentence in a news article; use a bus schedule to find the right route; use a calculator to figure the discount on a bill.	Interpret a phrase taken from a long article; explain in writing a simple statistical table; use a calculator to figure the cost of carpeting a room.

How people fared

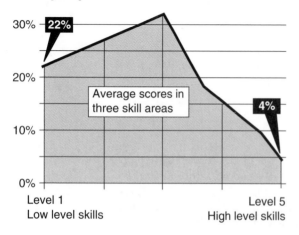

Average scores in three skill areas

Level 1
Low level skills

Level 5
High level skills

Types of literacy

The tests measured skills in three areas:

Prose: Understand basic written information such as editorials, news stories, poems and fiction.

Document: Use materials such as job applications, payroll forms, transportation schedules, maps, tables and graphs.

Quantitative: Use numbers for such tasks as balancing a checkbook, figuring out a tip, calculating interest from a loan advertisement.

One year, in the course of my career as an elementary teacher, I found myself wondering about two teaching and learning issues that I was sure were closely connected. The first issue was how to make real readers out of my students, and the second was how to improve my students' knowledge of social studies content, especially biography, history, and geography.

It was not that my students never read anything; each week during library period, many of them would check out several books to read, and, of course, I required the obligatory one-written-book-report-per-term from each student. Still, I wasn't satisfied with the way things were going, so I tried two ideas at once. The first idea was to drop the written book-report requirement. That idea was received with great joy by students, some of whom mentioned that they didn't mind reading but that they disliked having to write book reports. Now a teacher can't simply run a class just by asking the students their preference about whether to do something or not to do it. Still, it is important to listen to them and give them a feeling of some influence because it's their classroom. The reason their joy resonated with me was that I had bad memories of writing book reports myself. So, we agreed: no book reports.

The second idea I had was to develop a very simple (and that is the key) system of acknowledging and supporting their reading habits. To kick off this phase of my plan, I gave every student in class a green bookmark made from construction paper. They were an inch wide and six inches long, with one end cut at an angle. That was it—no fancy designs or anything else. I told the students that when they had finished reading a book, they were to record the date, title, and author. They were to inform me when they had finished their first book, and I would give them a red bookmark. After five books, they would be given a blue bookmark; after ten, a yellow bookmark; and so on, in increments of five.

Reading and Classroom Life

The amount and quality of reading done by those students literally exploded. The growth was exponential. They liked keeping track of their reading, and they *loved* the paper bookmarks. Why, I asked myself, hadn't I come up with something like this sooner? Napoleon himself once noted that the greatest discovery of his life was that soldiers would die for ribbons. Maybe that was the beginning of behavior modification. At any rate, I had learned that children would read for bookmarks. They loved to show me their growing lists, and it gave me a chance to listen to them tell me about their reading and to suggest biographies, historical fiction, histories, good fiction, and so on. Also, they were so proud of their bookmarks. It doesn't take much to make children happy if they know you care about them.

What happened that year was rather successful. I read more, the students read more, and even their parents started reading more. I got reports from parents who said their child used to watch television "all the time, but now he really wants to read." The nice thing about the bookmarks was that it gave every child his or her own measure of progress. It never became a competitive thing between students. Each child was able to compete against himself or herself and to improve the record. We had great class discussions about what it means to improve your own standards.

The Beneficial Outcomes

One of the beneficial outcomes of dropping the required book reports and supplying the students with the paper bookmarks was, as I noted, the increase in conversations I had with them as they told me about their goals and interests. I was able to get closer to the students and, as a result, felt much more comfortable about suggesting new books for them to read. It occurred to me that maybe I was really listening to them for the first time. The social fabric of the classroom was changing for the better. We were reaching toward one of those transcendent moments in teaching and learning that can only occur when people feel empowered to chart their educational destiny and to talk about it comfortably with others.

The Unexpected Happens

Soon, something unforeseen occurred. The much-hated book reports had become a thing of the past, but the children were actually reporting on their reading more than ever. The difference was that it had an easygoing informality about it; in other words, it was a much more natural process, and that was fine because we were getting at *why* someone might read rather than merely to comply with assignments. This is where the students' creativity emerged. They began to produce skits from books, do role-plays of famous characters, read brief excerpts from good books to the class, build model scenes depicting themes from books, draw elaborate posters advertising books they thought others should read, make bulletin-board displays, and a number of other things to share their knowledge.

Crossing a Frontier

These students had crossed a frontier that is seldom crossed in the annals of classroom life. Bringing me with them, they had crossed the frontier from teaching to learning. You think it was tough for the pioneers to cross the Rocky Mountains with their covered wagons? Yes, it was. But just try crossing the high barriers that separate true learning from teacher-centered instruction! Yet, once you've done it (and believe me, even most university students haven't done it), you won't want to go back to the low, swampy moral ground of just doing assignments that someone in charge wants you to carry out. True learning means freedom, and these children experienced it.

Becoming a Reader

I am convinced that becoming a reader takes a lot of practice. A few children do it without any outside help, but most do not. In fact, many who could have become readers give up. I think for most people, there is a threshhold that, once you cross it, you become a reader; no one has to tell you to read. I am also convinced that you and I and the textbook cannot "teach" students enough social studies to amount to very much. Piaget made it clear that telling is not teaching. What we can do is support children's learning, which is a very different thing—it's as different as dependence is to independence. A good book is the ultimate portable learning tool. It can be read in bed, in the bathtub, in a tree house, in the backseat of a car, and even in a chair. It can be set aside, picked up later, thrown in a backpack and carried to a park bench, and, best of all, it requires no batteries. The reader controls the pace. The great thing about it is that not only is it fun but the reader can also learn about prehistoric times, pioneers, other cultures, other children, famous women and men, great adventures, and who knows what else along the way.

The Importance of Reading at the Primary Level

For teachers of primary-age children, the challenge is especially fruitful. This is so because habits begin early in life, so it is easier to make reading, or anything else for that matter, a pattern if it is begun early. The parents are the key here. Somehow, you are going to have to convince them to read to their children. In fact, research illustrates that parents reading to children is vital to their cognitive growth. This procedure is most effective when the parent does three things:

1. Elaborates on the text, giving information and insight that might not be explicit
2. Refers to the child's own experiences, drawing him or her into the reading by comparing and contrasting events in the story with things the child knows from experience
3. Pauses from time to time to ask questions in order to actively involve the child, who may wish to guess what is going to happen next, compare this story with another one, or so on

Reading and Democracy

Returning to my earlier experience, the fact that my students were reading more was obvious to me, to them, and to others. The bookmarks seemed a small reward for all the energy and goodwill, and I was quite pleased with that result. Dropping the dreaded book reports had left me with a sense of ambivalence, because book reports are, and always have been, a part of reading—a kind of external obligation that "proves" you read the book. On the other hand, it seemed to have a liberating effect that was all to the good.

I was getting to know the children better because we spent time talking about books they were reading, which would lead inevitably to discussions of their interests. It became easier and more natural for me to suggest good books to them, and they seemed always to welcome the suggestions. I was gradually coming to realize that they *were* reporting on the books they read; it was just that the reporting was casual and informal, much the same way members of a book club might share their reading with one another.

The important thing was that the students were reading, and they wanted to communicate their reading—witness the skits, role-playing, and model making discussed earlier. We had somehow improved and expanded the whole theory of book reporting, at least for us, and the students had done much of it themselves. They had reached a stage of empowerment, and I began to understand what the term *facilitator* truly meant.

The level and quality of communication rose dramatically as the students shared their reading. The classroom was becoming one big book club that just happened to carry on some other business during the day as well—you know, stuff like

A children's book club discussion

spelling, math, science, and a few other subjects. But, in time, those subjects followed social studies and were swallowed up by the book club as well. The psychological edge that we all enjoyed was based on the premise that we were reading, discussing, writing, and calculating, not because of a routine based on teacher-centered assignments but because of self-direction and a social fabric that had brought us together and made us a community of learners.

Writing and Social Studies

Writer John Gardner stated that the best way to learn to write well is to read good books. He's perfectly right, of course. Good writing, both its substance and its style, are the best models for anyone of any age who aspires to write. This is an important point for any teacher of children. In order to get them to read good literature and to want to express themselves clearly in writing, a teacher must develop positive relationships with them. The relationship aspect in teaching and learning is key.

Novelist John Fowles, author of *The French Lieutenant's Woman*, *Daniel Martin*, and many other wonderful books, makes a very interesting point about reading and its effect not only on one's writing but also on one's thinking abilities. Fowles suggests that reading frees the imagination, allowing it to roam creatively. This is so, he says, because the reader must supply his or her own images, thus creating an ongoing mental process of interaction with the written text. Older people who listened to radio adventures when they were children say much the same thing: They had to supply the images in their mind. Of course, if you read to the children from a good book for 15 minutes or so after lunch (the favorite part of the school day for many children), they will supply the images as they listen to you read.

Fowles contrasts the image making of the reader with the captured imagination of the television viewer, who has both text and images supplied for him or her. There is little else to do in terms of mental construction. Now, this is all very important when it comes to writing. The person who has read a great deal of good literature has been tutored in how to use words and craft sentences so that the reader becomes actively involved in image making. Reading and writing, then, are actually a seamless process, each one supporting the other. For the child who finds it difficult to write the words that convey exactly what he or she wants to say, a greater appreciation for good writing is possible. Take a moment to read the few lines that follow from Ralph Waldo Emerson's poem "Concord Hymn," written to commemorate the beginning of the American Revolution. Allow yourself to create images of the scene.

> *By the rude bridge that arched the flood,*
> *Their flag to April's breeze unfurled,*
> *Here once the embattled farmers stood*
> *And fired the shot heard round the world.*

I suggest to you that any fifth-grade child who reads this poem, discusses it with a thoughtful teacher who supplies interesting historical information surrounding it, and draws pictures of the scene (see Figure 14.2) can probably write a description of the events that has more emotion and life in it than that found in the account in the social studies textbook.

Of course, the road to good writing and reading doesn't stop there. Children with whom you have a good relationship, who trust you and value your opinion, are

FIGURE 14.2

An 8-Year-Old Child's Interpretation of a Portion of the Poem "Concord Hymn" by Ralph Waldo Emerson

By the rude bridge that arched the flood...

Their flag to April's breeze unfurled...

Here once the embattled farmers stood...

And fired the shot heard round the world.

ready and eager to take cues from you. So when you suggest to a fifth-grade child that he or she read *Johnny Tremain, Little Women,* or some other well-written, worthwhile book, you are suggesting more than a book title; you are bringing the wealth of your goodwill and trust to a child who wants your advice. Believe me, it's great to have wonderful authors such as Louisa May Alcott helping you teach a child to write well.

When considering writing and reading for children, it is important to relate it to modes of thought. The work of Benjamin Whorf illustrates rather well that the language people are exposed to (both written and oral) decides in great measure what thoughts are possible to them. They cannot escape from it into any other way of perceiving the world. Whorf's work was done with such culture groups as Inuits (Eskimos) and Native Americans, primarily Hopis. He showed that the rich vocabularies of these two groups in certain areas gave them an expressive ability that is indeed remarkable. For example, Inuits have an amazing number of words for snow, depending on the exact type of snow that might be falling at a given time. They can, therefore, think thoughts about snow that most English speakers cannot.

The point of Whorf's research is that each individual can expand his or her vocabulary and, therefore, his or her range of thought and expression. There are four necessary components to this expansion: experience, discussion, reading, and writing.

Experience

In social studies, it is vital that children have direct experiences and vicarious experiences. Direct experiences build perceptions and ideas about reality. For example, a direct experience is taking primary-age children outside on a fall day to gather evidence of fall or allowing intermediate-level children to make a Native American meal with the guidance of a tribal member. Vicarious experiences about human behavior and environments are often best supplied through print, film, or pictures. Of course, it would be fantastic to take your class to visit Japan or to travel backward through time to visit a colonial village, but in the absence of such possibilities, a teacher learns to use print and film strategically to build experience.

Discussion

Experience is necessary, but for it to become imbedded intellectually and emotionally, you must use your most characteristically human trait: speech. Schools will not improve until teachers are willing to give over vast amounts of time to both small-group and whole-class discussion. Too often, teachers fail to capitalize on the opportunity to really reflect and personalize experience. Talking about what they do, how they feel, how their perceptions change, and so on enables people to use their experiences as a springboard to deeper insight about themselves and others. Discussion also exposes people to the thinking of others who may have had the same experience yet whose perceptions of the experience are quite different. This adds a richness and a sense of quality possible only when people take the time to discuss things with others. It sounds so simple, doesn't it? Unfortunately, research[2] shows that student-initiated talk accounts for only about 7 minutes out of a typical 300-minute school day.

Reading

A lot of time has been spent on this topic, but keep in mind that what a person reads determines to a considerable extent what he or she becomes in life. Just recently, I talked with a teacher who told me that reading was her first love, and that was why she thought it was such an important subject in the school curriculum. When I asked her what she had read recently, she couldn't think of anything. I guess she meant it was important for children to read, but that she had already done that. This attitude simply will not work. If you want your students to read, you must model it. As you read, you will grow, and the students will sense the excitement and the growth.

Writing

Take a moment to consider the relationship between reading and writing as it is portrayed in the following example. A fourth-grade teacher read a descriptive paragraph from E. B. White's classic book *Charlotte's Web:*

> The barn was very large. It was very old. It smelled of hay and it smelled of manure. It smelled of perspiration of tired horses and the wonderful sweet breath of patient cows. It often had a sort of peaceful smell—as though nothing bad could happen ever again in the world. It smelled of axle grease and of rubber boots and of new rope. And whenever the cat was given a fish head to eat, the barn would smell of fish. But mostly it smelled of hay, for there was always hay in the great loft up overhead.

Then the teacher asked the students to write a group composition describing their own classroom. Notice the learning effect that a piece of well-written prose had on the children:

> The schoolroom was very large and old. It smelled of chalk dust and children's clothes. It often had a quiet smell—as if nothing bad could happen in school. It smelled of pencil lead, ink, ink paste, watercolor paints, and crayons. Whenever it rained or snowed, the wet coats and boots in the dressing room smelled like a skunk. When the children walked into the room, it smelled like potato chips, candy, nuts, and pumpkin seeds. Most of the time it smelled like smoke and dust. The dust came from the windows. The smoke came from the chimneys.

Social Studies and Language Development

The great Austrian philosopher, Ludwig Wittgenstein, offers a compelling argument linking language development to thinking and, therefore, to expression, both written and oral. Wittgenstein maintained that the limits of a person's language are the limits of that person's world. Thus, an individual's (or group's) world view is limited and determined by the language he or she commands.

The meaning of all this for classroom learning is that children need to read good material (unfortunately, the average elementary social studies textbook hardly qualifies), to write extensively, and to be given ample opportunity for oral discourse. The practice in recent years of journal writing is an excellent example of how children can be helped along the road to building up their talents for written expression.

In his book *Thought and Language*, Russian psychologist Lev Vygotsky examined the relationship between language and cognition. Vygotsky came to the conclusion that experience added to social interaction, or group sharing of written and oral language, is a key to language development. What is often overlooked or underestimated is that the expressive abilities of children are the outcome of cognitive development, while they are at the same time an enhancer of cognitive development. In other words, you need to give your students as much practice as possible in reading, writing, and discussing.

Interpreting Text

A useful technique for combining reading and writing (and even oral discourse for that matter) is called *interpreting text*. In a superficial sense, it looks like note taking as one reads, but it is far more than that. Here's how it works: As a person reads a book, he or she actively interacts with the text. The interaction takes the form of responding to statements made by the author as well as adding the reader's knowledge, thoughts, feelings, impressions, questions, and insights. The purpose of interpreting text is to give the reader equal footing with the author, thereby giving the reader a participatory role. Thus, the role of the student is both reader and writer. Here is an example written by an 11-year-old student named Tony:

> I agree that the pioneers had to be tough and smart. Otherwise, they couldn't have made it with no roads and just covered wagons. So they are heroes for what they did. I never thought about it before, but maybe I get to live here because they settled our town. But I was just trying to think of how the Indians felt. Maybe they didn't know everything that happened. But they had lived there all their lives, and so had their grandparents back into history. It's hard for me to understand. Both the pioneers and the Indians had feelings. History is about the past, so when I read in this book everything I read about already happened. I still don't think the pioneers were wrong because they wanted to be farmers on different land. But I do think we should care about what happened to the Indians because they had a way of living that was good for them.

You can see in this child's writing a genuinely reflective viewpoint emerging. The child is bringing something to the text. The child has feelings of ambivalence that transcend the reading of text merely for information. He is on the way to becoming an involved, critical reader.

Journal Writing

One of the more productive avenues toward improved thought and expression is journal writing. A journal encourages metacognition, or thinking reflectively about the experiences the writer has. A good journal, like a good diary, includes thoughts, feelings, perspectives, insight, analyses, and other means of reflection. Some students like to imagine that their journals are ship's logs, and that they are making entries each day as the ship sails from September to June.

In social studies, a journal is useful as a way of reflecting on the ideas, skills, content, and values that are being considered. A journal should give a student a private avenue of expression for his or her personal growth. Take a moment to consider the journal entry written by a sixth-grade student:

February 17

I really enjoy sharing time when we get to tell about the biographies. Everybody tries to make it so interesting and it is so much fun that I never liked social studies as much as this year. Some days I look at the clock and wonder if it will ever turn two o'clock so we can get started, but today was the best of all when Maddie and Sean pretended they were Columbus and Chief Joseph who never really met but the way they did it made Columbus so surprised with the way things turned out. Now some of us are going to turn it into a play, I hope.

The Writing Process

In social studies, a useful place to begin the writing process is with descriptive writing. Remember that observing, recording, and explaining are three of the most basic social science processes. To make good descriptive writers of your students, you need to give them practice with the process itself. The writing process can be considered in four phases:

1. *Prewriting.* This is the initial, or warm-up, phase. In this phase, a young writer needs to consider the subject, think about who he or she is writing for, and create images of what he or she would like to say.
2. *Drafting.* The writer is ready to take the first written approach to the subject. At this stage, it is important that the writer says what he or she needs to say in rough form.
3. *Revising.* This is a good time to discuss the work with someone else, to get teacher comments, and to consider not merely *what* to say, but *how* to say it.
4. *Editing.* This is the phase where the finished product will emerge. Spelling, punctuation, elements of style, and so on are important, because others will read the product.

Let's go through the four phases with a specific example. In a third-grade class, the teacher decided that she would give each child a chestnut and ask him or her to write a description of the chestnut.

At phase 1, the children looked up information on chestnuts, and the teacher read some background from a botany text she had obtained from the library. More important, the children drew several pictures of their chestnuts and chestnut trees. They worked with a partner, telling their partner about their drawings and about their feelings as they drew their pictures.

At phase 2, each child began to write a description of his or her chestnut. These were rough drafts. The children shared their stories with their partners, and the teacher collected the rough drafts and made comments.

At phase 3, the children began helping each other with editing. They also considered the teacher's comments to help them with their expression.

At phase 4, each child wrote a finished paragraph about his or her chestnut and drew an accompanying illustration. The works were then displayed on the wall of the classroom.

Here is one child's finished paragraph:

Let me tell you about my chestnut. It is a kind of chestnut called a horse chestnut. People don't eat them, but squirrels like them. I know, because I have seen the squirrels eat them and bury them. The chestnut is brown with a smooth, shiny shell. It is about an inch wide. If you cut it open, you will see it is white, about the color of a piano key. The chestnut came from a blossom on the tree, and when it grew it had a green spiked cover. The spikes are sharp. The best time to find chestnuts is in the fall when they drop off the trees. If you study my drawings you will see the chestnut from beginning to end, even what a cut-open chestnut looks like. Good-bye.

The writing process served this child well. She learned about sequencing her ideas, about defining an object using words and pictures, and about conveying both form and function, in this case about chestnuts.

Like anything else, it takes time and practice to become proficient as a writer. The earlier children begin the process, the more they will see it as a natural extension of their ability to communicate with others. They need to do a lot of writing, especially descriptive writing, and they need to read or listen to good writing.

The Spoken Word

In the first century A.D., the Roman orator Quintilian noted that speech is our most purely human attribute. Nothing, he said, separates humans from other creatures more clearly than the ability to speak words and to listen to the spoken word. One could argue the point, citing other characteristics of the human condition as equally or more significant, but Quintilian's meaning is still well taken.

Sadly, many educators seem to have forgotten just how important it is for children to be given the opportunity to develop their speaking and listening skills. It is all too easy to overlook this form of literacy. In ancient times, people had little choice but to communicate using the spoken word. Many culture groups did not even have written language; others did, but had little means of storing the written word in an age before books. Today, the situation is quite the opposite. There are so many means of preserving the record that people tend to undervalue the spoken word. The poor speaking abilities of most politicians today serve as a reminder that no progress has been made in this area. In fact, great speakers in American history—such as Patrick Henry, Daniel Webster, Abraham Lincoln, and, more recently, Martin Luther King Jr.—seem no longer to be found.

Martin Luther King Jr.

Primary teachers usually do a better job than others in teaching speaking and listening skills, mainly because their students cannot write or read as well as they can speak and listen. Show and tell, dictating stories, and other oral moments of the curriculum are extremely useful in this regard. This is simply not enough, however. As children grow older and more self-conscious, it becomes crucial to encourage and nurture opportunities for oral discourse. To illustrate how significant this topic is, consider that certain surveys of adults have shown that their number one fear is speaking in front of a group. Four distinctly different strategies, effectively employed, will go a long way toward remedying this situation.

Public Speaking

It takes courage and skill to talk to a group, and, like any other skill, it can only be improved with practice. It is useful to bear in mind John Dewey's idea of the classroom as a learning laboratory where children are encouraged to take risks, to experiment, and to practice the skills that are needed in everyday life. Like any other complex task, speaking to groups needs to be approached using developmentally appropriate practice. A good place to begin is to have your students give brief one- or two-minute descriptive speeches in which they hold a prop and describe something (e.g., a chestnut, a baseball, a doll, or whatever). As success builds, as it will in a nurturing environment, students can be given more complex tasks, such as describing a certain river system, telling how to catch a ball, or explaining how to sew a particular stitch.

Small-Group Speaking

In real life, people often find themselves in relatively small groups, engaged in conversation with others. The art of speaking and listening in such a forum is perhaps best facilitated in school settings by having children work in collaborative groups. As they engage in answering questions, solving problems, or developing ideas, they will benefit from acquiring certain skills, such as showing courtesy to others, speaking in turn, talking quietly, asking questions, agreeing and disagreeing civilly, participating actively, encouraging others, contributing their share, being open to different perspectives, and so on. These skills need to be pointed out by you and discussed reflectively by the class. *Circles of Learning* by David and Roger Johnson is an excellent source of ideas and skills for promoting small group learning.

Informal Talks

Contrary to the opinion of those who think classrooms should always be so quiet that one can hear a pin drop, they should in fact be places of conversation. Of course, there is a time for quiet, but students should be encouraged to talk with each other as they work together on projects. For one thing, it encourages both language development and social intelligence. For another, it is natural behavior for human beings. Children benefit greatly from expressing themselves to each other as they build a colonial village, draw a mural, rehearse a play, organize a game, prepare a meal, and so forth. Ironically, there is far too little of this kind of shared activity in elementary school life, and your job is to make sure it happens. Social skills can be learned in such settings, especially if you and the class take the time to discuss appropriate behaviors for informal talk; in fact, the children will help you come up with rules governing their own behavior during these times.

Group Presentations

You need to be sure that your students engage in presentations in which they are part of a group. Examples of this are panel discussions, demonstrations, pageants, dramatizations, musical productions, debates, and such video productions as "news-casts" and "feature shows." The spoken word is invoked doubly with this procedure. First is the informal talk that goes along with planning, getting prepared, attending to details, orchestrating, making sure things are ready. Second is the presentation itself in which an audience is addressed, which involves deciding on roles, deter-mining who speaks when and how much, fielding questions from the audience, and other problematic issues.

These four strategies will go a long way toward putting the "social" back in so-cial studies. They are aimed directly at the development of thought and language, especially at its public expression. Constructivist approaches take a clear view on the distinction between information and knowledge and the need for public ex-pression of ideas. If a teacher employs only silent reading, worksheets, and paper and pencil tests, then *information* will serve the student well, at least until it's for-gotten. But *knowledge*, which implies the construction of meaning by learners—an activity that uses information as a way to build more complex social and intellec-tual structures—depends heavily on interaction, exchange, articulation, sharing of thoughts, reflection, and public expression of ideas.

Electronic Literacy

Without doubt, the invention of the printing press and movable type by the Ger-man inventor Johannes Gutenberg in the fifteenth century brought about the most profound revolution ever in the advancement of literacy. Everything changed as a result. Books became available to ordinary people, and stored knowledge became decentralized for the first time in history. Now, people are in the midst of another revolution in the annals of literacy. This revolution is brought about by electronic technology, especially in the form of the Internet. Sometimes called the Informa-tion Superhighway, the Internet provides a means of communication that affords people access to databases and on-line information systems of an incredible range. Although it is less than 10 years old, the Internet has become an indispensable tool for everyone from stockbrokers to school children. Using the Internet in the form of the World Wide Web, children in remote sites of Alaska or in crowded urban centers can connect to classrooms in other countries, access the Library of Con-gress, and examine news reports from around the globe. For social studies teach-ers, the Internet can create a kind of global village, allowing a teacher and his or her class to exchange pen-pal letters, stories, weather data, geography, history, and anything else of mutual interest. Useful websites for school purposes include the following:

- **The Globe Program** at http://www.globe.gov is a wonderful interdisciplinary source for teachers who wish to combine social studies, science, and related environmental issues. Some 3,000 classes around the world are collecting and posting environmental data to the site. Research scientists actually use the student data and offer feedback.
- **C-Span** at http://www.c-span.org gives you and your students access to the U.S. House of Representatives, allowing you to watch the actual process of debate, voting, and so on in the halls of Congress. C-Span also covers other political events and serious items in the news.
- **NCSSonline** at http://www.ncss.org gives you access to the National Council for the Social Studies, the largest organization in the country devoted solely to social studies education. NCSS provides members with networks for all the social science disciplines and for special topics as well, including law education, moral education, multicultural education, and others.

These are but a few of the thousands of electronic addresses available, and the list grows every day. The educational challenge of the Internet and the World Wide Web is one of the most exciting events of our lifetimes. I hope you will take advantage of the possibilities. Remember, Jean Piaget wrote that teaching is about possibilities, and the World Wide Web has created a new horizon of the possible. By the way, I'd love to hear from you. You can contact me at aellis@spu.com.

Summary

The key to this chapter is the interdependent relationship among reading, writing, and the spoken word as ways to communicate thoughts and feelings in social studies. Each of us constructs our own knowledge, but we do it best in social and intellectual contexts that provide access to productive ideas that allow us in turn to build structures of meaning. Children who become avid readers, willing writers, and confident public speakers are on the way to lifelong learning. Just imagine what a gift it is to a child to have a teacher who creates a learning landscape that offers nurture, support, and encouragement toward those ends. It is through the medium of language that people are able to define and express their hopes, fears, dreams, insights, and ambitions. Please make reading, writing, and the spoken word an integral part of your social studies curriculum.

ACTIVITIES

1. Select a good primary-level picture book with a social studies theme and develop a lesson around it—one that emphasizes discussion and reflection.
2. Create a webbing with a central theme (e.g., pioneers, Native Americans, families, culture, or whatever) and complete the webbing with some partners by brainstorming activities that students could do.

3. Create a step-by-step outline showing how you would establish a book club for students.
4. What qualities do you think a teacher should possess in order to create an environment where children feel that they can express themselves openly?
5. How comfortable are you with the Internet? If you are comfortable, teach someone else how to use it to improve their social studies teaching. If not, ask someone who is experienced on the Internet how you can improve your social studies teaching by using it.

SUGGESTED READINGS

Daley, P., and Allen, J. (2000). *The Most Riveting Read Alouds of All Time: Build Comprehension, Listening, and Higher-Order Thinking Skills with 10-Minute Read Alouds.* New York: Scholastic Professional Book Division.

Gregory, C. (2000). *Jeeves, I'm Bored: 25 Internet Adventures for Children.* Ask Jeeves, Inc.

Harvey, S. (1998). *Nonfiction Matters: Reading, Writing, and Research in Grades 3–8.* Stenhouse Publishers.

Hopkins, T. (2000). *1001 Best Website for Educators.* New York: Teacher Created Materials.

Irvin, J., Lunstrum, J., Lynch-Brown, C., and Shepard, M. (1995). *Enhancing Social Studies through Literacy Strategies.* Washington, DC: National Council for the Social Studies.

Lindquist, T., and Selwyn, D. (2000). *Social Studies at the Center: Integrating Kids, Content, and Literacy.* Portsmouth, NH: Heinneman.

Social Education. Each year the official journal of the National Council for the Social Studies publishes an edition containing notable children's tradebooks for social studies.

Social Studies and Current Events

The word *current* in current events has taken on new meaning in recent years. This is so primarily because new technologies have greatly accelerated the pace of change in our world. I remember talking with a woman whose grandmother was a young girl when President Abraham Lincoln was assassinated. She told me that her grandmother's family, living in rural Oregon in 1865, learned of Lincoln's death several days after it happened; and even then, the information they received was filled with hearsay accounts. Today, with global satellite telemetry and other advanced communication forms, news travels around the world almost as quickly as it happens. Children today are certainly more aware of current events on a worldwide scale than were children of past generations, and this makes the social studies teacher's role in interpreting current events crucial. In this chapter we will consider the following topics:

- Analysis of a current events discussion
- Criteria for successful current events analysis
- Content analyses of the news
- Examining the news from multiple perspectives
- News sources
- A theme approach to news reporting
- Current events interests of young learners
- Current events teaching and learning strategies

The newspaper is the first rough draft of history.

—Phil Bradley

CNN.com., USAToday.com., MSNBC.com.—news sources aren't what they used to be. A generation ago, you had to wait for the evening news on television to tell you what had happened that day, or wait for the morning paper to tell you what had happened the night before. Now, news coverage is 'round the clock, and the sheer quantity of it is overwhelming. If children learn nothing else from their study of current events, they will surely learn that we live in an information age. This is literally a time of information explosion.

Channel One brings television news reporting directly into the classroom, for better or worse. Children have access at home and at school to the Internet with its panoply of news sources. Cable television has transformed news reporting and analysis from scheduled coverage at six o'clock in the evening to continuous coverage. Only a few years ago, it was common knowledge among news people that the *New York Times*, by virtue of what it printed on its front page, pretty much dictated the evening newscasts of the major networks. News reporting in the past was primarily verbal—that is, written in newspapers and magazines, and spoken on radio and television (with a few pictures). With new technologies, we have witnessed the rise of iconographic representation in the form of television, video, and Internet coverage. Some analysts have pointed back to the Vietnam War as a turning point. It is one thing to read about armed conflict and quite another thing to watch it on television while eating dinner. Words and pictures tell different stories.

Phil Bradley, former editor of the *Washington Post*, once told his staff of reporters that their job was to write "the first rough draft of history." Imagine what he might tell them today when one considers that any large metropolitan newspaper exists not only in print editions but in continuous coverage on the Internet. In his day, there was no www.washingtonpost.com! But his point remains a valid one. What is written under the pressures of deadlines ultimately does find its way into the history books. Some events that seem rather significant at the time will drift away into oblivion, while others will become a significant part of the historical record. Just try to recall the coverage of the 2000 presidential election and the many stories that were reported, retracted, and re-reported. When the dust settles years from now and historians look back on that year, they will try to make sense of the massive amount of information generated by the news sources.

Here is an example of what I mean. Some years ago, I spent several days working in the archives room in a major university library. Much of my time was devoted to reading through old issues of the *San Francisco Chronicle*. As I was reading my way through the year 1943, I came across a small article buried in the back pages about a young U.S. Navy lieutenant named John F. Kennedy. His P.T. boat had been torpedoed and had sunk. Kennedy and his crew reached the shore of a Pacific Ocean island—a daring wartime rescue at sea. There it was—the first rough draft of history.

Today, people get their news from an incredible variety of sources. We have witnessed the decline of the newspaper as the primary source of people's information. Newspapers will always be around, but they must compete with on-line sources as well as radio and television. One lesson newspapers have learned is that while they may not be able to beat the electronic media in the area of rapid reporting, they can provide features that are useful to the social studies teacher—for example, in-depth stories on global warming, endangered species, and other topics. Ask yourself: What are the sources of news information that I most frequently use?

I urge you to make current events and news reporting an integral part of your social studies curriculum. You need to encourage your students to be aware of the news, to learn to distinguish the superficial from the significant, and, in the inquiry spirit of this book, to become reporters themselves. Let's begin by analyzing a current events discussion that took place in an elementary classroom.

After you read the following discussion, which took place in an elementary classroom, you will be asked to evaluate it.

> *Mrs. Carmichael:* Does anyone have any news to report this morning? (calls on Larry, who has his hand raised)
>
> *Larry:* (walks to front of room) There was a real bad wreck on the freeway yesterday—or maybe the day before yesterday.
>
> *Lisa:* Did anyone get killed?
>
> *Larry:* I think so. I'm not sure. Yeah, some people got hurt.
>
> *Mrs. Carmichael:* Larry, do you have a clipping from a newspaper?
>
> *Larry:* No, I heard my dad talking about it.
>
> *Mrs. Carmichael:* Class, you know that we've talked about being sure of our facts. Larry, I don't think you know what really happened. You may sit down.
>
> *Mrs. Carmichael:* Who else has some news to report? And let's be sure of our facts.
>
> *Anita:* Well, I have a story on the world food shortage. It says that people in many countries face starvation.
>
> *Mrs. Carmichael:* What else does it say?
>
> *Anita:* It says that the grain supplies in the United States are lower.
>
> *Mrs. Carmichael:* What do you think that means?
>
> *Anita:* That there won't be enough food? I don't know.
>
> *Mrs. Carmichael:* Thank you, Anita. We'll put your clipping up on the bulletin board.
>
> *Mrs. Carmichael:* Class, how many of you have heard of the world food shortage? (many hands are raised) Well, let's all do our part and not waste food. (pause) All right, class. Take out your math books and turn to page 41.

Take a few moments to react to this glimpse of a current events/news reporting session in an elementary classroom. Place a check near the point on the following continuum that reflects your opinion of the news session.

1	2	3	4	5
Really bad! No one learned anything about current events.	It's good to involve students in news reporting, but some improvements are definitely needed.	Not an in-depth analysis of the news—but about what you'd expect from elementary students.	Fairly good. Students are contributing and teacher is asking probing questions.	Excellent! Concise, conceptually oriented, good student involvement.

Now list two reasons for your opinion.

1. _____

   _____

   _____

2. _____

   _____

   _____

I gave Mrs. Carmichael a 2. It's good to involve students in news reporting, but some improvements are definitely needed. Whether your opinion coincides with mine or not, take a few moments to examine the following section, which deals with criteria for successful current events/news reporting sessions in elementary classrooms.

Criteria for Successful Current Events Sessions

Obviously, no set of suggestions is going to give you the perfect news period or current events session. You need to examine the following suggestions and decide for yourself how and to what extent they meet the needs of your unique situation. My purpose is to give you some general guidelines, which you and your students may find helpful as you strive to improve this important facet of the social studies curriculum.

Determining Whether News Is Important

A basic question to consider in selecting a news item for reporting and analysis is the following: To what extent is the news story of lasting importance? Sensational events, such as vehicle accidents and bizarre crimes, may be given considerable attention by the press and they may capture the fancy of a child looking for something to report on Monday morning, but these are often not items of lasting importance and they generally do not provide material for analysis by students. This is not to say that such topical events should never be reported. Rather, it is to say that students should learn not to be misled about what is newsworthy. Here are two strategies designed to help students consider the ultimate newsworthiness of items from the newspaper.

1. Select a newspaper from several years ago. You can probably borrow a copy from a library. Have the students list some headlines you have selected from the newspaper in order of their size. The largest headline is number 1, the second largest number 2, and so on. Then let small groups (or the entire class) list the headlines in the order of their importance today (in the students' opinion). Figure 15.1 illustrates this procedure. Examine the figure and do your own ranking.

2. Select a current newspaper and let students predict which stories will be of importance 1 year from now, 5 years from now, and 100 years from now.

FIGURE 15.1

*Newspaper
Headlines to Be
Ranked*

Fruits, veggies
can help

Illiteracy in America

PICASSO HEIST

SOUTH AFRICA PEACE

Low inflation

CELTICS, 108, BUCKS 100

RUSSIA will resume arms talks

Stuffing kids
with TV ads
for fatty foods

Making math add up

Tonight's TV listings

PCs flood market

Of course, the newspaper is only one source of news. These strategies could be applied to radio and television newscasts as an independent investigation for intermediate-age students.

Separating Facts from Opinions

Whether disseminated by newspapers, magazines, television, radio, or word of mouth, news contains both factual and opinion-oriented information. Most newspapers attempt to separate factual news from such opinion-oriented items as editorials and letters to the editor. However, rather than assume students know that (or even that it is true, for that matter), let students apply simple content analyses to articles and arrive at their own decisions as to whether articles are fact or opinion oriented. Figure 15.2 is a letter typical of the mixtures of fact and opinion one finds in the newspaper.

FIGURE 15.2

*A Letter to the
Editor*

To the Editor: Last Saturday a protest march was held on the Village Green. The newspapers and television reported that more than 2,000 people took part in the protest. I wasn't one of them. The people who do this kind of thing are bums. They shouldn't be allowed to live in our country. No arrests were made. A police captain was quoted as saying it was a peaceful demonstration. Well, we are sick and tired of people with beards carrying signs. The police should have put them in jail.

F. D. Jones
Midville

Take the following test. Put an *F* in front of each sentence you think is probably factual and an *O* for each sentence you think is probably the writer's opinion.

Content Analysis Guide

_____ 1. Last Saturday a protest march was held on the Village Green.

_____ 2. The newspapers and television reported that more than 2,000 people took part in the protest.

_____ 3. I wasn't one of them.

_____ 4. The people who do this kind of thing are bums.

_____ 5. They shouldn't be allowed to live in our country.

_____ 6. No arrests were made.

_____ 7. A police captain was quoted as saying that it was a peaceful demonstration.

_____ 8. Well, we are all sick and tired of people with beards carrying signs.

_____ 9. The police should have put them in jail.

Here is how I marked them. You may or may not agree, but your reasons for a response are crucial. (1) Fact; this could be verified. (2) Fact; the numbers could be wrong, but I assume the writer is right. (3) Fact; I take the writer's word for it. (4) Opinion; this is a sweeping inference. The writer used an emotion-laden term. (5) Opinion; our country guarantees people the right to protest. (6) Fact; I assume that is accurate—at least it could be verified. (7) Fact; same reason as for Number 6. (8) Opinion; inference is too sweeping. Everyone may not feel that way. (9) Opinion; I disagree. It would have been a questionable legality.

Considering Other Perspectives

Earlier, chronological perspective was alluded to as a measure of how important a news item might be. Cultural, attitudinal, and/or geographical perspective is also worth noting. For example, a college newspaper's report on a campus demonstration might be very different from the portrayal of the same event by a city newspaper. Papers from different regions of the United States may have different editorial opinions and different ways of reporting events. You can and should occasionally order newspapers from other cities around the country.

Also, other nations often see news of the United States from a different perspective. I recall talking to a man who returned to the United States from Europe during the World Trade Organization (WTO) "riot" in Seattle. He commented that the coverage in newspapers was quite extensive and (in his opinion) much more sympathetic to the cause than that in American papers he had seen. At any rate, cities in Canada, England, New Zealand, and other countries in which English-speaking newspapers are prevalent should be kept in mind as sources of news reporting that may offer alternatives to prevailing national views.

The study of current events creates the awareness that is necessary for good citizenship.

In this vein, Spanish-language newspapers, both domestic and foreign, are a valuable alternative news source if children speak Spanish, are learning it as a second language, or are studying countries in which Spanish is the national language.

Newspapers from around the world are available from Multinewspapers, Box DE, Dana Point, CA 92629.

Using a Theme Approach

The daily newspaper carries a little bit of everything: the signing of an international treaty to limit the production of nuclear weapons, a recipe for pineapple-upside-down cake, a summary and analysis of the Super Bowl game, an editorial on the hazards of chlorine in drinking water, the arrest of an alleged hijacker, tomorrow's weather forecast, and the latest cartoon adventures of Garfield. Therefore, what news to report can be confusing to a child. A solution to this problem is to let the students (with some help from you) select themes in the news and current events. When a theme has been selected, news reports are given for a week at a time on that theme. This approach will do two things for your study of current events. First, it will free students from wondering whether the news they have selected is fit to report. Second, it will allow sufficient coverage of a topic for students to develop an analysis of it. Possible themes include:

Air Pollution	International Treaties
Water Pollution	The Economy
New Stadium Proposal	School Busing
Controversial New Freeway	Agricultural Conditions

Presidential Election
Bond Issues (New Swimming
    Pool, Park, School, etc.)
Space Travel
School Consolidation

Traffic Problems
Labor Conditions
Transportation Issues
Other Countries

Unique local conditions in your area will add other possible themes.

Let's look in on a classroom in which a theme approach is being used in news reporting/current events. The class is studying a local controversy about whether a city should use a particular portion of its acreage to construct a municipal golf course or to develop a wildlife refuge/nature center.

Mrs. Olisinski: Class, since we've chosen the golf course/nature park controversy as next week's theme, I'd like to remind you to start clipping news items from the paper. We need to help Jerry and Elizabeth with material for their bulletin board.

Jerry: I've got quite a few stories. We need some more, though. And we need pictures and maps and stuff like that.

Editorial cartoons furnish students with excellent nonverbal material for the analysis and display of current events topics.

Doesn't anybody worry about the day when the stream might run dry?

Mrs. Olisinski: Melanie, has your committee on resource persons come up with anything?

Melanie: We're going to call City Hall this noon and ask who could come to talk to the class.

Mrs. Olisinski: Todd, what about your questions committee?

Todd: We've got a lot of questions ready. I think we have about 15 so far.

Mrs. Olisinski: Jackie, how is the research committee doing?

Jackie: Scott is writing a survey so we can find out parents' opinions—what they want. And Rachelle and Brenda are trying to describe the two different sides—the golf course side and the park side.

This teacher uses a theme approach to news reporting/current events several times a year. She usually spends one week getting committees started and the following week on the reporting and analysis of issues related to the theme. Obviously, these students have had experience with this procedure before this study. Also, the teacher has spent time with the various committees, reacting to their ideas and offering suggestions. Let's look at the next week's activities related to this theme. Each day, the class spent anywhere from 15 to 30 minutes on the project.

Monday

- The question committee read and posted its list of questions about the issue (for example: Which would be used by more people: a golf course or a nature park?).
- News clippings were reported and posted.
- The factual information committee (what, where, why, etc.) gave each student a dittoed sheet summarizing the situation.
- The resource committee reported that a city council member would visit the class on Thursday.

Tuesday

- The research committee gave students copies of its questionnaire for parents. They asked that the results be back by Thursday.
- More news reports were given and posted.
- The teacher asked students to begin thinking about which side of the issue they favored and why.
- The map committee showed maps and pictures of the site in question. They also showed the class some artist's sketches of the proposed golf course and the proposed nature park.

Wednesday

- The class was divided into groups of five. The groups discussed several questions selected from the list developed by the question committee. Each group reported the results of its discussion to the entire class.

Thursday

- A city council member presented a talk and a slide show on the issue. At the close of his talk, he answered students' questions. Also, the students showed the council member the results of their survey. They explained that they had selected a random sample of parents and other adults in a geographical area of the city they had marked on a map and had then polled people's opinions on the issue. The council member asked for a copy of their results to take to the next council meeting.

Friday
- A debate was held in the classroom, with the principal acting as moderator. When the debate was over, the class voted on the issue. Voting results were 11 in favor of the golf course and 21 in favor of the nature center.

Focusing on Students' Interests

Primary-age children often lack the experience and capabilities to do independent work, and they lack the world awareness of older elementary school students. However, it would be a mistake to assume that these younger children are ignorant of current events. They hear their parents talking of elections, pollution, the economy, and the weather. They watch a great deal of television and manage to hear and see the news as well as cartoons and family adventures. The teacher's role can be one of accurately informing and educating younger learners about current events.

A primary teacher may want to give a short summary of the news and weather each morning. The students will quickly see what kinds of news stories the teacher emphasizes. This is also an appropriate time to illustrate the differences between facts and opinions in stories from the newspaper. Gradually, students will begin to volunteer stories. As they do, it becomes increasingly appropriate to review sources of information and to introduce certain issues on which opinion is divided.

Holidays and other special observances are big news to younger elementary-age students. Current events time may be used to review the history and traditions of various special occasions. In addition, students may want to become involved in participating in some of the lesser known holidays and observances. The following holidays and special observances could provide the basis for current events investigations:

Martin Luther King's Birthday	Yom Kippur
March of Dimes Week	Citizenship Day
Brotherhood Week	American Indian Day
Black History Month	Fire Prevention Day
Valentine's Day	Columbus Day
Conservation Week	United Nations Day
Kindness to Animals Week	Veterans Day
Earth Week	Halloween
May Day	Book Week
Mother's Day	Election Day
Flag Day	Thanksgiving
Father's Day	Bill of Rights Day
Independence Day	Christmas
Labor Day	Presidents Day

Current Events Themes

A theme approach to current events discourages pupils from reporting on the scattered random and bizarre events often found in newspapers. In addition, the theme approach encourages concept learning by students because a variety of stories, features, and pictures that focus on one basic idea are brought to class. Thus, students can pursue an in-depth treatment of a topic for a period of time, generally one or two weeks. The materials students bring in support of a given theme should be displayed either on a bulletin board or at an interest center. Here is an illustrative list of themes.

Energy: Problems, new developments, controversial issues
Wild Animals: Endangered species, migratory and seasonal animals
Helpers: People in the news, community helpers, advice columns
History: Stories about the past, local histories, feature articles
Africa (or any other continent or world region): Government, places of interest, civil rights
Maps: Spatial concepts, rivers and oceans, mountain ranges
Cities: Current issues, urban renewal, transportation development
Transportation: New inventions, energy-saving ideas, people movers

Electronic Current Events

It's a Tuesday morning in Patricia Lerner's classroom and several children hover around the computer, typing in Web site addresses, scanning various electronic newspapers, and printing out pages, including worldwide weather reports, headlines, sports, and so on. The children are Patricia's on-line news team. Their responsibility is to put together the News Bulletin Board each day. It's a highly coveted job, and Patricia knows how important it is that every child gets a turn being a member of the on-line news team.

Electronic access to the world has brought a whole new meaning to the term *current events*. Students can find out the latest news in Russia, Japan, or Kenya; they can find out about the newest Library of Congress cultural exhibits; they can check weather patterns using earth images from orbiting weather satellites; they can learn the latest adventures of Dilbert or of comic characters from Disney; the possibilities are endless.

Here is a sampling of electronic news addresses:

CNN Interactive	http://www.cnn.com
Current Headlines	http://www.yahoo.com/
Electronic Newsstand	http://www.enews.com
USA Today Top News	http://www.usatoday.com/
Newspapers around the World	http://www.helsinki.fi/

This is not at all to say that other forms of news and current events reporting (newspapers, magazines, television, radio) are obsolete. Rather, the Internet takes its place as yet one more way to obtain access to information. Remember: Multiple modes of information access are vital to a democratic society.

Another electronic option is the news fax. Although it is still in its infancy, it has considerable promise for classroom use, especially in a day when many children come from homes where there is no newspaper available to them.

Current Events Strategies

Here are some teaching strategies for emphasizing the use of the daily newspaper in your classroom.

1. *Read the paper to your students.* Take a few minutes each morning to read the newspaper to your students. In addition to covering some of the day's important news stories, you may wish to emphasize different sections of the paper on different days.

2. *History headlines.* Ask your students to examine the headlines on the front page. There are usually five to eight stories. Have students play the role of historians whose task is to rank-order the headlines in terms of what they think will be their lasting importance. This exercise gives the students the opportunity to think about the signing of a major treaty, for example.

3. *Headline rewrite.* Headlines are written under the pressure of deadlines. They are also written to grab readers' attention. A simple exercise in creativity is to ask students to rewrite one or more headlines.

4. *The inverted pyramid* (▼). Journalistic style calls for the writer to tell who, what, when, where, and why (the five Ws) as quickly as possible in a news story. These facts should appear in the first paragraph of the story. The reader should be able to place an inverted pyramid over a news story and follow it from its most important items of information at the top to its least important facets near the end. You may wish to ask students to write a "five Ws" paragraph describing a news item from their day at school.

5. *Weather and climate.* Climate is weather over time. Each day, the paper carries a comprehensive summary of the weather, including temperature reports from major cities in the United States and Canada and from around the world. Assign each student a city and have the student record the high and low temperature for that city each day for two or three weeks. The students can then record their findings on graphs. During the study, each student writes to the city and requests information. When the study is in progress and completed, you will be able to introduce many factors of climate, including latitude, nearness to bodies of water, and mountains, for example.

6. *Comics.* This section of the paper is of great interest to many children. Ask the students to turn to the comics and find an example of humor they like. Perhaps you might wish to have them rewrite the captions for some of the cartoons.

7. *Sports.* The sports page contains a wealth of statistics. A motivating way for some students to learn decimals and percentages is to follow the exploits of different individual players and teams. Baseball batting averages, for example, are decimals carried out to the thousandths place.

8. *Plan a picnic.* Imagine the fun of taking the grocery ads and planning a picnic for two people, keeping the total cost under $5.00. This exercise involves quite a bit of decision making and mathematics.

9. *The Planet Zenna.* Imagine a scenario in which the technologically advanced people of another planet wanted to borrow from Earth. In this fantasy, the people of Zenna decide to take five people, five things, and five ideas from Earth to help them improve their own civilization. Each student should search the newspaper to come up with a list. Students then can work together in small groups of five to come up with an agreed upon list (consensus) from each group. Each group then shares its list with the rest of the class.

A Current Events Mini-Unit

This current events mini-unit for elementary students utilizes several different sections of the daily newspaper. It is adapted from Barbara Dewell, *Newspapers in Education.*[1]

▶ *Day I: What Is in a Newspaper?*

Student Objective. To use the index or table of contents to find out what is in a newspaper

Materials. Student copies of "What Is in a Newspaper" worksheet; newspaper for each student

Lesson Plan: Group Activity. Define an index. Have students locate the index in their newspapers. Discuss how an index is used. Discuss how the pages (or sections) of a newspaper are numbered. Locate several sections in the newspaper by having the students locate the page number in the index, and then turn to that page. Show students how to fold the newspaper after turning to a page so it can be read comfortably. Have students practice folding and then returning to the front page. (For younger students, it may be easier to work on the floor than to fold the newspaper.)

Individual Activity. Assign students to complete the following "What Is in the Newspaper" worksheet individually, in pairs, or in small groups.

WHAT IS IN THE NEWSPAPER?
Use the index to find out what is in the newspaper.

1. Weather   Find the high temperature in your city or town today.

        Page _____ High temperature _____

2. Television   Find a show that will be on television at 7 P.M. tonight.

        Page _____ Channel _____

        Show_____

3. Movies   Find a movie your family might want to see.

Movie _____ Page _____

Theater _____

4. Family Living   Find the name of a club or community event in the news (meeting, art show, etc.).

Page _____ Club or event _____

5. Business   Find the name of a company in the news.

Page _____ Company name _____

6. Sports   Find the name of an athlete in the news.

What sport does the athlete play? _____

Athlete's name _____ Page _____

7. Advertisements   Find something a mother or father would buy.

Page _____ Item _____

Store name _____

8. Editorial   Find an editorial and tell what it is about.

Page _____ What is it about? _____

_____

_____

_____

9. Comics   Find a comic strip you like to read.

Page _____ Title of comic _____

➤ *Day II: People in the News*

Student Objective. To learn about people in the news

Materials. Student copies of "People in the News" worksheet; newspaper for each student

Lesson Plan: Group Activity. Discuss what a person might do to get his or her name or picture in the newspaper. Students may answer only positively (e.g., win an election to office). Be sure students discuss that some people get their names in the news for doing something that does not make them proud (e.g., breaking the law).

Individual Activity. Have students complete the following "People in the News" worksheet individually, in pairs, or in small groups.

Learn about people in the news. People and what they do are important and interesting. Some people are described by the job they do. Some people are described by something they have done.

Each box names a kind of person who might be in the newspaper. See how many names you can find in the newspaper today to match with the boxes.

By Job

Job: Athlete

Name: _____

Sport: _____

Job: Entertainer

Name: _____

Job: (You Choose)

Name: _____

Job: Politician

Name: _____

Title: _____

Job: Politician (US)

Name: _____

Job: Dignitary

Name: _____

Title: _____

*Country:*_____

By Description

Lawbreaker

Name: _____

What did he or she do?

_____

Hero

Name: _____

What did he or she do?

_____

Accident Victim

Name: _____

Kind of accident:

_____

(You Choose)

Name: _____

Description: _____

_____

▶ *Day III: Shopping in the Newspaper*

Student Objective. To use newspaper advertisements to shop in the newspaper

Materials. Student copies of "Shopping in the Newspaper" worksheet; newspaper for each student

Lesson Plan: Group Activity. Discuss the three reasons advertising appears in the newspaper. Ask students to discuss why shopping in the newspaper first can save time and money.

Individual Activity. Have students shop in the newspaper by completing the following "Shopping in the Newspaper" worksheet.

Extra Credit Assignment. Design a newspaper ad for an existing (or invented) business.

SHOPPPING IN THE NEWSPAPER
Advertising is important to newspapers for three reasons:

1. Newspapers need advertising to make money for the newspaper business.
2. Businesses need advertising to tell people about their products and services.
3. Newspaper readers need advertising to learn about products, to learn about stores that sell products, and to know the prices of products.

Go shopping in the newspaper. Use your newspaper to find the information needed.

1. You want to take a parent out to eat as a special surprise. You have been saving your allowance so you can do this. Your parent likes seafood. Where can you go to eat?

   Name of restaurant: _____

   Address: _____

2. You want to have some friends come to a party. What food would your friends like? Find three party food items and the price of each. What will the total cost be?

   Food items: _____ *Cost:* _____

   _____ _____

   _____ _____

   Total: _____

3. Your father's birthday is next week and you do not have a gift yet. Shop in the newspaper for a gift. Your limit is $20.00.

   Gift: _____ *Price:* _____

   Store: _____

4. Can you find a business in the newspaper that sells each of the following items?

   Place to Buy

   Tires   _____

   Television   _____

   Used car   _____

   Jewelry   _____

Real estate _____

Shoes _____

Clothes _____

Football _____

Food _____

Toys _____

Furniture _____

▶▶ *Day IV: The Comics*

Student Objective. To learn about the kinds of comics in a newspaper

Materials. Student copies of "The Comics" worksheet; newspaper for each student

Lesson Plan: Group Activity. Discuss why different comics are in the newspaper. Why do people read comics?

Individual Activity. Have students complete the following "The Comics" worksheet.

THE COMICS

Some comics make us laugh. Some are not funny at all. Turn to the comic page of your newspaper and see if you can find the following:

*A comic character that is not human:*_____

A comic character who makes mistakes: _____

A comic with only one frame: _____

*A comic strip kids would like to read:*_____

A comic strip adults would like to read: _____

A comic strip that takes place in the past: _____

A comic character that is a child: _____

What is your favorite comic? _____

You become the comic strip creator! Show your favorite comic strip character as a student in your class at school. On a separate sheet of paper, draw your favorite comic strip character as a student in your classroom.

▶▶ *Day V: Getting the Facts*

Student Objective. To locate the facts in the news stories by identifying the five Ws

Materials. Student copies of "Getting the Facts" worksheets; newspaper for each student

Lesson Plan: Group Activity. Explain the importance of getting the facts from a news story. Find a story in the newspaper. Read the first few paragraphs aloud to the class. Locate the five Ws of the story as a class. Sometimes an answer is not in the story. Discuss why. Where are the answers to the five Ws found in a story?

Individual Activity. Assign three news stories for the activity. Tell students to put a number 1, 2, or 3 before each story in the newspaper. Have them complete the following "Getting the Facts" worksheet. Have students discuss the answers in pairs or in small groups. Were any of the answers missing? Why?

GETTING THE FACTS

A reporter must write all the facts in a news story. To get the facts, a reporter answers the five Ws questions in the story. The five Ws are:

WHO? WHEN? WHERE? WHAT? WHY?

Using three news stories selected by your teacher, get the facts of each story and complete the chart below.

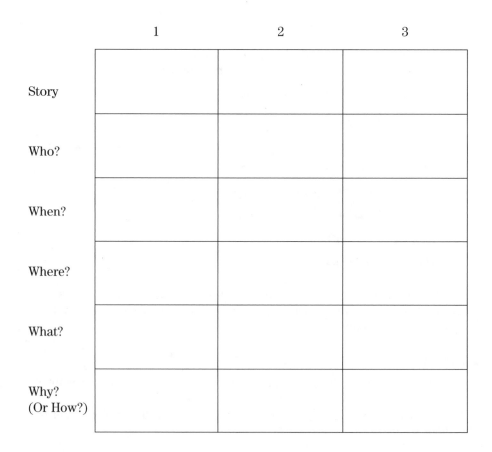

	1	2	3
Story			
Who?			
When?			
Where?			
What?			
Why? (Or How?)			

> ### *Other Resources*
>
> In addition to relying on newspapers, magazines, television, and radio for news information, students can take advantage of many commercial publications written at elementary levels.
>
> *My Weekly Reader* is available in separate editions for grades K–6 from American Education Publications Education Center, Columbus, OH 43216. *News Pilot, News Ranger, News Traits, News Explorer, Young Citizen,* and *Newstime* are available for grades 1–6 from Scholastic Magazines, 50 West 44th Street, New York, NY 10066

Summary

This chapter illustrated the importance of using current events from daily news sources in the social studies classroom. There are several different kinds of strategies to use to encourage students to read the newspaper. Some of these strategies include reading the newspapers to students, rewriting headlines, and locating areas with different weather patterns. A mini-unit is included at the end of the chapter for teachers wishing to experiment with using the newspaper in the classroom.

ACTIVITIES

1. Get on the Internet and read copies of several urban newspapers, such as the *New York Times, Atlanta Constitution,* and *Los Angeles Times.* Make your own comparisons. For example, try www.washingtonpost.com.
2. Read the coverage of a major, controversial event by newspapers with different perspectives, such as a student newspaper, a minority newspaper, and a socialist newspaper. Try to assess the differences in reporting.
3. Ask elementary-age students to give news reports or to write news articles on events that take place at and around the school.
4. How do teachers and students decide what is really worth studying in current events?

NOTE

1. Adapted from Barbara Dewell, *Newspapers in Education* (Boston: American Newspaper Publishers Association.

SUGGESTED READINGS

Harris, C., and Harris, R. (1993). *Make Your Own Newspaper.* Holbrook, MA: Bob Adams Media Services. (telephone: 1-800-872-5627)
International Reading Association. (1992). *Teaching Reading Skills through the Newspaper.* Washington, DC: Author.

Morton, J., and Cohn, A. (1998). *Kids on the 'Net: Conducting Research in K–5 Classrooms.* Portsmouth, NH: Heinneman.

On-line news services: cnn.com, usatoday.com, foxnews.com, washingtonpost.com. Also, any major newspaper has its own website.

Polly, J. (2002). *The Internet Kids and Family Yellow Pages.* New York: Osborne McGraw-Hill. Updated yearly.

Rhoades, L. (1994). "Quick Start Ideas for Teaching Events with Newspapers." *Social Education, 58* (Mar.): 173.

Sanderson, P. (1999). *Using Newspapers in the Classroom.* Cambridge: Cambridge University Press.

Cooperative Environments: The Hidden Curriculum

Certain aspects of the social studies curriculum, such as content and teaching style, are rather obvious; others take on subtler forms. This chapter on environments deals with alternative goal structures for social studies, strategies for group arrangements, and the physical setting of the classroom itself. Topics considered include the following:

- Competitive goal structures
- Individualistic goal structures
- Cooperative goal structures
- Characteristics of groups
- Types of groups
- A group activity
- The landscape of the classroom

*First one must establish the proper climate
for freedom and friendship to prevail.*

—Sarah Soon Kim

I n recent years, increased attention has been focused on the hidden curriculum of social studies. The *hidden curriculum* is the emotional, social, and intellectual environment fostered in a classroom. Although concern usually centers on the materials and subject matter of social studies, it is possible that less visible factors have an equally important effect on academic and attitudinal outcomes. Of course, there is an obvious relationship between good materials and a good learning environment. Materials designed to promote problem solving and communication among students will have a beneficial effect on the hidden curriculum of a classroom. However, in the final analysis, materials are subject to a wide variety of uses by teachers and cannot by themselves foster a positive learning environment. Johnson and Johnson, writing about alternative instructional goal structures, note that four possible types of goal structures exist: competitive, cooperative, individualistic, and none. They state:

> Each type of goal structure has an implicit value foundation which is taught subtly, as an unconscious curriculum, to the student who interacts within it. There is a great deal of evidence that the process by which students learn (i.e., the way in which students interact and behave in learning situations) and the outcomes of learning are both largely determined by the goal structure implemented by educators.[1]

Deutsch describes a *cooperative* situation as one in which the goals of the separate individuals are so linked together that there is a positive correlation between their goal attainments. He describes a *competitive* situation as one in which goal attainments are inversely related.[2]

There is no reason to believe that a social studies program needs to be based exclusively on cooperation. This is also true of competitive and individualistic approaches. Regardless of your preference for one or more of these environments, it is important that you attempt to develop a rationale for the kinds of environments you wish to establish with children in social studies. There are, however, compelling reasons for me to advise you to seriously consider cooperative learning.

Johnson and Johnson write that goal-structure research outcomes are available in the areas of achievement, problem-solving skills, and the cognitive development of students. They write that competition may prove superior to cooperative or individualistic goal structures when students are involved in simple drill activities or when "sheer quantity of work is desired on a mechanical or skill-oriented task that requires little if any help from another person."[3]

Numerous studies indicate that cooperative student efforts yield higher achievement in problem-solving activities and greater group productivity. Even memory work is more effectively facilitated by cooperative group discussions. Johnson and Johnson write:

> The research clearly indicates that the most desirable goal structure for promoting achievement in problem-solving tasks is a cooperative one. When working on problem-solving tasks within a cooperative goal structure students are also learning how to problem solve, how to cooperate, and how to join with other individuals to solve a common problem or to accomplish a common task.[4]

Little information is available regarding the effectiveness of individualistic goal structuring. The area of programmed learning, where subject-matter mastery or skill development is relevant, falls within this domain. The very nature of social studies, however, requires group interaction and sharing of ideas and skills. Watson and Johnson conclude that, on the basis of the available research, group cooperative structures are more effective than are individualistic structures in facilitating problem solving.[5]

Three Goal Structures for Social Studies

Much of what is taught (and presumably learned) in social studies methods courses is designed to help you interact with ideas and materials. This is particularly true in the case of inquiry methods. You are taught to facilitate children's learning by involving them in intellectually stimulating situations in which they manipulate artifacts, make original maps, play games, gather data, construct models, and so on. This way of learning is supported by a large and ever growing body of research. Another often overlooked dimension also bears examination: the classroom goal structure you create.

Johnson and Johnson clarify the meaning of classroom goal structure by posing the question "How should students interact with each other?" The basis on which your students interact is something you alone determine. Who gives you such power? The choice is yours by default. Even though you are often told what you must teach, you are seldom told how you must teach it.

Johnson and Johnson suggest that the basic generalization about goal structure is that how the teacher sets up the learning goals determines the teacher/student and student/student interaction patterns. The Johnsons identify three types of classroom goal structures: competitive, individualistic, and cooperative. (The Johnsons' definitions of the three terms are shown in Figure 16.1.) Each has its merits, and a teacher should probably use all three goal structures over the course of a year. But their own research and the research of other investigators that they reviewed led the Johnsons to conclude that the greatest potential academic and social good accrues from a cooperative goal structure. Curiously, however, it is seldom used by teachers because they do not understand how to implement it or have the mistaken idea that a cooperative goal structure makes it impossible to reward individual achievement. The following overview of three basic goal structures shows you how they work.

Competitive Goal Structure

In a competitive situation (whether academic or athletic, for example), one person can attain an individual goal only if others fail to obtain theirs. Thus, a negative correlation exists among goal attainments: If I win, you lose; and if you win, I lose. In this type of goal structure, each individual strives toward the highest marks. Evaluation is comparative or norm referenced. Grades are often based on a curve. Winners are rewarded. Losers are not exactly punished, but one wonders whether they know that.

The game of croquet provides an interesting illustration of an extreme competitive goal structure. You are trying to hit your own ball through the wicket, but you are also allowed to drive your opponent's ball away from the course. Closer to the classroom, researcher John Goodlad suggests that the natural outcome one might suspect in the typical school situation is the tendency on the part of the students to want to cheat.[6]

This is not to say that competition is inherently evil. All of us have enjoyed and benefited from certain types of competition. But you must learn to distinguish between appropriate and inappropriate competition.

Individualistic Goal Structure

In an individualistic situation, each person's goal attainment is unrelated to the goal attainment of others. No correlation among goal attainment exists. There is no linkage and therefore no support from one student to another. Each person is rewarded

FIGURE 16.1

Cooperation: We sink or swim together. I can attain my goal only if you attain your goal; there is a positive correlation among goal attainments.

Conditions:
- small, often heterogeneous groups
- other students as major resource
- teacher acts as consultant
- positive interdependence between group members
- individual accountability: all members must learn the material
- evaluation by comparison to a preset criterion

Individualization: We are each in this alone. My achieving my goal is unrelated to your achieving your goal; there is no correlation among goal attainments.

Conditions:
- separate working area
- separate work materials
- teacher is the primary source
- self-paced
- evaluate by a preset criterion

Competition: I swim, you sink; I sink, you swim. If I obtain my goal, you cannot obtain your goal and vice versa; there is a negative correlation among goal attainments.

Conditions:
- small, homogeneous groups
- maximize the number of winners
- compete against people at the same ability level
- not a life or death situation, but for fun and review, and a change of pace
- evaluate by comparison to others' work

Source: Based on D. W. Johnson and R. T. Johnson, *Learning the Cooperative School* (Edina, MN: Interaction Book Co., 1989), pp. 4, 5–7.

for an individual product. Evaluation is based on set standards, and everyone can therefore achieve mastery or the criterion of success.

This pattern is common in classrooms. It is seen in spelling and other subjects in which there are lists to learn. In social studies, if everyone memorizes all the capital cities, everyone receives a grade of A on the map test. A curious form of individualistic learning occurs in committee work, when each student does a particular piece of work and receives a personal reward.

Cooperative Goal Structure

In a cooperative learning environment, when one person achieves a goal, all others achieve their goals. Thus, a positive correlation exists among goal attainments. People sink or swim together. One thinks of Patrick Henry's stirring statement: "Let us all hang together, or we shall surely all hang separately."

In a cooperative goal structure, rewards are linked. Students may, for example, be given a common grade for a group project. But more than that, they may learn to help each other. Ellis and Fouts[7] cite the cumulative research findings that favor cooperative learning:

- Higher achievement, better retention
- Growth in moral and cognitive reasoning
- Enhanced motivation to learn
- Greater liking for school and school subjects
- Enhanced self-esteem
- Greater liking for each other regardless of individual differences

Take just a moment to go back over the list you just read. If these claims are true (and the evidence seems to point in that direction), then you simply cannot afford to ignore them. They go quickly to the heart of good education: moral and intellectual growth, increased motivation, greater liking for each other, and so on. Ellis and Fouts make two additional arguments that no social studies teacher can take lightly:

- Back to basics? There are few things in life that are more basic than working successfully with others.
- The single most common reason that people are fired from their jobs is failure to get along with others.

Grouping

Central to the idea of goal structuring are the opportunities you provide for various grouping patterns in social studies. The typical classroom provides a potential mix of academic, social, economic, and ethnic backgrounds that can be shared and integrated when a teacher is committed to that goal. The following pages are devoted to the principles of grouping, descriptions of various group structures, and strategies for their implementation in elementary social studies classes.

What Is a Group?

Watson and Johnson[8] characterize three essential features of a group:

- *Interaction* between and among group members
- *Satisfaction* derived from mutual meeting of needs
- *Recognition* of group unity and purpose by members

They define a *group* as "an aggregate of persons in face to face interaction, each aware of his own membership in the group, each aware of the others who belong in the group, and each obtaining some satisfactions from his participation with the others."[9]

Why Group in Social Studies?

The obvious answer to the question "Why group in social studies?" is that grouping of some kind is unavoidable. This is true even if you decide to keep all your

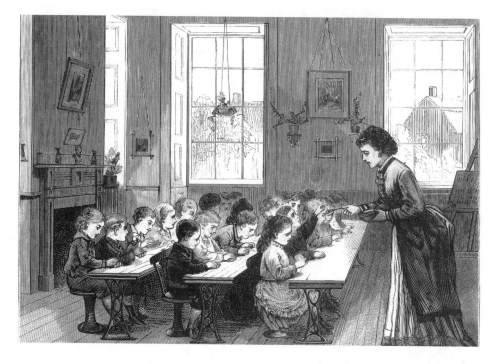

Classroom environments change, but deeper human needs remain the same.

students in one class-size group every day for all their social studies work. Social studies involves human beings and their interactions with one another. Perhaps the most effective way to get students to understand that concept is by strategically grouping them in situations where meaningful interactions are a logical outcome.

It is important to keep in mind that groups and grouping are means to certain ends, such as improved communication, better understanding of one another, and increased efficiency in completing tasks. Five small groups serve no better purpose than one large group unless a teacher has arrived at some meaningful reason for breaking down a larger unit. Thus, a crucial idea in grouping is the nature of the task to be completed. Group size ought to be a function of group task; similarly, group complexion (*who* makes up a given group) should be related to group task and its effective completion. Such characteristics as age and maturity as well as evidence of leadership and cooperation need to be taken into account. To summarize:

1. Groups are means to certain ends, such as improved communication and increased efficiency in the completion of tasks.
2. The particular task to be completed ought to determine such factors as group and group complexion.

Grouping Strategies

Dyads. A dyad, or group of two, is the simplest of groups and, in many ways, the best. Its interaction possibilities are limited to exchanges between its two members. Therefore, great potential exists in the dyad for group members to share feelings and ideas. Suppose, for example, that a teacher asks a class a question such as: "Name some things you'd like to learn about on our field trip tomorrow." The responses of the class at large would be very different from those of students in dyads. Although the small groups' list of "things to learn about" may not be any longer, more students will have had an opportunity to become actively involved in deciding what they want to learn about. Dyads provide a maximum potential for student input because there is less waiting time for a given participant while others speak. Its very strength, however, leads to its potential weakness: An insufficient pooling of student resources and ideas exists in such a small group.

Triads. Groups of three are often effective in short-term discussions, especially where roles are defined so one member is an arbitrator, the focus of a discussion, or a participant observer. A game suggested by Simon and colleagues, called the Focus Game,[10] lends itself to the triad. In the Focus Game, one person explains his or her feelings about an issue (such as birthday parties or holiday observances) while the other two group members attempt to keep the focus on that person by asking questions designed to further draw out that person's feelings. However, the triad is basically an unstable group arrangement,[11] because the potential exists for excluding one member. Thus, the triad is probably a less preferable grouping than either the dyad or groups of four or five for committee work and other long-range group tasks in social studies.

Other Small Groups. Findings by Bales indicate that potential participation by members of a group is a function of group size.[12] Observing group sessions at a Harvard laboratory, he found that, on the average, one member of a dyad talked 58 percent of the time while the other talked 42 percent of the time. The average talking time for triad members was 42 percent, 34 percent, and 24 percent. For groups of four, the percentages were 37 percent, 27 percent, 21 percent, and 16 percent. For groups of five, the percentages were 39 percent for the most talkative member and 9 percent for the least talkative. As group size was further increased, a pattern of dominance and withdrawal emerged. In groups of eight to ten, the most talkative member did approximately 50 percent of the talking while the least talkative spoke about 2 or 3 percent of the time. Obviously, in whole-class "discussions" some students will have very little opportunity for input.

Class-Size Groups. Perhaps the most common grouping arrangement in elementary social studies classrooms is the class-size group.[13] Certainly there are valid reasons for keeping a whole class together a certain amount of the time. However, a teacher must keep in mind that in so doing, he or she places severe restrictions on the possibilities for pupil input and interaction. Thus, one might question (given the criteria established earlier) whether a whole class is indeed a group or merely a collection of individuals in the same room. Here is a sample listing of situations in which you may wish to use class-size groups:

1. Viewing a film (Often films are available for short time periods and they contain information the whole class needs. This would not preclude the possibility of smaller groups meeting before or after the showing.)
2. Listening to a resource person present information related to a unit topic

3. Participating in class discussions when the teacher wishes to model questioning behavior and/or where the teacher wishes to ensure that students hear certain information, directions, and so on

4. Taking a field trip in a given site (although students may in fact be paired or placed in some small-group arrangement)

Although it is an often-used arrangement, the class-size group is hardly a natural grouping (notice the grouping behavior of people at parties). It is best used when a need exists to convey information or directions to large numbers of students at the same time.

Large Groups. Team teaching and other cooperative arrangements between two or more teachers and two or more classes of students occasionally provide opportunities for large-group instruction. As is the case with class-size instructional groups, large groups may logically be brought together to view films, hear resource persons, or perhaps initiate a unit when demonstrations, instructions, or certain items of information are necessary. Another reason for bringing large groups together is for viewing plays or student exhibitions related to a particular social studies unit.

In summary, it can be said that if efficient pupil interaction is to take place, small groups are necessary. There is no one perfect-sized grouping, and the criteria for grouping depend on a teacher's objectives, students' interests, and their perceived needs. A useful strategy to ensure that discussions occur is for a teacher to do a great deal of small-group work and to vary the size of the groups according to the tasks to be performed.

Role-Play Example: Westward Expansion

Role-playing fosters small-group interactions and decision making in hypothetical, nonthreatening situations. Role-play is a useful technique for dealing with moral dilemmas and related problems students face in classrooms, lunchrooms, hallways, playgrounds, the street, and at home. Role-play gives a student an opportunity to act out roles involving conflict, judgments, and actions from a point of view different from his or her own. In that regard, it is a useful tool for dealing with control problems and disputes between students. The simple technique of role reversal, in which students take a position that contrasts with a particular behavior or emotion they have exhibited, often enables students to see the complexity of an issue as well as an alternative point of view.

Role-play can also add a human dimension to historical periods, which, in children's minds, too often consist of a mixture of dates, names, sweeping events, and irreversible decisions made by larger-than-life individuals. The following role-play example humanizes the westward expansion of the United States.

A man and his wife emigrated to the United States 15 years ago and settled in Boston. Since that time, the wife's parents have joined the family. They are old and in poor health. During their 15 years in Boston, the man and his wife have had two children; the boy is age 13 and the girl is age 10. The man, who is a carpenter, has had little work lately. The family rents space in an apartment building in a run-down section of the city. The man and his wife have always been city dwellers.

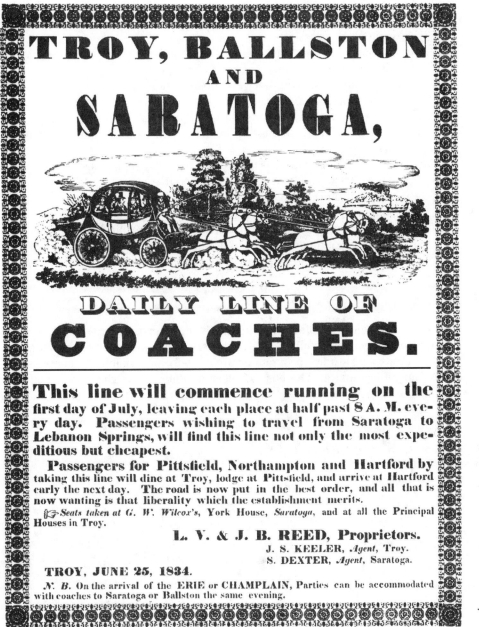

This poster advertising overland mail routes is similar to those the family in our role-play example might have seen.

Today, the husband has come home with a copy of a poster urging emigration to the West. The question is whether the family should move.

Let students work in small groups of six, with each student assuming one of the following roles. The task of each group is to role-play the family as the members discuss the move and try to decide whether or not they should leave Boston.

Father: You feel you are a good carpenter. But work has been hard to find. You have uprooted yourself and your wife once and you don't want to do it again if it wouldn't be wise.

Mother: Coming to the United States was difficult. Now this move would mean leaving Boston, which has been home for 15 years. Your sister and her family live here and you feel very close to her. Still, there has been little money for food and clothes.

Grandfather: You were a cabinetmaker in your day. You think maybe there would be work for you in this new land. But you are quite elderly and in poor health.

Grandmother: Your health has been poor. You've heard stories about the West and fear that it would be a difficult place to live.

Son: You are 13 and love adventure. But you have many friends you would have to leave.

Daughter: You are 10. You like Boston and city life. Your friends and cousins are here. But you know how hard it has been for your mother to cook and sew with little food and material. Perhaps things would be better in the West.

The Physical Environment

Goal structuring and grouping procedures are integral parts of the hidden curriculum in elementary social studies. They are every bit as important to the success of students in a social studies program as are such formal, visible elements as textbooks and subject matter. There is, however, another factor: the physical environment of the classroom. Like the other components of the hidden curriculum, the

Student-designed bulletin boards that are related to units being studied provide attractive and meaningful learning environments.

physical environment must reflect an articulated, well-defined rationale for the events that transpire during a year's social studies.

Just as geographers study land-use patterns in urban and agricultural areas, so might one look at the land-use patterns in an elementary classroom. Here is a series of questions you might ask to assess the geography of your classroom.

1. To what extent do the students participate in developing the classroom environment: interest centers, displays, bulletin boards, murals?
2. Are the desks, chairs, and other furniture (e.g., rocking chair) arranged to fit the needs of learning experiences? Do the arrangements change from time to time?
3. Are there interest centers in the room? Do the interest centers relate to the current course of study?
4. Are the bulletin boards integrated into the current course of study? Do the students share the responsibility for developing bulletin boards? Are the bulletin boards teaching/learning devices?
5. Is there a space in the classroom where students can be alone to think, study, or do nothing?
6. Are examples of student work (maps, pictures, charts, graphs, reports, models) prominently displayed?

Take a few minutes to study Figure 16.2, an aerial view of an ideal classroom learning environment as conceived by an elementary teacher. What does this teacher's drawing tell you about her sense of place? What does it tell you about her sense of relationships within places?

To what extent are your students involved in the planning of activities and investigations?

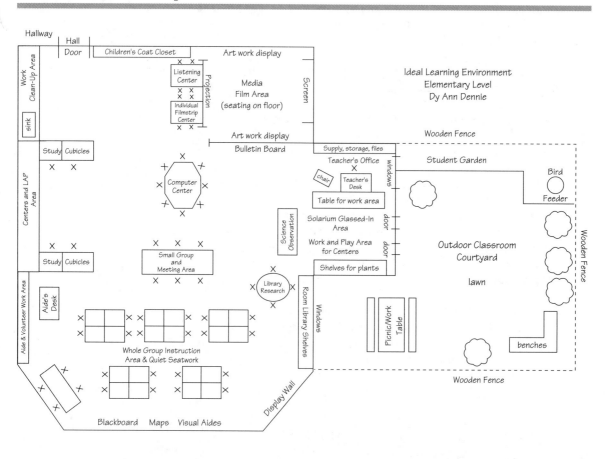

Summary

Your goal structures, grouping patterns, and physical setting are three key factors in the hidden social studies curriculum you establish. They are as crucial to the success of social studies teaching/learning as such obvious factors as content and teaching methods. As you seek to develop a rationale for what you do with students in social studies, you must give careful consideration to the kind of social/intellectual/physical environment you wish to develop.

ACTIVITIES

1. Write down five reasons that primary-age students cannot function effectively in small groups. Develop and try out some activities that disprove the reasons you listed.

2. Draw an elaborate sketch of the ideal classroom learning environment for social studies. Explain your sketch to someone.
3. Make a case for the effects that social studies ought to have on the rest of the school day, such as recess time, lunch, other subjects, and so on.

NOTES

1. David W. Johnson and Roger T. Johnson, "Instructional Goal Structure: Cooperative, Competitive, or Individualistic," *Review of Educational Research* (April 1974): 213.
2. M. Deutsch, "A Theory of Cooperation and Competition," *Human Relations*, *2* (1949): 129–152.
3. Johnson and Johnson, "Instructional Goal Structure," p. 231.
4. Ibid., p. 232.
5. Goodwin Watson and D. W. Johnson, *Social Psychology: Issues and Insights* (Philadelphia: Lippincott, 1972).
6. John Goodlad, *A Place Called School* (New York: McGraw-Hill, 1984).
7. Arthur K. Ellis and Jeffrey Fouts, *Research on Educational Innovations*, 2nd ed. (Princeton: Eye on Education, 1997).
8. Watson and Johnson, *Social Psychology*, p. 82.
9. Ibid., p. 82.
10. Sidney Simon, H. Kirschenbaum, and Leland Howe, *Values Clarification* (New York: Hart, 1973), pp. 171–173.
11. Watson and Johnson, *Social Psychology*, p. 58.
12. R. F. Bales, *Effects of Size of Problem-Solving Groups on the System of Interaction.* Report to the American Psychological Association, 1957.
13. Glen Heathers, "Grouping," *Encyclopedia of Educational Research* (New York: Crowell-Collier-Macmillan, 1964), pp. 564–670.

SUGGESTED READINGS

Cogan, J., Grossman, D., and Liu, M. (2000). "Citizenship: the Democratic Imagination in a Global/Local Context." *Social Education, 64* (Jan./Feb.): 48–52.

Deutsch, M, and Coleman, P. (2000). *The Handbook of Conflict Resolution.* San Francisco: Jossey-Bass.

Goleman, D. (2000). *Working with Emotional Intelligence.* New York: Bantam Books.

Johnson, D., and Johnson, R. (1998). *Learning Together and Alone: Cooperative, Competitive, and Individualistic Learning.* Boston: Allyn and Bacon.

Mandell, S. (1998). *Social Studies in the Cyberage: Applications with Cooperative Learning.* Skylight Publications.

Yeager, E. (2000). "Thoughts on Wise Practice in the Teaching of Social Studies." *Social Education, 64* (Oct.): 352–353.

Epilogue

Well, here we are. We've completed the journey through this text. I hope you are feeling that you've developed some purposeful ideas about teaching and learning social studies with elementary students. I also hope you are as excited about children's learning as I am and that your enthusiasm will continue to grow. I'd like to go back over the themes of this book in miniature. In order to do so, I'll leave you with the following thoughts.

Social studies should be activity centered, and it should be *social* above all. This means children working together, sharing, cooperating, planning, discussing, constructing, and being part of something they can't do on their own. Shared experience is the best experience.

Your students should be involved in every aspect of social studies learning. This includes planning, goal setting, active experience, reflection, and assessment. The more confidence you show in your students and their ability to take charge of their own learning, the more you come to realize how capable children are.

Knowledge is important, especially in the form of concepts, skills, and values. Information can feed each of these, but the good teacher knows that information is not an end in itself. Big ideas—important ideas—are what's at stake. Most of what we teach and learn is soon forgotten, so the question is: What *really* matters?

Inquiry, problem solving, and discovery are important because they model the activity and methods of historians, geographers, and other social scientists. That is, these types of learning enable students to ask their own questions, gather their own data, make applications, and think productively.

Projects, especially group projects, are crucial to childhood growth and development. Project learning elevates knowledge to the level of application. Knowledge becomes a needed instrument or tool. Projects demand careful planning and assessment—two valuable commodities in life. Projects have outcomes and often result in performance, giving students experience with living forms of knowledge.

Social studies ought to be the focal point of citizenship in your classroom. Students learn to work and play together, to experience the give and take so basic to a democratic society. A good classroom is a place of civil behavior; of government of, by, and for the people; and where rules are made, continually examined, and followed.

The hopes and dreams of each individual are nurtured in a good classroom. In our society, each individual is of supreme importance. Childhood is a brief season. Whatever you can do to make it a safe, secure, and happy time in the life of each child is all to the good. Remember, a teacher affects eternity. You never know where your influence will stop.

Index